ENGLISH
Verbs

Third Edition

by
Vincent F. Hopper

Professor of English
New York University

BARRON'S

BARRON'S EDUCATIONAL SERIES, INC.

All inquiries should be addressed to:
Barron's Educational Series, Inc.
250 Wireless Boulevard
Hauppauge, New York 11788
http://www.barronseduc.com

ISBN-13: 978-0-7641-2830-1
ISBN-10: 0-7641-2830-2

Library of Congress Catalog Card No. 2004041035

Library of Congress Cataloging-in-Publication Data

Hopper, Vincent Foster, 1906–
    Barron's English verbs / by Vincent F. Hopper.—3rd ed.
        p.   cm.
    ISBN 0-7641-2830-2
    1. English language—Verb—Tables.   I. Title: English verbs.
II. Title.
PE1315.I6H6   2004
428.2—dc22   2004041035

PRINTED IN CHINA
9 8 7 6 5 4 3

428.2
HOP

2.02

Book Sales

Austin

7-11-07

Contents

To the Reader

This book is meant to help both native English speakers and those learning English as a second language to avoid many common pitfalls of English grammar and usage. The main requirements of so-called "standard" written English are described and illustrated within these pages. Spoken language is, of course, less formal than written discourse. Readers should note, therefore, that many usages considered incorrect in writing are perfectly acceptable in casual conversation.

It is assumed that readers are familiar with grammatical terms common to most languages: for example, the parts of speech, such as nouns, adjectives, and conjunctions, as well as such concepts as plural and singular, verb tenses, idioms, sentence structure, and punctuation.

To use the book efficiently, review the Table of Contents to see what the book contains. Afterward, keep the book by your side as a convenient guide to using correct English while speaking and especially while writing. When in doubt about correct usage, let the book steer you to the proper choice.

In a world that values shortcuts and efficiency, abbreviations are bound to flourish. In fact, it's hard to imagine modern life without them. What follows are some of the most common abbreviations encountered in conversation, in print, and in the media.

Note that many technical abbreviations have been deliberately omitted from the list which does not contain commercial and business abbreviations, such as GM, IBM, and CBS.

AA	Alcoholics Anonymous	AM, A.M.	Master of Arts
AAA	American Automobile Association	Amb.	Ambassador
AARP	American Association of Retired People	a.m.	before noon (*ante meridian*)
A.B.	Bachelor of Arts	A.M.A., AMA	American Medical Association
A.B.A.	American Bar Association	AMEX	American Stock Exchange
AC., A.C.	alternating electric current	amt.	amount
ACLU	American Civil Liberties Union	AP, A.P.	Associated Press Assistant Principal
AD, A.D.	Anno Domini	apt.	apartment
ad inf	to infinity (*ad infinitum*)	A.R.C., ARC	American Red Cross
adj.	adjective	arith.	arithmetic
Adm.	Admiral	Ariz., AZ	Arizona
admin.	administrator, administration	Ark., AR	Arkansas
adv.	adverb	ASAP	as soon as possible
advt.	advertisement	assn.	association
AFL/CIO	American Federation of Labor, Congress of Industrial Organization	assoc.	association, associate
		asst.	assistant
		A.T.F.	Alcohol, Tobacco, and Firearms
AG, A.G.	Attorney General	Atl.	Atlantic
AIDS	Auto-Immune Deficiency Syndrome	ATM	Automated Teller Machine
AK	Alaska	att.	attention
A.L.	American League	attrib.	attribution, attributed to
Ala., AL	Alabama	atty.	attorney
alt.	alternate altitude	Aug.	August
		Ave.	Avenue
		AWOL	absent without leave

Abbreviations

b.	born	CPA	Certified Public Accountant
B.A.	Bachelor of Arts	CRT	cathode ray tube
BC, B.C.	before Christ	CT	Central Time
bibliog.	bibliography	Ct.	Court
bio.	biology	cu.	cubic
biog.	biography	cyl.	cylinder
Blvd.	Boulevard		
B.O., BO	body odor	d.	died
b/r	bedroom	DA., D.A.	District Attorney
bro, bros.	brother, brothers	DAR, D.A.R.	Daughters of the American Revolution
B.S.	Bachelor of Science	D.C., DC	District of Columbia
BTU	British Thermal Unit		direct electrical current
C	Celsius, centigrade carbon	DDS	Doctor of Dental Surgery
c.	about (*circa*)	Dec.	December
ca.	approximately	Del., DE	Delaware
Calif., CA	California	Dem.	Democrat
Capt.	Captain	dept.	department
cc.	carbon copy copy to cubic centimeter	Det.	Detective
		dipl.	diplomat diploma
CD	compact disk	dir.	director
C.D.C., CDC	Center for Disease Control	DIY	do it yourself
cent.	century center	DMV	Department of Motor Vehicles
C.E.O., CEO	Chief Executive Officer	DOA	dead on arrival
cf.	compare		Department of Agriculture
CIA	Central Intelligence Agency	DOC	Department of Commerce Department of Corrections
cm.	centimeter		
Co.	company	DOD	Department of Defense
C.O.D., COD	Collect on Delivery	DOE	Department of Energy
Colo., CO	Colorado	DOL	Department of Labor
Comsat	Communications satellite	DOS	disk operating system
Conn., CT	Connecticut		
Corp.	Corporation		

DOT	Department of Transportation		f.	and the following page
doz.	dozen		ff.	and the following pages
dpi	dots per inch		F, F.	Fahrenheit
Dr.	Doctor		F.A.A., FAA	Federal Aviation Administration
d/r	dining room			
DSL	direct service line		FAQ	frequently asked questions
DUI	driving under the influence		F.B.I., FBI	Federal Bureau of Investigation
DVD	digital video disk			
DWI	driving while intoxicated		FCC	Federal Communications Commission
			FDA	Food and Drug Administration
E, E.	East			
econ.	economics		F.D.I.C., FDIC	Federal Deposit Insurance Corporation
ed.	editor			
EDT	Eastern Daylight Time		FDR	Franklin Delano Roosevelt
e.g.	for example (*exempli gratia*)			
			Feb.	February
EKG	electro-cardiogram		FEMA	Federal Emergency Management Administration
Email	electronic mail			
Engl.	English			
E.P.A., EPA	Environmental Protection Agency		FHA	Federal Housing Authority
			fig.	figure
equiv.	equivalent		fl.	fluid
E.R.A., ERA	Earned Run Average, Equal Rights Amendment		Fla., FL	Florida
			flgt.	flight
ESL	English as a Second Language		FM	frequency modulation
esp.	especially		f/p	fireplace
ESP	extrasensory perception		fps	feet per second
			Fri.	Friday
Esq.	Esquire		ft.	foot, feet
EST	Eastern Standard Time		Ft.	Fort
ETA	estimated time of arrival		FYI	for your information
et al.,	and others (*et alia*)			
etc.	and so forth (*et cetera*)		G., g.	gram
ex.	example		Ga., GA	Georgia

Abbreviations

gal.	gallon	*ibid.*	in the same place
GB	gigabyte		(*ibidem*)
	Great Britain	ICC, I.C.C.	Interstate Commerce
Gen.	General		Commission
gm.	gram	ID	Idaho
GMT	Greenwich Mean Time	id.	the same (*idem*)
GNP	Gross National	i.e.	that is
	Product	Ill., IL	Illinois
GOP, G.O.P.	Grand Old Party	IMF, I.M.F.	International
	(Republican)		Monetary Fund
Gov.	Governor	in.	inch
govt.	government	inc.	incorporated
GPO	Government Printing	Ind., IN	Indiana
	Office	*in loc cit*	*in loco citato* (in the
G.P.S., GPS	Global Positioning		place cited)
	System	IQ, I.Q.	intelligence quotient
GW	George Washington	I.R.A., IRA	Individual Retirement
			Account
HazMat	Hazardous materials		Irish Republican Army
HHS	Department of Health	I.R.S., IRS	Internal Revenue
	and Human Services		Service
HI	Hawaii		
Hon.	Honorable	JAG	Judge Advocate
hp, h.p.	horsepower		General
hr., hrs.	hours	Jan.	January
HR	home run	j.g., jg	junior grade
	House of	Jr.	junior
	Representatives		
HS, H.S.	High School	K.	kilo
ht.	height		kilometer
HTML	Hypertext Markup		1,000
	Language	Kans., KS	Kansas
HUD	Department of	KB	kilobyte
	Housing and Urban	kg.	kilograms
	Development	kHz	kilohertz
hwy.	highway	km.	kilometers
		kw.	kilowatt
I., Is.	Island	Ky., KY	Kentucky
I-5, I-70, I-95	Interstate Highways 5,		
	70, 95	l.	liter
IA	Iowa	Lieut.	Lieutenant

4

La., LA	Louisiana	Mme.	Madame
L.A.	Los Angeles	Mo., MO	Missouri
L.A.P.D.	Los Angeles Police Department	Mon.	Monday
Lat.	Latin	Mont., MT	Montana
lat.	latitude	MP, M.P.	Military Police
lb.	pound		Member of Parliament
lbs.	pounds	mph, m.p.h.	miles per hour
log.	logarithm	Mr.	Mister
long.	longitude	M.R.I., MRI	magnetic resonance imaging
l/r	living room	Mrs.	Mistress, Missus
Lt.	Lieutenant	Ms.	(no spelled out version)
ltd.	Limited	M.S., MS	multiple sclerosis
LWV	League of Women Voters	ms., mss.	manuscript, manuscripts
		MSG	monosodium glutamate
m.	meter	MSW	Master of Social Work
	married	mt.	mountain
	mile	M.T., MT	Mountain Time
M.	Monsieur		Montana
M.A.	Master of Arts	mtg.	meeting
Maj.	Major	mtge.	mortgage
Mass., MA	Massachusetts	mtn.	mountain
MAT	Miller Analogy Test	MVP	most valuable player
MB	megabyte		
M.B.A., MBA	Master of Business Administration	N, N.	North
M.D.	medical doctor	N.A., NA	North America
Md., MD	Maryland	N.A.A.C.P.,	National Association
mdse.	merchandise	NAACP	for the Advancement
Me., ME	Maine		of Colored People
Messrs.	plural of *Mr.*	N.A.F.T.A.,	North American
MFA	Master of Fine Arts	NAFTA	Free Trade Alliance
mfr.	manufacturer	N.A.S.A.,	National Aeronautical
mg.	milligram	NASA	and Space
	megabytes		Administration
mgr.	manager	NATO	North Atlantic Treaty Organization
Mich., MI	Michigan		
Minn., MN	Minnesota	N.B.	note well (*nota bene*)
Miss., MS	Mississippi	N.B.A., NBA	National Basketball
Mlle.	Madamoiselle		Association

Abbreviations

	National Boxing Association	OH	Ohio
N.C., NC	North Carolina	OK, O.K.	okay, all right
n.d.	no date	Okla., OK	Oklahoma
N.D., ND	North Dakota	*op. cit.*	work cited
NE	North East, New England	op., *opus*	(work of art)
N.E.A., NEA	National Education Association	Ore., OR	Oregon
		org.	organization
	National Endowment of the Arts	oz.	ounce
Nebr., NE	Nebraska	p., pp.	page, pages
Nev., NV	Nevada	Pa., PA	Pennsylvania
N.F.L., NFL	National Football League	Pacif.	Pacific
N.H., NH	New Hampshire	par.	paragraph
N.H.L. NHL	National Hockey League	Pat. Off.	Patent Office
N.I.H, NIH	National Institutes of Health	P.C., PC	personal computer political correctness
N.J., NJ	New Jersey	pd.	paid
N.L., NL	National League	P.D., PD	Police Department
N.M., NM	New Mexico	PDT	Pacific Daylight Time
no.	number	Ph.D.	Doctor of Philosophy
non seq	out of sequence; it does not follow (*non sequitur*)	P.I.	private investigator
		pkg.	package
Nov.	November	pkwy.	parkway
N.P.S., NPS	National Park Service	pl.	plural
N.R.A., NRA	National Rifle Association	p.m., pm	afternoon (*post meridian*)
N.R.C., NRC	Nuclear Regulatory Commission	P.M., PM	Postmaster
NW	North West	PMS	pre-menstrual syndrome
N.Y., NY	New York	P.O., PO	Post Office
N.Y.C., NYC	New York City	P.O.W., POW	Prisoner of War
NYSE	New York Stock Exchange	ppd.	postpaid
		p.r.	public relations
		P.R., PR	Puerto Rico
		Prin.	Principal
		Prof.	Professor
		P.S.	post script
		PSAT	Preliminary Scholastic Assessment Test
O.A.S., OAS	Organization of American States	pseud.	pseudonym
Oct.	October	p.s.f.	pounds per square foot

p.s.i.	pounds per square inch	SAT	Scholastic Assessment Test
PST	Pacific Standard Time		
Pt.	Point	Sat.	Saturday
p/t	part time	S.C., SC	South Carolina
P.T.A., PTA	Parent Teacher Association	S. Dak., SD	South Dakota
		S.E., SE	Southeast
pub.	published	S.E.C., SEC	Securities and Exchange Commission
Q.E.D.	which was to be demonstrated (*quod erat demonstrandum*)	sec.	secretary
		sect.	section
		Sen.	Senator
qt.	quart	Sept.	September
Q.T.	secret; quiet	*seq.*	the following (*sequentia*)
q.v.	which see (*quod vide*)		
		S.P.C.A., SPCA	Society for the Prevention of Cruelty to Animals
R.	River		
R and R	rest and relaxation		
RBI	runs batted in	sq.	square
R.C.	Roman Catholic	S.R.O., SRO	standing room only single room occupancy
Rd.	Road		
reg.	registered	Sr.	Senior
REM	rapid eye movement	St.	Street
Rep.	Representative	St., Ste.	Saint, Saint (feminine, French)
Rev.	Reverend		
R.F.D.	Rural Free Delivery	Sun.	Sunday
R.I., RI	Rhode Island	SW	Southwest
R.I.P.	rest in peace	syn.	synonym
rm.	room		
R.N.	registered nurse	T.B., TB	tuberculosis
R.O.T.C., ROTC	Reserve Officers Training Corps	t.b., tb.	
		Tenn., TN	Tennessee
rpm, r.p.m.	revolutions per minute	Tex., TX	Texas
R.R., RR	railroad rural route	T.K.O., TKO	technical knockout
		TM	trademark
RSVP	please reply (*repondez, s'il vous plait*)	Thurs.	Thursday
		tr.	translated by
		Tues.	Tuesday
S., S	South	TV	television
SAM	surface to air missile		
SASE	self-addressed stamped envelope	UHF	ultra-high frequency
		U.K., UK	United Kingdom

Abbreviations

U.N., UN	United Nations
U.P., UP	United Press
UPC	Universal Product Code
URL	Universal Resource Locator
US, U.S.	United States
USA, U.S.A.	United States of America
USAF	U.S. Air Force
USAFA	U.S. Air Force Academy
USB	Universal S-Band
USCG	U.S. Coast Guard
USDA	U.S. Department of Agriculture
USDC	U.S. Department of Commerce
USDI	U.S. Department of the Interior
USDL	U.S. Department of Labor
USMA	U.S. Military Academy
USMC	U.S. Marine Corps
USN	U.S. Navy
USNA	U.S. Naval Academy
U.S.S., USS	United States Ship
USSC	U.S. Supreme Court
UT	Utah
uv, UV	ultra-violet
v.	volt(s)
v., vs.	against (*versus*)
Va., VA	Virginia
V.A., VA	Veterans Administration
vb.	verb
V.F.W., VFW	Veterans of Foreign Wars
VHF	very high frequency
VIP	very important person
viz.	namely (*videlicet*)
vol.	volume
V.P., VP	Vice-President
Vt., VT	Vermont
W., W	West
Wash., WA	Washington
Wed.	Wednesday
W.H.O., WHO	World Health Organization
Wis., WI	Wisconsin
Wm.	William
W.T.O., WTO	World Trade Organization
W.Va., WV	West Virginia
www.	World Wide Web
Wyo., WY	Wyoming
yd.	yard

Adjectives and Adverbs

Adjectives and adverbs are descriptive words like *sweet, big, ripe, tender* (adjectives); *sweetly, beautifully, softly, tenderly* (adverbs).

> Adjectives modify nouns or pronouns: *sweet* Sue. (describes Sue)
> Adjective: *sweet*
> Adverbs modify verbs: She *sang* sweetly. (how she sang) Adverb: *sweetly*
> Or adjectives: very *sweet* Sue. (how sweet) Adverb: *very*
> Or other adverbs: She sang very *sweetly*. (how sweetly) Adverb: *very*
> Adverbs usually describe how, why, when, or where.

Adjectives and adverbs are said to limit the meaning of the words they describe, and they usually do in the sense that the word *woman* applies to all females while the addition of an adjective like *beautiful* limits the noun *woman* by excluding all the women who are not beautiful.

Comparison of Adjectives

POSITIVE	COMPARATIVE	SUPERLATIVE

Most one-syllable adjectives add *er* for the comparative form and *est* for the superlative form.

sweet	sweeter	sweetest
rich	richer	richest

One-syllable adjectives ending in *e* add *r* for the comparative form and *st* for the superlative form.

late	later	latest
bright	brighter	brightest

Two-syllable adjectives ending in *e*—if the accent is on the first syllable—add *r* for the comparative form and *st* for the superlative form.

little	littler	littlest
gentle	gentler	gentlest

Two-syllable adjectives ending in *y* preceded by a consonant change the *y* to *i* before adding *er* or *est*.

pretty	prettier	prettiest
handy	handier	handiest

Most other adjectives of two or more syllables form the comparative and superlative by the use of the auxiliary adverbs *more* and *most*.

sedate	more sedate	most sedate
beautiful	more beautiful	most beautiful

Adjectives and Adverbs

IRREGULAR FORMS

bad	worse	worst
ill	worse	worst
good	better	best
much	more	most

Predicate Adjectives

Adjectives usually precede the words they describe: *deep* river; *efficient, intelligent* woman. To make statements or sentences out of these phrases, place the adjectives after copulative verbs such as *is*.

The river is *deep*.	(Adjective modifies *river*.)
The woman is *efficient* and *intelligent*.	(Adjectives modify *woman*.)
She is *efficient* and *intelligent*.	(Adjectives modify *She*.)

Articles

The most commonly used adjectives are the articles, *a, an,* and *the*.

A and *an* are known as indefinite articles because they refer to any single member of the class specified by whatever noun they modify: *a* tree, *an* apple.

The is the definite article. It calls attention to a specific person, place, or thing: *the* boy, *the* city, *the* typewriter.

Use *a* before words beginning with a consonant sound: *a* cat, *a* train.

Use *an* before words beginning with a vowel sound: *an* artist, *an* elephant.

NOTE: It is the sound, not the letter, which determines whether *a* or *an* should be used: *a* uniform, *an* L-shaped room, *an* 80-year-old man.

Adverbs are frequently formed from adjectives by adding *ly* to the adjective.

careful	*carefully*
quick	*quickly*

BUT many adjectives also end in *ly* (*lovely, elderly*). A common error, therefore, occurs when an adjective is used where an adverb is required. The reverse—using an adverb in place of an adjective—also occurs, but less often.

Several principles govern the choice between adjectives and adverbs:

Most adverbs form the comparative and superlative by the use of the auxiliaries more and most: *more quickly, most quickly*.

A few words like *fast, slow, early, late,* and *well* function as either adverbs or adjectives depending on what they modify or, occasionally, on what they mean. For example, when *well* means *healthy*, it is always an adjective, and when *late* means *no longer alive*, it is always an adjective.

ADJECTIVE	ADVERB
a *fast* train [modifies *train*]	He ran *fast*. [modifies *ran*]
a *slow* watch [modifies *watch*]	Go *slow*. [modifies *go*]
an *early* bird [modifies *bird*]	She came *early*. [modifies *came*]
the *late* student [modifies *student*]	They slept *late*. [modifies *slept*]
a *well* child [modifies *child*]	She played *well*. [modifies *played*]

    Good, along with some other adjectives, sometimes causes trouble when used after a verb. Because *good* should not be used after most verbs, avoid *talks good*, *drives good*, *writes good*, and so on. *Good*, as well as other adjectives, however, may be used after some verbs, called *linking verbs*, such as *look, smell, taste, feel, appear, stay, seem, remain, grow, become,* and all forms of *to be*. Thus, it is correct to say *sounds good, feels good, is good,* and so forth. (Notice that many, but not all, linking verbs refer to the senses.)

    Occasionally linking verbs are used as active verbs. *Look*, for instance, is a linking verb when referring to someone's health or to the appearance of things, as in *The day looks good for a picnic.* But it is an active verb when it refers to the act of looking, as in *Mary looked proudly at her son.* To check whether a verb is a linking verb or an active verb, substitute a form of the verb *to be* in its place. If the sentence retains its basic meaning, the verb is probably a linking verb. For example:

The pizza *tastes* good.	The pizza *is* good.
She will *stay* asleep until noon.	She *will be* asleep until noon.

In both examples, the substitute verb maintains the essential meaning of the sentence. Therefore, *tastes* and *stay* are linking verbs and may be followed by any adjective you choose: *sour, sweet, tart, spoiled, happy, satisfied, cool, depressed,* and many, many others.

    Adverbs usually describe, or modify, verbs, adjectives, or other adverbs. They often give answers to such questions as How? When? How much? Where? In what sequence? To what extent? In what manner?

    How does Richard run? Richard runs *well*. (The adverb *well* modifies the verb *run*.)

    When should Martha go to the store? Martha should go *now*. (The adverb *now* modifies the verb *go*.)

    How much did it rain last night? It rained *enough* to flood the basement. (The adverb *enough* modifies the verb *rain*.)

    In what manner did Juan sit down? Juan sat down *quickly*. (The adverb *quickly* modifies the verb *sat*.)

Adjectives and Adverbs

Review: Whenever a choice must be made between an adjective or an adverb, determine whether the verb is a linking verb. If it is, use the adjective. If it isn't, use the adverb. Also, if the word modifies an adjective or another adverb, you must use the adverb. If it modifies a noun or pronoun, use the adjective. Most errors involving adjective/adverb usage occur when no clear distinction is evident between the linking verbs and the active verbs being modified.

Use adverbs to modify active verbs:

> The dancer spun swiftly around the stage. (*Swiftly* is an adverb; it explains how the dancer spun; therefore, *swiftly* modifies, or clarifies, the active verb *spun*.)

When the verb is clearly active, it must be followed by an adverb, never by an adjective. But when the verb is a linking verb, use an adjective:

> Onion soup tastes good. (*Good* is an adjective; it describes the soup. If *tastes* were an active verb, the adverb *well* would be needed. To say that the soup tastes *well* is nonsense, however.)

The first word of a sentence is always capitalized.

The pronoun *I* is always capitalized: "John and *I* are good friends."

Proper nouns are always capitalized. The individual title of any person, place, or thing is a proper noun. A good dictionary indicates proper nouns by capitalizing them. Some examples of proper nouns are: *James Madison High School, The Pine Tree Tavern, Hamilton College, Florida, Crescent City, New York State, African, France, Mary Roberts Rinehart, Second Avenue, Mr. Smith, Judge Black, Elm Street.* Notice that words like *school* and *city* are capitalized when they are part of the title. So are honorary or distinguishing titles (whether abbreviated or not) when placed before names: *Miss Halpern, Mrs. Smith, Doctor Johnson, Dr. Johnson, Capt. Darcy, Professor Edwards, Prof. Edwards.* Remember that titles are not capitalized when they come after the person's name: *Jonathan Edwards, professor of theology; Martha Johnson, doctor of pediatric cardiology.*

Titles of books, plays, poems, themes, essays, etc. are capitalized. The first word of the title is always capitalized and all other words except the articles (*a, an, the*) and short prepositions and conjunctions (like *and, but, in, of*). The last word of the title is always capitalized: *The Phantom of the Opera, Back to the Future, A Rose for Emily, For Whom the Bell Tolls.*

The names of geographical regions are capitalized: the *Southwest,* the *South.* Such words are not capitalized when they merely indicate direction: "He went *west.*" BUT "He settled in the *West.*"

Days of the week, months of the year, holidays are capitalized: *Monday, Tuesday, January, February, Easter, Martin Luther King's Birthday.* But names of the seasons are not capitalized: *spring, autumn, fall, winter.*

Common nouns are capitalized when they become proper nouns by being used to identify a specific person, place, or thing. For example, *history* is a common noun. But *History of the United States* or *History 201* might be names of academic courses. *Mother* is a common noun in a phrase like *my mother.* But in the sentence *I will ask Mother,* the absence of the identifying word *my* makes *Mother* the identification of one specific person. In similar identifications like *Uncle John* or *President Smith,* the nouns *uncle* and *president* become proper nouns because they are part of the identifications of specific people.

Abbreviations of titles, usually placed after a name, are capitalized: *John Larkin, M.D., Frank Loeser, Jr., James Donovan, Ph.D.*

The first word of a line of verse is usually capitalized.

The word or opening words used for the salutation of a letter are capitalized: *Gentlemen: Dear Madam: Dear Sir: My dear Mrs. Smith: Dear Fred, Dear Mr. Strong,.*

The opening word of the complimentary close of a letter is capitalized: *Sincerely, Sincerely yours, Yours very truly, Cordially yours,.*

Conjunctions

Coordinating Conjunctions

Coordinating conjunctions join words, phrases, and clauses of equal value. The coordinating conjunctions are: *and, but, or, nor, for, whereas, yet, so.*

and	He likes bread and butter.
	She bought a black-and-white dress.
	He did it quickly and well.
	Over the fence and into the woods went the ball.
	They sang and danced all night.
	The crowds were inside and outside the church.
	Drinking too much and eating too little was bad for him.
	Mary prepared the salad, and Jane made the cake.
but	(As a preposition it means *except*.)
	He did it quickly but well.
	Over the net but into the woods went the ball.
	They did not sing but danced all night.
	The crowd was angry but not ready to take action.
	Drinking too much but eating too title was bad for him.
	Mary prepared the salad, but Jane made the cake.
for	They decided to leave, for they could see that a storm was coming.
nor	He didn't mind leaving the party, nor would anyone miss him.
or	Do you want tea or coffee?
	I want a red or a green dress.
	Do it immediately or not at all.
	I will do it quickly or carefully, whichever you please.
	Put it on the table or on the counter.
	They sang or danced all night long.
	Are you for or against this proposal?
	Eating too much or drinking too much was bad for him.
	Get dressed quickly, or I won't wait for you.
so	The driver explained the reason for the delay, so everybody was willing to wait patiently.
whereas	(formal usage)
	Whereas the council has deliberated this matter for several weeks, be it resolved that no sensible action can be taken.
yet	She was a pretty, yet not very attractive girl.
	She did it quickly, yet well.
	He heard the clock strike, yet did not pay attention to the time.
	Speaking with apparent frankness, yet concealing his inner thoughts, he swayed the crowd.

Again and again he cried for help, yet nobody paid any attention to him.

Correlative Conjunctions

Correlative conjunctions are pairs of words used to join sentence elements of equal importance.

as	The tree was as tall as the house.
. . . as	He did it as well as he could.
both	Both the men and the women took part in the sports.
. . . and	He was both older and wiser as a result of long experience.
either	Either John or Fred is at home.
. . . or	Either John or his sisters are at home.
	Either his sisters or John is at home.
	We can either walk or ride to the picnic.
neither	Neither John nor Fred is at home.
. . . nor	Neither John nor his sisters are at home.
	Neither his sisters nor John is at home.
	We can neither walk nor ride to the picnic.
not only	He played not only jazz but also classical music.
. . . but	He not only worked hard, but he also played hard.
also	
so	He was not so tall as his sister.
. . . as	He was not so happy as he pretended to be.

NOTE: *So . . . as* is used after a negative construction instead of *as . . . as*.

Subordinating Conjunctions

Subordinating conjunctions join sentence elements of unequal rank. They are: *as, after, although, because, before, if, since, that, though, unless, until, when, where, while*. Subordinating conjunctions are most frequently used to join dependent clauses to independent clauses.

He whistled *while* he worked.

A few words like *after* function both as prepositions and conjunctions.

He came *after* me. [preposition]
He came *after* I did. [conjunction]

The conjunctions *as* and *than* are sometimes confused with prepositions because they frequently introduce elliptical clauses (clauses where words are omitted because the meaning is clear without them).

He worked as rapidly *as* I [worked].
I worked more rapidly *than* he [worked].
She disliked him as much *as* [she disliked] me.
The rain soaked him more *than* [it soaked] me.

The relative pronouns (*who, which, that*) frequently act as subordinating conjunctions.

John, *who* was ill, recovered.
He did not know *which* of the girls he liked best.
The cake *that* she made was good.

When indicating a causal relationship, the conjunctions *because, since,* and *as* are preferable in that order. *Since* is weaker than *because,* for it also refers to time (*She has been unhappy since she left the city.*). *As* is the weakest because it also refers both to time and comparison (*He tackled each problem as he came to it. He played as hard as he worked.*).

Most of the subordinating conjunctions frequently introduce participial phrases.

After cleaning the house, she took a nap.
He read the paper *while* eating his breakfast.
Although driven to the wall, he kept calm.

Conjunctive Adverbs

A few adverbs, like *consequently, furthermore, however, moreover, nevertheless, then, therefore,* function with the effect of conjunctions because they refer to the subject matter of the preceding sentence. They are not actually conjunctions because they may not be used to join sentence elements of either equal or unequal value.

He was sick. *Consequently,* he did not go to work.
It costs more than it's worth. *Furthermore,* I don't need it.
He was not poor. He was glad, *however,* to inherit the money.
He was tired from lack of sleep. *Moreover,* he had a bad cold.
She hated the town. *Nevertheless,* she was willing to live there.

aren't	are not	shan't	shall not
can't	cannot	she'd	she would, she had
couldn't	could not	she'll	she will
didn't	did not	she's	she is, she has
doesn't	does not	shouldn't	should not
don't	do not	they'd	they would, they had
hadn't	had not	they'll	they will
hasn't	has not	they're	they are
haven't	have not	wasn't	was not
he'd	he would, he had	we'd	we would, we had
he'll	he will	we're	we are
he's	he is, he has	weren't	were not
I'd	I would, I had	we've	we have
I'll	I shall, I will	won't	will not
I'm	I am	wouldn't	would not
I've	I have	you'd	you would, you had
isn't	is not	you'll	you will
it's	it is	you're	you are
mightn't	might not	you've	you have
mustn't	must not		

Glossary of Troublesome Words and Phrases

Diction

Diction means word choice. Faulty diction occurs when a word is used that means something other than what is intended (*e.g.*, *infer* instead of *imply*, or *eminent* instead of *imminent*). Faulty word choice also occurs when an inappropriate word is used (*e.g.*, a slang expression like *chill out* or *you guys* in a formal context), or when a grammatically incorrect word is used (*e.g.*, *good* instead of *well* after a certain verb, or *where* instead of *when*, as in "the time where you lost your wallet").

a, an	Use *a* before words beginning with a consonant sound: *a book*, *a unique ring*. Use *an* before words beginning with a vowel sound: *an apple, an urchin*.
accept, except	*Accept* means to *receive*: "Please *accept* my offer." The verb *except* means to leave out or omit: "Will you *except* the last provision of the contract?"
adapt, adopt	*Adapt* means to modify and make suitable; *adopt* is to choose or select, as in "We adopted a style of play which had been adapted from one used by the New York Giants."
adverse, averse	*Adverse* means *opposing*: *adverse circumstances*. *Averse* means *opposed to*: "He was *averse* to my proposal." *Adverse* usually relates to actions or things. *Averse* usually applies to people (who have an aversion).
advert, avert	*Advert* means *refer*: "The speaker *adverted* to an earlier talk he had given." *Avert* means *ward off*: "He narrowly *averted* a bad fall."
advice, advise	*Advice* is a noun meaning recommendation concerning an action or decision: "Few people will take my *advice* when I give it to them." *Advise* is a verb: "I *advise* you to take fewer courses next year."
affect, effect	*Affect* means to *influence*: "His attitude in class *affected* his grade." *Affect* is never used as a noun except in psychological terminology. *Effect* as a noun means *result*: "The *effect* of the explosion was disastrous." *Effect* as a verb means to *accomplish*: "The new machinery *effected* a decided improvement in the product."
aggravate	Do not use *aggravate* to mean *irritate*. *Aggravate* means to make a bad situation worse: "I was *irritated* by his behavior when he came in, but he *aggravated* the situation when he slammed the door when he went out."
aggravation	*Aggravation* means an act or circumstance that increases the gravity or seriousness of a situation: "His job was difficult enough in itself without the unexpected *aggravation* of the addition of overtime work."

Glossary of Troublesome Words and Phrases

aid, aide
: *Aid* can mean "assistance" or "to assist," but *aide* is always a noun meaning an assistant.

almost, most
: *Almost* means *nearly*: "He was *almost* ready when we called for him." "*Almost* every girl in the class had long hair." *Most* as an adjective or adverb means *in the greatest degree*: "A *most* difficult problem was presented." "*Most* people prefer sunny climates." *Most* as a noun means the largest number or the greatest quantity: "The *most* I can give you is $2."

all ready, already
: *All ready* (two words) is used in such sentences as "They are *all ready* to go." *Already* is an adverb meaning *previously*: "We ran to catch the train but it had *already* left."

all right, alright
: *Alright* is illiterate for *all right*. Do not confuse the spelling with words like *almost, already, altogether*.

a lot, allot
: *Allot* is a verb meaning *to apportion, to share out*. When speaking of a large quantity, use *a lot*. Never write it as a single word (*alot*). There is no such word in standard English.

altogether, all together
: *All together* (two words) is used in such sentences as "They were *all together* in the same room." *Altogether* is an adverb, meaning *completely*: "You are *altogether* wrong in your assumption."

allusion, illusion, delusion
: *Allusion* means reference to: "She made an *allusion* to last week's meeting." *Illusion* is an unreality: "That a pair of railroad tracks seems to meet in the distance is an optical *illusion*." *Delusion* is a false belief: "Convinced that he was the King of Spain, Tom lived in a *delusion*."

alternative, alternate
: *Alternative* means a choice in a situation where a choice must be made between two possibilities: "If you can't take the test on Thursday, your only *alternative* is to take it next week." *Alternate* means substitute, as in: "Because the main road was under construction, they took an *alternate* route to town."

alumnus, alumna, alumni, alumnae
: An *alumnus* is a male graduate. *Alumni* is the plural. An *alumna* is a female graduate. *Alumnae* is the plural. *Alumni* is used for male and female combined.

among, between
: *Between* is used in connection with two persons or things: "He divided the money *between* his two children." *Among* is used for more than two. "He divided the money *among* his three children." EXCEPTIONS: If more than two are involved in a united situation, *between* is used: "*Between* the four of us we raised a thousand dollars." If a comparison or an opposition is involved,

19

Glossary of Troublesome Words and Phrases

between is used: "There was great rivalry *between* the three colleges. It was difficult to choose *between* them."

amount, number
Amount refers to bulk or quantity: *amount* of sugar, grain, flour, money. *Number* refers to objects which are thought of as individual units: *number* of oranges, children, diamonds. Notice that most words following *amount* are singular (*coal, butter, water*) and that most words following *number* are plural (*apples, bottles, glasses*).

and/or
Although this usage is becoming common, it is unnecessary and should be avoided. *Or* alone carries the same meaning.

ante- anti-
These similar prefixes carry different meanings. *Ante-* means "before" and *anti-* means "against" or "opposed to." Notice *antebellum* (before the war) and *antiwar* (against war).

any one, anyone
Any one means any single person or thing of a group: "*Any one* of the students in the class was capable of passing the course." *Anyone* is an indefinite pronoun meaning *anybody:* "*Anyone* can tell that you are not as stupid as you pretend."

appraise, apprise
Appraise means to make an estimate: "Will you *appraise* the value of this ring?" *Apprise* means *inform* (usually in a formal sense): "He was *apprised* by registered mail that his lease would not be renewed."

apt, liable, likely
Apt refers to a habitual disposition: "Having a good brain, he is *apt* to get good grades." *Likely* merely expresses probability: "It is *likely* to rain." *Liable* implies the probability of something unfortunate: "The firm is *liable* to fail."

as . . . as, so . . . as
As . . . as is used for affirmative comparisons. "He was *as* tall *as* his father." *So . . . as* is used for negative comparisons: She was not *so* tall *as* her mother."

as, like
When used as a preposition, *like* should never introduce a clause (NOT *like I was saying*). When introducing a clause, *as* is used (*as I was saying*) even if some of the words of the clause are implied: "He did it as well *as* I [did]."

beside, besides
Beside means *by the side of:* "Ask him to sit *beside* me." *Besides* means *in addition:* "She was an expert secretary. *Besides*, she had a wonderful disposition."

bimonthly, semimonthly
Bimonthly magazines are published once every two months. *Semimonthly* ones are published twice a month.

bring, take
Bring refers to movement toward the speaker: "*Bring* me a ham sandwich, please." *Take* refers to movement away from the speaker: "*Take* this book over to the shelf near the window."

Glossary of Troublesome Words and Phrases

can, may	*Can* implies ability: "*Can* you (are you able to) lift that heavy box?" *May* denotes permission: "*May* I (Have I permission to) swim in your pool?"
cite, site	To *cite* is to make a reference to a source in a term paper. The noun *site* refers to a space of ground, as in "the *site* of a new dormitory."
claim, assert	*Claim* refers to a justified demand or legal right: "I *claim* this piece of property." "I *claim* the prize." It should not be used when only an assertion is intended: "He *asserted* (not *claimed*) that his demands were reasonable."
common, mutual	*Common* means shared by two or more people or things: "The classmates had a *common* admiration for their school." "All the houses in the development had a big recreation area in *common*." *Mutual* means *reciprocal*: "The classmates had a *mutual* admiration for each other."
compare to, compare with	*Compare to* is used to indicate a definite resemblance: "He *compared* the railroad *to* a highway." *Compare with* is used to indicate an examination of similarities and dissimilarities: "He *compared* the middle ages *with* modern times."
complement, compliment	*Complement* as a verb means *complete*: "He needed a typewriter to *complement* his office equipment." As a noun *complement* means whatever is needed for completion: "I am sending you fifty books as a *complement* to your law library." It can also mean whatever is needed to complete an operation: "The officers and crew are the *complement* of a ship." *Compliment* is a noun meaning an expression of admiration: "He paid her the *compliment* of saying that she had exquisite taste in clothes."
confidant, confident	A *confidant* (*confidante*, if female) is a trusted friend in whom one can "confide." *Confident* is an adjective meaning you are certain, e.g., you are *confident* he or she will not betray your trust.
consul, council, counsel	A *consul* is a government agent who lives in a foreign country to protect the interests of the citizens of his own country: "When I lost my passport, I went immediately to the *consul*." *Council* is a *group* of individuals who act in an advisory capacity or who meet for the purposes of discussion or decision-making: "The mayor met with the *council*." "They called a *council* to make plans for the future." *Counsel* as a noun means *advice*, or, in legal parlance, a lawyer or lawyers: "He sought my *counsel*." "He retained *counsel* to represent him at the trial." As a verb *counsel* means *advise*: "I would *counsel* you to accept his offer."

Glossary of Troublesome Words and Phrases

contemptuous, contemptible
: *Contemptuous* means showing contempt: "My teacher was *contemptuous* of my performance." *Contemptible* means deserving of contempt: "His rude behavior at the wedding was *contemptible*."

continual, continuous
: *Continual* means *constantly with interruptions*: "She smoked *continually*." *Continuous* means *without interruptions*: "The water flows *continuously* over Niagara Falls."

councilor, counselor
: A *councilor* is a member of a council. A *counselor* is an adviser. The term is also used to denote a leader, guardian, or supervisor of children or young people as at a summer camp.

credible, creditable, credulous
: *Credible* means *believable*: "His story was entirely *credible*." *Creditable* means *meritorious, praiseworthy*—but not outstanding: "His performance was *creditable*, but I wouldn't pay admission to hear him again." *Credulous* means *ready to believe*: "Being a *credulous* person, he believed everything he read."

different from, differ from, differ with
: *Different from* is the correct idiom, NOT *different than*. *Differ from* applies to differences between one person or thing and another or others: "My car *differs from* his because it is a newer model." *Differ with* means to have a difference in opinion: "I *differ with* him in his views about government."

discreet, discrete
: *Discreet* means careful in avoiding mistakes, as in "He was *discreet* in his habits." *Discrete* means separate, or detached, as in "Each grain of rice was *discrete*, not clinging to the rest in a glutinous mass."

disinterested, uninterested
: *Disinterested* means impartial: "The two sides chose a *disinterested* party to settle the dispute between them." *Uninterested* means apathetic: "Some people are *uninterested* in modern art."

dominate, domineer
: *Dominate* means to rule over: "He *dominated* the audience with his oratory." *Domineer* means to rule tyrannically: "One of his daughters *domineered* over the entire family."

don't
: *Don't* is the contraction of *do not: I don't, you don't, we don't, they don't*. Do not confuse it with *doesn't*, the contraction of *does not: He doesn't, she doesn't, it doesn't*.

dual, duel
: *Dual* means double: "Since he was born in England of American parents, he could lay claim to *dual* citizenship." A *duel* is a combat between two men: "He challenged his enemy to a *duel* with pistols."

due to
: *Due to* acts grammatically as an adjective and must therefore modify a specific noun or pronoun: "The flood was *due to* the rapid spring thaw." If there is no specific noun or pronoun for *due* to modify, use the phrase *because of*: "He was late *because*

of an accident." Or rephrase the sentence: "His *lateness* [noun] was *due to* an accident."

elicit,
illicit

Elicit means to draw or bring forth: "After hours of questioning, they *elicited* the truth from him." *Illicit* is an adjective meaning not permitted or illegal: "Traffic in drugs is *illicit*."

emigrant,
immigrant

A *migrant* is a member of a mass movement of people from one region to another. A migrant who leaves a country or place of residence is called an *emigrant*; one who comes in is an *immigrant*.

eminent,
imminent

Eminent means famous or prominent; *imminent* means soon to take place: "The Christmas season is *imminent*."

famous,
infamous

Famous means well-known: "After medical school, she became a *famous* surgeon." *Infamous* also means well-known but for a negative reason: "He participated in the *infamous* art theft at the museum."

fewer, less

Fewer is used in connection with people or with objects which are thought of as individual units: *fewer oranges, fewer children, fewer books, fewer dollars. Less* is used in connection with the concept of bulk: *less money, less coal, less weight, less grain.* Notice that most words following *fewer* are plural (*oranges, books, dollars*); most words following *less* are singular (*money, coal, weight*).

flaunt, flout

Flaunt means to display in an ostentatious fashion: "He *flaunted* his learning before his friends." *Flout* means to treat with contempt: "They *flouted* the law by parking in front of a hydrant."

forcible,
forceful

Forcible means effected by force, no matter how much or how little force is used: "Since the key wouldn't fit, they made a *forcible* entry into the house by breaking a window." *Forceful* means full of force: "He was a very *forceful* speaker."

former,
latter

Former and *latter* are used to designate one of two persons or things: "Of the two possibilities, I prefer the *former* to the *latter*." If more than two persons or things are involved, *first* or *first named* and *last* or *last named* are used: "He had a choice of yellow, rose, pink, and brown. He preferred the *first* and *last* to the others."

formerly,
formally

Formerly means at an earlier time: "He is a rich man, but he was *formerly* poor." *Formally* means done in a very correct manner: "He was *formally* inducted into the lodge."

fortuitous,
fortunate

That which is *fortuitous* happens by accident and may or may not be a favorable event. The word is often misused as a synonym for *fortunate*, but it does not have this meaning.

Glossary of Troublesome Words and Phrases

had ought	*Ought* is known as a defective verb because it has only one form and cannot be used with an auxiliary: "They *ought* (NOT *had ought*) to have told her."
hanged, hung	*Hanged* is used in connection with executions: "He was condemned to be *hanged* by the neck until dead." *Hung* is the past tense of *hang* and denotes any other kind of suspension: "The pictures were *hung* on the wall."
hardly	Like *barely* and *scarcely, hardly* should not be used with a negative. "He was *hardly* (*barely, scarcely*) able to do it." (NOT *not hardly, barely, scarcely*.)
healthful, healthy	*Healthful* means *health-giving:* a *healthful* climate. *Healthy* means *in a state of health:* "She was a *healthy* young girl."
imply, infer	*Imply* means to throw out a hint or suggestion: "She *implied* by her manner that she was unhappy." *Infer* means to take in a hint or suggestion: "I *inferred* from her manner that she was unhappy."
in, into	*In* means within or inside: "Old correspondence is stored *in* this file." *Into* refers to motion from outside to inside: "Put the pickles *into* the glass jar."
indict, indite	*Indict* means to make a formal charge of an offense as a means of bringing a suspect to trial: "He was *indicted* for evasion of income tax." *Indite* means to compose a formal or literary work: "Robert Frost *indited* many poems about New England."
ingenious, ingenuous	*Ingenious* means possessing unusual powers of invention when applied to a person and showing the result of clever inventiveness when applied to a thing: "The *ingenious* inventor perfected a most *ingenious* mechanical toy." *Ingenuity* is the noun. *Ingenuous* means naive or unsophisticated: "He was so *ingenuous* that he believed everything he read."
its, it's	*Its* (no apostrophe) is the possessive case of *it:* "The pig suckled *its* young." *It's* is the contraction of *it is:* "*It's* too late to go to church."
kind, sort, type, variety	When these words are singular in number, they should never be prefaced by plural modifiers: *This kind of book* (Not *these* kind of book). If you want a plural construction, you must make sure all parts are plural: *These kinds of books.*
kind of, sort of, type of, variety of	Never place an article after these expressions: *This kind of pistol* (NOT this kind of *a* pistol).

last, latest	*Last* means that which comes at the end: "It is the *last* game of the season." *Latest* is the last in time, but not necessarily the final occurrence: "That was the *latest* insult in a series of indignities."
lay, lie	*Lay, laid, laid* are the principal parts of the transitive verb which means *to put down*: "I shall *lay* the rug." "I *laid* the rug." "I have *laid* the rug." "I *am laying* the rug." *Lie, lay, lain* are the principal parts of the intransitive verb (it cannot take an object) which means *to recline* or *repose*: "She will *lie* in the hammock." "She *lay* in the hammock yesterday." "She *has lain* there all afternoon." "She *is lying* in the hammock."
lead, led	When pronounced alike, the noun *lead* is the metal; *led* is the past tense and past participle of the verb *to lead* (*pronounced leed*).
learn, teach	*Learn* means to acquire information or knowledge: "I *learned* my lesson." *Teach* means to impart information or knowledge: "I intend to *teach* him as much as he *taught* me."
liable	See *apt.*
like	See *as.*
likely	See *apt.*
loose, lose	*Loose* is an adjective meaning *not completely attached*: "The screw is *loose*." *Lose* is a verb meaning *to be deprived of*: "I *lost* a lot of money at the race track and I don't intend to *lose* any more."
majority, plurality	In voting, *majority* means the number of votes constituting more than half of the total number cast. "Since fifty-one of the one hundred members voted for Jane, she won by a *majority*." *Plurality* is used when there are three or more candidates. It means the excess of votes received by the leading candidate over those received by the next most popular candidate: "The results of the ballot are as follows: Smith, 254; Jones, 250; Marshall, 243; Edwards, 23. Therefore Smith won by a *plurality* of 4. *Plurality* is also used to mean the largest number of votes received by a single candidate: "In the results listed above, Smith received a *plurality* but not a *majority*."
mean, median	*Mean* is the middle point between extremes (computed mathematically by dividing the sum of the quantities in a set by the number of terms in the set). *Median* refers to the middle value in a series of numbers, ranged from smallest to largest.
militate, mitigate	*Militate* (connected with *military*) means to have a strong influence for or against, usually against: "His grouchy manner

Glossary of Troublesome Words and Phrases

militated against his success as a salesman." *Mitigate* means to lessen: "The cold compress on his leg *mitigated* the pain."

miner, minor
A *miner* is one who extracts minerals from the earth. When used as a noun a *minor* means one who is under age. As an adjective *minor* means *unimportant*. "Since he was a *minor*, the judge let him off with a *minor* penalty."

moral, morale
Moral is an adjective meaning pertaining to the accepted customs of a society with reference to right or wrong: "I know that he didn't steal my book because he is a very *moral* young man." *Morality* is the noun. *Morale* means a *state of well being*: "The *morale* of the employees was very good."

myself
Myself (like *yourself, himself, herself, itself, yourselves, themselves*) is an intensive and reflexive pronoun. It should never be used in a sentence without its corresponding noun or pronoun: "*I myself* will do it." "*I* hurt *myself*." "They sent for John and *me* (NOT *myself*).

nauseated, nauseous
Nauseated means sick: "After the roller coaster ride, Susan felt *nauseated*." *Nauseous* refers to something that evokes disgust: "The rotten eggs left a *nauseous* odor in the refrigerator."

personal, personnel
Personal is an adjective meaning *pertaining to an individual*: "The watch was his *personal* property." *Personnel* is a noun meaning the group of people employed in an organization: "The *personnel* manager is in charge of the welfare of the *personnel* of the firm."

plain, plane
Plain is an adjective meaning *simple* or *unadorned*: "Carl Sandburg loved the *plain* people." *Plain* is also a noun meaning flat country. *Plane* is a noun meaning *a flat surface*. It is also a tool used to make a flat surface smooth. It is also an accepted abbreviation for *airplane*. "When he went by *plane* to the great *plain* between the mountains, he took several *planes* with him along with his other carpenter's tools."

plurality
See *majority*.

practicable, practical
Practicable means capable of being put into practice: "He found a *practicable* way of depositing money without going to the bank." *Practical* means *useful* or *related to actual experience* as opposed to *theoretical*: "The *practical* nurse knew several *practical* methods to stop the flow of blood."

principal, principle
Principal is usually an adjective meaning *main*: *principal* cities, *principal* people. It has become a noun in a few usages where the noun it formerly modified is understood. "He was the *principal* (teacher) of the school." "I withdrew the

DANVILLE PUBLIC LIBRARY
DANVILLE, INDIANA

principal (amount) and interest from my savings account."
"He acted as the *principal* (person) rather than as an agent."
The noun *principle* means a *basic law* or *doctrine*: "The country
was founded on the *principle* that all men are created free and
equal."

prone, supine
: *Prone* means reclining with the face downward: "He slept in
a *prone* position to keep the sun out of his eyes." *Supine*
means reclining with the face upward (note the word *up* in
supine): "He lay *supine* on the ground all morning watching the
clouds."

quiet, quite
: *Quiet* means free from noise: "*Quiet* must be preserved in the
library." *Quite* means either *fully* or *to a considerable extent*,
depending on the sense of the sentence: "By the time the doctor
arrived, the mother was *quite* upset because she thought her
child was *quite* ill."

rare, scarce
: *Rare* and *scarce* refer to hard-to-find items in short supply.
Rare usually implies exceptional quality, as in a "*rare* book."
Scarce can be applied to ordinary things like potatoes that are
usually abundant.

reason is, because
: The words *reason is* (*was*, etc.) should be followed by a
statement of the reason: "The *reason* for his failure *was* illness."
"The *reason* for the strict rules *is* to enforce discipline." Similar
statements can be made by using *because*: "He failed *because* of
illness." "The rules are strict *because* it is necessary to enforce
discipline." *Reason* and *because* convey the same sense. It is
illogical to use both words to indicate the same meaning.

recommend, refer
: *Recommend* means *to present as worthy of confidence*: "Do
you know any doctor you could *recommend* to me?" *Refer* means
to direct attention to: "Can you *refer* me to a good doctor?"

regardless, irregardless
: *Regardless* means in spite of: "*Regardless* of the strike, they
will go to work." *Irregardless* is a non-standard synonym for
regardless and should not be used.

same
: Do not use *same* as a pronoun: "I have your order and will send
it (NOT will send *same*)."

sensory, sensuous, sensual
: *Sensory* pertains to one or more of the five senses: "Walking
through the rose garden was a *sensory* delight." *Sensuous*
means gratifying to the senses: "A vase with a *sensuous* shape
stood on the shelf." *Sensual* refers to the pleasures of the senses,
especially the pleasures of the flesh: "It is clearly wrong to
broadcast *sensual* advertisements during Saturday morning
cartoons."

Glossary of Troublesome Words and Phrases

stationary, stationery	*Stationary* is an adjective meaning *fixed* or *attached*: "The benches are *stationary* because they are fastened to the floor." *Stationery* is writing paper used in correspondence: "He bought a box of *stationery* at the *stationery* store so that he could write to his friends." Notice that the *er* in *stationery* corresponds to the *er* in *paper*.
terse, trite	*Terse* means *concise*: "Francis Bacon wrote in a very *terse* style." *Trite* means *hackneyed, worn out from overuse*: "*As different as night and day* is a *trite* expression."
than, then	*Than* is a conjunction: "She was wealthier *than* her sister." *Then* is an adverb denoting time, past or future: "She remembered her youth because her sister was richer *then*. But *then* she herself fell heir to a fortune."
their, there	Be careful to distinguish the spelling of the possessive case of the pronoun *their* (*their* books) from the spelling of the adverb and expletive *there*. "I got *there* before I knew it." "*There* are forty oranges in the crate."
therefor, therefore	*Therefor* means *for that, for it, for them*: "I sent the manuscript by registered mail and have the receipt *therefor*." *Therefore* means for that reason: "He was sick. *Therefore*, he did not go to work."
to, too, two	*To* is a preposition meaning *direction toward*: "Take this package *to* the store." It is used to make the infinitive when combined with the root of a verb: *to eat, to sing. Too* is an adverb meaning *more than enough*: "He was *too* tired to eat." *Two* is the number 2.
tortuous, torturous	*Tortuous* means full of twists or bends: "The car was moving too fast for such a *tortuous*, crooked road." *Torturous* means inflicting great pain in a cruel manner.
unique	*Unique* means the only one of its kind: "His was a *unique* personality." It cannot logically be used in a comparative or superlative form. Something may be more or most odd, rare, unusual, peculiar, remarkable, etc., but NOT more or most *unique*.
verbal, oral	*Verbal* means *pertaining to words*; *oral* means *pertaining to spoken words*: "She nodded assent, but gave no *verbal* confirmation, either written or *oral*."
waist, waste	*Waist* is the middle section of the body. "He wore a belt around his *waist*." As a verb *waste* means *to squander*; as a noun it means *that which is squandered or useless*: "He *wasted* his money." "Reading that stupid novel was a *waste* of time."

| who's, whose | *Who's* is the contraction for *who is* and *who has*: "I don't know *who's* coming." "*Who's* taken my matches?" *Whose* is the possessive form of *who*: "We knew the family *whose* house was robbed." |
| your, you're | *Your* is the possessive case of *you*: "I have read *your* notes." *You're* is the contraction of *you are*: "*You're* sure to be there on time if you leave now." |

Avoiding Errors in Diction

When in doubt about a correct word choice, consult a dictionary. A comprehensive dictionary will not only define each word but illustrate its use in a sentence or phrase. The famous *Oxford English Dictionary* is the most complete dictionary in existence, but other, more modest, dictionaries will serve most people equally well.

Be wary of a dictionary or thesaurus of synonyms found in most computer word-processing programs. The dictionary will check spelling but won't differentiate among misused words. The thesaurus will offer a list of synonyms. But use the thesaurus cautiously because many words only approximate the meaning of other words. Don't be misguided into thinking that any word listed as a synonym will be the equivalent of any other word. In the previous sentence, take the word *misguided*, for example. The thesaurus in Microsoft Word lists the following as synonyms: *mistaken, foolish, ill-advised, unwise, erroneous, injudicious, imprudent*, and *wrong*. All these words come close to the key word *misguided*, but not one of these so-called synonyms can properly serve as a substitute in the given sentence—not without making another revision to eliminate an awkward use of the word. Keep this caution in mind whenever you use the thesaurus for help.

Every language has its own idioms. An idiom usually consists of a group of words which is either meaningless or absurd if the words are understood to mean what they usually do. For example, *catch* is a simple and common word in such sentences as "He will catch a fish" and "He will catch the ball." But in English it is commonplace to say, "He will catch the train," meaning that he will be at the station in time to board the train before it leaves. Similarly, a common English idiom for suffering from a common winter ailment is "to catch cold." People are not being proud of their abilities when they say, "I caught a bad cold." Actually, the cold caught them.

The list of common idioms which begins on p. 30 is arranged alphabetically according to the key word in the idiom. The usual meaning of the key word can be found in any dictionary. Only the idiomatic meanings are described in this section.

Idioms

Idioms

ABOUT

The store is *about* five miles from here. (approximately)

I was *about to invite* you to the party. (on the verge of inviting)

It is *about* time you decided to pay back what you owe me. (certainly)

AFRAID

My sister would like to join us, but *I'm afraid* she has another engagement. (I regret that it is likely that)

AFTER

Who will *look after* the dog while we are on vacation? (take care of)

John won't be able to join us *after all*. (in spite of previous expectation)

Nellie asked *after you* when I saw her yesterday. (about you)

BACK

The mayor *backed* my brother for councilman. (supported)

The councilman had the mayor's *backing*. (support)

The tree stood *in back of* the house. (behind)

BALL

Stop loafing and *get on the ball*. (become efficient)

The gay and noisy young people were having *a ball*. (a good time)

After losing his money, John found himself *behind the 8-ball*. (in serious trouble)

BLUE

The departure of her friend left Mary feeling *blue*. (depressed, melancholy)

BUCK

It is foolish to try to *buck* an established system. (battle against)

BRIGHT

All *bright* young people should go to college. (intelligent)

CAR

The entire family went for a long ride in the *car*. (automobile)

CATCH

Take off your wet shoes and socks before you *catch cold*. (become ill from a cold)

They were late in leaving the house, but they *caught* the train. (arrived in time to board it before it left)

CHISEL

The dishonest storekeeper tried to *chisel* the customer. (cheat)

The storekeeper had the reputation of being a *chiseler*. (cheater)

COME

Father *came to grief* when he invested in a new speculative stock. (suffered misfortune)

The skeptical employee finally *came to believe* in the business. (acquired faith)

The dogmatic professor got *his comeuppance* when he was proved to be entirely wrong. (what he deserved)

Yellow tomatoes are *hard to come by*. (difficult to find)

COOL

Only a few of the people *kept cool* during the panic. (remained unexcited)

After his friend's apology, John *cooled down*. (lost his anger)

The labor arbitrator ordered *a cooling-off period*. (time to think calmly)

Cool off with a glass of cold beer. (lower body temperature)

DEAD

They were startled by the sound of sirens in the *dead* of night. (darkest hours)

I should have taken Fred's advice; he was *dead* right. (entirely)

The bus came to a *dead* stop at the railroad crossing. (complete)

DESERT

The judge gave the convicted criminal his *just deserts*. (justified punishment)

DISH

Mother asked me to *dish up* the peas. (serve from a bowl or pot)

DO

Good morning, my friend. How *do you do*? (are you)

Will you please *do up* my package? (wrap)

The soldiers *did away with* their prisoner. (killed)

Numbers *have to do* with arithmetic. (are connected)

Thank you. That *will do*. (is enough, is satisfactory)

I have eaten so much that I *can do without* dessert. (am willing to omit)

That steak is really *well done*. (thoroughly cooked)

The job was *well done* by the efficient clerk. (excellently completed)

It is time for us to *have done with* childish toys. (abandon)

Most missionaries are *do-gooders* at heart. (determined to help others)

Idioms

DOWN

Fearing the dark, my mother hoped to arrive by *sundown*. (dusk)

Amy went *downtown* to buy some new clothes. (business section or southern part of a town or city)

I made a *down* payment on the car and will pay the rest in installments. (first, initial)

I paid $500 *down* and will pay $10 a week for three years. (as a first payment)

DRIVE

After taking lessons, she learned to *drive* our car. (operate)

The entire family has gone out for *a drive*. (an automobile ride)

I don't understand what you are *driving at*. (trying to convey)

The vigorous young woman had lots of *drive*. (energy and determination)

DROP

Drop in (by) to see me some day. (make a casual visit)

The dull-eyed boy was a *high school dropout*. (left school before graduating)

EYE

The detective *eyed* the shopper suspiciously. (scrutinized)

The pretty girl *gave me the eye*. (flirted with me)

My shrewd friend *has his eyes open*. (isn't easily fooled)

My little daughter was *all eyes* when she saw her birthday presents. (amazed and delighted)

My father and I hardly ever *see eye to eye*. (agree)

That decaying old building is certainly *an eyesore*. (ugly)

The plane flew into the *eye* of the hurricane. (center)

FACE

Let him *face up to* his mistakes. (admit)

If he does, he will have to *face the music*. (be responsible for past errors)

Your explanation puts a new *face on* the matter. (interpretation of)

Most pompous people are apt to be *two-faced*. (hypocritical)

FALL

John and Mary *fell in love*. (became enamoured of each other)

The baby will soon *fall asleep*. (be)

FIRE

The employee was *fired* because of his inefficiency. (dismissed)

FIX

The automobile mechanic *fixed* our car. (repaired)

I was really in a *fix* when I lost my job. (difficult predicament)

FOOT

John was so naive that he was always *putting his foot in it*. (making embarrassing blunders)

Our wealthy friend offered to *foot* the bill at the hotel. (pay)

GET

The patient is feeling better and will soon *get* well. (become)

There are so many clouds that it is *getting* dark. (becoming)

Please try to *get along* with what you have. (manage)

It will be difficult, but we will try to *get along* without you. (manage)

Instead of talking so much, let's *get on with it*. (make progress)

The cheated customer *got even with* the salesman by calling the police. (avenged himself on)

Not knowing that he was being observed, the student expected to *get away with* his cheating. (evade discovery of)

GIVE

After several useless attempts, they *gave up*. (stopped trying)

During the earthquake a corner of the building *gave way*. (broke off)

GO

Tomorrow I *am going to* finish my work. (shall)

My energetic wife is always *on the go*. (active)

The mediator of the dispute acted as a *go-between*. (intermediary)

I believe the baby is *going to sleep*. (will soon be asleep)

It *goes without saying* that winters are cold in the north. (is self-evident)

The new fall styles are *all the go*. (popular)

The manufacturing company is a *going* concern. (thriving)

If you were only older, I could *go for* you. (fall in love with)

The job may be difficult, but let's *have a go at* it. (attempt)

We tried to finish the job, but it was *no go*. (unsuccessful)

HARD

The feeble old man was *hard of hearing*. (partially deaf)

The planning expert was a *hard-headed* man. (clear thinking)

The boss was too *hard-hearted* to raise my salary. (unsympathetic)

Being paid so little, I was always *hard up*. (poor)

Idioms

HAVE

The construction workers *have to* be careful. (must)

The *haves* and the *have-nots* have been studied by sociologists. (rich and poor)

HEART

Agnes *learned* the entire poem *by heart*. (memorized)

When his friend deserted him, he *took it to heart*. (was deeply troubled)

Mother couldn't resist a beggar, because she was *all heart*. (emotionally generous)

HIGH

After several cocktails our guests became quite *high*. (intoxicated)

The professor was very *high-handed* in assigning grades. (arrogant and arbitrary)

Emerson was a *high-minded* American author. (idealistic)

It is *high time* for all of us to go to bed. (latest reasonable time)

His experiences in the war left him very *high strung*. (nervous and hypersensitive)

The *highbrows* usually scorn the ordinary lowbrow people. (intellectuals)

After being awarded the Nobel prize, he became very *high hat*. (snobbish)

I'll meet you at the station at *high noon*. (on the dot of 12 noon)

HOLD

The lecturer *held forth* on the subject for nearly an hour. (orated)

How long can the enemy *hold out*? (endure)

The bandits *held up* the train. (stopped and robbed)

KNOW

Max was *in the know about* his sister's plans. (acquainted with)

After forty years in his firm, he had a lot of *know-how*. (expert knowledge)

LOOK

She gave him an angry *look*. (stare)

The boys like her because of her *good looks*. (attractive appearance)

That is another way of saying that she is *good looking*. (pleasant to look at)

Please *look after* my dog while I am away. (take care of)

Please *take a look at my oil*. (verify the level on the oil gauge)

It *looks like rain*. (appears as if rain was imminent)

LONG

The people at the beach basked in the sunshine *all day long*. (the entire day)

On vacation my brother had nothing to do *all the livelong day*. (the entire day)

MAKE

The shy young man was too timid to *try to make love* to her. (attempt sexual advances)

After their lover's quarrel, they kissed and *made up*. (were reconciled)

If we don't really have a good time, let's *make believe* it was fun. (pretend)

This hammer isn't really satisfactory, but I'll try to *make do* with it. (serve my purpose)

The salesman *made good* on the defective merchandise he sold us. (corrected the defect either by refunding money or substituting a satisfactory product)

I hearby *make it known* that I have divorced my wife. (publish the fact)

Let us eat, drink, and *make merry*. (have a good time)

After finishing college, he had to *make his way* in the world. (succeed)

The three men who robbed the bank *made off with* nearly a million dollars. (ran away with)

She *made up to* the professor, hoping that she would pass the course. (flattered)

MOUTH

He was so nervous at the meeting that he *mouthed his words*. (talked indistinctly)

I didn't read it in the newspaper; I heard it *by word of mouth*. (orally)

My brother was really *down in the mouth* after his house was robbed. (depressed)

OUT

The new book on outer space has just *come out*. (been published)

Mary and Jane quarreled a week ago; they are still *on the outs*. (unfriendly)

I never believe what he says because he is an *out-and-out* liar. (complete)

Your outrageous demands are *out of the question*. (impossible to fulfill)

I'll mend your rug tomorrow; I can't do it *out of hand*. (immediately or without preparation)

The Chinese have been growing rice since *time out of mind*. (extremely remote past)

Idioms

PASS

His grandfather *passed away* six months ago. (died)

One of the guests became so drunk that he *passed out*. (became unconscious)

The counterfeiter tried to *pass* one of his bills at the bank. (have it accepted)

It *came to pass* that there was a new prophet in Israel. (happened)

The clever actor *passed himself off as* a woman. (convinced the public that he was)

Things will come to a *pretty pass* if we don't act immediately. (critical situation)

PRETTY

After several months of practice, he became *pretty* good at golf. (quite)

Considering the short time he studied, he learned the lesson *pretty* well. (quite)

After her wealthy husband died, she found herself *sitting pretty*. (in an affluent position)

PUT

James was very much *put out* when the bank refused to give him a loan. (annoyed)

I can't believe you; you must be *putting me on*. (fooling me)

It is so late now that we will have to *put up with* this miserable hotel. (tolerate)

"*Put up or shut up*," said my partner when I argued about my share of the business. (Produce or be quiet.)

RED

The young man *saw red* when he was evicted from his room. (became very angry)

There is too much *red tape* involved in registering for this course. (tiresome details)

The thief was caught *red-handed* as he exited from the bank. (in the act)

Te threw a *red herring* into the case by pretending deafness. (misleading clue)

REST

Rest assured that I will do everything I can to help you. (Be)

36

RUN

When my father became ill, I had to *run* the establishment. (manage)

I believe that we will succeed *in the long run*. (over an extended period of time)

Our competitor is not exactly thriving, but he is still *in the running*. (competitive)

The splinter on the chair caused a *run* in Mary's stocking. (long vertical tear)

Don't you dare *run down* my achievement. (deprecate)

He *ran up* a big bill at the hotel. (accumulated)

The old building on the corner is in a *run-down* condition. (deteriorating)

The gambler decided to give his friend a *run* for his money. (contest)

SET

Early in the morning, they *set off* for the country. (departed)

The angry heirs had a real *set-to* about dividing the estate. (dispute)

SHARP

The millionaire was very *sharp* in running his business. (shrewd, clever)

With your new suit, you are really looking *sharp*. (well-groomed)

SHORT

I'll pay you tomorrow when I won't be so *short of* funds. (lacking in)

The business operation was *short-handed* during vacation periods. (deficient in number of employees)

He left the main road and took a *shortcut* to his house. (shorter way)

It never pays to be *shortsighted*. (remiss in foreseeing the future)

SHUT

"Shut up," said the angry father to his argumentative son. (Be quiet)

SMALL

I hate to go to the store with nothing but *small change* in my pocket. (pennies, nickels, dimes)

Bothered by his many worries, he stayed awake during the *small hours* of the night. (1, 2, 3 A.M.)

STAND

In spite of strong opposition, he took a firm *stand* on the matter. (position)

He left home because he couldn't *stand* his wife's friend. (endure)

Don't stand on ceremony; take off your jackets. (Be informal)

Throughout the entire trial, the attorney *stood up for* his client. (supported)

Idioms

He asserted his rights and *stood up to* the boss. (was firm in his attitude toward)

The snow was so heavy that everything came to a *standstill*. (complete stop)

The *standing* committee gave its annual report. (permanent)

STICK

Our best plan to avoid trouble is for all of us to *stick* together. (stay)

There is no point in *sticking at* trifles. (making an issue of)

TAKE

I expect to *take a train* to Boston. (go on a train)

It doesn't seem sensible to *take* the time to pack. (use)

The strange dog *took to* me right away. (liked)

Both of the children *take after* their mother. (resemble)

I am so tired of this job that I think I'll *take off*. (leave)

It is impossible to *take* you seriously when you talk so wildly. (consider)

TIE

At 8 to 8 the score was *tied*. It was a *tie* score. (even)

The busy executive was *tied up* at the office. (too busy to leave)

The ballplayer was *fit to be tied* when the umpire ruled against him. (extremely angry)

TIME

It isn't a perfect job, but it will do for the *time being*. (present)

If the plane isn't *on time*, we will have to wait. (punctual in arriving)

Once upon a time, there was a fairy princess. (in the remote past)

EXPRESSIONS OF TIME

8:30   Eight-thirty, half-past eight

9:15   Nine-fifteen, a quarter after (past) nine

10:45 Ten-forty-five, a quarter to eleven

2:50   Two-fifty, ten of (to) three

4:20   Four-twenty, twenty minutes past four, twenty after four

TRY

The tailor asked me to *try on* the suit. (put it on for fitting and appearance)

I met so many difficult customers that I had a *trying* day. (nerve-wracking)

TURN

He did me a *good turn* by mowing my lawn when I was away. (favor)

The old car *turned out* to be in good condition. (was actually)

I *turned over* my account to another bank. (transferred)
Our whole success in this undertaking *turns* on his ability. (depends)
Appearing so suddenly, you gave me quite a *turn*. (fright)

USE

I *used to enjoy* drinking milk, but now I prefer coffee. (formerly
enjoyed)
The new stove is very difficult to *get used to*. (become adjusted to)

WEATHER

It is raining, snowing, hailing, thundering and lightning, fair, warm, dry,
humid, etc.
It *looks like* rain, snow, etc. (appears likely that it will rain, etc.)
It has been a rainy, snowy, etc. day.

Interjections

The word *interjection* means *thrown in*. Interjections are words which either stand alone or are thrown into a sentence without becoming a part of the grammatical structure of the sentence. They are such words as *yes*, *no*, *oh*, *goodbye*, *hello* or sometimes phrases like *oh my*.

Since interjections are not properly parts of sentence structure, they either stand alone or are separated from the remainder of the sentence by commas.

> *Hello.* How are you?
> *No! Please!* Don't say it!
> *Yes,* I'll come with you.
> *Oh,* you can't mean it!
> I was resigned, *alas,* to failing the course.
> *Wow,* that is terrific news.

No and *not* are the usual words to express negation.

> He has *no* money left.
> They have *not* done what was expected of them.

In informal usage the contraction *n't* is more frequently used than *not*.

CONTRACTION	NEGATIVE	EXAMPLE
aren't	are not	They *aren't* able to come.
can't	cannot	They *can't* come.
couldn't	could not	He *couldn't* care less about his future.
doesn't	does not	He *doesn't* want to join the club.
don't	do not	They *don't* want to join the club.
hasn't	has not	He *hasn't* any money.
hadn't	had not	He *hadn't* enough time to pack before the train came.
haven't	have not	We *haven't* anything in the house for dessert.
isn't	is not	He *isn't* interested in her.
mustn't	must not	They *mustn't* think that we avoided them.
shan't	shall not	He *shan't* get any of my money.
shouldn't	should not	He *shouldn't* expect the impossible.
wasn't	was not	She *wasn't* able to complete her assignment.
weren't	were not	They *weren't* expecting him to come.
wouldn't	would not	He insisted that he *wouldn't* do the job.
won't	will not	She *won't* come even if you beg her to be agreeable.

Double Negatives

In some languages two negative words reinforce the negative sense; in standard English two negatives may not be used in the same statement.

> They *didn't* do *nothing* wrong.

Because both *didn't* and *nothing* are negatives, the sense of the sentence is the reverse of what was probably intended. Accurately stated:

> They *didn't* do anything wrong. or
> They did *nothing* wrong.

In some constructions, particularly when *not* modifies an adjective with a negative prefix such as *un*, *in*, and *im*, a double negative pairs words to make a positive statement:

> It was *not uncommon* for Lilah to wake up before dawn.
> For the train to arrive on time is *not impossible*.
> The schedule was *not at all incomplete*.

Negatives in English

Be vigilant for words like *hardly* and *scarcely*. They, too, are considered negative words.

You *can't hardly* tell one tree from another without a guidebook.

Both *can't* and *hardly* are negative words.

Likewise, stay alert for negative words followed by *but*, a word that is also regarded as negative. An expression like *can't help but* violates the double-negative rule. Therefore, "Harvey *can't help but* tell everyone what to do" should properly be "Harvey *can't help* telling everyone what to do."

Plurals

	SINGULAR	PLURAL
Most nouns form their plurals by adding *s* to the singular. Nouns ending in *s*, *sh*, *x*, or *z* add *es* to the singular.	son	sons
	house	houses
	boss	bosses
	gas	gases
	dish	dishes
	tax	taxes
	waltz	waltzes
Many nouns ending in *f* or *fe* change the *f* to *v* when forming their plurals. Nouns ending in *y* preceded by a consonant change the *y* to *i* and add *es*.	half	halves
	wife	wives
	penny	pennies
	laboratory	laboratories
The following nouns ending in *o* add *es* when forming their plurals.	buffalo	buffaloes
	calico	calicoes
	cargo	cargoes
	desperado	desperadoes
	domino	dominoes
	embargo	embargoes
	hero	heroes
	mosquito	mosquitoes

Nouns With Irregular Plurals

SINGULAR	PLURAL	SINGULAR	PLURAL
addendum	addenda	child	children
alumna (fem.)	alumnae	curriculum	curricula
alumnus (masc.)	alumni	datum	data
analysis	analyses	deer	deer
antithesis	antitheses	die	dice
appendix	appendices	elf	elves
axis	axes	ellipsis	ellipses
bacterium	bacteria	emphasis	emphases
basis	bases	fish	fish (*fishes*— different kinds)
beef	beeves	focus	foci
cannon	cannon	foot	feet
cherub	cherubim		

Nouns

SINGULAR	PLURAL	SINGULAR	PLURAL
fungus	fungi	phenomenon	phenomena
goose	geese	radius	radii
half	halves	self	selves
hoof	hooves	seraph	seraphim
hypothesis	hypotheses	sheaf	sheaves
knife	knives	sheep	sheep
leaf	leaves	swine	swine
life	lives	synopsis	synopses
loaf	loaves	synthesis	syntheses
louse	lice	terminus	termini
man	men	thesis	theses
maximum	maxima	thief	thieves
metamorphosis	metamorphoses	tooth	teeth
minimum	minima	vertebra	vertebrae
mouse	mice	virtuoso	virtuosi
oasis	oases	yourself	yourselves
ourself	ourselves	wife	wives
ox	oxen	wolf	wolves
parenthesis	parentheses	woman	women

Possessive Nouns

The possessive case of nouns, meaning *belonging to*, is usually formed by adding the apostrophe and *s* to words which do not end with an *s* or *z* sound and by adding only the apostrophe to words which end with an *s* or *z* sound:

> the boy's room   the children's school
> the boys' room   Dickens' novels

EXCEPTION: In singular one-syllable nouns ending in the *s* or *z* sound, it is customary to add the apostrophe and *s* and to pronounce the possessive as if it ended in *es: the boss's hat*.

To be certain about the correct placing of the apostrophe, remember that it always means belonging to whatever immediately precedes it:

> *the boy's suit*   belonging to the boy
> *the boys' room*   belonging to the boys
> *the boss's office*   belonging to the boss
> *the bosses' office*   belonging to the bosses
> *the women's department*   belonging to the women

When possession is shared by two or more nouns, this fact is indicated by using the possessive case for the last noun in the series: *John, Fred, and Edward's canoe.* They all own the same canoe. If each one separately owns a canoe, each name is placed in the possessive case: *John's, Fred's, and Edward's canoes.*

Inanimate objects are not capable of possession. The relationship meaning *a part of* is indicated by the use of the preposition *of*:

> *the wall of the castle* NOT *the castle's wall*

EXCEPTIONS: Objects which are personified, such as ships and airplanes, may use the possessive case: *the ship's compass, the plane's gyroscope.* Idiomatic usage also allows the possessive case for time and money: *a day's work, a dollar's worth, three years' time.* In such instances be careful in placing the apostrophe to observe whether the noun is singular or plural: *a month's vacation, two months' vacation.*

Numbers

Cardinal and Ordinal Numbers

NUMERALS	CARDINAL NUMBERS	ORDINAL NUMBERS
1	one	first
2	two	second
3	three	third
4	four	fourth
5	five	fifth
6	six	sixth
7	seven	seventh
8	eight	eighth
9	nine	ninth
10	ten	tenth
11	eleven	eleventh
12	twelve	twelfth
13	thirteen	thirteenth
14	fourteen	fourteenth
15	fifteen	fifteenth
16	sixteen	sixteenth
17	seventeen	seventeenth
18	eighteen	eighteenth
19	nineteen	nineteenth
20	twenty	twentieth
21	twenty-one	twenty-first
30	thirty	thirtieth
40	forty	fortieth
50	fifty	fiftieth
60	sixty	sixtieth
70	seventy	seventieth
80	eighty	eightieth
90	ninety	ninetieth
100	one hundred	one hundredth
1000	one thousand	one thousandth
1001	one thousand one	one thousand and first
1,000,000	one million	one millionth
1,000,000,000	one billion (U.S.)	one billionth (U.S.)

Word Elements Meaning Number

WORD ELEMENT	MEANING	EXAMPLES
uni	one	unit, universe, unicycle
du, bi, di	two	duet, bicycle, disect
tri	three	tricycle, tri-semester
quadr, quart	four	quadrangle, quartet
quint, penta	five	quintuplet, pentagon
ses, sext, hexa	six	sestet, sextet, hexagon
sept	seven	septennial, septuple
oct	eight	octagon, octet
non, nov	nine	nonagenarian, November
deca	ten	decade, decasyllable
centi	hundred	centipede
	hundredth	centimeter
mille	thousand	millennium
milli	thousandth	milliampere

Prepositions

Prepositions are connecting words used to show the relationship of one word to another. The word *preposition* means *placed before*. It is so named because it is usually placed before a noun or a pronoun or a noun phrase or clause.

> The river is *at* the edge *of* town.
> He acted *like* a friend *of* the family.

The principal prepositions are:

about	She walked about the town for an hour.
	He inquired about my health.
	I must be about my business.
above	The birds flew above the house.
	Look at the sentence above the last one.
	He was above suspicion.
across	They rowed across the river.
after	After the storm, the sun shone brightly.
	The son was after his father's money.
	In the procession a captain comes after a general.
against	He leaned against the wall.
	The enemy is always against us.
	The teacher is against talking in class.
	He is saving his money against a rainy day.
	He charged twenty dollars against the customer's account.
ahead of	The fastest car was ahead of the others.
	He was ahead of his brother in school because he was more intelligent.
along	They drove along the road while others rowed along the shore.
along with	The boy went along with his parents.
	Along with my loose change, I have $41.53.
	I am willing to go along with you in your beliefs.
around	He ran around the farm.
	The baseball player ran around the bases.
	Twenty-four and twenty-six are around twenty-five.
as	He went to the masquerade dressed as a king.
	The boy was as tall as his father.
	He was not so tall as his uncle.
at	The store was at the corner of Vine Street and First Avenue.
	His sister was away at college.
	At nine o'clock he had breakfast.

	He usually read at night.
	The audience applauded at the entrance of the star.
	Do it at your own convenience.
	The oranges are priced at sixty cents a dozen.
	The prisoner was at the mercy of the jailer.
	During vacations I find myself at leisure.
	He gave the command to fire at will.
away from	He swam away from the boat.
	You are far away from the answer.
	He stayed away from home.
in back of	The firehouse was in back of the city center.
	When he changed his plans we did not know what was in back of his mind.
before	He put the cart before the horse.
	He got out of bed before sunrise.
	Page 40 comes before page 50.
	Job asked to come before the presence of God.
behind	The caboose was behind all the other cars on the train.
	He was behind his brother in finishing the job.
	The books were hidden behind the fence.
below	The cellar was below the first floor.
	The temperature dropped below twenty degrees.
	He thought that laughter was below his dignity.
	His performance was below his usual standard.
beneath	They put rafters beneath the roof.
	Cheating on examinations was beneath him.
	They lived beneath the rule of a dictator.
between	On a piano the black keys are between the white keys.
	The bus ran between New York and San Francisco.
	He divided the money between his two sons.
	He felt as if he were between the frying pan and the fire.
	Just between you and me, I think we're in trouble.
	The audience went out for refreshments between the acts.
but	(meaning *except*)
	Nobody was left but me.
	All but one were able to get on the bus.
by	He passed by the bank on his way home.
	He was assisted by his friends.
	He was paid by the week, but he paid his rent by the month.
	Coal is sold by the ton.

	He is not a carpenter by choice; he would rather be an electrician.
down	It was easy to run down the hill.
	He played down the scale from f to c.
down from	He dropped down from the roof to the ground.
down to	After paying for lunch he was down to his last nickel.
except	Everybody sang except John.
for	He took aspirin for his headache.
	She would do anything for a friend.
	This is a perfect location for a store.
	She is hoping for a prize.
	He has a talent for painting.
	I voted for him in the last election.
	I paid twenty dollars for my shoes.
	He failed for many reasons.
	He was bedridden for seven months.
	I would not cross the ocean for anything.
	Father bought a new suit for me.
	The son was named for his father.
	As for me, I would rather not say what I think.
from	He jumped from the boat.
	They took my money from me.
	John drove from Washington to New York.
	He was a good man from birth to death.
	I can tell a good play from a bad one.
	His unusual knowledge came from intensive studying.
in front of	I stood in front of the theater.
in	He lived in a hotel in Washington when he was in the army.
	Let us cut the apple in half.
	America was discovered in 1492.
	I hope to be ready in a few minutes.
	In fact, it may take me longer.
	The boat was twenty feet in length.
	In my opinion, the enemy will soon be defeated.
	He read the book in German.
	She delighted in the sunshine of a warm spring day.
	She spoke in opposition to the views of the majority.
	He owned property in addition to his cash assets.
	His writing was in connection with his job.
inside	Put the milk inside the refrigerator.

into	He walked into the store.
	I shall look into the matter.
	Put the carrots into the stew.
	He tried to change lead into gold.
like	She looks like her sister.
	It looks like rain.
	It would be like him to do it.
	He ate like a horse.
of	That is the tower of Pisa.
	He was the owner of the yacht.
	He lived where he did of necessity.
	Give me a glass of water.
	He lived in the village of Ilion.
	She was a woman of many talents.
	He got tired of working very quickly.
	Nothing good was said of him after he left.
	There have been very few thunderstorms of late.
off	Take the books off the table.
	The theater was off Broadway.
on	Put the bread on the counter.
	She played on the cello.
	He piled one box on the other.
	They had a house on the Mississippi River.
	He owned a watch on a chain.
	He set sail on the twentieth of May.
	I will let you have it on your assurance that it will be returned.
	On my word I will not be late.
	The detective was on my track.
	The house faced on the street.
	He went on record in stating his belief in capital punishment.
	She was working on a new book.
	He was writing a book on witchcraft.
out	He ran out the door.
out of	He was out of money.
	The elevator was out of order.
out with	He had a falling out with his father over money matters.
outside	Put the garbage outside the house.
	Being unpopular, he was always outside the group.

Prepositions

over
    The plane flew over the city.
    The boss has power over his employees.
    Put a blanket over you when you go to bed.
    He jumped over the fence.
    They drove over the fields.
    The river rose over its banks.
    The students went home over the holidays.
    We laughed over his description of his embarrassment.
    She talked to me over the telephone.
    The dress costs over fifty dollars.
    Nuclear physics is over my head.

past
    It is past ten o'clock.
    He drove past the restaurant without stopping.
    He has become so ill that he is past hope.

through
    He shot a bullet through the door.
    He read through the entire newspaper.
    She aged gracefully through the years.
    He succeeded through the help of his father.

throughout
    He was happy throughout his entire life.

to
    He traveled to the fair.
    He found out to his sorrow that his house had fallen down.
    The final bill came to fifty dollars.
    He owed duty to his family.
    They stood back to back.
    This is the key to the car.
    It is twenty minutes to five.
    Let us drink to his health.
    To my knowledge she has not left the city.
    The race is not always to the swift.
    Two is to four as four is to eight.

under
    The sheet was under the blanket.
    He built a house under the cliff.
    He took her under his guidance.
    You will find definitions under *U* in the dictionary.
    He fought under General Clark.
    She insisted that her age was under forty.
    He felt nothing because he was under ether.
    Under the terms of the contract, you must complete the job quickly.

underneath
    You will find paper underneath the book.
    She kept the brushes underneath the sink.

until	I won't leave until six o'clock.
up	We walked slowly up the hill.
	They sailed their boat up the river.
	The beauty parlor is up the street.
	She kept her diary up to date.
upon	He stacked the books upon the table.
with	I shall go to the store with you.
	He reached the airport with twenty minutes to spare.
	In the military service he is with the Navy.
	He looked with sorrow on his wasted life.
	She swept the floor with a broom.
	He was sick with influenza.
	She was believed to be a person with sound principles.
	I hate to part with my money.
	I am angry with you because of your neglect.
within	He resided within the city limits.
	She always drove within the speed limits.
	She was within her rights in doing so.
without	He went without food for two days.
	I left the house without my coat.

Pronouns

Personal Pronouns

The personal pronouns are distinguished by person, case, and number. First Person (the person speaking or writing):

CASE	SINGULAR	PLURAL
Nominative	I	we
Possessive	my, mine	our, ours
Objective	me	us

Second Person (the person addressed):

Nominative	you	you
Possessive	your, yours	your, yours
Objective	you	you

Third Person (the person, place, or thing spoken or written about); singular pronouns also distinguished by gender:

	MASCULINE	FEMININE	NEUTER	
Nominative	he	she	it	they
Possessive	his	her, hers	its	their, theirs
Objective	him	her	it	them

Relative Pronouns

The relative pronouns, *who*, *which*, and *that*, are used to relate a dependent clause of a sentence to a word in the independent clause.

> The tools *which he used* were rusty.

The pronoun *who* is used to refer to persons; *which* refers to things; *that* refers to both persons and things. For references to persons it is preferable to use the pronoun *who* rather than *that*.

Like the personal pronouns, *who* takes different forms depending on its case.

CASE	SINGULAR AND PLURAL
Nominative	who
Possessive	whose
Objective	whom

Interrogative Pronouns

The interrogative pronouns, *who*, *which*, *what*, are used to ask a question. Their antecedents are the answers to the questions.

Who is the presiding officer?   Answer: Joan [the antecedent].
What is he carrying?   Answer: a suitcase [the antecedent].

Who as an interrogative pronoun is distinguished by case.
Nominative: *Who* is coming to dinner?
Possessive: *Whose* gloves are these?
Objective: *Whom* were you talking to? [object of preposition *to*]

Demonstrative Pronouns

SINGULAR	PLURAL
this	these
that	those

The demonstrative pronouns are used to point out people, places, or things without naming them. The antecedent of a demonstrative pronoun is whoever or whatever is being pointed out.

I like *this*.   *Those* are good to eat.

Intensive and Reflexive Pronouns

SINGULAR	PLURAL
myself	ourselves
yourself	yourselves
himself, herself, itself	themselves

Intensive Usage: I *myself* will do it.   He *himself* was the culprit.
Reflexive Usage: I hurt *myself*.   They fooled *themselves*.

Indefinite Pronouns

The indefinite pronouns are so named because their antecedents are vague or unknown. They are such words as *each*, *all*, *either*, *anyone*, *everyone*, *everybody*, *somebody*, *nobody*.

Determining Correct Case for Pronouns

The subject of a verb should be in the nominative case.

I, we, you, he, she, it, they fell down.

Pronouns

Put a predicate pronoun (following any finite form of the verb *to be*) in the nominative case.

> They suspected that the masquerader was *I, you, he, she.*
> They suspected that the masqueraders were *we, you, they.*

Put the appositive of a subject in the nominative case.

> The clergy, *we* of the cloth, are dedicated people.

The object of a verb should be in the objective case.

> A bolt of lightning struck *me, him, her, it, you, them.*

Put the object of a participle in the objective case.

> She spent her whole life hating *me, him, her, it, you, them.*

Put the object of an infinitive in the objective case.

> He tried very hard to understand *me, him, her, it, you, them.*

Put the subject of an infinitive in the objective case.

> They asked *me* to do it.
> They trained *him* to be a doctor.

The object of a preposition should be in the objective case.

> He aimed the rifle at *me, him, her, it, you, them.*

Elliptical Clauses

In elliptical clauses introduced by *as* or *than*, part of the clause is omitted because it would be repetitious. To determine the case of the pronoun, supply the omitted words (in brackets below) in your mind.

> He doesn't work as hard as *I* [do].
> Nobody in the class is taller than *he* [is].
> He likes me better than [he likes] *him.*
> He praised me as much as [he praised] *her.*

Who or Whom?

The principles for determining the case for all pronouns are the same for *who* (nominative case) and *whom* (objective case).

SUBJECT OF A VERB: *Who* is going to the party? [subject of *is*] My friend, *who* is a doctor, is very clever. [subject of *is*]

OBJECT OF A VERB: *Whom* have they invited? [object of *invited*] My friend, *whom* you know, is a doctor. [object of *know*]

OBJECT OF A PREPOSITION: The man from *whom* I got it is honest.
[object of *from*]
To *whom* it may concern: [object of *to*]
Whom did you give it to? [object of *to*]

Pronoun-Antecedent Agreement

A pronoun must agree with its antecedent in person, number, and gender. The antecedent is the noun or pronoun to which it refers.

SINGULAR MASCULINE PRONOUNS FOLLOWING INDEFINITE SINGULAR ANTECEDENTS: Indefinite singular pronouns like *each, everyone, everybody, anyone, anybody, nobody, no one, someone, either, neither* have traditionally been treated as masculine unless the situation is such (as in a woman's college) that the reference is clearly feminine or unless (as it might be for *each* or *either* or *neither*) the reference is neuter.

CORRECT: Everybody in the fraternity has to clean up *his* own room.
CORRECT: Nobody in the Girl Scouts shirks *her* duty.
CORRECT: Either of the plans should be considered on *its* merits.

To avoid sexism when indefinite pronouns refer to a group composed of both men and women, try to rewrite the sentence in the plural. This avoids the awkward and ungainly *his or her* construction.

AWKWARD: Each of the lawyers had his or her briefcase with him or her.
BETTER: All of the lawyers had their briefcases with them.

PLURAL PRONOUNS FOLLOWING TWO OR MORE SINGULAR ANTECEDENTS JOINED BY *and:*   When the pronoun refers to more than one person, place, or thing, it must be a plural pronoun.

CORRECT: Fred and Nancy ate *their* dinner quickly.
CORRECT: The church and the school had a playground which *they* shared in common.

SINGULAR PRONOUNS AFTER TWO OR MORE SINGULAR ANTECEDENTS JOINED BY *or* OR *nor:*   When the pronoun refers to only one of two or more from which a selection is to be made, the pronoun is singular.

CORRECT: Either Jack or Pearl is bound to forget *his* appointment.
CORRECT: Neither the train nor the plane can be expected to keep *its* schedule.

SINGULAR PRONOUNS AFTER COLLECTIVE NOUNS THE SENSE OF WHICH IS SINGULAR: Many nouns like *army, class, committee, group,* refer to more than one person, place, or thing. When such a group is considered as a single unit, as is usual, pronouns referring to the unit should be singular, neuter in gender.

Pronouns

CORRECT: The class elected *its* officers at the end of the term.
CORRECT: An army marches on *its* stomach.

Only when a group is thought of as made up of many individuals should a plural pronoun be used.

CORRECT: The choir sang *their* different parts perfectly.

FEMININE PRONOUNS FOR SOME NEUTER ANTECEDENTS: Traditionally, a few inanimate and actually sexless things have been referred to as feminine: ships, airplanes, nations, colleges. Hurricanes are now both masculine and feminine. Neuter pronouns are correct when referring to such antecedents, but feminine pronouns are sometimes used.

CORRECT: The plane took off for *its* second flight that day.
CORRECT: The plane took off for *her* second flight that day.

AN IMPOSSIBLE SITUATION: SINGULAR AND PLURAL ANTECEDENTS JOINED BY *or* OR *nor:* When there are two possible antecedents, one of which is singular and the other plural, English offers no grammatical solution.

EXAMPLE: Either the *boy* or his *parents* have lost *his*? *their*? mind.

The only escape from such a dilemma is to recast the sentence.

SOLUTION: Either the *boy* has lost *his* mind or his *parents* are out of *their* wits.

Pronoun Reference Problems

Since a pronoun has no meaning without an antecedent, it is important that the antecedent of every pronoun be clearly stated and unmistakable. Apart from such obvious idiomatic usage as "*It* is raining" or the deliberate indefiniteness of "*They* say . . ." or the lazy vagueness of "Why don't *they* repair this sidewalk?" or a conversational situation where the antecedent is obvious ("It won't start."), the exact antecedent of every pronoun must be made clear.

AVOID AMBIGUOUS REFERENCE: Be sure that a pronoun cannot be taken to refer to more than one possible antecedent.

AMBIGUOUS: My mother told our maid that *she* had made a mistake.
QUESTION: Who made a mistake? *She* could refer to *mother* or *maid*.
SOLUTION: My mother scolded our maid for making a mistake.
SOLUTION: My mother said to our maid, "You have made a mistake."

AVOID REMOTE REFERENCE: Be sure that a pronoun is reasonably close to its antecedent.

REMOTE: The curtain rose on *Carmen* which is a very popular opera with lively music, a colorful cast of characters, and a large chorus. *It* is made of a heavy brocade.

PROBLEM: The *it* is so far from its antecedent *curtain* that the reader is put to unnecessary effort in clarifying the meaning of the pronoun.

SOLUTION: The *curtain, which* is made of a heavy brocade, rose ...

AVOID INDEFINITE REFERENCE: Be sure that a pronoun has a definite antecedent instead of a vague idea.

VAGUE: He played golf all morning and tennis all afternoon *which* was probably bad for his health.

SOLUTION: He played golf all morning and tennis all afternoon. So much exertion was bad for his health.

VAGUE: They asked me to join them at six o'clock in the morning, but *this* is something I can't stand.

SOLUTION: They asked me to join them at six o'clock in the morning, but early rising is something I can't stand.

AVOID REFERENCE TO A NOUN IN THE POSSESSIVE CASE: However clear such reference may be, usage of this kind constitutes slovenly English.

EXAMPLE: Goethe's *Faust* has been called the epic of modern man. *He* was particularly fitted to write such an epic because of his extraordinarily broad experiences.

SOLUTION: Goethe's *Faust* has been called the epic of modern man. *Goethe* was particularly ...

Punctuation

Commas

MAXIM: *When in doubt, leave it out.* This well-known maxim makes relatively good sense because most uncertain punctuators annoy their readers by scattering commas at random through their writings.

A BETTER MAXIM: *Master the few definite principles of correct comma usage.*

COMMAS TO SEPARATE PARTS OF A SERIES: When the parts of a series are not joined by a connecting word like *and* or *or*, commas keep the parts of the series apart.

She was tall, young, beautiful.

The last term of any series is usually preceded by the conjunction *and* or *or*. The conjunction takes the place of a comma, but since it is not unusual for an *and* to occur within one element of the series, careful writers place a comma before the final *and* or *or* to indicate the termination of the series.

A SERIES WITH *and's*:	For breakfast he had orange juice, ham and eggs, toast and butter, and coffee.
A SERIES WITH *or's*:	When he invested his money, he had choices of buying common or preferred stock, safe or speculative stock, or corporate or municipal bonds.
A SERIES OF WORDS:	This bus goes to Trenton, Baltimore, and Washington.
A SERIES OF PHRASES:	They ran into the house, through the living room, and up to his room.
A SERIES OF VERBS:	He combed his hair, put on a clean shirt, and went to the party.
A SERIES OF CLAUSES:	The food was good, the service was excellent, and the dinner-music was enchanting.
A SERIES OF ADJECTIVES:	It was a big, ugly, unfriendly dog.

NOTE: Frequently a single adjective modifying a noun is so much a part of the identification that the adjective-noun is thought of as a single word: *oak tree*, *dress shirt*, *straw hat*. Whenever such combinations are thought of as units, no comma is required to separate a preceding adjective: *tall oak tree*, *dirty dress shirt*, *old straw hat*. Similarly, when an adjective is used only for identification, it is felt to be part of the noun: She wore her old *red dress*. If the intention is to emphasize the color of the dress instead of merely identifying it, a comma is used: *her old, red dress*.

COMMA TO SEPARATE THE CLAUSES OF A COMPOUND SENTENCE: In a compound sentence all but very short clauses joined by a coordinating conjunction are separated by a comma immediately preceding the conjunction (*and, but, or, nor, for, yet, so, whereas*).

COMPOUND SENTENCE: My father was born and raised on a large farm in New England, and I learned a great deal about rural life from him.

COMPOUND SENTENCE: I have been studying French for the last seven years, so I am sure that I shall feel at home in Paris.

SHORT CLAUSES: He wrote to me and I answered his letter.

COMMA TO SEPARATE AN INTERJECTION OR TERM OF DIRECT ADDRESS: When a word or phrase is clearly not a part of the structure of a sentence, separate it from the sentence by a comma; by two commas if necessary.

INTERJECTION: *Hello,* I didn't expect to see you.

INTERJECTION: *Oh no,* you can't expect me to do that!

INTERJECTION: He's going to be late again, *darn it!*

DIRECT ADDRESS: *John,* come over here at once!

DIRECT ADDRESS: That vegetable soup, *Mother,* is delicious!

COMMA TO SET OFF A SENTENCE MODIFIER: Instead of modifying a single word, a sentence modifier modifies the whole sentence in which it occurs because it usually refers the sense of the entire sentence to something preceding that sentence. Common sentence modifiers are *however, moreover, therefore, nevertheless, furthermore, in addition, on the other hand, on the contrary*.

He made no effort to take care of his health. *Nevertheless,* he was never sick.

She cooked all the meals, kept the house clean, and raised four children. *In addition,* she was a member of three clubs.

Banks observe a shorter business day than almost any other kind of commercial operation. Bankers, *on the other hand,* often work longer than other businessmen.

Another kind of sentence modifier is the absolute phrase, made up of a noun or pronoun and a participle.

ABSOLUTE PHRASE: *The sun having risen,* we set forth on our journey.

ABSOLUTE PHRASE: It seemed entirely reasonable, *things being what they were,* to expect a disastrous outcome of the affair.

Punctuation

COMMA AFTER A LONG PHRASE OR A CLAUSE PRECEDING THE SUBJECT: Since the subject of a sentence is usually expected at the beginning, any phrase or clause of more than five words which precedes the subject is ended with a comma to assist the reader in determining the subject.

> LONG PHRASE: *After a long afternoon of tedious debate,* the meeting was adjourned.
>
> LONG CLAUSE: *When I think of all the things I might have done,* I feel very discouraged.

COMMAS TO INDICATE INTERRUPTIONS OF NORMAL WORD ORDER: When unexpected or interrupted word order occurs, commas are very helpful to the reader.

> UNEXPECTED: The chaplain, loved and respected by all, went to his rest.
>
> COMMENT: Adjectives (*loved, respected*) usually precede the word they modify.
>
> INTERRUPTION: The price of the eggs, *ninety cents a dozen,* was exhorbitant.
>
> INTERRUPTION: He was lazy and shiftless and, *to put it bluntly,* untrustworthy.

COMMAS TO SET OFF NONRESTRICTIVE ELEMENTS: Any word, phrase, or clause that is not essential to the meaning of a sentence is called nonrestrictive. Such elements may be highly informative, but the fact that they are not essential is indicated by setting them off with commas.

> RESTRICTIVE: Fielding's novel *Tom Jones* was made into a motion picture.
>
> COMMENT: Since Fielding wrote more than one novel, the title, *Tom Jones,* is essential in this sentence.
>
> NONRESTRICTIVE: Dante's epic, *The Divine Comedy,* is an undisputed masterpiece.
>
> COMMENT: Dante wrote only one epic. Supplying its name is useful but not essential.
>
> RESTRICTIVE: The people *who came by train* missed the first race.
>
> COMMENT: No commas because *who came by train* is obviously essential to the meaning.
>
> NONRESTRICTIVE: The people, *who came by train,* enjoyed their vacations at the summer resort.

NOTE: By the use of commas, the writer makes clear whether the word, phrase, or clause in question is intended to be restrictive or not. The preceding sentence implies that everybody came by train. The information is added but it is not essential. If some people came by other means of transportation and only the people who came by train enjoyed their vacations, the commas should not be used.

COMMAS TO EMPHASIZE CONTRASTS: If one part of the meaning of a sentence is in contrast to the other, a comma emphasizes the contrast.

    CONTRAST: She was beautifully, yet inexpensively dressed.
    CONTRAST: The singing was noisy, not melodious.
    CONTRAST: They ran to the dock, but found that the boat had left.

COMMAS TO PREVENT MISREADING: Occasionally, a comma is used when none of the above principles is involved, but when it is helpful to avoid possible confusion on the part of the reader.

MOMENTARY POSSIBLE CONFUSION:	"Whatever is, is right."
COMMENT:	If Pope had omitted the comma from this famous quotation, the reader might have been momentarily troubled by the repetition of *is*.
MOMENTARY CONFUSION:	During the winter nights become longer.
INSTANTLY CLARIFIED:	During the winter, nights become longer.

Conventional Comma Usages

There are a few comma usages which have been established by convention. These are entirely arbitrary.

After the salutation of an informal letter: *Dear John,*   *Dear Mr. Smith,*
    Dear Mrs. Jones,
After the complimentary close of a letter: *Yours truly,*   *Sincerely,*
    With love,
Separating dates of the month from the year: *July 16, 1948*
Separating parts of an address: *Mrs. Andrew Clark,*   *142 South Street,*
    New Lebanon, Indiana, 10765
Separating numbered or lettered divisions or subdivisions: *Book VII,*
    Canto 42, Stanza 17; Section B, 4, d
Separating distinguishing titles from names: *John J. Darcy, Jr.*
    Jacob Elson, M.D.
Separating thousands in large figures: *7,639,420*

Placed before introductory words and abbreviations such as i.e., e.g.: *Some colleges are coeducational, for example, Cornell. Some books need to be digested, i.e., they must be read slowly and thoughtfully.*

Punctuation

Pitfalls in Comma Usage

THE COMMA SPLICE: Don't separate two sentences or two independent clauses by using a comma.

INCORRECT: The robins came early that spring, the weather was unusually warm.

CORRECT: The robins came early that spring. The weather was unusually warm.

CORRECT: The robins came early that spring; the weather was unusually warm.

THE COMMA INTERRUPTER: Don't interrupt a natural flow of thought with a comma.

INCORRECT: The many hours of painstaking effort that she spent in completing her term paper, were rewarded when it was highly praised.

CORRECT: The many hours of painstaking effort that she spent in completing her term paper were rewarded when it was highly praised.

INCORRECT: He said, that he was anxious to see me.

CORRECT: He said that he was anxious to see me.

THE MISPLACED COMMA: Place a comma before, not after, the coordinating conjunction in a compound sentence.

INCORRECT: The architects drew excellent plans for the building but, the builder was unwilling to follow them.

CORRECT: The architects drew excellent plans for the building, but the builder was unwilling to follow them.

THE MISTAKEN COMMA: Do not mistake a compound predicate for a compound sentence. A compound predicate does not require a comma.

INCORRECT: The doctor spent the entire day driving about town, and was able to visit nearly all his patients.

CORRECT: The doctor spent the entire day driving about town and was able to visit nearly all his patients.

CORRECT: The doctor spent the entire day driving about town, and he was able to visit nearly all his patients. [compound sentence]

Terminal Punctuation

THE PERIOD: If a sentence is not a question or an exclamation, it should always be terminated by a period.

> There are forty students in the room. [statement]
> I asked if she was ready. [indirect question]
> Please write to me. [request or command]

Even when a sentence is not involved, the period is used for terminal purposes.

> Hello. I am delighted to see you.

In an enumerated list:

1. The Manager
2. The Foremen
3. The Workers

The period is used to terminate most abbreviations: *Mr., Mrs., Rev., Mass., i.e., etc.*

Three spaced periods are used to indicate the omission of one or more words or sentences in a quotation:

> "In the beginning God created . . . the earth."

When the omission occurs after the end of a sentence, the three spaced periods are added after the period which terminates the sentence.

> "The Lord is my shepherd. . . . Surely, goodness and mercy . . ."

THE QUESTION MARK: The question mark is used to terminate a direct question:

> Where are you going? Why? You are? May I come with you?

The question mark enclosed in parentheses is used to indicate uncertainty or doubt.

> He was born in 1914 (?) and died in 1967.

THE EXCLAMATION MARK: The exclamation mark is used to emphasize a strong expression of feeling.

> Never! I will never sign that document!
> Don't you dare take the car without my permission!

Semicolons and Colons

The semicolon is used to separate the clauses in a compound sentence when they are not joined by a coordinating conjunction.

> The judge instructed the jury; the jurors listened patiently.
> The professor was an expert in his subject; nevertheless, he was a dull lecturer.

Punctuation

Since the semicolon is a stronger punctuation mark than the comma, it is sometimes used to separate parts of a series when commas are included within one or more of the parts.

> She bought a rib roast of beef, ten lamb chops, and a pound of liver at the butcher shop; potatoes, apples, and oranges at the grocery store; and tooth paste and hand lotion at the drug store.

The colon is usually the signal for introducing a list. It is frequently used after such words as *as follows* or *following*.

> The following members of the committee were present: James Anderson, Mary Montgomery, Nelson Danforth, John Winters, and Sarah Dunn.
> The most important rules of this organization are:
> 1. Attendance is required at two-thirds of the regular meetings.
> 2. Dues must be paid during the first month of every year.
> 3. All members must be willing to serve on committees.

The colon is used after the salutation of a business letter: *Gentlemen*: *Dear Sirs*: *My dear Mr. Holstead*:

The colon is used to divide subdivisions from major divisions when indicating the time of day [7:25], or when making references to Biblical passages [Genesis 12:2].

Dashes, Hyphens, and Apostrophes

THE DASH: The dash indicates a sudden, and usually unexpected, break in the anticipated sequence of thought. Since most typewriters do not have a dash on the keyboard, two connected hyphens are used (- -).

> I believed that my country—but why should I have believed it?—was always right.

The dash can be used to indicate hesitation or a suspension or breaking off of thought.

> I always wanted to—. But it's too late now to want anything.

The dash sometimes separates parenthetical material from the main body of a sentence.

> His hopeless condition—it seemed hopeless at the time—caused his wife intolerable anguish.

The dash is useful to indicate that a remark at the end of a sentence has been inserted as an afterthought, sometimes with ironic effect.

The president of the firm was a man of absolute integrity—or so it seemed to the stockholders before the firm collapsed.

The dash is used for lists in apposition to avoid confusion.

She invited her cousins—Albert, Arthur, and Englebert—for a visit.

THE HYPHEN: The hyphen is used to make a compound word out of two or more words which are to be thought of as a single unit.

The 1990-91 academic year
The Princeton-Yale game
A blue-green dress
He played a better-than-average game.

The hyphen is used where a word must be broken (hyphenated) at the end of a line because there is not enough space to write, type, or print all of it. Words must not be divided arbitrarily; they may be hyphenated only between syllables. Syllables are the parts of a word which are pronounced as units. When in doubt about correct hyphenation, consult a good dictionary.

Samuel Johnson, who was an outstanding literary figure of the eighteenth century in England, was known as the great lexicographer. He compiled the first real English dictionary.

The hyphen is sometimes required to eliminate misreading when a prefix ends with the same letter as the initial letter of the word to which it is added.

re-estimate   co-ownership   de-escalate

The hyphen is used in compound numbers from twenty-one to ninety-nine.

The hyphen is used to separate dates of birth and death: James Finch (1714-1778); scores of games: Princeton-Dartmouth, 78-67; and similar opposing or terminal relationships: Nearly everything goes in pairs: sun-moon, day-night, man-woman, winter-summer.

THE APOSTROPHE: The apostrophe is used to indicate the possessive case of a noun. Add the apostrophe and *s* to words which do not end with an *s* or *z* sound. Add only the apostrophe to words which end with an *s* or *z* sound:

the boy's room   the children's school
the boys' room   Dickens' novels

EXCEPTION: In singular one-syllable nouns ending in the *s* or *z* sound, it is customary to add the apostrophe and *s* and to pronounce the possessive as if it ended in *es*: *the boss's hat*.

Punctuation

The apostrophe is used to indicate missing letters in a contraction:

> *He's* ready to join us. [He is]
> Martha *can't* be with us. [cannot]

The apostrophe is used to form plurals of letters or symbols when simply adding an *s* could cause confusion.

> Remember to dot your i's.

Parentheses and Brackets

Parentheses ( ) and brackets [ ] are both used to exclude extraneous or interrupting material from a sentence or from a paragraph.

PARENTHESES: Parentheses are used to enclose anything that interrupts the sense of what is being written.

> I was born in 1906. (That was the year of the San Francisco earthquake.)
> I met my future wife (my first date, incidentally) at a high school dance.
> The dam was built (1) to provide water for irrigation, (2) to prevent flooding, and (3) to provide power for the generation of electricity.
> His seventh novel, *The Errant Wife* (1836), was a failure.

BRACKETS: Brackets are used only to enclose additions by an editor of any kind of quoted material.

> "The composer [Brahms] was frequently entertained by the nobility."
> "Jonathan Swift [1667–1745] lived during the War of the Spanish Succession."

Quotation Marks

QUOTATION MARKS TO INDICATE TITLES: Quotation marks should enclose titles of short pieces such as essays, articles in magazines, chapters in books, short stories, one-act plays, short musical compositions, short poems, etc.

> "The Afternoon of a Faun" [short musical composition]
> "The Killers" [short story]
> "Ode to the West Wind" [short poem]

NOTE: Titles of lengthier works are placed in italics, indicated by underlining in typed or handwritten material: Shakespeare's *Macbeth*.

DIRECT QUOTATIONS: The exact words of a quotation, spoken or written, should be placed in quotation marks. A paraphrase of what someone spoke or wrote (indirect quotation) does not require and should not be indicated by quotation marks.

DIRECT: She said, "I am not going to wait for my husband."

INDIRECT: She said that she wasn't going to wait for her husband.

DIRECT: Dickens introduces his novel *David Copperfield* by saying, "Whether I shall turn out to be the hero of my own life, or whether that station will be held by anybody else, these pages must show."

INDIRECT: Dickens introduces his novel *David Copperfield* by saying that the pages which follow will show whether he will be the hero of his own life or whether that position will be held by somebody else.

OTHER PUNCTUATION MARKS WITH DIRECT QUOTATIONS: In the reporting of speech or dialogue, reference to the speaker (*I said*, *he answered*) are separated from the quotation by a comma. Two commas are required if the reference to the speaker is inserted within the quotation.

> "Let me know where I can reach you," I said.
> "I'm not at all sure," she replied," that I want you to reach me."
> I answered abruptly, "Then don't bother."

The comma is omitted if a question mark or an exclamation mark is required where the comma would ordinarily be placed.

> "Why can't you finish your dinner?" I asked.
> "I refuse to see anybody!" he shouted.

If the quotation consists of more than one sentence, only one sentence is joined by a comma to the reference to the speaker.

> "I have come home after a long journey," he said. "I want to rest."

QUOTATIONS OTHER THAN DIALOGUE: When quoting printed or written subject-matter, reproduce the punctuation and capitalization of what is quoted exactly as it originally appeared.

> Benjamin Franklin believed that "A penny saved is a penny earned."
> The author expressed "a sinking feeling about our domestic problems."

If the quotation is longer than one paragraph, no end-quotation marks are placed at the conclusion of the first paragraph. All succeeding paragraphs are prefaced by quotation marks, but only the final paragraph is concluded with end-quotation marks.

In the following excerpt from Cervantes' *Don Quixote*, notice that only at the end of the third paragraph are the end-quotation marks used.

"While Don Quixote was singing a ballad about the noble Marquis of Mantua, a neighbor from his own village happened to come along. Amazed at the appearance of Don Quixote and wondering about the sadness of his song, he asked what was the matter with him.

"Don Quixote was firmly persuaded that this was the Marquis of Mantua so his only answer was to go on singing his ballad.

"The neighbor was amazed at such nonsense, and taking off Don Quixote's helmet, he recognized him as Senor Don Quixada which had been his real name when he was still possessed of his senses."

Long quotations (five lines or more) from writings are not usually enclosed in quotation marks. They are indicated as quotations by being indented at both right and left sides. Smaller typeface is customary for printed matter and single spacing for typescript.

Charles Dickens' *Child's History of England* is written in a very simple and vivid style. As a way of delineating the character of Oliver Cromwell, Dickens describes Cromwell's leadership of the Irish campaign:

> Oliver had been appointed by the Parliament to command the army in Ireland, where he took a terrible vengeance for the sanguinary rebellion, and made tremendous havoc, particularly in the siege of Drogheda, where no quarter was given, and where he found at least a thousand of the inhabitants shut up together in the great church, every one of whom was killed by his soldiers, usually known as Oliver's Ironsides. There were numbers of friars and priests among them; and Oliver gruffly wrote home in his dispatch that these were "knocked on the head" like the rest.

QUOTATIONS WITHIN QUOTATIONS: Single quotation marks are used to set off a quotation within another quotation.

"Have you read Poe's 'Ulalume' lately?" I asked.

At the trial the star witness testified, "On the night of the murder I distinctly heard Mrs. Knox say, 'I would give anything to get him out of the way.'"

QUOTATION MARKS RELATED TO OTHER PUNCTUATION: Without regard to logic, periods and commas are always placed inside quotation marks; colons and semicolons are always placed outside quotation marks.

"They insisted that I go with them," she said. "So I did."

There are four characters in the Brome "Abraham and Isaac": God, the angel, Abraham, and Isaac.

He glanced rapidly through Frost's "Mending Wall"; he was in a hurry to finish his assignment.

Other punctuation marks are placed where they logically belong: inside the quotation marks if they punctuate the quotation, outside if they punctuate the entire sentence of which the quotation is a part.

> What is the theme of Longfellow's "Excelsior"?
> She inquired, "Is this the road to Denver?"
> Don't let me catch you reading "The Love Song of Alfred Prufrock"!
> As he fell off the dock, the child screamed, "Help!"

PUNCTUATION OF DIALOGUE: When a dialogue between two or more persons is set down (usually in a story or novel), a new paragraph is used for each new speaker. Descriptive or other matter relevant to the speaker is placed in the same paragraph as the quotation. When only two speakers are involved, the alternation of paragraphs makes it unnecessary to identify the speaker every time and so permits the dialogue to proceed more rapidly and without interruption.

> "Herbert," said I, after a short silence, in a hurried way, "can you see me best by the light of the window, or the light of the fire?"
> "By the firelight," answered Herbert, coming close again.
> "Look at me."
> "I do look at you, my dear boy."
> "Touch me."
> "I do touch you, my dear boy."
> "You are not afraid that I am in any fever, or that my head is much disordered by the accident of last night?"
> "N-no, my dear boy," said Herbert, after taking time to examine me. "You are rather excited, but you are quite yourself."
>
> —Charles Dickens, *Great Expectations*

The Sentence and Its Parts

A sentence is a group of words that makes sense. It says something definite. It must contain a verb because the verb is the asserting word. It ends with a period (.), a question mark (?), or an exclamation mark (!). A sentence can be made of only one word if that word is a verb: *Go!* On the other hand, many words even if they are related to each other cannot form a sentence without a verb: *all the friends of my family in their best clothes and on their best behavior.* What *about* all the friends of my family, etc., etc.?

THE SUBJECT: The subject is what is being talked or written about.

>*She* is sick.
>*The clever student* completed the test before all the others.

The simple subject is the basic word, usually a noun or a pronoun. The complete subject is the simple subject together with any modifiers it may have. In the sentence above, *student* is the simple subject; *the clever student* is the complete subject. In the following sentence *dispute* is the simple subject; the complete subject is italicized:

>*A lengthy dispute about wages and hours of employment* led to a strike.

In an interrogative sentence, the subject is the person, place, or thing about whom or which the question is being asked.

>Is *my book* lying on the table?

If in doubt, you can usually find the subject of such a sentence by answering the question: *My book* is lying on the table.

When talking directly to another person or persons (*you*), the subject is frequently omitted because it is understood.

>[You] Come to the table. Dinner is getting cold.

A compound subject contains two or more subjects joined by coordinating or correlative conjunctions.

>*The boys* and *the girls* played nicely together.
>*Dogs, cats, goats,* and *mules* were all over the street.
>Neither *an apartment in the city* nor *a house in the country* could serve to keep him happy.

THE PREDICATE: Everything in a sentence besides the complete subject is the predicate. It says whatever there is to be said about the subject. In an interrogative sentence it asks the question.

>The house *was falling apart because nobody lived in it any longer.*
>*Why is* the house *falling apart?*

The simple predicate is the principal verb of the sentence (*was falling*). All the other words except the complete subject constitute the complete predicate.

A compound predicate contains two or more predicates joined by coordinating or correlative conjunctions.

> He *eats* and *drinks* heartily every day.
>
> My friends either *go to Europe on their vacations* or *stay at home in their air-conditioned apartments.*

PHRASES: Phrases are closely joined groups of words that function in sentences as single parts of speech.

A prepositional phrase contains a preposition, the object of the preposition, and often modifiers of the object. The whole phrase functions as an adjective or an adverb.

> The man *in the blue suit* worked *at the bank.*

In this sentence, *in the blue suit* is an adjective phrase modifying *man*; *at the bank* is an adverbial phrase modifying *worked*.

A participial phrase contains a participle and either a complement or one or more modifiers or both.

> *Happily singing an old familiar song*, he wandered down the country road.

This is a present participial phrase used as an adjective to modify *he*. *Singing* is the present participle. *Happily* is an adverb modifying *singing*. The remainder of the phrase is the complement of *singing*.

> *Driven into a corner by the dog*, the cat hissed defiance.

This is a past participial phrase used as an adjective to modify *cat*. *Driven* is the past participle. *Into the corner* and *by the dog* are prepositional phrases modifying *driven*.

An infinitive phrase contains an infinitive and possible modifiers or an object or both. It functions as a noun, an adjective, or an adverb.

> *To live a good life* was his only ambition.

Functioning as a noun, this phrase is the subject of the verb *was*. *To live* is the infinitive. *Life* is the object of the infinitive. A and *good* are adjectives modifying *life*.

> She had a lifetime ambition *to live in style.*

This is an adjective phrase modifying *ambition* (describing her ambition). *In style* is an adverbial prepositional phrase modifying the infinitive.

> It was much too cold *to go outdoors.*

This is an adverbial phrase modifying the adjective *cold*. *Outdoors* is an adverb modifying the infinitive.

A verb phrase is any group of verbal units that functions as a single verb.

> I *can do* it.   You *should be* happily *married*.

A gerund phrase is introduced by a gerund and acts as a noun.

> *Flying a kite* is easy at the seashore.

Flying is the gerund. *Kite* is its object. The phrase is the subject of the sentence.

CLAUSES: A clause is a group of words containing a subject and a predicate. It is not a sentence only because it is part of a sentence and so is not complete in itself. An independent clause (sometimes called a main clause) is one that could stand by itself and be written as a sentence.

> *I am always late to dinner* because the bus is so slow.

A dependent (or subordinate) clause cannot stand alone because it depends on something else in the complete sentence.

> I am always late to dinner *because the bus is so slow.*

Since they depend on something else in the sentence, dependent clauses function as nouns, adjectives, or adverbs.

Noun Clauses

> He hoped *that he would pass the course.* (object of verb *hoped*)
> *Why he did it* was not clear to anybody. (subject of verb *was*)

Adjective Clauses

> The money *that I lost* was quickly replaced. (modifies noun *money*)
> I admire a person *who knows his way around.* (modifies noun *person*)

Adverbial Clauses

> He was pleased *that he could master the problem.* (modifies adjective *pleased*)
> She cried *when he went away.* (modifies verb *cried*)

TYPES OF SENTENCES: A simple sentence is the same as an independent clause standing alone. It actually contains no clauses:

> They all enjoyed their trip to Canada.

A complex sentence is composed of one independent clause and one or more dependent clauses. The dependent clauses are italicized in the following complex sentences:

The opera, *which was written by Wagner*, didn't end until midnight.
While I was waiting for the train, an old man *who reminded me of my grandfather* entertained me with stories of people *who had lived in the neighborhood years ago*.

A compound sentence contains two or more independent clauses and no dependent clauses. Numbers in parentheses indicate the beginnings of the clauses in the following sentences:

(1) The flowers were blooming, (2) the birds were singing, (3) and spring was in the air.
(1) There is one important rule in this factory: (2) haste makes waste.
(1) Lord Gladstone rose to speak; (2) the house listened attentively.

A compound-complex sentence contains two or more independent clauses and one or more dependent clauses. In the following sentences, the dependent clauses are italicized:

Men *who are wise* are often mistaken, and fools are sometimes right.
The captain, *who was standing on the bridge*, thought he saw a shape looming ahead in the fog, but it turned out to be only an illusion *which fooled his tired eyes*.

Sentences that ask questions are *interrogative*.

PRESENT TENSE:	*Is* he *coming* to dinner?
	Does he *know* the way?
	May I *borrow* your eraser?
	What *do* they *have* for breakfast?
FUTURE TENSE:	*Will* he *come* to dinner?
	What *will* they *have* for breakfast?
PAST TENSE:	*Was* he *eating* his dinner?
	Did he *know* the way?
	What *did* they *have* for breakfast?
PRESENT PERFECT TENSE:	*Has* he *eaten* his dinner?
	Have I *finished* the assignment?
PAST PERFECT TENSE:	*Had* he *eaten* his dinner?
	Had I *finished* the assignment?
FUTURE PERFECT TENSE:	*Will* he *have eaten* his dinner?
	Shall I *have finished* the assignment?

Idiomatic question after statement:

He won't be here after all, *will he*?
They have all gone to the movies, *haven't they*?

In phrasing a question, put the subject after the verb.

> Have *you* any money?   (subject of verb *have*)
> Was the *train* on time?   (subject of verb *was*)
> Is there a *doctor* in the house?   (subject of verb *is*)

A declarative sentence used as a question is so indicated by a rising voice inflection in speaking or by a question mark in writing.

> You believe that I am not telling the truth?

Sometimes a declarative sentence is followed by a question phrased in the negative.

> She has a lovely voice, hasn't she?
> The shirt is very dirty, isn't it?

Pitfalls in Sentence Construction

Do not write a "sentence" without a finite verb.

> WRONG: All the little children miserable and poor and hungry.
> CORRECT: All the little children *were* miserable and poor and hungry.

Do not omit any part of a finite verb.

> WRONG: All the little children singing and dancing in the garden.
> CORRECT: All the little children *were* singing and dancing in the garden.

Do not write a dependent clause without a complete independent clause in the same sentence.

> WRONG: No point in doing anything if nothing could be done about it.
> CORRECT: *There was* no point in doing anything if nothing could be done about it.

Do not consider an infinitive phrase to be a complete sentence.

> WRONG: To visit every famous museum in the world and take my time in every one.
> CORRECT: To visit every famous museum in the world and take my time in every one *is my ambition.*

Do not mistake a prepositional phrase for a complete sentence.

> WRONG: Over the hills and dales and mountains and valleys.
> CORRECT: He roamed over the hills and dales and mountains and valleys.

Do not separate one part of a compound predicate from the sentence in which it belongs.

WRONG:	The weary clerk finally completed the tally of all his accounts. And then went home for a good meal and a long night's sleep.
CORRECT:	The weary clerk finally completed the tally of all his accounts and then went home for a good meal and a long night's sleep.

Do not combine two sentences into one by attempting to make a single word do double duty.

WRONG:	It is difficult to explain what he came for he was extremely bewildered about everything.
CORRECT:	It is difficult to explain what he came for. For he was extremely bewildered about everything.
BETTER:	It is difficult to explain what he came for because he was extremely bewildered about everything.

Agreement of Subject and Verb

A singular subject requires a singular form of the verb.
A plural subject requires a plural form of the verb.

SINGULAR PRONOUNS: Even when the sense of the subject seems to be plural, the following pronouns are singular: *each, every, everybody, anybody, anyone, nobody, no one, someone, either, neither.*

CORRECT:	Everybody *is coming* to the party.
	Neither of the two sisters *is* really attractive.

With *some, most,* and *none,* a singular verb is used when the sense is a single quantity. Use a plural verb when a number of individual units seem to be implied.

CORRECT:	Most of the sugar *is* stored in the warehouse.
	Most of the apples *are* rotten.
	None of the cereal *has* been eaten.
	None of the guests *are* going to stay all night.

COMPOUND SUBJECTS: When the parts of a compound subject are joined by *and,* the verb must be plural because at least two subjects are involved.

CORRECT:	The house and the barn *are* for sale.
CORRECT:	The captain and his men *are* ready to set sail.
CORRECT:	The men and their captain *are* ready to set sail.

When the parts of a compound subject are joined by *either . . . or* or *neither . . . nor,* the verb agrees with the part of the compound subject which is nearest to it.

CORRECT:	Either the whole engine or some of its parts *are* defective.
CORRECT:	Neither the students nor the instructor *agrees* with the principal.

NOTE: The sentence usually sounds better if the plural noun is second, allowing a plural verb.

PROBLEMS WITH SINGULAR-PLURAL NOUNS AS SUBJECTS: Some nouns like *committee*, *crew*, *jury*, *club* are sometimes singular and sometimes plural in meaning. Use a singular verb if all the members of the named group are acting as a unit. Use a plural verb if they are being thought of as individuals.

    CORRECT: The club *meets* every Friday.

    CORRECT: The jury *find* themselves in disagreement.

As a general principle, use a singular verb if the form of the noun is singular. If the sense is plural, it is usually less awkward to substitute another noun.

    CORRECT: The *jurors* find themselves in disagreement.

    CORRECT: The *members of the jury* find themselves in disagreement.

SUBJECTS SEPARATED FROM OR FOLLOWING VERBS: Use special care when the subject does not immediately precede the verb. Be sure the verb agrees with the subject wherever it appears in the sentence.

    WRONG: The *house* which is surrounded by junkyards and filling stations *are* going to be sold.

    CORRECT: The *house* which is surrounded by junkyards and filling stations *is* going to be sold.

    WRONG: The *leader* together with his twenty followers *are* approaching the town.

    CORRECT: The *leader* together with his twenty followers *is* approaching the town.

    WRONG: How many coats, shoes, and dresses *do she* own?

    CORRECT: How many coats, shoes, and dresses *does she* own?

    WRONG: There *is* too many *cars* in the city streets.

    CORRECT: There *are* too many *cars* in the city streets.

NOTE: *There* is called an expletive. It is not to be confused with the subject although it usually immediately precedes the verb. When a sentence is introduced by *there*, the verb nearly always precedes the subject.

THE PROBLEM WITH NUMBER WHEN A PREDICATE NOMINATIVE IS INVOLVED: On rare occasions the subject of a sentence and the predicate nominative may not agree in number. Nevertheless, the verb must agree with the subject in number. The sentence generally sounds better if the plural noun is used as the subject.

    CORRECT: Our greatest *asset is* the many loyal customers who buy regularly from us.

    BETTER: Our many loyal *customers are* our greatest asset.

Clarity in Sentence Construction

A good sentence is a tightly constructed sentence where the meaning is unmistakably clear. To avoid flabby sentences keep all modifiers close to the words they modify and be sure that no modifier is left without a definite word to modify.

WATCH OUT FOR DANGLING PHRASES: Such phrases are called *dangling* because they are connected to nothing. The writer knows what they refer to and the reader can usually guess, but the reader will know that he is reading the work of an inept writer.

DANGLING:	Driving through the rain, the street lights were scarcely visible.
AMUSED READER:	Were the street lights driving a car or a bus?
TIGHTENED:	Driving through the rain, I could hardly see the street lights.
DANGLING:	To learn how to care for pets, hamsters are ideal to begin with.
AMUSED READER:	I didn't know that hamsters had pets.
TIGHTENED:	To learn how to care for pets, children should begin with hamsters.

WATCH OUT FOR REMOTE MODIFIERS:

REMOTE:	He said that he was willing to sign the contract *yesterday*.
COMMENT:	Clear if *yesterday* is meant to apply to the signing of the contract, but misleading if the intended meaning was that he made the remark *yesterday*.
TIGHTENED:	He said yesterday that he was willing to sign the contract.
REMOTE:	He took two aspirin tablets to cure his headache which made him feel much better.
COMMENT:	If his headache made him feel much better, why did he want to cure it?
TIGHTENED:	To cure his headache, he took two aspirin tablets which made him feel much better.

WATCH OUT FOR AMBIGUOUS MODIFIERS: Avoid placing modifiers in such a position in a sentence that they may apply to either a preceding or following word.

AMBIGUOUS:	We decided *in the morning* to pack the car and take a long trip.
QUESTION:	Was the decision made in the morning or is the packing planned for the morning?
SOLUTION:	In the morning, we decided to pack the car and take a long trip.
SOLUTION:	We decided to pack the car in the morning and take a long trip.

The Sentence and Its Parts

MEANINGLESS REPETITION: If a connecting word has already been used, don't repeat it even though it seems to come naturally.

> REPEATED: He had so many friends that there were scores of people *to* whom he thought he could appeal *to* for advice.
>
> CORRECTION: He had so many friends that there were scores of people *to* whom he thought he could appeal for advice.

MIXED VERB TENSES: Don't mix verb tenses without reason. Keep all verbs in the same tense in relating a sequence of events.

> MIXED TENSES: John *ran* to the store, *bought* a bag of oranges, and *walked* slowly home. The grocer *noticed* that he *had* a Canadian nickel in his till and *wonders* if he *had gotten* it from John.
>
> CORRECTION: *wonders* should be *wondered*.
>
> COMMENT: *had gotten* is past perfect tense because the event occurred before he wondered.

MIXED CLAUSE STRUCTURE: Don't combine clauses that make a statement with clauses that ask a question.

> MIXED CLAUSES: They asked me [declarative] would I run for councilman [interrogative].
>
> CORRECTED: They asked me if I would run for councilman.

OMISSION OF *other*: Do not omit *other* after *than* when comparing two members of the same class.

> OMITTED: She was taller than any girl in her club.
>
> QUESTION: Taller even than herself? She was a member of the club.
>
> CORRECTED: She was taller than any *other* girl in her club.

INCONSISTENT COMPARISONS: Even though the meaning is understandable, do not compare things which are not really comparable.

> INCONSISTENT: The motor in the Elixir Vacuum Cleaner is more powerful than any other cleaner.
>
> QUESTION: A motor is more powerful than a cleaner?
>
> SOLUTION: The motor in the Elixir Vacuum Cleaner is more powerful than *that* of any other cleaner.

COMPARATIVE FOR TWO; SUPERLATIVE FOR THREE OR MORE: Do not use the comparative form to compare more than two; do not use the superlative form to compare fewer than three.

INCORRECT COMPARATIVE:	He is the *oldest* of the two brothers.
CORRECT COMPARATIVE:	He is the *older* of the two brothers.
INCORRECT SUPERLATIVE:	She is the *older* of the three sisters.
CORRECT SUPERLATIVE:	She is the *oldest* of the three sisters.

OMISSION OF NECESSARY ARTICLES OR POSSESSIVE PRONOUNS: When two or more terms are in parallel construction and refer to separate people or things, be sure to supply an article or appropriate possessive pronoun for each of the terms.

OMITTED ARTICLE:	He bought a brown and gray coat.
COMMENT:	This is correct if the same coat was brown and gray.
SUPPLIED ARTICLE:	He bought a brown and *a* gray coat.
OMITTED PRONOUN:	She always consulted her maid and accountant about her income tax.
COMMENT:	This is correct if the maid was her accountant.
SUPPLIED PRONOUN:	She always consulted her maid and *her* accountant about her income tax.

OMISSION OF NECESSARY PREPOSITIONS: Usually it is sufficient to use a single preposition to connect two parallel words to the object of the preposition, but occasionally because of idiomatic prepositional usage, the same preposition is not suitable to both of the parallel words.

CORRECT:	She spoke about her love and admiration *for* her father.
COMMENT:	*Love for her father* and *admiration for her father* are both correct.
INCOMPLETE:	She spoke of her confidence and love *for* her father.
COMMENT:	The idiom is *confidence in*, not *confidence for*.
COMPLETE:	She spoke of her confidence *in* and love for her father.

OMISSION OF PART OF A VERB PHRASE: When two parts of a compound verb are in different tenses, be sure that each tense is completely expressed.

INCOMPLETE:	It will probably rain for the annual picnic because it always has.
COMPLETE:	It will probably rain for the annual picnic because it always has *rained*.
INCOMPLETE:	Many of our clients have and probably will be unable to pay their bills.
COMPLETE:	Many of our clients have *been* and probably will be unable to pay their bills.

The Sentence and Its Parts

OMISSION OF *that* AFTER CERTAIN VERBS.   When verbs like *saying, thinking, hoping, feeling, wishing* introduce a dependent noun clause as object of the verb, the dependent clause should be introduced by *that* to avoid possible confusion.

OMITTED: She felt her husband was not good enough for her.
CORRECTED: She felt *that* her husband was not good enough for her.
OMITTED: He believed his friend would not desert him.
CORRECTED: He believed *that* his friend would not desert him.

Normal English Word Order

Normal sentence word order in English is subject—verb—complement.

John ate *dinner*.   (object of verb *ate*)
John is *boss*.   (predicate noun)
John is *sick*.   (predicate adjective)

Indirect objects usually precede direct objects.

We gave *him* the check.   (gave the check to him)

The expletives *here* and *there* usually precede the verb which is followed by the subject.

Here is your *hat*.   (subject in italics)
There are *dozens* of roses in the garden.   (subject in italics)

Modifiers are placed as close as possible to the words they modify. Adjectives usually precede the words they modify.

the *tall* building   the *sick old* man

Adjective phrases or clauses usually follow the words they modify.

The man *in the dark suit*   (adjective phrase)
The woman *who was in the grocery store*   (adjective clause)

Adverbs usually follow the verbs they modify.

She ran *rapidly*.   (adverb)
She ran *into the house*.   (adverbial phrase)
She ran *when she saw her mother coming*.   (adverbial clause)

Single adverbs sometimes precede the verbs they modify.

They *rapidly* took advantage of the situation.

Single adverbs are usually inserted after the first element of a verb phrase.

They *will* really *have* trouble.   (verb phrase in italics)
He *has* certainly *been trying* hard.   (verb phrase in italics)

Single adverbs modifying adjectives or other adverbs precede the words they modify.

> His uncle was *very* rich.   (modifies adjective *rich*)
> The train was *extraordinarily* fast.   (modifies adjective *fast*)
> He finished his work *more* quickly than the others.   (modifies adverb *quickly*)

EXAMPLE OF A DECLARATIVE SENTENCE WITH MODIFIERS: The strong smell of gas which pervaded all the rooms of the house quickly drove the guests at the party out into the street.

For variety of sentence structure, or for emphasis, dependent phrases and clauses frequently precede the subject.

> *In the late afternoon*, Father usually took a nap.   (dependent phrase)
> *When they discovered their mistake*, the workmen tried to correct it. (dependent clause)

Spelling

The Sounds of English

Sounds and spellings in English are frequently at variance with each other. Only the following sounds are dependable in English spelling. They are almost invariably represented by the corresponding letters of the alphabet.

B	bat	SH	shut
D	dog	T	toy
L	love	TH	think *or* then
P	push	V	vat

The following sounds are listed in alphabetical order, followed by suggestions of what letters may represent these sounds in English (and, consequently, how you may look up words in the dictionary that are apparently not spelled as they should be).

When looking for a word, if you do not find it spelled phonetically:

1. Sound it out carefully,
2. Then consult the following list of sounds, and
3. Check the corresponding letters in your dictionary.

Vowel Sounds

SOUND	AS IN	MAY BE REPRESENTED BY	ILLUSTRATION
A	wake	A	able
		AE	aerial
		AI	aid
		E	crepe
		EI	eight
A	fat	A	atom
AH	start	A	art
		O	octave
AW	straw	AW	awful
		AU	auto
		O	office
		OU	ought
E	he	E	emotion
		EA	each
		EE	eel
		EI	either
		EY	money
		I	unique
		IE	mien
		Y	carry

SOUND	AS IN	MAY BE REPRESENTED BY	ILLUSTRATION
E	wet	E	edify
		AE	aesthetic
		AI	said
		EA	dead
I	white	I	idea
		IE	pie
		AI	aisle
		AY	aye
		EI	height
		Y	fly
I	hid	I	if
		A	stoppage
		Y	myth
O	slow	O	obey
		OA	oak
		OW	low
OI	boil	OI	ointment
		OY	boy
OW	plow	OW	owl
		OU	out
OO	mood	OO	ooze
		EW	news
		U	astute
		UI	fruit
OO	foot	OO	took
		OU	would
U	mute	U	unity
		EAU	beauty
		EU	eulogy
		EW	ewe
UH	but	U	until
		A	above
		E	her
		O	oven
		OU	rough

Consonant Sounds

CH	child	CH	chill
		TCH	stretch

Spelling

SOUND	AS IN	MAY BE REPRESENTED BY	ILLUSTRATION
F	after	F	far
		GH	tough
		PH	philosophy
G	drag	G	game
		GH	ghost
GS	legs	X	exist
H	hoot	H	house
		WH	who
J	reject	J	jet
		G	gentle (usually before *E*)
		G	giant (usually before *I*)
		G	gyroscope (sometimes before *Y*)
		DG	pledge
K	kitten	K	key
		C	cat, cot, cut, clip (usually before *a*, *o*, *u*, or consonants)
		CH	chorus
KS	ducks	X	expert
M	mad	M	mad
		MN	condemn
N	noon	N	now
		GN	gnome
		KN	know
		PN	pneumatic
R	art	R	reach
		WR	write
S	sing	S	sun
		SC	science
		ST	fasten
		C	cease, city (usually before *e* and *i*)
		PS	psalm

SOUND	AS IN	MAY BE REPRESENTED BY	ILLUSTRATION
SF	glassful	SPH	sphere
SH	wish	SH	shirt
		SS	mission
		T	fiction
SK	flask	SK	skirt
		SC	scandal
		SCH	school
		SQ	squirrel
SW	sweet	SW	swim
		SU	suede
W	wind	W	waste
		WH	white
		O	one
X(KS)	expert	X	wax
Y	you	Y	yet
		U	unit
		EU	eulogy
		EW	ewe
Z	ooze	Z	zip
		S	cosy
		X	xylophone
ZH		Z	seizure
		S	division

Some Spelling Principles

Use *i* before *e* except after *c*, if the sound is *ee*.

If the sound is *ee*, use *ie*, as in *achieve, believe, siege, field, relief,* and *niece,* except after *c*, as in *ceiling, receive, deceit, perceive,* and *conceit.* EXCEPTIONS: *either, neither, leisure, caffeine, protein, seize, weird, counterfeit, plebeian, species, financier*

If the sound is NOT *ee*, use *ei*, as in *neighbor, height, weigh, weight, foreign,* and *heir.* EXCEPTIONS: *friend, sieve, mischief,* and *handkerchief*

Common Prefixes

When adding a prefix to a word, the spelling of the base word remains unchanged, although for convenience of pronunciation, prefix spellings are sometimes slightly altered.

Spelling

PREFIX	MEANING	EXAMPLES
a	not	amoral, atypical, anomalous
ab	away from	abduct, abstain, abjure
ad	to	adapt, adhere, adroit
bi	two	biennial, bi-weekly, bicycle
circum	around	circumnavigate, circumscribe, circumvent
co	with, together with	combine, coeditor, coincide
contra	against	contrary, contradict, controversy
de	down, away from	debase, deflate, depose
dis	not	distrust, dissociate, disinterested
ex	out	expel, exit, exhume
	former	ex-wife, ex-convict, ex-president
extra	outside	extracurricular, extraterritorial, extraordinary
in	in	induct, invert, implicit
	not	insane, improper, inarticulate
inter	between, among	interstate, international, intervene
intra	within	intrastate, intramural, introvert
mal	bad	malevolent, malediction, malefactor
mis	wrong	mistake, miscalculation, misadventure
omni	all	omnipotent, omniscient, omniverous
post	after	postpone, postgraduate, postoperative
pre	before	predate, preface, premarital
re	again	remake, restate, reimburse
retro	back	retroactive, retro-rockets, retrospect
sub	under	subway, substandard, subordinate
super	over	superintendent, superstructure, supervise
sym, syn	together	synthetic, symphony, sympathy
trans	across	transfer, transmit, transom
un	not	unnatural, uncivilized, unobtrusive

When a prefix adapts to the first letter of the base word or root, use a double letter, as in ir + regular = *irregular*, and in such words as *appoint*, *announce*, *correspond*, *collect*, *illegal*, *immortal*, *occur*, *oppose*, *suffer*, and *suppose*.

Common Suffixes

NOUN SUFFIXES:

SUFFIX	MEANING	EXAMPLES
ance, ence, ancy, ency	act of, state of, condition of	attendance, precedence, hesitancy, presidency
dom	state or condition of	wisdom, kingdom
er, or, ar, eer, ist	one who	painter, governor, bursar, profiteer, segregationist
ess	one who (feminine)	poetess, actress
hood	state of	manhood, nationhood, falsehood
ism	doctrine or practice of	totalitarianism, mannerism
ment	state, quality, act of	wonderment, treatment, payment
ness	state of	fullness, shyness, sickness

ADJECTIVE SUFFIXES:

SUFFIX	MEANING	EXAMPLES
able, ible	capable of	eatable, visible
ful	full of	hopeful, meaningful
ish, y, ic, ac, al	like, pertaining to	childish, sandy, demonic, cardiac, practical
less	without	careless, comfortless
ory, ary	relating	sensory, funerary
ous, ose	full of, like	cancerous, verbose
ward	in the direction of	upward, homeward

When adding a suffix that begins with a consonant, the spelling of the base word remains the same:

> sad + ness = sadness
> hope + less = hopeless
> care + ful = careful

Also: excitement, meanness, drunkenness, government

Changing the Final Y to I Before Adding Suffixes

With base words ending in *y*, the *y* is usually changed to *i* before the suffix is added, as *happiness*, *loneliness*, *beautifully* and *happily*. EXCEPTIONS: one-syllable words ending in *y*, such as *dryness* and *shyly*, and when adding the suffix *ing*, as in *carrying*.

Spelling

Dropping the Final E Before Adding Suffixes

Words ending in a silent *e* drop the *e*, as in *stare-staring, spare-spared, come-coming, excite-exciting, argue-arguing*. EXCEPTIONS: Words ending in *oe*, such as *canoeing, hoeing*. Also words ending in *ce* and *ge*: *notice-noticeable, manage-manageable, courage-courageous* (The *e* keeps the sound "soft" like *j* and *s*.), and words ending in *ic* or *ac* insert a *k* before the *ing: picnic-picnicking, panic-panicked, traffic-trafficker*.

Note that words ending in double e (ee) never drop the final ee, as in *agree-agreeing*.

Adding Other Endings

When adding an *ly* ending to turn an adjective into an adverb, normally just add *ly*, as in *extreme + ly = extremely, definite + ly = definitely, careful + ly = carefully, beautiful + ly = beautifully*, and *accidental + ly = accidentally*.

Words ending in *ic* form adverbs by adding *ally*, as in *basically, terrifically*, and *fantastically*. EXCEPTION: *publicly*.

Words ending in *y* preceded by a consonant change the *y* to *i*, as in *happy-happily* and *necessary-necessarily*.

Words ending in *ble* and *ple* drop the *e*, as in *probable-probably* and *simple-simply*.

Words ending in *ue* drop the *e* and add *ly*, as in *true-truly* and *due-duly*.

In words of one syllable ending in a single vowel followed by a single consonant, double the final letter of the base word: *tap-tapping, hop-hopping, scar-scarred, spar-sparring*.

In words of more than one syllable that end in one vowel and one consonant (such as *happen, occur, prefer, commit*) double the consonant before adding *ing, ed, able, er* **only** when the emphasis falls on the last vowel, as in *begin-beginning, refer-referring, occur-occurring, regret-regrettable, forget-forgettable*. But do not double the consonant if the emphasis shifts, as in *prefer-preference*, and not before the suffixes *ity* and *ize*, as in *equality-equalize*. Similarly, do not double the consonant if the emphasis is anywhere but on the last syllable before the suffix, as in *happen-happening, offer-offered, travel-traveler*. EXCEPTIONS: *handicapped, kidnapped*.

Turning Singular Nouns into Plurals

Most singular nouns are turned into plurals by adding *s*, as in *dog-dogs* and *picture-pictures*. After *s, x, ch, sh*, and *z*, add *es*, as in *dress-dresses* and *sex-sexes*. If the noun ends in a consonant followed by *y*, drop the *y* and add *ies*, as in *liberty-liberties, monastery-monasteries, lady-ladies, story-stories, ally-allies*.

If the noun ends in a vowel followed by *y*, simply add *s*, as in *donkey-donkeys*, *valley-valleys*, *chimney-chimneys*, *boy-boys*, *tray-trays*. For nouns ending in *i*, add *s*, as in *alibis* and *rabbis*.

For nouns ending in *o*, add *s*, as in *pianos*, *dynamos*, *photos*. EXCEPTIONS: *tomatoes*, *potatoes*, *heroes*, *mosquitoes*, *echoes*, *mottoes*, *torpedoes*, *cargoes*, *volcanoes*, *vetoes*, *embargoes*, *tornadoes*, *dominoes*, *buffaloes*, *desperadoes*, *haloes*, *noes*.

Some nouns ending in *f* and *fe* are made plural by turning the *f* to *v* before adding *s*, as in *calf-calves*, *wife-wives*, *knife-knives*, *half-halves*, *shelf-shelves*, *thief-thieves*, *loaf-loaves*. Some of these words may be spelled either way: *hoofs-hooves*, *wharfs-wharves*.

Some English nouns of foreign origin keep their original plurals, as in *crisis-crises*, *oasis-oases*, *criterion-criteria*, *phenomenon-phenomena*, *alumnus-alumni*, *larva-larvae*, *medium-media*, *ox-oxen*.

Plurals of hyphenated compound nouns usually add the *s* to the main noun part, as in *passers-by* and *mothers-in-law*.

Some nouns have the same form in both singular and plural, as in *sheep*, *aircraft*, *moose*, *deer*, *fish*, and *swine*.

For some nouns, the difference between the singular and plural form lies in their vowels, as in *foot-feet*, *goose-geese*, *man-men*, *tooth-teeth*, and *woman-women*.

Words Frequently Misspelled

abbreviation
abscess
absence
accede
acceptable
accessible
accidentally
accommodate
accompanied
according
accustomed
achievement
acknowledgment
acquaintance
across
address
advertisement
advice (noun)

advise (verb)
aggravate
agreeable
aisle
allotment
altar
altogether
always
among
amount
analyze
annual
answer
anxious
arguing
arrangement
arrive
article

ashamed
assignment
athlete
attendance
author
awful
awkward
beginning
behavior
benefited
breath (noun)
breathe (verb)
calendar
candidate
captain
carrying
cemetery
characteristic

Spelling

coarse
college
color
committed
compel
complexion
conceivable
conference
conscience
conscientious
conscious
consistent
continuous
convenience
courteous
criticize
cupboard
dealt
descent
describe
despair
dessert
develop
dictionary
dining
disappear
disappoint
disastrous
discipline
discuss
dissatisfied
divide
divine
division
doesn't
earnest
efficient
eighteen
eighth
embarrass
eminent

envelope
environment
equipped
especially
etc.
exaggerate
excellent
exhilarate
existence
extraordinary
familiar
fascinate
February
fiery
finally
foreign
foresee
forty
fourth
government
grammar
guarantee
headache
height
heroes
hypocrisy
imaginary
independence
indispensable
interest
irrelevant
jewelry
judgment
knowledge
laboratory
likelihood
likely
loneliness
luncheon
maintenance
manual

marriage
mathematics
miniature
misspell
mortgage
murmur
naturally
necessary
neighborhood
niece
ninety
ninth
nuclear
occasion
occur
occurrence
optimism
pageant
parallel
parliament
particular
peaceable
perceive
perform
permissible
perseverance
personnel
persuade
playwright
poison
possess
potatoes
precede
preferred
prejudice
prevalent
previously
privilege
probably
procedure
psychology

pursue
recognize
recommend
referred
religious
restaurant
rhythm
salary
schedule
secretary
seize
sensitive
separate

sergeant
shepherd
sincerely
stopped
strength
stretch
studying
succeed
superintendent
supersede
temperament
temperature
therefore

tragedy
tremendous
truly
twelfth
vacuum
vengeance
villain
warranty
Wednesday
whether
wholesale
withhold
yield

Verbs

Correct Verb Usage

Verbs *are* the asserting words. Without a verb it *is* impossible to make a sentence. On the other hand, a sentence *can be made* of a single verb: *Go. Eat. Wait.* These *are* one-word sentences. All the italicized words above are verbs.

An assertion can involve action (*Write* me a letter.) or a state of being (I *feel* sick.) or it can be nothing more than a device for making a statement (Gold *is* valuable.) or asking a question (*Are* you happy?).

But since action or state of being or even a statement involves time—past, present, future—verbs have tenses to indicate the time. A very few verbs like *ought* do not have a complete sequence of tenses and are therefore known as defective verbs.

PRINCIPAL PARTS OF VERBS: The essential forms of a verb are known as its principal parts:

Infinitive:	to go OR go
Present Tense:	go
Past Tense:	went
Present Participle:	going
Past Participle:	gone

MUMBER AND PERSON RELATED TO VERBS: Most English verbs have very easy conjugations because for nearly all verbs the forms for number (singular and plural) are the same. For example:

Singular: I sing   Plural: We sing

Person alludes to the subject of the verb.
First person is the person speaking or writing:

Singular: I   Plural: we

Second person is the person spoken or written to:

Singular: you   Plural: you

Third person is anybody or anything else:

Singular: he, she, it	Plural: they
street	streets
beauty	beauties

In nearly all verbs the only change of form occurs in the third person singular of the present and present perfect tenses and in the first person of the future and future perfect tenses. For example:

PRESENT TENSE: I, you, we, they *go* BUT he, she, it *goes.*
PRESENT PERFECT TENSE: I, you, we, they *have gone* BUT he, she, it *has gone.*

FUTURE TENSE:	you, he, she, it, they *will go* BUT I, *we shall go*.
FUTURE PERFECT TENSE:	you, he, she, it, they *will have gone* BUT I, we *shall have gone*.
PAST TENSE (*no change*):	I, you, he, she, it, we, they *went*.
PAST PERFECT TENSE (*no change*):	I, you, he, it, we, they *had gone*.
EXCEPTION:	An important exception is the verb *to be* which has several different forms.

MOOD OF VERBS: Differences in the intention of the speaker or writer are shown by mood.

Indicative Mood: The indicative mood is used to make a statement or ask a question.

> The old man *walked* slowly down the street.
> Why *do* you *eat* so rapidly?

Conjugations of English verbs are usually in the indicative mood.

Imperative Mood: The imperative mood of English verbs is identical with the infinitive (without the *to*): *be, work, eat, run*.

It is used for commands, requests, or directions:

COMMAND:	*Sit* down and *eat* your supper.
REQUEST:	Please *be* on time, and *bring* your lunch.
DIRECTION:	*Fold* the paper vertically and *put* your name at the top.

Subjunctive Mood: The subjunctive mood is rarely used in modern English. The following usages are listed in order of frequency of occurrence from most frequent to least frequent:

To express a wish or to describe a condition contrary to fact, the verb form is the same as in the indicative mood except for the verb *to be* where the form *were* is used for all persons.

WISH:	I wish I *were* as healthy as I used to be.
CONDITION CONTRARY TO FACT:	If she *were* younger, we could give her the job.

A second use of the subjunctive, rare and very formal, occurs in a dependent clause after a verb that expresses determination or a command or a request. In this usage, the subjunctive form is the same as the imperative.

DETERMINATION:	I insist that he *meet* me at the bank.
COMMAND:	The general commanded that all troops *be* in dress uniform.
REQUEST:	I request that I *be allowed* to leave after the wedding. (passive voice)

The same form of the subjunctive is used in formal parliamentary procedure to introduce a motion or resolution.

I move that this resolution *be* adopted: "*Be* it resolved that the Senate *go* on record as endorsing Article Seven of the Constitution."

TRANSITIVE AND INTRANSITIVE VERBS: The distinction between transitive and intransitive verbs is useful principally for the grammatical purpose of determining the case of a pronoun which follows a verb. Is it correct to say "It is I" or "It is me"? The answer is *I* because *is* is an intransitive verb. Transitive verbs are followed by the objective case (*me*); intransitive verbs are followed by the nominative case (*I*).

When a verb indicates a motion or a passing over from one person or thing to another, it is called *transitive*: He *hit* the ball. She *ate* her dinner. Usually, something is being done to something or somebody.

Many verbs are both transitive and intransitive, depending on the meaning of the sentence in which they are used. "He *is* still *breathing*" means that he is alive. "He *is breathing* the fresh air of the seashore" implies that he is having a fine vacation. The first *is breathing* is intransitive; the action is self-contained. The second *is breathing* is a transitive verb because the sense of the verb requires the object *air*.

A simple test for a transitive verb is to find out if the sentence can be reversed by being stated in the passive voice, since only transitive verbs have a passive voice:

ACTIVE VOICE: He is breathing the air.
PASSIVE VOICE: The air is being breathed by him.

If the object of the verb (*air*) cannot be made the subject and the subject expressed in a "by-phrase" (*by him*), the verb is not transitive.

An intransitive verb makes an assertion without requiring any object.

The bell *rings*.
The church *stands* on the top of a little hill.
The books *are* on the desk.

This distinction is important grammatically only for one small class of intransitive verbs known as *linking*, or *copulative*, verbs. Such verbs link a sentence subject to a noun, pronoun, or adjective in the predicate. *To be* is the most frequently used linking verb. Pronouns following linking verbs should be in the nominative case.

It is *I, we, you, he, she, it, they*.

Adjectives, not adverbs, follow linking verbs in the predicate.

He is *tall, good, bad, weak, sick, strong*.

Besides *to be*, the most frequently used linking verbs are *become*, *seem*, *smell*, *look*, *grow*, *feel*, *sound*, *get*, *taste*, *appear*.

> The food smells bad.   (not *badly*)
> The orchestra sounded *good*.   (not *well*)
> I feel *well*.   (*Well* is here an adjective meaning "not sick.")
> I feel *good*.   (in good spirits)

WARNING: The subject and object of an infinitive—even the infinitive *to be*—are always in the objective case.

> At the masquerade they all believed *him* to be *me*.

VOICE OF VERBS: Transitive verbs—and only transitive verbs—depend on voice to indicate whether the emphasis in a sentence should be placed on the doer or the receiver of the action stated by the verb.

ACTIVE VOICE   emphasizes the doer.

> Andrew plays the piano.

The sentence implies that one of Andrew's talents is piano playing since *Andrew* is the subject of the transitive verb *plays* in the active voice. *Piano* is the object of the verb.

PASSIVE VOICE   emphasizes the receiver of the action.

> The piano is played by Andrew.

This sentence implies that someone has asked who uses the piano which is part of the furniture of a room. Therefore *piano* is the subject of the sentence. But the piano isn't doing anything; something is being done to it. Therefore the passive form *is played* of the transitive verb *play* is followed by the prepositional phrase *by Andrew* to explain the use of the piano.

The passive voice is necessary on occasions where the doer is unknown or where it is preferable that he remain anonymous.

> The wine was spilled on the floor.

It is also used when the doer is of no importance or when his identity is already known, or on occasions where the performer of the action is obvious.

> The programs were distributed during the concert.
> The cellar was flooded.

THE PRESENT TENSE: Use the present tense to indicate that something is so at the moment of speaking or writing.

> He *is* sorry.   That *looks* like an expensive dress.

Use the present tense to describe something that is true regardless of time.

> Justice *is* important.   Bees *sting*.

Verbs

The present tense is frequently used to refer to artistic productions which exist in the present even though they were created in the past and to make statements about artists (in the sense that they continue to live because of their works). Similarly, synopses of plots are usually given in the present tense.

> In *Romeo and Juliet*, Shakespeare's verse *has* a lyric quality.
> Verdi *is* one of the greatest composers of all time.
> At the beginning of *The Divine Comedy*, Dante *is* lost in a forest.
> He *attempts* to climb a nearby hill.

Use the progressive form of the present tense to indicate a continuing action or situation.

> The clock *is striking.*   The organ *is playing.*   The people *are listening.*

When the progressive form is not used for such continuing events, a dramatic effect is produced.

> The clock *strikes*, the organ *plays*, the people *listen.*

Use the intensive form of the present tense to secure emphasis.

> I *do work* hard.   He *does dress* well.   They *do understand* you.

THE FUTURE TENSE: Use the future tense to indicate an event predicted to occur in the future. In informal conversation, many people use only the auxiliary verb *will* for all persons, or else they use contractions.

> I (we) will do it.   I'll do it.   We'll do it.
> You will do it.   You'll do it.
> He (she, it, they) will do it.   He'll, she'll, they'll do it.

In formal usage, use *shall* in the first person and *will* in the second and third.

> I (we) *shall* write.
> You *will* write.
> He (she, it, they) *will* write.

To indicate intensity, implying a promise or determination, reverse the above formal usage by using *will* in the first person and *shall* in the second and third.

> I (we) *will* succeed.
> You *shall* succeed.
> He (she, it, they) *shall* succeed.

THE PAST TENSE: Use the past tense to refer to something that occurred at a definite time in the past.

> He *opened* a bank account two years ago.

Use the progressive form of the past tense to indicate that the event in the past continued over a period of time.

When he was seven years old, he *was learning* to write.

Use the intensive form of the past tense to secure emphasis.

It took a long time, but he *did learn* to write.

THE PRESENT PERFECT TENSE: Use the present perfect tense when the emphasis is on the fact that something that occurred once or several times in the past is considered from a present point of view. "I *have been* in London" gives no indication of when the event occurred or even how many times it occurred except that it happened in the past. The emphasis is on the fact that at the present time a trip to London is a part of the speaker's or writer's experience.

Use the present perfect tense to describe an event which began at some time in the past and which has just been completed.

I *have finished* my homework.

Use the progressive form of the present perfect tense to indicate a continuing action.

I *have been looking* all over for you.

THE PAST PERFECT TENSE: Use the past perfect tense to refer to an event which was terminated prior to some definite time in the past.

She *had finished* her work before she went to bed.

Since the past perfect tense implies a past event before another past event, it is usually accompanied by another verb in the past tense (*went* in the example above) though not necessarily in the same sentence.

He *caught* a bad cold.   He *had been* out in the rain all day.

Use the progressive form of the past perfect tense to indicate a continuing action.

He *had been waiting* a long time when the train came.

THE FUTURE PERFECT TENSE: Use the future perfect tense to indicate that something will be completed before some definite time in the future.

By the time she gets married, she *will have learned* to cook.

The use of *shall* and *will* in forming the future perfect tense is the same as in the future tense.

Use the progressive form of the future perfect tense to indicate a continuing action.

When we reach the top of the mountain, we *shall have been climbing* for more than seven hours.

Verbs

Verbals

Verbals are words which are derived from verbs but which function as other parts of speech. Unlike finite verbs they do not have tense nor are they limited by person and number.

INFINITIVES:

Present Infinitive:	*to be, to go*
Prefect Infinitive:	*to have been, to have gone*
Progressive Forms:	*to be going, to have been going*

The *to* is sometimes omitted because of idiomatic usage: *Let him go.* (*Ask him to go.*)

Infinitives usually function as nouns. In the sentence *To die is common*, the infinitive *to die* could be replaced by the noun *death*. But since infinitives are nouns and verbs at the same time, they may also, like verbs, have modifiers and complements:

> *To sing* beautifully was her ambition.

[The adverb *beautifully* modifies *to sing*; *to sing* is the subject of *was*.]

> He loved *to eat* candy.

[*Candy* is the object of *to eat*; *to eat candy* is the object of *loved*.]

THE GERUND: A gerund is a present participle that functions as a noun. It is the name of an action or state of being. Like the infinitive it may have modifiers and complements.

> He enjoyed *driving* the car.
> Heavy *drinking* was his only bad habit.
> *Being* sensible was difficult for him.
> She enjoyed *cooking* on her new stove.

PRESENT AND PRESENT PERFECT PARTICIPLES: With or without complements or modifiers, present and present perfect participles function as adjectives.

> The *sinking* ship.   The *rising* sun. [modify *ship* and *sun*]
> *Having lost* his notebook, he failed the test. [modifies *he*]

PAST AND PAST PERFECT PARTICIPLES: Past and past perfect participles (with or without complements or modifiers) also function as adjectives, but they describe an action happening *to* the noun or pronoun being modified.

> The robber, *shot* by the police, was in critical condition. [modifies *robber*]
> The lobsters, *flown* in from the ocean, were delicious. [modifies *lobsters*]
> *Having been drenched* by the rain, he caught a cold. [modifies *he*]

VERB CONJUGATIONS

Regular Verbs

Irregular Verbs

In the conjugations of the future tense, (P) indicates forms that imply a promise, and (C) indicates forms that imply a command. Note that the verb *shall* is now rare in conversation, though it is still used in formal written English.

Conjugation of a Regular Verb

to push (active voice)

Principal Parts: push, pushing, pushed, pushed

Infinitive: to push, push
Perfect Infinitive: to have pushed

Present Participle: pushing
Past Participle: pushed

INDICATIVE MOOD

Pres.	I push	we push
	you push	you push
	he (she, it) pushes	they push
Pres. Prog.	I am pushing	we are pushing
	you are pushing	you are pushing
	he (she, it) is pushing	they are pushing
Pres. Int.	I do push	we do push
	you do push	you do push
	he (she, it) does push	they do push
Fut.	I shall push	we shall push
	you will push	you will push
	he (she, it) will push	they will push
Fut.	I will push *(P)*	we will push *(P)*
	you shall push *(C)*	you shall push *(C)*
	he (she, it) shall push *(C)*	they shall push *(C)*
Past	I pushed	we pushed
	you pushed	you pushed
	he (she, it) pushed	they pushed
Past Prog.	I was pushing	we were pushing
	you were pushing	you were pushing
	he (she, it) was pushing	they were pushing
Past Int.	I did push	we did push
	you did push	you did push
	he (she, it) did push	they did push
Pres. Perf.	I have pushed	we have pushed
	you have pushed	you have pushed
	he (she, it) has pushed	they are pushed
Past Perf.	I had pushed	we had pushed
	you had pushed	you had pushed
	he (she, it) had pushed	they had pushed
Fut. Perf.	I shall have pushed	we shall have pushed
	you will have pushed	you will have pushed
	he (she, it) will have pushed	they will have pushed

IMPERATIVE MOOD
push

SUBJUNCTIVE MOOD

Pres.	if I push	if we push
	if you push	if you push
	if he (she, it) push	if they push
Past	if I pushed	if we pushed
	if you pushed	if you pushed
	if he (she, it) pushed	if they pushed
Fut.	if I should push	if we should push
	if you should push	if you should push
	if he (she, it) should push	if they should push

Infinitive: to be pushed, be pushed *Present Participle:* being pushed
Perfect Infinitive: to have been pushed *Past Participle:* been pushed

INDICATIVE MOOD

Pres.	I am pushed	we are pushed
	you are pushed	you are pushed
	he (she, it) is pushed	they are pushed
Pres.	I am being pushed	we are being pushed
Prog.	you are being pushed	you are being pushed
	he (she, it) is being pushed	they are being pushed
Pres.	I do get pushed	we do get pushed
Int.	you do get pushed	you do get pushed
	he (she, it) does get pushed	they do get pushed
Fut.	I shall be pushed	we shall be pushed
	you will be pushed	you will be pushed
	he (she, it) will be pushed	they will be pushed
Fut.	I will be pushed *(P)*	we will be pushed *(P)*
	you shall be pushed *(C)*	you shall be pushed *(C)*
	he (she, it) shall be pushed *(C)*	they shall be pushed *(C)*
Past	I was pushed	we were pushed
	you were pushed	you were pushed
	he (she, it) was pushed	they were pushed
Past	I was being pushed	we were being pushed
Prog.	you were being pushed	you were being pushed
	he (she, it) was being pushing	they were being pushed
Past	I did get pushed	we did get pushed
Int.	you did get pushed	you did get pushed
	he (she, it) did get pushed	they did get pushed
Pres.	I have been pushed	we have been pushed
Perf.	you have been pushed	you have been pushed
	he (she, it) has been pushed	they have been pushed
Past	I had been pushed	we had been pushed
Perf.	you had been pushed	you had been pushed
	he (she, it) had been pushed	they had been pushed
Fut.	I shall have been pushed	we shall have been pushed
Perf.	you will have been pushed	you will have been pushed
	he (she, it) will have been pushed	they will have been pushed

IMPERATIVE MOOD
be pushed

SUBJUNCTIVE MOOD

Pres.	if I be pushed	if we be pushed
	if you be pushed	if you be pushed
	if he (she, it) be pushed	if they be pushed
Past	if I were pushed	if we were pushed
	if you were pushed	if you were pushed
	if he (she, it) were pushed	if they were pushed
Fut.	if I should be pushed	if we should be pushed
	if you should be pushed	if you should be pushed
	if he (she, it) should be pushed	if they should be pushed

Verbs

Irregularities of Some Regular Verbs

Regular verbs ending in a consonant (push, cook float):

> form the present participle by adding *ing* (pushing, cooking, floating).
>
> form the past tense and past participle by adding *ed* (pushed, cooked, floated).

Regular verbs ending in a vowel (veto):

> form the present participle by adding *ing* (vetoing).
>
> form the past tense and past participle by adding *ed* (vetoed).

BUT

Regular verbs ending in *e* preceded by a single consonant (make, smoke):

> form the present participle by dropping the *e* before adding *ing* (making, smoking).
>
> form the past tense and past participle by adding only *d* (raked, smoked).

Regular verbs ending in a single consonant preceded by a single vowel (drop, grip):

> double the final consonant before adding *ing* or *ed* (dropping, dropped, gripping, gripped).

Regular verbs ending in *y* preceded by a consonant (try, hurry):

> change the *y* to *i* before adding *ed* (tried, hurried).
>
> change the *y* to *i* for third person singular (tries, hurries).

Principal Auxiliary Verbs

PRONOUN	PRES. TENSE	PAST TENSE
I, you, he, she, it, we, they	can	could
I, you, we, they	do	did
he, she, it	does	did
I, you, we, they	have	had
he, she, it	has	had
I, you, he, she, it, we, they	may	might
I, you, he, she, it, we, they	must	had to
I, you, he, she, it, we, they	ought ·	should have
I, we	shall (future)	
I, you, he, she, it, we, they	should	should have
you, he, she, it, they	will (future)	
I, you, he, she, it, we, they	would	would have

104

Conjugation of Irregular Verbs

to arise (active voice)

Principal Parts: arise, arising, arose, arisen

Infinitive: to arise

Present Participle: arising

Perfect Infinitive: to have arisen

Past Participle: arisen

INDICATIVE MOOD

Pres.	I arise	we arise
	you arise	you arise
	he (she, it) arises	they arise

Pres. Prog.	I am arising	we are arising
	you are arising	you are arising
	he (she, it) is arising	they are arising

Pres. Int.	I do arise	we do arise
	you do arise	you do arise
	he (she, it) does arise	they do arise

Fut.	I shall arise	we shall arise
	you will arise	you will arise
	he (she, it) will arise	they will arise

Fut.	I will arise *(P)*	we will arise *(P)*
	you shall arise *(C)*	you shall arise *(C)*
	he (she, it) shall arise *(C)*	they shall arise *(C)*

Past	I arose	we arose
	you arose	you arose
	he (she, it) arose	they arose

Past Prog.	I was arising	we were arising
	you were arising	you were arising
	he (she, it) was arising	they were arising

Past Int.	I did arise	we did arise
	you did arise	you did arise
	he (she, it) did arise	they did arise

Pres. Perf.	I have arisen	we have arisen
	you have arisen	you have arisen
	he (she, it) has arisen	they have arisen

Past Perf.	I had arisen	we had arisen
	you had arisen	you had arisen
	he (she, it) had arisen	they had arisen

Fut. Perf.	I shall have arisen	we shall have arisen
	you will have arisen	you will have arisen
	he (she, it) will have arisen	they will have arisen

IMPERATIVE MOOD

arise

SUBJUNCTIVE MOOD

Pres.	if I arise	if we arise
	if you arise	if you arise
	if he (she, it) arise	if they arise

Past	if I arose	if we arose
	if you arose	if you arose
	if he (she, it) arose	if they arose

Fut.	if I should arise	if we should arise
	If you should arise	if you should arise
	if he (she, it) should arise	if they should arise

to awake (active voice)   *Principal Parts:* awake awaking, awoke
(awaked), awaked (awakened)

Infinitive: to awake   *Present Participle:* awaking
Perfect Infinitive: to have awakened   *Past Participle:* awaked, awakened

Pres.	I awake	we awake
	you awake	you awake
	he (she, it) awakes	they awake
Pres.	I am awaking	we are awaking
Prog.	you are awaking	you are awaking
	he (she, it) is awaking	they are awaking
Pres.	I do awake	we do awake
Int.	you do awake	you do awake
	he (she, it) does awake	they do awake
Fut.	I shall awake	we shall awake
	you will awake	you will awake
	he (she, it) will awake	they will awake
Fut.	I will awake *(P)*	we will awake *(P)*
	you shall awake *(C)*	you shall awake *(C)*
	he (she, it) shall awake *(C)*	they shall awake *(C)*
Past	I awoke, awaked	we awoke, awaked
	you awoke, awaked	you awoke, awaked
	he (she, it) awoke awaked	they awoke, awaked
Past	I was awaking	we were awaking
Prog.	you were awaking	you were awaking
	he (she, it) was awaking	they were awaking
Past	I did awake	we did awake
Int.	you did awake	you did awake
	he (she, it) did awake	they did awake
Pres.	I have awaked, awakened	we have awaked, awakened
Perf.	you have awaked, awakened	you have awaked, awakened
	he (she, it) has awaked, awakened	they have awaked, awakened
Fut.	I shall have awaked, awakened	we shall have awaked, awakened
Perf.	you will have awaked, awakened	you will have awaked, awakened
	he (she, it) will have awaked, awakened	they will have awaked, awakened

awake

Pres.	if I awake	if we awake
	if you awake	if you awake
	if he (she, it) awake	if they awake
Past	if I awoke	if we awoke
	if you awoke	if you awoke
	if he (she, it) awoke	if they awoke
Fut.	if I should awake	if we should awake
	if you should awake	if you should awake
	if he (she, it) should awake	if they should awake

(passive voice)

Infinitive: to be awakened   *Present Participle:* being awakened
Perfect Infinitive: to have been awakened *Past Participle:* been awakened

INDICATIVE MOOD

Pres.	I am awakened	we are awakened
	you are awakened	you are awakened
	he (she, it) is awakened	they are awakened
Pres. Prog.	I am being awakened	we are being awakened
	you are being awakened	you are being awakened
	he (she, it) is being awakened	they are being awakened
Pres. Int.	I do get awakened	we do get awakened
	you do get awakened	you do get awakened
	he (she, it) does get awakened	they do get awakened
Fut.	I shall be awakened	we shall be awakened
	you will be awakened	you will be awakened
	he (she, it) will be awakened	they will be awakened
Fut.	I will be awakened *(P)*	we will be awakened *(P)*
	you shall be awakened *(C)*	you shall be awakened *(C)*
	he (she, it) shall be awakened *(C)*	they shall be awakened *(C)*
Past	I was awakened	we were awakened
	you were awakened	you were awakened
	he (she, it) was awakened	they were awakened
Past Prog.	I was being awakened	we were being awakened
	you were being awakened	you were being awakened
	he (she, it) was being awakened	they were being awakened
Past Int.	I did get awakened	we did get awakened
	you did get awakened	you did get awakened
	he (she, it) did get awakened	they did get awakened
Pres. Perf.	I have been awakened	we have been awakened
	you have been awakened	you have been awakened
	he (she, it) has been awakened	they have been awakened
Past Perf.	I had been awakened	we had been awakened
	you had been awakened	you had been awakened
	he (she, it) had been awakened	they had been awakened
Fut. Perf.	I shall have been awakened	we shall have been awakened
	you will have been awakened	you will have been awakened
	he (she, it) will have been awakened	they will have been awakened

IMPERATIVE MOOD
be awakened

SUBJUNCTIVE MOOD

Pres.	if I be awakened	if we be awakened
	if you be awakened	if you be awakened
	if he (she, it) be awakened	if they be awakened
Past	if I were awakened	if we were awakened
	if you were awakened	if you were awakened
	if he (she, it) were awakened	if they were awakened
Fut.	if I should be awakened	if we should be awakened
	if you should be awakened	if you should be awakened
	if he (she, it) should be awakened	if they should be awakened

to be

Infinitive: to be, be   *Present Participle:* being
Perfect Infinitive: to have been   *Past Participle:* been

INDICATIVE MOOD

Pres.	I am	we are
	you are	you are
	he (she, it) is	they are
Fut.	I shall be	we shall be
	you will be	you will be
	he (she, it) will be	they will be
Fut.	I will be *(P)*	we will be *(P)*
	you shall be *(C)*	you shall be *(C)*
	he (she, it) shall be *(C)*	they shall be *(C)*
Past	I was	we were
	you were	you were
	he (she, it) was	they were
Pres. *Perf.*	I have been	we have been
	you have been	you have been
	he (she, it) has been	they have been
Past *Perf.*	I had been	we had been
	you had been	you had been
	he (she, it) had been	they had been
Fut. *Perf.*	I shall have been	we shall have been
	you will have been	you will have been
	he (she, it) will have been	they will have been

IMPERATIVE MOOD
be

SUBJUNCTIVE MOOD

Pres.	if I be	if we be
	if you be	if you be
	if he (she, it) be	if they be
Past	if I were	if we were
	if you were	if you were
	if he (she, it) were	if they were
Fut.	if I should be	if we should be
	if you should be	if you should be
	if he (she, it) should be	if they should be

Common Uses of *To Be*

The basic meaning of *to be* is *to exist* as in Hamlet's well-known soliloquy "To be or not to be: that is the question."

The principal use of *to be* is to make an assertion. An observation like "cold ice" becomes an assertion by adding the appropriate form of the verb *to be:* Ice *is* cold.

To be is called a copulative verb because it joins many kinds of sentence elements: nouns as in "Mr. Price *is* the mayor," nouns and predicate adjectives as in "The girl *was* beautiful," infinitives and predicate adjectives as in "To err *is* human," expletives and phrases as in "There *would be* many more people in the hall tonight if it *were* not raining," etc.

To be is also used to create the progressive forms of other verbs: "The water *is flowing*" as well as the passive voice: "I *was beaten*."

to bear (active voice)   *Principal Parts:* bear, bearing, bore, borne

Infinitive: to bear   *Present Participle:* bearing
Perfect Infinitive: to have borne   *Past Participle:* borne

INDICATIVE MOOD

Pres.	I bear	we bear
	you bear	you bear
	he (she, it) bears	they bear
Pres.	I am bearing	we are bearing
Prog.	you are bearing	you are bearing
	he (she, it) is bearing	they are bearing
Pres.	I do bear	we do bear
Int.	you do bear	you do bear
	he (she, it) does bear	they do bear
Fut.	I shall bear	we shall bear
	you will bear	you will bear
	he (she, it) will bear	they will bear
Fut.	I will bear *(P)*	we will bear *(P)*
	you shall bear *(C)*	you shall bear *(C)*
	he (she, it) shall bear *(C)*	they shall bear *(C)*
Past	I bore	we bore
	you bore	you bore
	he (she, it) bore	they bore
Past	I was bearing	we were bearing
Prog.	you were bearing	you were bearing
	he (she, it) was bearing	they were bearing
Past	I did bear	we did bear
Int.	you did bear	you did bear
	he (she, it) did bear	they did bear
Pres.	I have borne	we have borne
Perf.	you have borne	you have borne
	he (she, it) had borne	they had borne
Past	I had borne	we had borne
Perf.	you had borne	you had borne
	he (she, it) had borne	they had borne
Fut.	I shall have borne	we shall have borne
Perf.	you will have borne	you will have borne
	he (she, it) will have borne	they will have bone

IMPERATIVE MOOD
bear

SUBJUNCTIVE MOOD

Pres.	if I bear	if we bear
	if you bear	if you bear
	if he (she, it) bear	if they bear
Past	if I bore	if we bore
	if you bore	if you bore
	if he (she, it) bore	if they bore
Fut.	if I should bear	if we should bear
	if you should bear	if you should bear
	if he (she, it) should bear	if they should bear

Infinitive: to be borne, to be born
Perfect Infinitive: to have been borne,
to have been born

Present Participle: being borne,
being born
Past Participle: been borne,
been born

INDICATIVE MOOD

Pres. I am borne, born
you are borne, born
he (she, it) is borne, born

we are borne, born
you are borne, born
they are borne, born

Pres.
Prog. I am being borne, born
you are being borne, born
he (she, it) is being borne, born

we are being borne, born
you are being borne, born
they are being borne, born

Pres.
Int. I do get borne, born
you do get borne, born
he (she, it) does get borne, born

we do get borne, born
you do get borne, born
they do get borne, born

Fut. I shall be borne, born
you will be borne, born
he (she, it) will be borne, born

we shall be borne, born
you will be borne, born
they will be borne, born

Fut. I will be borne, born *(P)*
you shall be borne, born *(C)*
he (she, it) shall be borne, born *(C)*

we will be borne, born *(P)*
you shall be borne, born *(C)*
they shall be borne, born *(C)*

Past I was borne, born
you were borne, born
he (she, it) were borne, born

we were borne, born
you were borne, born
they were borne, born

Past
Prog. I was being borne, born
you were being borne, born
he (she, it) was being borne, born

we were being borne, born
you were being borne, born
they were being borne, born

Past
Int. I did get borne, born
you did get borne, born
he (she, it) did get borne, born

we did get borne, born
you did get borne, born
they did get borne, born

Pres.
Perf. I have been borne, born
you have been borne, born
he (she, it) had been borne, born

we have been borne, born
you have been borne, born
they had been borne, born

Past
Perf. I had been borne, born
you had been borne, born
he (she, it) had been borne, born

we had been borne, born
you had been borne, born
they had been borne, born

Fut.
Perf. I shall have been borne, born
you will have been borne, born
he (she, it) will have been borne,
born

we shall have been borne, born
you will have been borne, born
they will have been borne, born

IMPERATIVE MOOD
be borne, be born

SUBJUNCTIVE MOOD

Pres. if I be borne, born
if you be borne, born
if he (she, it) be borne, born

if we be borne, born
if you be borne, born
if they be borne, born

Past if I were borne, born
if you were borne, born
if he (she, it) were borne, born

if we were borne, born
if you were borne, born
if they were borne, born

Fut. if I should be borne, born
if you should be borne, born
if he (she, it) should be borne, born

if we should be borne, born
if you should be borne, born
if they should be borne, born

to beat (active voice) *Principal Parts:* beat, beating, beat, beaten

Infinitive: to beat *Present Participle:* beating
Perfect Infinitive: to have beaten *Past Participle:* beaten

INDICATIVE MOOD

Pres.	I beat	we beat
	you beat	you beat
	he (she, it) beats	they beat
Pres.	I am beating	we are beating
Prog.	you are beating	you are beating
	he (she, it) is beating	they are beating
Pres.	I do beat	we do beat
Int.	you do beat	you do beat
	he (she, it) does beat	they do beat
Fut.	I shall beat	we shall beat
	you will beat	you will beat
	he (she, it) will beat	they will beat
Fut.	I will beat *(P)*	we will beat *(P)*
	you shall beat *(C)*	you shall beat *(C)*
	he (she, it) shall beat *(C)*	they shall beat *(C)*
Past	I beat	we beat
	you beat	you beat
	he (she, it) beat	they beat
Past	I was beating	we were beating
Prog.	you were beating	you were beating
	he (she, it) was beating	they were beating
Past	I did beat	we did beat
Int.	you did beat	you did beat
	he (she, it) did beat	they did beat
Pres.	I have beaten	we have beaten
Perf.	you have beaten	you have beaten
	he (she, it) had beaten	they had beaten
Past	I had beaten	we had beaten
Perf.	you had beaten	you had beaten
	he (she, it) had beaten	they had beaten
Fut.	I shall have beaten	we shall have beaten
Perf.	you will have beaten	you will have beaten
	he (she, it) will have beaten	they will have beaten

IMPERATIVE MOOD
beat

SUBJUNCTIVE MOOD

Pres.	if I beat	if we beat
	if you beat	if you beat
	if he (she, it) beat	if they beat
Past	if I beat	if we beat
	if you beat	if you beat
	if he (she, it) beat	if they beat
Fut.	if I should beat	if we should beat
	if you should beat	if you should beat
	if he (she, it) should beat	if they should beat

(passive voice)

Infinitive: to be beaten   *Present Participle:* being beaten
Perfect Infinitive: to have been beaten   *Past Participle:* been beaten

INDICATIVE MOOD

Pres.	I am beaten	we are beaten
	you are beaten	you are beaten
	he (she, it) is beaten	they are beaten
Pres. *Prog.*	I am being beaten	we are being beaten
	you are being beaten	you are being beaten
	he (she, it) is being beaten	they are being beaten
Pres. *Int.*	I do get beaten	we do get beaten
	you do get beaten	you do get beaten
	he (she, it) does get beaten	they do get beaten
Fut.	I shall be beaten	we shall be beaten
	you will be beaten	you will be beaten
	he (she, it) will be beaten	they will be beaten
Fut.	I will be beaten *(P)*	we will be beaten *(P)*
	you shall be beaten *(C)*	you shall be beaten *(C)*
	he (she, it) shall be beaten *(C)*	they shall be beaten *(C)*
Past	I was beaten	we were beaten
	you were beaten	you were beaten
	he (she, it) was beaten	they were beaten
Past *Prog.*	I was being beaten	we were being beaten
	you were being beaten	you were being beaten
	he (she, it) was being beaten	they were being beaten
Past *Int.*	I did get beaten	we did get beaten
	you did get beaten	you did get beaten
	he (she, it) did get beaten	they did get beaten
Pres. *Perf.*	I have been beaten	we have been beaten
	you have been beaten	you have been beaten
	he (she, it) has been beaten	they have been beaten
Past *Perf.*	I had been beaten	we had been beaten
	you had been beaten	you had been beaten
	he (she, it) had been beaten	they had been beaten
Fut. *Perf.*	I shall have been beaten	we shall have been beaten
	you will have been beaten	you will have been beaten
	he (she, it) will have been beaten	they will have been beaten

IMPERATIVE MOOD
be beaten

SUBJUNCTIVE MOOD

Pres.	if I be beaten	if we be beaten
	if you be beaten	if you be beaten
	if he (she, it) be beaten	if they be beaten
Past	if I were beaten	if we were beaten
	if you were beaten	if you were beaten
	if he (she, it) were beaten	if they were beaten
Fut.	if I should be beaten	if we should be beaten
	if you should be beaten	if you should be beaten
	if he (she, it) should be beaten	if they should be beaten

to begin (active voice)   *Principal Parts:* begin, beginning, began, begun

Infinitive: to begin	*Present Participle:* beginning
Perfect Infinitive: to have begun	*Past Participle:* begun

INDICATIVE MOOD

Pres.	I begin	we begin
	you begin	you begin
	he (she, it) begins	they begin
Pres. Prog.	I am beginning	we are beginning
	you are beginning	you are beginning
	he (she, it) is beginning	they are beginning
Pres. Int.	I do begin	we do begin
	you do begin	you do begin
	he (she, it) does begin	they do begin
Fut.	I shall begin	we shall begin
	you will begin	you will begin
	he (she, it) will begin	they will begin
Fut.	I will begin *(P)*	we will begin *(P)*
	you shall begin *(C)*	you shall begin *(C)*
	he (she, it) shall begin *(C)*	they shall begin *(C)*
Past	I began	we began
	you began	you began
	he (she, it) began	they began
Past Prog.	I was beginning	we were beginning
	you were beginning	you were beginning
	he (she, it) was beginning	they were beginning
Past Int.	I did begin	we did begin
	you did begin	you did begin
	he (she, it) did begin	they did begin
Pres. Perf.	I have begun	we have begun
	you have begun	you have begun
	he (she, it) has begun	they have begun
Past Perf.	I had begun	we had begun
	you had begun	you had begun
	he (she, it) had begun	they had begun
Fut. Perf.	I shall have begun	we shall have begun
	you will have begun	you will have begun
	he (she, it) will have begun	they will have begun

IMPERATIVE MOOD
begin

SUBJUNCTIVE MOOD

Pres.	if I begin	if we begin
	if you begin	if you begin
	if he (she, it) begin	if they begin
Past	if I began	if we began
	if you began	if you began
	if he (she, it) began	if they began
Fut.	if I should begin	if we should begin
	if you should begin	if you should begin
	if he (she, it) should begin	if they should begin

(passive voice)

Infinitive: to be begun   *Present Participle:* being begun
Perfect Infinitive: to have been begun   *Past Participle:* been begun

INDICATIVE MOOD

Pres.	I am begun	we are begun
	you are begun	you are begun
	he (she, it) is begun	they are begun
Pres.	I am being begun	we are being begun
Prog.	you are being begun	you are being begun
	he (she, it) is being begun	they are being begun
Pres.	I do get begun	we do get begun
Int.	you do get begun	you do get begun
	he (she, it) does get begun	they do get begun
Fut.	I shall be begun	we shall be begun
	you will be begun	you will be begun
	he (she, it) will be begun	they will be begun
Fut.	I will be begun *(P)*	we will be begun *(P)*
	you shall be begun *(C)*	you shall be begun *(C)*
	he (she, it) shall be begun *(C)*	they shall be begun *(C)*
Past	I was begun	we were begun
	you were begun	you were begun
	he (she, it) was begun	they were begun
Past	I was being begun	we were being begun
Prog.	you were being begun	you were being begun
	he (she, it) was being begun	they were being begun
Past	I did get begun	we did get begun
Int.	you did get begun	you did get begun
	he (she, it) did get begun	they did get begun
Pres.	I have been begun	we have been begun
Perf.	you have been begun	you have been begun
	he (she, it) has been begun	they have been begun
Past	I had been begun	we had been begun
Perf.	you had been begun	you had been begun
	he (she, it) had been begun	they had been begun
Fut.	I shall have been begun	we shall have been begun
Perf.	you will have been begun	you will have been begun
	he (she, it) will have been begun	they will have been begun

IMPERATIVE MOOD
be begun

SUBJUNCTIVE MOOD

Pres.	if I be begun	if we be begun
	if you be begun	if you be begun
	if he (she, it) be begun	if they be begun
Past	if I were begun	if we were begun
	if you were begun	if you were begun
	if he (she, it) were begun	if they were begun
Fut.	if I should be begun	if we should be begun
	if you should be begun	if you should be begun
	if he (she, it) should be begun	if they should be begun

to bend (active voice)   *Principal Parts:* bend, bending, bent, bent

Infinitive: to bend   *Present Participle:* bending
Perfect Infinitive: to have bent   *Past Participle:* bent

INDICATIVE MOOD

Pres.	I bend	we bend
	you bend	you bend
	he (she, it) bends	they bend
Pres.	I am bending	we are bending
Prog.	you are bending	you are bending
	he (she, it) is bending	they are bending
Pres.	I do bend	we do bend
Int.	you do bend	you do bend
	he (she, it) does bend	they do bend
Fut.	I shall bend	we shall bend
	you will bend	you will bend
	he (she, it) will bend	they will bend
Fut.	I will bend *(P)*	we will bend *(P)*
	you shall bend *(C)*	you shall bend *(C)*
	he (she, it) shall bend *(C)*	they shall bend *(C)*
Past	I bent	we bent
	you bent	you bent
	he (she, it) bent	they bent
Past	I was bending	we were bending
Prog.	you were bending	you were bending
	he (she, it) was bending	they were bending
Past	I did bend	we did bend
Int.	you did bend	you did bend
	he (she, it) did bend	they did bend
Pres.	I have bent	we have bent
Perf.	you have bent	you have bent
	he (she, it) has bent	they have bent
Past	I had bent	we had bent
Perf.	you had bent	you had bent
	he (she, it) had bent	they had bent
Fut.	I shall have bent	we shall have bent
Perf.	you will have bent	you will have bent
	he (she, it) will have bent	they will have bent

IMPERATIVE MOOD
bend

SUBJUNCTIVE MOOD

Pres.	if I bend	if we bend
	if you bend	if you bend
	if he (she, it) bend	if they bend
Past	if I bent	if we bent
	if you bent	if you bent
	if he (she, it) bent	if they bent
Fut.	if I should bend	if we should bend
	if you should bend	if you should bend
	if he (she, it) should bend	if they should bend

(passive voice)

Infinitive: to be bent

Perfect Infinitive: to have been bent

Present Participle: being bent

Past Participle: been bent

INDICATIVE MOOD

Pres.	I am bent you are bent he (she, it) is bent	we are bent you are bent they are bent
Pres. *Prog.*	I am being bent you are being bent he (she, it) is being bent	we are being bent you are being bent they are being bent
Pres. *Int.*	I do get bent you do get bent he (she, it) does get bent	we do get bent you do get bent they do get bent
Fut.	I shall be bent you will be bent he (she, it) will be bent	we shall be bent you will be bent they will be bent
Fut.	I will be bent *(P)* you shall be bent *(C)* he (she, it) shall be bent *(C)*	we will be bent *(P)* you shall be bent *(C)* they shall be bent *(C)*
Past	I was bent you were bent he (she, it) was bent	we were bent you were bent they were bent
Past *Prog.*	I was being bent you were being bent he (she, it) was being bent	we were being bent you were being bent they were being bent
Past *Int.*	I did get bent you did get bent he (she, it) did get bent	we did get bent you did get bent they did get bent
Pres. *Perf.*	I have been bent you have been bent he (she, it) has been bent	we have been bent you have been bent they have been bent
Past *Perf.*	I had been bent you had been bent he (she, it) had been bent	we had been bent you had been bent they had been bent
Fut. *Perf.*	I shall have been bent you will have been bent he (she, it) will have been bent	we shall have been bent you will have been bent they will have been bent

IMPERATIVE MOOD

be bent

SUBJUNCTIVE MOOD

Pres.	if I be bent if you be bent if he (she, it) be bent	if we be bent if you be bent if they be bent
Past	if I were bent if you were bent if he (she, it) were bent	if we were bent if you were bent if they were bent
Fut.	if I should be bent if you should be bent if he (she, it) should be bent	if we should be bent if you should be bent if they should be bent

to bid (active voice)   *Principal Parts:* bid, bidding, bid, bid
(as at an auction)

Infinitive: to bid   *Present Participle:* bidding
Perfect Infinitive: to have bid   *Past Participle:* bid

INDICATIVE MOOD

Pres.	I bid	we bid
	you bid	you bid
	he (she, it) bids	they bid
Pres. *Prog.*	I am bidding	we are bidding
	you are bidding	you are bidding
	he (she, it) is bidding	they are bidding
Pres. *Int.*	I do bid	we do bid
	you do bid	you do bid
	he (she, it) does bid	they do bid
Fut.	I shall bid	we shall bid
	you will bid	you will bid
	he (she, it) will bid	they will bid
Fut.	I will bid *(P)*	we will bid *(P)*
	you shall bid *(C)*	you shall bid *(C)*
	he (she, it) shall bid *(C)*	they shall bid *(C)*
Past	I bid	we bid
	you bid	you bid
	he (she, it) bid	they bid
Past *Prog.*	I was bidding	we were bidding
	you were bidding	you were bidding
	he (she, it) was bidding	they were bidding
Past *Int.*	I did bid	we did bid
	you did bid	you did bid
	he (she, it) did bid	they did bid
Pres. *Perf.*	I have bid	we have bid
	you have bid	you have bid
	he (she, it) has bid	they have bid
Past *Perf.*	I had bid	we had bid
	you had bid	you had bid
	he (she, it) had bid	they had bid
Fut. *Perf.*	I shall have bid	we shall have bid
	you will have bid	you will have bid
	he (she, it) will have bid	they will have bid

IMPERATIVE MOOD
bid

SUBJUNCTIVE MOOD

Pres.	if I bid	if we bid
	if you bid	if you bid
	if he (she, it) bid	if they bid
Past	if I bid	if we bid
	if you bid	if you bid
	if he (she, it) bid	if they bid
Fut.	if I should bid	if we should bid
	if you should bid	if you should bid
	if he (she, it) should bid	if they should bid

Infinitive: to be bid   *Present Participle:* being bid
Perfect Infinitive: to have been bid   *Past Participle:* been bid

INDICATIVE MOOD

Pres.	I am bid	we are bid
	you are bid	you are bid
	he (she, it) is bid	they are bid
Pres.	I am being bid	we are being bid
Prog.	you are being bid	you are being bid
	he (she, it) is being bid	they are being bid
Pres.	I do get bid	we do get bid
Int.	you do get bid	you do get bid
	he (she, it) does get bid	they do get bid
Fut.	I shall be bid	we shall be bid
	you will be bid	you will be bid
	he (she, it) will be bid	they will be bid
Fut.	I will be bid *(P)*	we will be bid *(P)*
	you shall be bid *(C)*	you shall be bid *(C)*
	he (she, it) shall be bid *(C)*	they shall be bid *(C)*
Past	I was bid	we were bid
	you were bid	you were bid
	he (she, it) was bid	they were bid
Past	I was being bid	we were being bid
Prog.	you were being bid	you were being bid
	he (she, it) was being bid	they were being bid
Past	I did get bid	we did get bid
Int.	you did get bid	you did get bid
	he (she, it) did get bid	they did get bid
Pres.	I have been bid	we have been bid
Perf.	you have been bid	you have been bid
	he (she, it) has been bid	they have been bid
Past	I had been bid	we had been bid
Perf.	you had been bid	you had been bid
	he (she, it) had been bid	they had been bid
Fut.	I shall have been bid	we shall have been bid
Perf.	you will have been bid	you will have been bid
	he (she, it) will have been bid	they will have been bid

IMPERATIVE MOOD
be bid

SUBJUNCTIVE MOOD

Pres.	if I be bid	if we be bid
	if you be bid	if you be bid
	if he (she, it) be bid	if they be bid
Past	if I were bid	if we were bid
	if you were bid	if you were bid
	if he (she, it) were bid	if they were bid
Fut.	if I should be bid	if we should be bid
	if you should be bid	if you should be bid
	if he (she, it) should be bid	if they should be bid

to bid (active voice)

Principal Parts: bid, bidding, bade, bidden
(order or command)

Infinitive: to bid

Present Participle: bidding

Perfect Infinitive: to have bidden

Past Participle: bidden

INDICATIVE MOOD

Pres.	I bid	we bid
	you bid	you bid
	he (she, it) bids	they bid
Pres. Prog.	I am bidding	we are bidding
	you are bidding	you are bidding
	he (she, it) is bidding	they are bidding
Pres. Int.	I do bid	we do bid
	you do bid	you do bid
	he (she, it) does bid	they do bid
Fut.	I shall bid	we shall bid
	you will bid	you will bid
	he (she, it) will bid	they will bid
Fut.	I will bid *(P)*	we will bid *(P)*
	you shall bid *(C)*	you shall bid *(C)*
	he (she, it) shall bid *(C)*	they shall bid *(C)*
Past	I bade	we bade
	you bade	you bade
	he (she, it) bade	they bade
Past Prog.	I was bidding	we were bidding
	you were bidding	you were bidding
	he (she, it) was bidding	they were bidding
Past Int.	I did bid	we did bid
	you did bid	you did bid
	he (she, it) did bid	they did bid
Pres. Perf.	I have bid	we have bid
	you have bid	you have bid
	he (she, it) has bid	they have bid
Past Perf.	I had bid	we had bid
	you had bid	you had bid
	he (she, it) had bid	they had bid
Fut. Perf.	I shall have bid	we shall have bid
	you will have bid	you will have bid
	he (she, it) will have bid	they will have bid

IMPERATIVE MOOD
bid

SUBJUNCTIVE MOOD

Pres.	if I bid	if we bid
	if you bid	if you bid
	if he (she, it) bid	if they bid
Past	if I bade	if we bade
	if you bade	if you bade
	if he (she, it) bade	if they bade
Fut.	if I should bid	if we should bid
	if you should bid	if you should bid
	if he (she, it) should bid	if they should bid

(passive voice)

Infinitive: to be bidden
Perfect Infinitive: to have been bidden

Present Participle: being bidden
Past Participle: been bidden

INDICATIVE MOOD

Pres. I am bidden	we are bidden
you are bidden	you are bidden
he (she, it) is bidden	they are bidden

Pres. I am being bidden	we are being bidden
Prog. you are being bidden	you are being bidden
he (she, it) is being bidden	they are being bidden

Pres. I do get bidden	we do get bidden
Int. you do get bidden	you do get bidden
he (she, it) does get bidden	they do get bidden

Fut. I shall be bidden	we shall be bidden
you will be bidden	you will be bidden
he (she, it) will be bidden	they will be bidden

Fut. I will be bidden *(P)*	we will be bidden *(P)*
you shall be bidden *(C)*	you shall be bidden *(C)*
he (she, it) shall be bidden *(C)*	they shall be bidden *(C)*

Past I was bidden	we were bidden
you were bidden	you were bidden
he (she, it) was bidden	they were bidden

Past I was being bidden	we were being bidden
Prog. you were being bidden	you were being bidden
he (she, it) was being bidden	they were being bidden

Past I did get bidden	we did get bidden
Int. you did get bidden	you did get bidden
he (she, it) did get bidden	they did get bidden

Pres. I have been bidden	we have been bidden
Perf. you have been bidden	you have been bidden
he (she, it) has been bidden	they have been bidden

Past I had been bidden	we had been bidden
Perf. you had been bidden	you had been bidden
he (she, it) had been bidden	they had been bidden

Fut. I shall have been bidden	we shall have been bidden
Perf. you will have been bidden	you will have been bidden
he (she, it) will have been bidden	they will have been bidden

IMPERATIVE MOOD
be bidden

SUBJUNCTIVE MOOD

Pres. if I be bidden	if we be bidden
if you be bidden	if you be bidden
if he (she, it) be bidden	if they be bidden

Past if I were bidden	if we were bidden
if you were bidden	if you were bidden
if he (she, it) were bidden	if they were bidden

Fut. if I should be bidden	if we should be bidden
if you should be bidden	if you should be bidden
if he (she, it) should be bidden	if they should be bidden

to bind (active voice)   *Principal Parts:* bind, binding, bound, bound

Infinitive: to bind   *Present Participle:* binding
Perfect Infinitive: to have bound   *Past Participle:* bound

INDICATIVE MOOD

Pres.	I bind	we bind
	you bind	you bind
	he (she, it) binds	they bind
Pres.	I am binding	we are binding
Prog.	you are binding	you are binding
	he (she, it) is binding	they are binding
Pres.	I do bind	we do bind
Int.	you do bind	you do bind
	he (she, it) does bind	they do bind
Fut.	I shall bind	we shall bind
	you will bind	you will bind
	he (she, it) will bind	they will bind
Fut.	I will bind *(P)*	we will bind *(P)*
	you shall bind *(C)*	you shall bind *(C)*
	he (she, it) shall bind *(C)*	they shall bind *(C)*
Past	I bound	we bound
	you bound	you bound
	he (she, it) bound	they bound
Past	I was binding	we were binding
Prog.	you were binding	you were binding
	he (she, it) was binding	they were binding
Past	I did bind	we did bind
Int.	you did bind	you did bind
	he (she, it) did bind	they did bind
Pres.	I have bound	we have bound
Perf.	you have bound	you have bound
	he (she, it) has bound	they have bound
Past	I had bound	we had bound
Perf.	you had bound	you had bound
	he (she, it) had bound	they had bound
Fut.	I shall have bound	we shall have bound
Perf.	you will have bound	you will have bound
	he (she, it) will have bound	they will have bound

IMPERATIVE MOOD
bind

SUBJUNCTIVE MOOD

Pres.	if I bind	if we bind
	if you bind	if you bind
	if he (she, it) bind	if they bind
Past	if I bound	if we bound
	if you bound	if you bound
	if he (she, it) bound	if they bound
Fut.	if I should bind	if we should bind
	if you should bind	if you should bind
	if he (she, it) should bind	if they should bind

Infinitive: to be bound   *Present Participle:* being bound
Perfect Infinitive: to have been bound   *Past Participle:* been bound

INDICATIVE MOOD

Pres.	I am bound	we are bound
	you are bound	you are bound
	he (she, it) is bound	they are bound
Pres. Prog.	I am being bound	we are being bound
	you are being bound	you are being bound
	he (she, it) is being bound	they are being bound
Pres. Int.	I do get bound	we do get bound
	you do get bound	you do get bound
	he (she, it) does get bound	they do get bound
Fut.	I shall be bound	we shall be bound
	you will be bound	you will be bound
	he (she, it) will be bound	they will be bound
Fut.	I will be bound *(P)*	we will be bound *(P)*
	you shall be bound *(C)*	you shall be bound *(C)*
	he (she, it) shall be bound *(C)*	they shall be bound *(C)*
Past	I was bound	we were bound
	you were bound	you were bound
	he (she, it) was bound	they were bound
Past Prog.	I was being bound	we were being bound
	you were being bound	you were being bound
	he (she, it) was being bound	they were being bound
Past Int.	I did get bound	we did get bound
	you did get bound	you did get bound
	he (she, it) did get bound	they did get bound
Pres. Perf.	I have been bound	we have been bound
	you have been bound	you have been bound
	he (she, it) has been bound	they have been bound
Past Perf.	I had been bound	we had been bound
	you had been bound	you had been bound
	he (she, it) had been bound	they had been bound
Fut. Perf.	I shall have been bound	we shall have been bound
	you will have been bound	you will have been bound
	he (she, it) will have been bound	they will have been bound

IMPERATIVE MOOD
bind

SUBJUNCTIVE MOOD

Pres.	if I be bound	if we be bound
	if you be bound	if you be bound
	if he (she, it) be bound	if they be bound
Past	if I were bound	if we were bound
	if you were bound	if you were bound
	if he (she, it) were bound	if they were bound
Fut.	if I should be bound	if we should be bound
	if you should be bound	if you should be bound
	if he (she, it) should be bound	if they should be bound

to bite (active voice)

Principal Parts: bite, biting, bit, bitten (bit)

Infinitive: to bite

Present Participle: biting

Perfect Infinitive: to have bitten, bit

Past Participle: bitten (bit)

INDICATIVE MOOD

Pres.	I bite	we bite

Pres.   I bite   we bite
        you bite   you bite
        he (she, it) bites   they bite

Pres.   I am biting   we are biting
Prog.   you are biting   you are biting
        he (she, it) is biting   they are biting

Pres.   I do bite   we do bite
Int.   you do bite   you do bite
        he (she, it) does bite   they do bite

Fut.   I shall bite   we shall bite
        you will bite   you will bite
        he (she, it) will bite   they will bite

Fut.   I will bite *(P)*   we will bite *(P)*
        you shall bite *(C)*   you shall bite *(C)*
        he (she, it) shall bite *(C)*   they shall bite *(C)*

Past   I bit   we bit
        you bit   you bit
        he (she, it) bit   they bit

Past   I was biting   we were biting
Prog.   you were biting   you were biting
        he (she, it) was biting   they were biting

Past   I did bite   we did bite
Int.   you did bite   you did bite
        he (she, it) did bite   they did bite

Pres.   I have bitten, bit   we have bitten, bit
Perf.   you have bitten, bit   you have bitten, bit
        he (she, it) has bitten, bit   they have bitten, bit

Past   I had bitten, bit   we had bitten, bit
Perf.   you had bitten, bit   you had bitten, bit
        he (she, it) had bitten, bit   they had bitten, bit

Fut.   I shall have bitten, bit   we shall have bitten, bit
Perf.   you will have bitten, bit   you will have bitten, bit
        he (she, it) will have bitten, bit   they will have bitten, bit

IMPERATIVE MOOD
bite

SUBJUNCTIVE MOOD

Pres.   if I bite   if we bite
        if you bite   if you bite
        if he (she, it) bite   if they bite

Past   if I bit   if we bit
        if you bit   if you bit
        if he (she, it) bit   if they bit

Fut.   if I should bite   if we should bite
        if you should bite   if you should bite
        if he (she, it) should bite   if they should bite

(passive voice)

Infinitive: to be bitten

Perfect Infinitive: to have been
bitten (bit)

Present Participle: being bitten (bit)

Past Participle: been bitten (bit)

INDICATIVE MOOD

Pres.	I am bitten	we are bitten
	you are bitten	you are bitten
	he (she, it) is bitten	they are bitten
Pres.	I am being bitten	we are being bitten
Prog.	you are being bitten	you are being bitten
	he (she, it) is being bitten	they are being bitten
Pres.	I do get bitten	we do get bitten
Int.	you do get bitten	you do get bitten
	he (she, it) does get bitten	they do get bitten
Fut.	I shall be bitten	we shall be bitten
	you will be bitten	you will be bitten
	he (she, it) will be bitten	they will be bitten
Fut.	I will be bitten *(P)*	we will be bitten *(P)*
	you shall be bitten *(C)*	you shall be bitten *(C)*
	he (she, it) shall be bitten *(C)*	they shall be bitten *(C)*
Past	I was bitten	we were bitten
	you were bitten	you were bitten
	he (she, it) was bitten	they were bitten
Past	I was being bitten	we were being bitten
Prog.	you were being bitten	you were being bitten
	he (she, it) was being bitten	they were being bitten
Past	I did get bitten	we did get bitten
Int.	you did get bitten	you did get bitten
	he (she, it) did get bitten	they did get bitten
Pres.	I have been bitten	we have been bitten
Perf.	you have been bitten	you have been bitten
	he (she, it) has been bitten	they have been bitten
Past	I had been bitten	we had been bitten
Perf.	you had been bitten	you had been bitten
	he (she, it) had been bitten	they had been bitten
Fut.	I shall have been bitten	we shall have bitten
Perf.	you will have been bitten	you will have been bitten
	he (she, it) will have been bitten	they will have been bitten

IMPERATIVE MOOD
be bitten

SUBJUNCTIVE MOOD

Pres.	if I be bitten	if we be bitten
	if you be bitten	if you be bitten
	if he (she, it) be bitten	if they be bitten
Past	if I were bitten	if we were bitten
	if you were bitten	if you were bitten
	if he (she, it) were bitten	if they were bitten
Fut.	if I should be bitten	if we should be bitten
	if you should be bitten	if you should be bitten
	if he (she, it) should be bitten	if they should be bitten

to blow (active voice)

Principal Parts: blow, blowing, blew, blown

Infinitive: to blow
Perfect Infinitive: to have blown

Present Participle: blowing
Past Participle: blown

INDICATIVE MOOD

Pres.	I blow	we blow
	you blow	you blow
	he (she, it) blows	they blow
Pres.	I am blowing	we are blowing
Prog.	you are blowing	you are blowing
	he (she, it) is blowing	they are blowing
Pres.	I do blow	we do blow
Int.	you do blow	you do blow
	he (she, it) does blow	they do blow
Fut.	I shall blow	we shall blow
	you will blow	you will blow
	he (she, it) will blow	they will blow
Fut.	I will blow *(P)*	we will blow *(P)*
	you shall blow *(C)*	you shall blow *(C)*
	he (she, it) shall blow *(C)*	they shall blow *(C)*
Past	I blew	we blew
	you blew	you blew
	he (she, it) blew	they blew
Past	I was blowing	we were blowing
Prog.	you were blowing	you were blowing
	he (she, it) was blowing	they were blowing
Past	I did blow	we did blow
Int.	you did blow	you did blow
	he (she, it) did blow	they did blow
Pres.	I have blown	we have blown
Perf.	you have blown	you have blown
	he (she, it) has blown	they have blown
Past	I had blown	we had blown
Perf.	you had blown	you had blown
	he (she, it) had blown	they had blown
Fut.	I shall have blown	we shall have blown
Perf.	you will have blown	you will have blown
	he (she, it) will have blown	they will have blown

IMPERATIVE MOOD
blow

SUBJUNCTIVE MOOD

Pres.	if I blow	if we blow
	if you blow	if you blow
	if he (she, it) blow	if they blow
Past	if I blew	if we blew
	if you blew	if you blew
	if he (she, it) blew	if they blew
Fut.	if I should blow	if we should blow
	if you should blow	if you should blow
	if he (she, it) should blow	if they should blow

(passive voice)

Infinitive: to be blown   *Present Participle:* being blown
Perfect Infinitive: to have been blown   *Past Participle:* been blown

INDICATIVE MOOD

Pres.	I am blow	we are blown
	you are blown	you are blown
	he (she, it) is blown	they are blown
Pres. Prog.	I am being blown	we are being blown
	you are being blown	you are being blown
	he (she, it) is being blown	they are being blown
Pres. Int.	I do get blown	we do get blown
	you do get blown	you do get blown
	he (she, it) does get blown	they do get blown
Fut.	I shall be blown	we shall be blown
	you will be blown	you will be blown
	he (she, it) will be blown	they will be blown
Fut.	I will be blown *(P)*	we will be blown *(P)*
	you shall be blown *(C)*	you shall be blown *(C)*
	he (she, it) shall be blown *(C)*	they shall be blown *(C)*
Past	I was blown	we were blown
	you were blown	you were blown
	he (she, it) was blown	they were blown
Past Prog.	I was being blown	we were being blown
	you were being blown	you were being blown
	he (she, it) was being blown	they were being blown
Past Int.	I did get blown	we did get blown
	you did get blown	you did get blown
	he (she, it) did get blown	they did get blown
Pres. Perf.	I have been blown	we have been blown
	you have been blown	you have been blown
	he (she, it) has been blown	they have been blown
Past Perf.	I had been blown	we had been blown
	you had been blown	you had been blown
	he (she, it) had been blown	they had been blown
Fut. Perf.	I shall have been blown	we shall have been blown
	you will have been blown	you will have been blown
	he (she, it) will have been blown	they will have been blown

IMPERATIVE MOOD
be blown

SUBJUNCTIVE MOOD

Pres.	if I be blown	if we be blown
	if you be blown	if you be blown
	if he (she, it) be blown	if they be blown
Past	if I were blown	if we were blown
	if you were blown	if you were blown
	if he (she, it) were blown	if they were blown
Fut.	if I should be blown	if we should be blown
	if you should be blown	if you should be blown
	if he (she, it) should be blown	if they should be blown

to break (active voice) *Principal Parts:* break, breaking, broke, broken

Infinitive: to break   *Present Participle:* breaking
Perfect Infinitive: to have broken   *Past Participle:* broken

INDICATIVE MOOD

Pres.	I break	we break
	you break	you break
	he (she, it) breaks	they break
Pres.	I am breaking	we are breaking
Prog.	you are breaking	you are breaking
	he (she, it) is breaking	they are breaking
Pres.	I do break	we do break
Int.	you do break	you do break
	he (she, it) does break	they do break
Fut.	I shall break	we shall break
	you will break	you will break
	he (she, it) will break	they will break
Fut.	I will break *(P)*	we will break *(P)*
	you shall break *(C)*	you shall break *(C)*
	he (she, it) shall break *(C)*	they shall break *(C)*
Past	I broke	we broke
	you broke	you broke
	he (she, it) broke	they broke
Past	I was breaking	we were breaking
Prog.	you were breaking	you were breaking
	he (she, it) was breaking	they were breaking
Past	I did break	we did break
Int.	you did break	you did break
	he (she, it) did break	they did break
Pres.	I have broken	we have broken
Perf.	you have broken	you have broken
	he (she, it) has broken	they have broken
Past	I had broken	we had broken
Perf.	you had broken	you had broken
	he (she, it) had broken	they had broken
Fut.	I shall have broken	we shall have broken
Perf.	you will have broken	you will have broken
	he (she, it) will have broken	they will have broken

IMPERATIVE MOOD
break

SUBJUNCTIVE MOOD

Pres.	if I break	if we break
	if you break	if you break
	if he (she, it) break	if they break
Past	if I broke	if we broke
	if you broke	if you broke
	if he (she, it) broke	if they broke
Fut.	if I should break	if we should break
	if you should break	if you should break
	if he (she, it) should break	if they should break

Infinitive: to be broken   *Present Participle:* being broken
Perfect Infinitive: to have been broken   *Past Participle:* been broken

INDICATIVE MOOD

Pres.	I am broken	we are broken
	you are broken	you are broken
	he (she, it) is broken	they are broken
Pres.	I am being broken	we are being broken
Prog.	you are being broken	you are being broken
	he (she, it) is being broken	they are being broken
Pres.	I do get broken	we do get broken
Int.	you do get broken	you do get broken
	he (she, it) does get broken	they do get broken
Fut.	I shall be broken	we shall be broken
	you will be broken	you will be broken
	he (she, it) will be broken	they will be broken
Fut.	I will be broken *(P)*	we will be broken *(P)*
	you shall be broken *(C)*	you shall be broken *(C)*
	he (she, it) shall be broken *(C)*	they shall be broken *(C)*
Past	I was broken	we were broken
	you were broken	you were broken
	he (she, it) was broken	they were broken
Past	I was being broken	we were being broken
Prog.	you were being broken	you were being broken
	he (she, it) was being broken	they were being broken
Past	I did get broken	we did get broken
Int.	you did get broken	you did get broken
	he (she, it) did get broken	they did get broken
Pres.	I have been broken	we have been broken
Perf.	you have been broken	you have been broken
	he (she, it) has been broken	they have been broken
Past	I had been broken	we had been broken
Perf.	you had been broken	you had been broken
	he (she, it) had been broken	they had been broken
Fut.	I shall have been broken	we shall have been broken
Perf.	you will have been broken	you will have been broken
	he (she, it) will have been broken	they will have been broken

IMPERATIVE MOOD
be broken

SUBJUNCTIVE MOOD

Pres.	if I be broken	if we be broken
	if you be broken	if you be broken
	if he (she, it) be broken	if they be broken
Past	if I were broken	if we were broken
	if you were broken	if you were broken
	if he (she, it) were broken	if they were broken
Fut.	if I should be broken	if we should be broken
	if you should be broken	if you should be broken
	if he (she, it) should be broken	if they should be broken

129

to bring (active voice)

Principal Parts: bring, bringing, brought

Infinitive: to bring
Perfect Infinitive: to have brought

Present Participle: bringing
Past Participle: brought

INDICATIVE MOOD

Pres.	I bring	we bring
	you bring	you bring
	he (she, it) brings	they bring
Pres.	I am bringing	we are bringing
Prog.	you are bringing	you are bringing
	he (she, it) is bringing	they are bringing
Pres.	I do bring	we do bring
Int.	you do bring	you do bring
	he (she, it) does bring	they do bring
Fut.	I shall bring	we shall bring
	you will bring	you will bring
	he (she, it) will bring	they will bring
Fut.	I will bring *(P)*	we will bring *(P)*
	you shall bring *(C)*	you shall bring *(C)*
	he (she, it) shall bring *(C)*	they shall bring *(C)*
Past	I brought	we brought
	you brought	you brought
	he (she, it) brought	they brought
Past	I was bringing	we were bringing
Prog.	you were bringing	you were bringing
	he (she, it) was bringing	they were bringing
Past	I did bring	we did bring
Int.	you did bring	you did bring
	he (she, it) did bring	they did bring
Pres.	I have brought	we have brought
Perf.	you have brought	you have brought
	he (she, it) has brought	they have brought
Past	I had brought	we had brought
Perf.	you had brought	you had brought
	he (she, it) had brought	they had brought
Fut.	I shall have brought	we shall have brought
Perf.	you will have brought	you will have brought
	he (she, it) will have brought	they will have brought

IMPERATIVE MOOD
bring

SUBJUNCTIVE MOOD

Pres.	if I bring	if we bring
	if you bring	if you bring
	if he (she, it) bring	if they bring
Past	if I brought	if we brought
	if you brought	if you brought
	if he (she, it) brought	if they brought
Fut.	if I should bring	if we should bring
	if you should bring	if you should bring
	if he (she, it) should bring	if they should bring

Infinitive: to be brought   *Present Participle:* being brought
Perfect Infinitive: to have been brought   *Past Participle:* been brought

INDICATIVE MOOD

Pres.	I am brought	we are brought
	you are brought	you are brought
	he (she, it) is brought	they are brought
Pres.	I am being brought	we are being brought
Prog.	you are being brought	you are being brought
	he (she, it) is being brought	they are being brought
Pres.	I do get brought	we do get brought
Int.	you do get brought	you do get brought
	he (she, it) does get brought	they do get brought
Fut.	I shall be brought	we shall be brought
	you will be brought	you will be brought
	he (she, it) will be brought	they will be brought
Fut.	I will be brought *(P)*	we will be brought *(P)*
	you shall be brought *(C)*	you shall be brought *(C)*
	he (she, it) shall be brought *(C)*	they shall be brought *(C)*
Past	I was brought	we were brought
	you were brought	you were brought
	he (she, it) was brought	they were brought
Past	I was being brought	we were being brought
Prog.	you were being brought	you were being brought
	he (she, it) was being brought	they were being brought
Past	I did get brought	we did get brought
Int.	you did get brought	you did get brought
	he (she, it) did get brought	they did get brought
Pres.	I have been brought	we have been brought
Perf.	you have been brought	you have been brought
	he (she, it) has been brought	they have been brought
Past	I had been brought	we had been brought
Perf.	you had been brought	you had been brought
	he (she, it) had been brought	they had been brought
Fut.	I shall have been brought	we shall have been brought
Perf.	you will have been brought	you will have been brought
	he (she, it) will have been brought	they will have been brought

IMPERATIVE MOOD
be brought

SUBJUNCTIVE MOOD

Pres.	if I be brought	if we be brought
	if you be brought	if you be brought
	if he (she, it) be brought	if they be brought
Past	if I were brought	if we were brought
	if you were brought	if you were brought
	if he (she, it) were brought	if they were brought
Fut.	if I should be brought	if we should be brought
	if you should be brought	if you should be brought
	if he (she, it) should be brought	if they should be brought

131

to broadcast (active voice)

Principal Parts: broadcast, broadcasting, broadcast (broadcasted) broadcast (broadcasted)

Infinitive: to broadcast
Perfect Infinitive: to have broadcast

Present Participle: broadcasting
Past Participle: broadcast

INDICATIVE MOOD

Pres.	I broadcast	we broadcast
	you broadcast	you broadcast
	he (she, it) broadcasts	they broadcast
Pres.	I am broadcasting	we are broadcasting
Prog.	you are broadcasting	you are broadcasting
	he (she, it) is broadcasting	they are broadcasting
Pres.	I do broadcast	we do broadcast
Int.	you do broadcast	you do broadcast
	he (she, it) does broadcast	they do broadcast
Fut.	I shall broadcast	we shall broadcast
	you will broadcast	you will broadcast
	he (she, it) will broadcast	they will broadcast
Fut.	I will broadcast *(P)*	we will broadcast *(P)*
	you shall broadcast *(C)*	you shall broadcast *(C)*
	he (she, it) shall broadcast *(C)*	they shall broadcast *(C)*
Past	I broadcast(ed)	we broadcast(ed)
	you broadcast(ed)	you broadcast(ed)
	he (she, it) broadcast(ed)	they broadcast(ed)
Past	I was broadcasting	we were broadcasting
Prog.	you were broadcasting	you were broadcasting
	he (she, it) was broadcasting	they were broadcasting
Past	I did broadcast	we did broadcast
Int.	you did broadcast	you did broadcast
	he (she, it) did broadcast	they did broadcast
Pres.	I have broadcast(ed)	we have broadcast(ed)
Perf.	you have broadcast(ed)	you have broadcast(ed)
	he (she, it) has broadcast(ed)	they have broadcast(ed)
Past	I had broadcast(ed)	we had broadcast(ed)
Perf.	you had broadcast(ed)	you had broadcast(ed)
	he (she, it) had broadcast(ed)	they had broadcast(ed)
Fut.	I shall have broadcast(ed)	we shall have broadcast(ed)
Perf.	you will have broadcast(ed)	you will have broadcast(ed)
	he (she, it) will have broadcast(ed)	they will have broadcast(ed)

IMPERATIVE MOOD
broadcast

SUBJUNCTIVE MOOD

Pres.	if I broadcast	if we broadcast
	if you broadcast	if you broadcast
	if he (she, it) broadcast	if they broadcast
Past	if I broadcast(ed)	if we broadcast(ed)
	if you broadcast(ed)	if you broadcast(ed)
	if he (she, it) broadcast(ed)	if they broadcast(ed)
Fut.	if I should broadcast	if we should broadcast
	if you should broadcast	if you should broadcast
	if he (she, it) should broadcast	if they should broadcast

Infinitive: to be broadcast(ed)   *Present Participle:* being broadcast(ed)

Perfect Infinitive: to have been   *Past Participle:* been broadcast(ed)
         broadcast(ed)

INDICATIVE MOOD

Pres.	I am broadcast(ed)	we are broadcast(ed)
	you are broadcast(ed)	you are broadcast(ed)
	he (she, it) is broadcast(ed)	they are broadcast(ed)
Pres.	I am being broadcast(ed)	we are being broadcast(ed)
Prog.	you are being broadcast(ed)	you are being broadcast(ed)
	he (she, it) is being broadcast(ed)	they are being broadcast(ed)
Pres.	I do get broadcast(ed)	we do get broadcast(ed)
Int.	you do get broadcast(ed)	you do get broadcast(ed)
	he (she, it) does get broadcast(ed)	they do get broadcast(ed)
Fut.	I shall be broadcast(ed)	we shall be broadcast(ed)
	you will be broadcast(ed)	you will be broadcast(ed)
	he (she, it) will be broadcast(ed)	they will be broadcast(ed)
Fut.	I will be broadcast(ed) *(P)*	we will be broadcast(ed) *(P)*
	you shall be broadcast(ed) *(C)*	you shall be broadcast(ed) *(C)*
	he (she, it) shall be broadcast(ed) *(C)*	they shall be broadcast(ed) *(C)*
Past	I was broadcast(ed)	we were broadcast(ed)
	you were broadcast(ed)	you were broadcast(ed)
	he (she, it) was broadcast(ed)	they were broadcast(ed)
Past	I was being broadcast(ed)	we were being broadcast(ed)
Prog.	you were being broadcast(ed)	you were being broadcast(ed)
	he (she, it) was being broadcast(ed)	they were being broadcast(ed)
Past	I did get broadcast(ed)	we did get broadcast(ed)
Int.	you did get broadcast(ed)	you did get broadcast(ed)
	he (she, it) did get broadcast(ed)	they did get broadcast(ed)
Pres.	I have been broadcast(ed)	we have been broadcast(ed)
Perf.	you have been broadcast(ed)	you have been broadcast(ed)
	he (she, it) has been broadcast(ed)	they have been broadcast(ed)
Past	I had been broadcast(ed)	we had been broadcast(ed)
Perf.	you had been broadcast(ed)	you had been broadcast(ed)
	he (she, it) had been broadcast(ed)	they had been broadcast(ed)
Fut.	I shall have been broadcast(ed)	we shall have been broadcast(ed)
Perf.	you will have been broadcast(ed)	you will have been broadcast(ed)
	he (she, it) will have been broadcast(ed)	they will have been broadcast(ed)

IMPERATIVE MOOD
be broadcast

SUBJUNCTIVE MOOD

Pres.	if I be broadcast(ed)	if we be broadcast(ed)
	if you be broadcast(ed)	if you be broadcast(ed)
	if he (she, it) be broadcast(ed)	if they be broadcast(ed)
Past	if I were broadcast(ed)	if we were broadcast(ed)
	if you were broadcast(ed)	if you were broadcast(ed)
	if he (she, it) were broadcast(ed)	if they were broadcast(ed)
Fut.	if I should be broadcast(ed)	if we should be broadcast(ed)
	if you should be broadcast(ed)	if you should be broadcast(ed)
	if he (she, it) should be broadcast(ed)	if they should be broadcast(ed)

to build (active voice)   *Principal Parts:* build, building, built, built

Infinitive: to build   *Present Participle:* building
Perfect Infinitive: to have built   *Past Participle:* built

INDICATIVE MOOD

Pres.	I build	we build
	you build	you build
	he (she, it) builds	they build
Pres. *Prog.*	I am building	we are building
	you are building	you are building
	he (she, it) is building	they are building
Pres. *Int.*	I do build	we do build
	you do build	you do build
	he (she, it) does build	they do build
Fut.	I shall build	we shall build
	you will build	you will build
	he (she, it) will build	they will build
Fut.	I will build *(P)*	we will build *(P)*
	you shall build *(C)*	you shall build *(C)*
	he (she, it) shall build *(C)*	they shall build *(C)*
Past	I built	we built
	you built	you built
	he (she, it) built	they built
Past *Prog.*	I was building	we were building
	you were building	you were building
	he (she, it) was building	they were building
Past *Int.*	I did build	we did build
	you did build	you did build
	he (she, it) did build	they did build
Pres. *Perf.*	I have built	we have built
	you have built	you have built
	he (she, it) has built	they have built
Past *Perf.*	I had built	we had built
	you had built	you had built
	he (she, it) had built	they had built
Fut. *Perf.*	I shall have built	we shall have built
	you will have built	you shall have built
	he (she, it) will have built	they will have built

IMPERATIVE MOOD
build

SUBJUNCTIVE MOOD

Pres.	if I build	if we build
	if you build	if you build
	if he (she, it) build	if they build
Past	if I built	if we built
	if you built	if you built
	if he (she, it) built	if they built
Fut.	if I should build	if we should build
	if you should build	if you should build
	if he (she, it) should build	if they should build

Infinitive: to be built   *Present Participle:* being built
Perfect Infinitive: to have been built   *Past Participle:* been built

INDICATIVE MOOD

Pres.	I am built	we are built
	you are built	you are built
	he (she, it) is built	they are built
Pres.	I am being built	we are being built
Prog.	you are being built	you are being built
	he (she, it) is being built	they are being built
Pres.	I do get built	we do get built
Int.	you do get built	you do get built
	he (she, it) does get built	they do get built
Fut.	I shall be built	we shall be built
	you will be built	you will be built
	he (she, it) will be built	they will be built
Fut.	I will be built *(P)*	we will be built *(P)*
	you shall be built *(C)*	you shall be built *(C)*
	he (she, it) shall be built *(C)*	they shall be built *(C)*
Past	I was built	we were built
	you were built	you were built
	he (she, it) was built	they were built
Past	I was being built	we were being built
Prog.	you were being built	you were being built
	he (she, it) was being built	they were being built
Past	I did get built	we did get built
Int.	you did get built	you did get built
	he (she, it) did get built	they did get built
Pres.	I have been built	we have been built
Perf.	you have been built	you have been built
	he (she, it) has been built	they have been built
Past	I had been built	we had been built
Perf.	you had been built	you had been built
	he (she, it) had been built	they had been built
Fut.	I shall have been built	we shall have been built
Perf.	you will have been built	you will have been built
	he (she, it) will have been built	they will have been built

IMPERATIVE MOOD
be built

SUBJUNCTIVE MOOD

Pres.	if I be built	if we be built
	if you be built	if you be built
	if he (she, it) be built	if they be built
Past	if I were built	if we were built
	if you were built	if you were built
	if he (she, it) were built	if they were built
Fut.	if I should be built	if we should be built
	if you should be built	if you should be built
	if he (she, it) should be built	if they should be built

to burst (active voice)   *Principal Parts:* burst, bursting, burst, burst

Infinitive: to burst   *Present Participle:* bursting
Perfect Infinitive: to have burst   *Past Participle:* burst

INDICATIVE MOOD

Pres.	I burst	we burst
	you burst	you burst
	he (she, it) bursts	they burst
Pres. Prog.	I am bursting	we are bursting
	you are bursting	you are bursting
	he (she, it) is bursting	they are bursting
Pres. Int.	I do burst	we do burst
	you do burst	you do burst
	he (she, it) does burst	they do burst
Fut.	I shall burst	we shall burst
	you will burst	you will burst
	he (she, it) will burst	they will burst
Fut.	I will burst *(P)*	we will burst *(P)*
	you shall burst *(C)*	you shall burst *(C)*
	he (she, it) shall burst *(C)*	they shall burst *(C)*
Past	I burst	we burst
	you burst	you burst
	he (she, it) burst	they burst
Past Prog.	I was bursting	we were bursting
	you were bursting	you were bursting
	he (she, it) was bursting	they were bursting
Past Int.	I did burst	we did burst
	you did burst	you did burst
	he (she, it) did burst	they did burst
Pres. Perf.	I have burst	we have burst
	you have burst	you have burst
	he (she, it) has burst	they have burst
Past Perf.	I had burst	we had burst
	you had burst	you had burst
	he (she, it) had burst	they had burst
Fut. Perf.	I shall have burst	we shall have burst
	you will have burst	you will have burst
	he (she, it) will have burst	they will have burst

IMPERATIVE MOOD
burst

SUBJUNCTIVE MOOD

Pres.	if I burst	if we burst
	if you burst	if you burst
	if he (she, it) burst	if they burst
Past	if I burst	if we burst
	if you burst	if you burst
	if he (she, it) burst	if they burst
Fut.	if I should burst	if we should burst
	if you should burst	if you should burst
	if he (she, it) should burst	if they should burst

(passive voice)

Infinitive: to be burst   *Present Participle:* being burst
Perfect Infinitive: to have been burst   *Past Participle:* been burst

INDICATIVE MOOD

Pres.	I am burst	we are burst
	you are burst	you are burst
	he (she, it) is burst	they are burst
Pres.	I am being burst	we are being burst
Prog.	you are being burst	you are being burst
	he (she, it) is being burst	they are being burst
Pres.	I do get burst	we do get burst
Int.	you do get burst	you do get burst
	he (she, it) does get burst	they do get burst
Fut.	I shall be burst	we shall be burst
	you will be burst	you will be burst
	he (she, it) will be burst	they will be burst
Fut.	I will be burst *(P)*	we will be burst *(P)*
	you shall be burst *(C)*	you shall be burst *(C)*
	he (she, it) shall be burst *(C)*	they shall be burst *(C)*
Past	I was burst	we were burst
	you were burst	you were burst
	he (she, it) was burst	they were burst
Past	I was being burst	we were being burst
Prog.	you were being burst	you were being burst
	he (she, it) was being burst	they were being burst
Past	I did get burst	we did get burst
Int.	you did get burst	you did get burst
	he (she, it) did get burst	they did get burst
Pres.	I have been burst	we have been burst
Perf.	you have been burst	you have been burst
	he (she, it) has been burst	they have been burst
Past	I had been burst	we had been burst
Perf.	you had been burst	you had been burst
	he (she, it) had been burst	they had been burst
Fut.	I shall have been burst	we shall have been burst
Perf.	you will have been burst	you will have been burst
	he (she, it) will have been burst	they will have been burst

IMPERATIVE MOOD
be burst

SUBJUNCTIVE MOOD

Pres.	if I be burst	if we be burst
	if you be burst	if you be burst
	if he (she, it) be burst	if they be burst
Past	if I were burst	if we were burst
	if you were burst	if you were burst
	if he (she, it) were burst	if they were burst
Fut.	if I should be burst	if we should be burst
	if you should be burst	if you should be burst
	if he (she, it) should be burst	if they should be burst

to buy (active voice)   *Principal Parts:* buy, buying bought, bought

Infinitive: to buy   *Present Participle:* buying
Perfect Infinitive: to have bought   *Past Participle:* bought

INDICATIVE MOOD

Pres.	I buy	we buy
	you buy	you buy
	he (she, it) buys	they buy
Pres.	I am buying	we are buying
Prog.	you are buying	you are buying
	he (she, it) is buying	they are buying
Pres.	I do buy	we do buy
Int.	you do buy	you do buy
	he (she, it) does buy	they do buy
Fut.	I shall buy	we shall buy
	you will buy	you will buy
	he (she, it) will buy	they will buy
Fut.	I will buy *(P)*	we will buy *(P)*
	you shall buy *(C)*	you shall buy *(C)*
	he (she, it) shall buy *(C)*	they shall buy *(C)*
Past	I bought	we bought
	you bought	you bought
	he (she, it) bought	they bought
Past	I was buying	we were buying
Prog.	you were buying	you were buying
	he (she, it) was buying	they were buying
Past	I did buy	we did buy
Int.	you did buy	you did buy
	he (she, it) did buy	they did buy
Pres.	I have bought	we have bought
Perf.	you have bought	you have bought
	he (she, it) has bought	they have bought
Past	I had bought	we had bought
Perf.	you had bought	you had bought
	he (she, it) had bought	they had bought
Fut.	I shall have bought	we shall have bought
Perf.	you will have bought	you will have bought
	he (she, it) will have bought	they will have bought

IMPERATIVE MOOD
buy

SUBJUNCTIVE MOOD

Pres.	if I buy	if we buy
	if you buy	if you buy
	if he (she, it) buy	if they buy
Past	if I bought	if we bought
	if you bought	if you bought
	if he (she, it) bought	if they bought
Fut.	if I should buy	if we should buy
	if you should buy	if you should buy
	if he (she, it) should buy	if they should buy

Infinitive: to be bought	*Present Participle:* being bought
Perfect Infinitive: to have been bought	*Past Participle:* been bought

INDICATIVE MOOD

Pres.	I am bought	we are bought
	you are bought	you are bought
	he (she, it) is bought	they are bought
Pres. Prog.	I am being bought	we are being bought
	you are being bought	you are being bought
	he (she, it) is being bought	they are being bought
Pres. Int.	I do get bought	we do get bought
	you do get bought	you do get bought
	he (she, it) does get bought	they do get bought
Fut.	I shall be bought	we shall be bought
	you will be bought	you will be bought
	he (she, it) will be bought	they will be bought
Fut.	I will be bought *(P)*	we will be bought *(P)*
	you shall be bought *(C)*	you shall be bought *(C)*
	he (she, it) shall be bought *(C)*	they shall be bought *(C)*
Past	I was bought	we were bought
	you were bought	you were bought
	he (she, it) was bought	they were bought
Past Prog.	I was being bought	we were being bought
	you were being bought	you were being bought
	he (she, it) was being bought	they were being bought
Past Int.	I did get bought	we did get bought
	you did get bought	you did get bought
	he (she, it) did get bought	they did get bought
Pres. Perf.	I have been bought	we have been bought
	you have been bought	you have been bought
	he (she, it) has been bought	they have been bought
Past Perf.	I had been bought	we had been bought
	you had been bought	you had been bought
	he (she, it) had been bought	they had been bought
Fut. Perf.	I shall have been bought	we shall have been bought
	you will have been bought	you will have been bought
	he (she, it) will have been bought	they will have been bought

IMPERATIVE MOOD

be bought

SUBJUNCTIVE MOOD

Pres.	if I be bought	if we be bought
	if you be bought	if you be bought
	if he (she, it) be bought	if they be bought
Past	if I were bought	if we were bought
	if you were bought	if you were bought
	if he (she, it) were bought	if they were bought
Fut.	if I should be bought	if we should be bought
	if you should be bought	if you should be bought
	if he (she, it) should be bought	if they should be bought

to cast (active voice)　　　　　*Principal Parts:* cast, casting, cast, cast

Infinitive: to cast　　　　　　　　　　*Present Participle:* casting
Perfect Infinitive: to have cast　　　　　*Past Participle:* cast

INDICATIVE MOOD

Pres.	I cast	we cast
	you cast	you cast
	he (she, it) casts	they cast
Pres.	I am casting	we are casting
Prog.	you are casting	you are casting
	he (she, it) is casting	they are casting
Pres.	I do cast	we do cast
Int.	you do cast	you do cast
	he (she, it) does cast	they do cast
Fut.	I shall cast	we shall cast
	you will cast	you will cast
	he (she, it) will cast	they will cast
Fut.	I will cast *(P)*	we will cast *(P)*
	you shall cast *(C)*	you shall cast *(C)*
	he (she, it) shall cast *(C)*	they shall cast *(C)*
Past	I cast	we cast
	you cast	you cast
	he (she, it) cast	they cast
Past	I was casting	we were casting
Prog.	you were casting	you were casting
	he (she, it) was casting	they were casting
Past	I did cast	we did cast
Int.	you did cast	you did cast
	he (she, it) did cast	they did cast
Pres.	I have cast	we have cast
Perf.	you have cast	you have cast
	he (she, it) has cast	they have cast
Past	I had cast	we had cast
Perf.	you had cast	you had cast
	he (she, it) had cast	they had cast
Fut.	I shall have cast	we shall have cast
Perf.	you will have cast	you will have cast
	he (she, it) will have cast	they will have cast

IMPERATIVE MOOD
cast

SUBJUNCTIVE MOOD

Pres.	if I cast	if we cast
	if you cast	if you cast
	if he (she, it) cast	if they cast
Past	if I cast	if we cast
	if you cast	if you cast
	if he (she, it) cast	if they cast
Fut.	if I should cast	if we should cast
	if you should cast	if you should cast
	if he (she, it) should cast	if they should cast

(passive voice)

Infinitive: to be cast   *Present Participle:* being cast
Perfect Infinitive: to have been cast   *Past Participle:* been cast

INDICATIVE MOOD

Pres.	I am cast	we are cast
	you are cast	you are cast
	he (she, it) is cast	they are cast
Pres. Prog.	I am being cast	we are being cast
	you are being cast	you are being cast
	he (she, it) is being cast	they are being cast
Pres. Int.	I do get cast	we do get cast
	you do get cast	you do get cast
	he (she, it) does get cast	they do get cast
Fut.	I shall be cast	we shall be cast
	you will be cast	you will be cast
	he (she, it) will be cast	they will be cast
Fut.	I will be cast *(P)*	we will be cast *(P)*
	you shall be cast *(C)*	you shall be cast *(C)*
	he (she, it) shall be cast *(C)*	they shall be cast *(C)*
Past	I was cast	we were cast
	you were cast	you were cast
	he (she, it) was cast	they were cast
Past Prog.	I was being cast	we were being cast
	you were being cast	you were being cast
	he (she, it) was being cast	they were being cast
Past Int.	I did get cast	we did get cast
	you did get cast	you did get cast
	he (she, it) did get cast	they did get cast
Pres. Perf.	I have been cast	we have been cast
	you have been cast	you have been cast
	he (she, it) has been cast	they have been cast
Past Perf.	I had been cast	we had been cast
	you had been cast	you had been cast
	he (she, it) had been cast	they had been cast
Fut. Perf.	I shall have been cast	we shall have been cast
	you will have been cast	you will have been cast
	he (she, it) will have been cast	they will have been cast

IMPERATIVE MOOD
be cast

SUBJUNCTIVE MOOD

Pres.	if I be cast	if we be cast
	if you be cast	if you be cast
	if he (she, it) be cast	if they be cast
Past	if I were cast	if we were cast
	if you were cast	if you were cast
	if he (she, it) were cast	if they were cast
Fut.	if I should be cast	if we should be cast
	if you should be cast	if you should be cast
	if he (she, it) should be cast	if they should be cast

to catch (active voice)   *Principal Parts:* catch, catching, caught, caught

Infinitive: to catch   *Present Participle:* catching
Perfect Infinitive: to have caught   *Past Participle:* caught

INDICATIVE MOOD

Pres.	I catch	we catch
	you catch	you catch
	he (she, it) catches	they catch
Pres.	I am catching	we are catching
Prog.	you are catching	you are catching
	he (she, it) is catching	they are catching
Pres.	I do catch	we do catch
Int.	you do catch	you do catch
	he (she, it) does catch	they do catch
Fut.	I shall catch	we shall catch
	you will catch	you will catch
	he (she, it) will catch	they will catch
Fut.	I will catch *(P)*	we will catch *(P)*
	you shall catch *(C)*	you shall catch *(C)*
	he (she, it) shall catch *(C)*	they shall catch *(C)*
Past.	I caught	we caught
	you caught	you caught
	he (she, it) caught	they caught
Past	I was catching	we were catching
Prog.	you were catching	you were catching
	he (she, it) was catching	they were catching
Past	I did catch	we did catch
Int.	you did catch	you did catch
	he (she, it) did catch	they did catch
Pres.	I have caught	we have caught
Perf.	you have caught	you have caught
	he (she, it) has caught	they have caught
Past	I had caught	we had caught
Perf.	you had caught	you had caught
	he (she, it) had caught	they had caught
Fut.	I shall have caught	we shall have caught
Perf.	you will have caught	you will have caught
	he (she, it) will have caught	they will have caught

IMPERATIVE MOOD
catch

SUBJUNCTIVE MOOD

Pres.	if I catch	if we catch
	if you catch	if you catch
	if he (she, it) catch	if they catch
Past	if I caught	if we caught
	if you caught	if you caught
	if he (she, it) caught	if they caught
Fut.	if I should catch	if we should catch
	if you should catch	if you should catch
	if he (she, it) should catch	if they should catch

Infinitive: to be caught   *Present Participle:* being caught
Perfect Infinitive: to have been caught   *Past Participle:* been caught

INDICATIVE MOOD

Pres.	I am caught	we are caught
	you are caught	you are caught
	he (she, it) is caught	they are caught
Pres.	I am being caught	we are being caught
Prog.	you are being caught	you are being caught
	he (she, it) is being caught	they are being caught
Pres.	I do get caught	we do get caught
Int.	you do get caught	you do get caught
	he (she, it) does get caught	they do get caught
Fut.	I shall be caught	we shall be caught
	you will be caught	you will be caught
	he (she, it) will be caught	they will be caught
Fut.	I will be caught *(P)*	we will be caught *(P)*
	you shall be caught *(C)*	you shall be caught *(C)*
	he (she, it) shall be caught *(C)*	they shall be caught *(C)*
Past	I was caught	we were caught
	you were caught	you were caught
	he (she, it) was caught	they were caught
Past	I was being caught	we were being caught
Prog.	you were being caught	you were being caught
	he (she, it) was being caught	they were being caught
Past	I did get caught	we did get caught
Int.	you did get caught	you did get caught
	he (she, it) did get caught	they did get caught
Pres.	I have been caught	we have been caught
Perf.	you have been caught	you have been caught
	he (she, it) has been caught	they have been caught
Past	I had been caught	we had been caught
Perf.	you had been caught	you had been caught
	he (she, it) had been caught	they had been caught
Fut.	I shall have been caught	we shall have been caught
Perf.	you will have been caught	you will have been caught
	he (she, it) will have been caught	they will have been caught

IMPERATIVE MOOD
be caught

SUBJUNCTIVE MOOD

Pres.	if I be caught	if we be caught
	if you be caught	if you be caught
	if he (she, it) be caught	if they be caught
Past	if I were caught	if we were caught
	if you were caught	if you were caught
	if he (she, it) were caught	if they were caught
Fut.	if I should be caught	if we should be caught
	if you should be caught	if you should be caught
	if he (she, it) should be caught	if they should be caught

to choose (active voice)

Infinitive: to choose
Perfect Infinitive: to have chosen

Present Participle: choosing
Past Participle: chosen

INDICATIVE MOOD

Pres.	I choose	we choose
	you choose	you choose
	he (she, it) chooses	they choose
Pres. Prog.	I am choosing	we are choosing
	you are choosing	you are choosing
	he (she, it) is choosing	they are choosing
Pres. Int.	I do choose	we do choose
	you do choose	you do choose
	he (she, it) does choose	they do choose
Fut.	I shall choose	we shall choose
	you will choose	you will choose
	he (she, it) will choose	they will choose
Fut.	I will choose *(P)*	we will choose *(P)*
	you shall choose *(C)*	you shall choose *(C)*
	he (she, it) shall choose *(C)*	they shall choose *(C)*
Past	I chose	we chose
	you chose	you chose
	he (she, it) chose	they chose
Past Prog.	I was choosing	we were choosing
	you were choosing	you were choosing
	he (she, it) was choosing	they were choosing
Past Int.	I did choose	we did choose
	you did choose	you did choose
	he (she, it) did choose	they did choose
Pres. Perf.	I have chosen	we have chosen
	you have chosen	you have chosen
	he (she, it) has chosen	they have chosen
Past Perf.	I had chosen	we had chosen
	you had chosen	you had chosen
	he (she, it) had chosen	they had chosen
Fut. Perf.	I shall have chosen	we shall have chosen
	you will have chosen	you will have chosen
	he (she, it) will have chosen	they will have chosen

IMPERATIVE MOOD
choose

SUBJUNCTIVE MOOD

Pres.	if I choose	if we choose
	if you choose	if you choose
	if he (she, it) choose	if they choose
Past	if I chose	if we chose
	if you chose	if you chose
	if he (she, it) chose	if they chose
Fut.	if I should choose	if we should choose
	if you should choose	if you should choose
	if he (she, it) should choose	if they should choose

(passive voice)

Infinitive: to be chosen

Perfect Infinitive: to have been chosen

Present Participle: being chosen

Past Participle: been chosen

INDICATIVE MOOD

Pres.
I am chosen
you are chosen
he (she, it) is chosen

we are chosen
you are chosen
they are chosen

Pres.
Prog.
I am being chosen
you are being chosen
he (she, it) is being chosen

we are being chosen
you are being chosen
they are being chosen

Pres.
Int.
I do get chosen
you do get chosen
he (she, it) does get chosen

we do get chosen
you do get chosen
they do get chosen

Fut.
I shall be chosen
you will be chosen
he (she, it) will be chosen

we shall be chosen
you will be chosen
they will be chosen

Fut.
I will be chosen *(P)*
you shall be chosen *(C)*
he (she, it) shall be chosen *(C)*

we will be chosen *(P)*
you shall be chosen *(C)*
they shall be chosen *(C)*

Past
I was chosen
you were chosen
he (she, it) was chosen

we were chosen
you were chosen
they were chosen

Past
Prog.
I was being chosen
you were being chosen
he (she, it) was being chosen

we were being chosen
you were being chosen
they were being chosen

Past
Int.
I did get chosen
you did get chosen
he (she, it) did get chosen

we did get chosen
you did get chosen
they did get chosen

Pres.
Perf.
I have been chosen
you have been chosen
he (she, it) has been chosen

we have been chosen
you have been chosen
they have been chosen

Past
Perf.
I had been chosen
you had been chosen
he (she, it) had been chosen

we had been chosen
you had been chosen
they had been chosen

Fut.
Perf.
I shall have been chosen
you will have been chosen
he (she, it) will have been chosen

we shall have been chosen
you will have been chosen
they will have been chosen

IMPERATIVE MOOD
be chosen

SUBJUNCTIVE MOOD

Pres.
if I be chosen
if you be chosen
if he (she, it) be chosen

if we be chosen
if you be chosen
if they be chosen

Past
if I were chosen
if you were chosen
if he (she, it) were chosen

if we were chosen
if you were chosen
if they were chosen

Fut.
if I should be chosen
if you should be chosen
if he (she, it) should be chosen

if we should be chosen
if you should be chosen
if they should be chosen

Principal Parts: cling, clinging, clung, clung

Infinitive: to cling *Present Participle:* clinging
Perfect Infinitive: to have clung *Past Participle:* clung

INDICATIVE MOOD

Pres.	I cling	we cling
	you cling	you cling
	he (she, it) clings	they cling
Pres.	I am clinging	we are clinging
Prog.	you are clinging	you are clinging
	he (she, it) is clinging	they are clinging
Pres.	I do cling	we do cling
Int.	you do cling	you do cling
	he (she, it) does cling	they do cling
Fut.	I shall cling	we shall cling
	you will cling	you will cling
	he (she, it) will cling	they will cling
Fut.	I will cling *(P)*	we will cling *(P)*
	you shall cling *(C)*	you shall cling *(C)*
	he (she, it) shall cling *(C)*	they shall cling *(C)*
Past	I clung	we clung
	you clung	you clung
	he (she, it) clung	they clung
Past	I was clinging	we were clinging
Prog.	you were clinging	you were clinging
	he (she, it) was clinging	they were clinging
Past	I did cling	we did cling
Int.	you did cling	you did cling
	he (she, it) did cling	they did cling
Pres.	I have clung	we have clung
Perf.	you have clung	you have clung
	he (she, it) has clung	they have clung
Past	I had clung	we had clung
Perf.	you had clung	you had clung
	he (she, it) had clung	they had clung
Fut.	I shall have clung	we shall have clung
Perf.	you will have clung	you will have clung
	he (she, it) will have clung	they will have clung

IMPERATIVE MOOD

cling

SUBJUNCTIVE MOOD

Pres.	if I cling	if we cling
	if you cling	if you cling
	if he (she, it) cling	if they cling
Past	if I clung	if we clung
	if you clung	if you clung
	if he (she, it) clung	if they clung
Fut.	if I should cling	if we should cling
	if you should cling	if you should cling
	if he (she, it) should cling	if they should cling

Infinitive: to come   *Present Participle:* coming
Perfect Infinitive: to have come   *Past Participle:* come

INDICATIVE MOOD

Pres.	I come	we come
	you come	you come
	he (she, it) comes	they come
Pres.	I am coming	we are coming
Prog.	you are coming	you are coming
	he (she, it) is coming	they are coming
Pres.	I do come	we do come
Int.	you do come	you do come
	he (she, it) does come	they do come
Fut.	I shall come	we shall come
	you will come	you will come
	he (she, it) will come	they will come
Fut.	I will come *(P)*	we will come *(P)*
	you shall come *(C)*	you shall come *(C)*
	he (she, it) shall come *(C)*	they shall come *(C)*
Past	I came	we came
	you came	you came
	he (she, it) came	they came
Past	I was coming	we were coming
Prog.	you were coming	you were coming
	he (she, it) was coming	they were coming
Past	I did come	we did come
Int.	you did come	you did come
	he (she, it) did come	they did come
Pres.	I have come	we have come
Perf.	you have come	you have come
	he (she, it) has come	they have come
Past	I had come	we had come
Perf.	you had come	you had come
	he (she, it) had come	they had come
Fut.	I shall have come	we shall have come
Perf.	you will have come	you will have come
	he (she, it) will have come	they will have come

IMPERATIVE MOOD
come

SUBJUNCTIVE MOOD

Pres.	if I come	if we come
	if you come	if you come
	if he (she, it) come	if they come
Past	if I came	if we came
	if you came	if you came
	if he (she, it) came	if they came
Fut.	if I should come	if we should come
	if you should come	if you should come
	if he (she, it) should come	if they should come

Infinitive: to creep   *Present Participle:* creeping
Perfect Infinitive: to have crept   *Past Participle:* crept

INDICATIVE MOOD

Pres.	I creep	we creep
	you creep	you creep
	he (she, it) creeps	they creep
Pres.	I am creeping	we are creeping
Prog.	you are creeping	you are creeping
	he (she, it) is creeping	they are creeping
Pres.	I do creep	we do creep
Int.	you do creep	you do creep
	he (she, it) does creep	they do creep
Fut.	I shall creep	we shall creep
	you will creep	you will creep
	he (she, it) will creep	they will creep
Fut.	I will creep *(P)*	we will creep *(P)*
	you shall creep *(C)*	you shall creep *(C)*
	he (she, it) shall creep *(C)*	they shall creep *(C)*
Past	I crept	we crept
	you crept	you crept
	he (she, it) crept	they crept
Past	I was creeping	we were creeping
Prog.	you were creeping	you were creeping
	he (she, it) was creeping	they were creeping
Past	I did creep	we did creep
Int.	you did creep	you did creep
	he (she, it) did creep	they did creep
Pres.	I have crept	we have crept
Perf.	you have crept	you have crept
	he (she, it) has crept	they have crept
Past	I had crept	we had crept
Perf.	you had crept	you had crept
	he (she, it) had crept	they had crept
Fut.	I shall have crept	we shall have crept
Perf.	you will have crept	you will have crept
	he (she, it) will have crept	they will have crept

IMPERATIVE MOOD
creep

SUBJUNCTIVE MOOD

Pres.	if I creep	if we creep
	if you creep	if you creep
	if he (she, it) creep	if they creep
Past	if I crept	if we crept
	if you crept	if you crept
	if he (she, it) crept	if they crept
Fut.	if I should creep	if we should creep
	if you should creep	if you should creep
	if he (she, it) should creep	if they should creep

To creep is an intransitive verb.

It does not take an object.

It describes action, but the action is self-contained.

Like other intransitive verbs, it may be followed by adverbs, adverbial phrases and clauses describing the how, why, when, and where of the action:

HOW: The baby crept *quietly*. (adverb)

WHY: The baby crept *because it could not walk*. (adverbial clause)

WHEN: The baby will creep *soon*. (adverb)

WHERE: The baby crept *around the room*. (adverbial phrase)

to cut (active voice)   *Principal Parts:* cut, cutting, cut, cut

Infinitive: to cut   *Present Participle:* cutting
Perfect Infinitive: to have cut   *Past Participle:* cut

INDICATIVE MOOD

Pres.	I cut	we cut
	you cut	you cut
	he (she, it) cuts	they cut
Pres.	I am cutting	we are cutting
Prog.	you are cutting	you are cutting
	he (she, it) is cutting	they are cutting
Pres.	I do cut	we do cut
Int.	you do cut	you do cut
	he (she, it) does cut	they do cut
Fut.	I shall cut	we shall cut
	you will cut	you will cut
	he (she, it) will cut	they will cut
Fut.	I will cut *(P)*	we will cut *(P)*
	you shall cut *(C)*	you shall cut *(C)*
	he (she, it) shall cut *(C)*	they shall cut *(C)*
Past	I cut	we cut
	you cut	you cut
	he (she, it) cut	they cut
Past	I was cutting	we were cutting
Prog.	you were cutting	you were cutting
	he (she, it) was cutting	they were cutting
Past	I did cut	we did cut
Int.	you did cut	you did cut
	he (she, it) did cut	they did cut
Pres.	I have cut	we have cut
Perf.	you have cut	you have cut
	he (she, it) has cut	they have cut
Past	I had cut	we had cut
Perf.	you had cut	you had cut
	he (she, it) had cut	they had cut
Fut.	I shall have cut	we shall have cut
Perf.	you will have cut	you will have cut
	he (she, it) will have cut	they will have cut

IMPERATIVE MOOD
cut

SUBJUNCTIVE MOOD

Pres.	if I cut	if we cut
	if you cut	if you cut
	if he (she, it) cut	if they cut
Past	if I cut	if we cut
	if you cut	if you cut
	if he (she, it) cut	if they cut
Fut.	if I should cut	if we should cut
	if you should cut	if you should cut
	if he (she, it) should cut	if they should cut

(passive voice)

Infinitive: to be cut　　　　　　　　　　*Present Participle:* being cut
Perfect Infinitive: to have been cut　　　　　*Past Participle:* been cut

INDICATIVE MOOD

Pres.	I am cut	we are cut
	you are cut	you are cut
	he (she, it) is cut	they are cut
Pres.	I am being cut	we are being cut
Prog.	you are being cut	you are being cut
	he (she, it) is being cut	they are being cut
Pres.	I do get cut	we do get cut
Int.	you do get cut	you do get cut
	he (she, it) does get cut	they do get cut
Fut.	I shall be cut	we shall be cut
	you will be cut	you will be cut
	he (she, it) will be cut	they will be cut
Fut.	I will be cut *(P)*	we will be cut *(P)*
	you shall be cut *(C)*	you shall be cut *(C)*
	he (she, it) shall be cut *(C)*	they shall be cut *(C)*
Past	I was cut	we were cut
	you were cut	you were cut
	he (she, it) was cut	they were cut
Past	I was being cut	we were being cut
Prog.	you were being cut	you were being cut
	he (she, it) was being cut	they were being cut
Past	I did get cut	we did get cut
Int.	you did get cut	you did get cut
	he (she, it) did get cut	they did get cut
Pres.	I have been cut	we have been cut
Perf.	you have been cut	you have been cut
	he (she, it) has been cut	they have been cut
Past	I had been cut	we had been cut
Perf.	you had been cut	you had been cut
	he (she, it) had been cut	they had been cut
Fut.	I shall have been cut	we shall have been cut
Perf.	you will have been cut	you will have been cut
	he (she, it) will have been cut	they will have been cut

IMPERATIVE MOOD
be cut

SUBJUNCTIVE MOOD

Pres.	if I be cut	if we be cut
	if you be cut	if you be cut
	if he (she, it) be cut	if they be cut
Past	if I were cut	if we were cut
	if you were cut	if you were cut
	if he (she, it) were cut	if they were cut
Fut.	if I should be cut	if we should be cut
	if you should be cut	if you should be cut
	if he (she, it) should be cut	if they should be cut

to deal (active voice) *Principal Parts:* deal, dealing, dealt, dealt

Infinitive: to deal   *Present Participle:* dealing
Perfect Infinitive: to have dealt   *Past Participle:* dealt

INDICATIVE MOOD

Pres.	I deal	we deal
	you deal	you deal
	he (she, it) deals	they deal
Pres.	I am dealing	we are dealing
Prog.	you are dealing	you are dealing
	he (she, it) is dealing	they are dealing
Pres.	I do deal	we do deal
Int.	you do deal	you do deal
	he (she, it) does deal	they do deal
Fut.	I shall deal	we shall deal
	you will deal	you will deal
	he (she, it) will deal	they will deal
Fut.	I will deal *(P)*	we will deal *(P)*
	you shall deal *(C)*	you shall deal *(C)*
	he (she, it) shall deal *(C)*	they shall deal *(C)*
Past	I dealt	we dealt
	you dealt	you dealt
	he (she, it) dealt	they dealt
Past	I was dealing	we were dealing
Prog.	you were dealing	you were dealing
	he (she, it) was dealing	they were dealing
Past	I did deal	we did deal
Int.	you did deal	you did deal
	he (she, it) did deal	they did deal
Pres.	I have dealt	we have dealt
Perf.	you have dealt	you have dealt
	he (she, it) has dealt	they have dealt
Past	I had dealt	we had dealt
Perf.	you had dealt	you had dealt
	he (she, it) had dealt	they had dealt
Fut.	I shall have dealt	we shall have dealt
Perf.	you will have dealt	you will have dealt
	he (she, it) will have dealt	they will have dealt

IMPERATIVE MOOD
deal

SUBJUNCTIVE MOOD

Pres.	if I deal	if we deal
	if you deal	if you deal
	if he (she, it) deal	if they deal
Past	if I dealt	if we dealt
	if you dealt	if you dealt
	if he (she, it) dealt	if they dealt
Fut.	if I should deal	if we should deal
	if you should deal	if you should deal
	if he (she, it) should deal	if they should deal

(passive voice)

Infinitive: to be dealt

Perfect Infinitive: to have been dealt

Present Participle: being dealt

Past Participle: been dealt

INDICATIVE MOOD

Pres.	I am dealt	we are dealt
	you are dealt	you are dealt
	he (she, it) is dealt	they are dealt

Pres. Prog.	I am being dealt	we are being dealt
	you are being dealt	you are being dealt
	he (she, it) is being dealt	they are being dealt

Pres. Int.	I do get dealt	we do get dealt
	you do get dealt	you do get dealt
	he (she, it) does get dealt	they do get dealt

Fut.	I shall be dealt	we shall be dealt
	you will be dealt	you will be dealt
	he (she, it) will be dealt	they will be dealt

Fut.	I will be dealt *(P)*	we will be dealt *(P)*
	you shall be dealt *(C)*	you shall be dealt *(C)*
	he (she, it) shall be dealt *(C)*	they shall be dealt *(C)*

Past	I was dealt	we were dealt
	you were dealt	you were dealt
	he (she, it) was dealt	they were dealt

Past Prog.	I was being dealt	we were being dealt
	you were being dealt	you were being dealt
	he (she, it) was being dealt	they were being dealt

Past Int.	I did get dealt	we did get dealt
	you did get dealt	you did get dealt
	he (she, it) did get dealt	they did get dealt

Pres. Perf.	I have been dealt	we have been dealt
	you have been dealt	you have been dealt
	he (she, it) has been dealt	they have been dealt

Past Perf.	I had been dealt	we had been dealt
	you had been dealt	you had been dealt
	he (she, it) had been dealt	they had been dealt

Fut. Perf.	I shall have been dealt	we shall have been dealt
	you will have been dealt	you will have been dealt
	he (she, it) will have been dealt	they will have been dealt

IMPERATIVE MOOD
be dealt

SUBJUNCTIVE MOOD

Pres.	if I be dealt	if we be dealt
	if you be dealt	if you be dealt
	if he (she, it) be dealt	if they be dealt

Past	if I were dealt	if we were dealt
	if you were dealt	if you were dealt
	if he (she, it) were dealt	if they were dealt

Fut.	if I should be dealt	if we should be dealt
	if you should be dealt	if you should be dealt
	if he (she, it) should be dealt	if they should be dealt

Infinitive: to dive *Present Participle:* diving
Perfect Infinitive: to have dived *Past Participle:* dived

INDICATIVE MOOD

Pres.	I dive	we dive
	you dive	you dive
	he (she, it) dives	they dive
Pres. *Prog.*	I am diving	we are diving
	you are diving	you are diving
	he (she, it) is diving	they are diving
Pres. *Int.*	I do dive	we do dive
	you do dive	you do dive
	he (she, it) does dive	they do dive
Fut.	I shall dive	we shall dive
	you will dive	you will dive
	he (she, it) will dive	they will dive
Fut.	I will dive *(P)*	we will dive *(P)*
	you shall dive *(C)*	you shall dive *(C)*
	he (she, it) shall dive *(C)*	they shall dive *(C)*
Past	I dived, dove	we dived, dove
	you dived, dove	you dived, dove
	he (she, it) dived, dove	they dived, dove
Past *Prog.*	I was diving	we were diving
	you were diving	you were diving
	he (she, it) was diving	they were diving
Past *Int.*	I did dive	we did dive
	you did dive	you did dive
	he (she, it) did dive	they did dive
Pres. *Perf.*	I have dived	we have dived
	you have dived	you have dived
	he (she, it) has dived	they have dived
Past *Perf.*	I had dived	we had dived
	you had dived	you had dived
	he (she, it) had dived	they had dived
Fut. *Perf.*	I shall have dived	we shall have dived
	you will have dived	you will have dived
	he (she, it) will have dived	they will have dived

IMPERATIVE MOOD
dive

SUBJUNCTIVE MOOD

Pres.	if I dive	if we dive
	if you dive	if you dive
	if he (she, it) dive	if they dive
Past	if I dived, dove	if we dived, dove
	if you dived, dove	if you dived, dove
	if he (she, it) dived, dove	if they dived, dove
Fut.	if I should dive	if we should dive
	if you should dive	if you should dive
	if he (she, it) should dive	if they should dive

To dive is an intransitive verb.

It does not take an object.

It describes action, but the action is self-contained.

Like other intransitive verbs, it may be followed by adverbs, adverbial phrases and clauses describing the how, why, when, and where of the action:

HOW: She dived *beautifully*. (adverb)

WHY: The submarine dived *because an enemy ship was in sight*. (adverbial clause)

WHEN: The boys dived *until late in the afternoon*. (adverbial phrases)

WHERE: I dived *into the pool*. (adverbial phrase)

to do (active voice)   *Principal Parts:* do, doing, did, done

Infinitive: to do   *Present Participle:* doing
Perfect Infinitive: to have done   *Past Participle:* done

INDICATIVE MOOD

Pres.	I do	we do
	you do	you do
	he (she, it) does	they do
Prog.	I am doing	we are doing
Pres.	you are doing	you are doing
	he (she, it) is doing	they are doing
Pres.	I do do	we do do
Int.	you do do	you do do
	he (she, it) does do	they do do
Fut.	I shall do	we shall do
	you will do	you will do
	he (she, it) will do	they will do
Fut.	I will do *(P)*	we will do *(P)*
	you shall do *(C)*	you shall do *(C)*
	he (she, it) shall do *(C)*	they shall do *(C)*
Past	I did	we did
	you did	you did
	he (she, it) did	they did
Past	I was doing	we were doing
Prog.	you were doing	you were doing
	he (she, it) was doing	they were doing
Past	I did do	we did do
Int.	you did do	you did do
	he (she, it) did do	they did do
Pres.	I have done	we have done
Perf.	you have done	you have done
	he (she, it) has done	they have done
Past	I had done	we had done
Perf.	you had done	you had done
	he (she, it) had done	they had done
Fut.	I shall have done	we shall have done
Perf.	you will have done	you will have done
	he (she, it) will have done	they will have done

IMPERATIVE MOOD
do

SUBJUNCTIVE MOOD

Pres.	if I do	if we do
	if you do	if you do
	if he (she, it) do	if they do
Past	if I did	if we did
	if you did	if you did
	if he (she, it) did	if they did
Fut.	if I should do	if we should do
	if you should do	if you should do
	if he (she, it) should do	if they should do

156

Infinitive: to be done   *Present Participle:* being done
Perfect Infinitive: to have been done   *Past Participle:* been done

INDICATIVE MOOD

Pres.	I am done	we are done
	you are done	you are done
	he (she, it) is done	they are done
Pres. Prog.	I am being done	we are being done
	you are being done	you are being done
	he (she, it) is being done	they are being done
Pres. Int.	I do get done	we do get done
	you do get done	you do get done
	he (she, it) does get done	they do get done
Fut.	I shall be done	we shall be done
	you will be done	you will be done
	he (she, it) will be done	they will be done
Fut.	I will be done *(P)*	we will be done *(P)*
	you shall be done *(C)*	you shall be done *(C)*
	he (she, it) shall be done *(C)*	they shall be done *(C)*
Past	I was done	we were done
	you were done	you were done
	he (she, it) was done	they were done
Past Prog.	I was being done	we were being done
	you were being done	you were being done
	he (she, it) was being done	they were being done
Past Int.	I did get done	we did get done
	you did get done	you did get done
	he (she, it) did get done	they did get done
Pres. Perf.	I have been done	we have been done
	you have been done	you have been done
	he (she, it) has been done	they have been done
Past Perf.	I had been done	we had been done
	you had been done	you had been done
	he (she, it) had been done	they had been done
Fut. Perf.	I shall have been done	we shall have been done
	you will have been done	you will have been done
	he (she, it) will have been done	they will have been done

IMPERATIVE MOOD
be done

SUBJUNCTIVE MOOD

Pres.	if I be done	if we be done
	if you be done	if you be done
	if he (she, it) be done	if they be done
Past	if I were done	if we were done
	if you were done	if you were done
	if he (she, it) were done	if they were done
Fut.	if I should be done	if we should be done
	if you should be done	if you should be done
	if he (she, it) should be done	if they should be done

to draw (active voice)   *Principal Parts:* draw, drawing, drew, drawn

Infinitive: to draw   *Present Participle:* drawing
Perfect Infinitive: to have drawn   *Past Participle:* drawn

INDICATIVE MOOD

Pres.	I draw	we draw
	you draw	you draw
	he (she, it) draws	they draw
Pres.	I am drawing	we are drawing
Prog.	you are drawing	you are drawing
	he (she, it) is drawing	they are drawing
Pres.	I do draw	we do draw
Int.	you do draw	you do draw
	he (she, it) does draw	they do draw
Fut.	I shall draw	we shall draw
	you will draw	you will draw
	he (she, it) will draw	they will draw
Fut.	I will draw *(P)*	we will draw *(P)*
	you shall draw *(C)*	you shall draw *(C)*
	he (she, it) shall draw *(C)*	they shall draw *(C)*
Past	I drew	we drew
	you drew	you drew
	he (she, it) drew	they drew
Past	I was drawing	we were drawing
Prog.	you were drawing	you were drawing
	he (she, it) was drawing	they were drawing
Past	I did draw	we did draw
Int.	you did draw	you did draw
	he (she, it) did draw	they did draw
Pres.	I have drawn	we have drawn
Perf.	you have drawn	you have drawn
	he (she, it) has drawn	they have drawn
Past	I had drawn	we had drawn
Perf.	you had drawn	you had drawn
	he (she, it) had drawn	they had drawn
Fut.	I shall have drawn	we shall have drawn
Perf.	you will have drawn	you will have drawn
	he (she, it) will have drawn	they will have drawn

IMPERATIVE MOOD
draw

SUBJUNCTIVE MOOD

Pres.	if I draw	if we draw
	if you draw	if you draw
	if he (she, it) draw	if they draw
Past	if I drew	if we drew
	if you drew	if you drew
	if he (she, it) drew	if they drew
Fut.	if I should draw	if we should draw
	if you should draw	if you should draw
	if he (she, it) should draw	if they should draw

(passive voice)

Infinitive: to be drawn   *Present Participle:* being drawn
Perfect Infinitive: to have been drawn   *Past Participle:* been drawn

INDICATIVE MOOD

Pres.	I am drawn	we are drawn
	you are drawn	you are drawn
	he (she, it) is drawn	they are drawn
Pres.	I am being drawn	we are being drawn
Prog.	you are being drawn	you are being drawn
	he (she, it) is being drawn	they are being drawn
Pres.	I do get drawn	we do get drawn
Int.	you do get drawn	you do get drawn
	he (she, it) does get drawn	they do get drawn
Fut.	I shall be drawn	we shall be drawn
	you will be drawn	you will be drawn
	he (she, it) will be drawn	they will be drawn
Fut.	I will be drawn *(P)*	we will be drawn *(P)*
	you shall be drawn *(C)*	you shall be drawn *(C)*
	he (she, it) shall be drawn *(C)*	they shall be drawn *(C)*
Past	I was drawn	we were drawn
	you were drawn	you were drawn
	he (she, it) was drawn	they were drawn
Past	I was being drawn	we were being drawn
Prog.	you were being drawn	you were being drawn
	he (she, it) was being drawn	they were being drawn
Past	I did get drawn	we did get drawn
Int.	you did get drawn	you did get drawn
	he (she, it) did get drawn	they did get drawn
Pres.	I have been drawn	we have been drawn
Perf.	you have been drawn	you have been drawn
	he (she, it) has been drawn	they have been drawn
Past	I had been drawn	we had been drawn
Perf.	you had been drawn	you had been drawn
	he (she, it) had been drawn	they had been drawn
Fut.	I shall have been drawn	we shall have been drawn
Perf.	you will have been drawn	you will have been drawn
	he (she, it) will have been drawn	they will have been drawn

IMPERATIVE MOOD
be drawn

SUBJUNCTIVE MOOD

Pres.	if I be drawn	if we be drawn
	if you be drawn	if you be drawn
	if he (she, it) be drawn	if they be drawn
Past	if I were drawn	if we were drawn
	if you were drawn	if you were drawn
	if he (she, it) were drawn	if they were drawn
Fut.	if I should be drawn	if we should be drawn
	if you should be drawn	if you should be drawn
	if he (she, it) should be drawn	if they should be drawn

to drink (active voice)   *Principal Parts:* drink, drinking, drank, drunk

Infinitive: to drink   *Present Participle:* drinking
Perfect Infinitive: to have drunk   *Past Participle:* drunk

INDICATIVE MOOD

Pres.	I drink	we drink
	you drink	you drink
	he (she, it) drinks	they drink
Pres.	I am drinking	we are drinking
Prog.	you are drinking	you are drinking
	he (she, it) is drinking	they are drinking
Pres.	I do drink	we do drink
Int.	you do drink	you do drink
	he (she, it) does drink	they do drink
Fut.	I shall drink	we shall drink
	you will drink	you will drink
	he (she, it) will drink	they will drink
Fut.	I will drink *(P)*	we will drink *(P)*
	you shall drink *(C)*	you shall drink *(C)*
	he (she, it) shall drink *(C)*	they shall drink *(C)*
Past	I drank	we drank
	you drank	you drank
	he (she, it) drank	they drank
Past	I was drinking	we were drinking
Prog.	you were drinking	you were drinking
	he (she, it) was drinking	they were drinking
Past	I did drink	we did drink
Int.	you did drink	you did drink
	he (she, it) did drink	they did drink
Pres.	I have drunk	we have drunk
Perf.	you have drunk	you have drunk
	he (she, it) has drunk	they have drunk
Past	I had drunk	we had drunk
Perf.	you had drunk	you had drunk
	he (she, it) had drunk	they had drunk
Fut.	I shall have drunk	we shall have drunk
Perf.	you will have drunk	you will have drunk
	he (she, it) will have drunk	they will have drunk

IMPERATIVE MOOD
drink

SUBJUNCTIVE MOOD

Pres.	if I drink	if we drink
	if you drink	if you drink
	if he (she, it) drink	if they drink
Past	if I drank	if we drank
	if you drank	if you drank
	if he (she, it) drank	if they drank
Fut.	if I should drink	if we should drink
	if you should drink	if you should drink
	if he (she, it) should drink	if they should drink

(passive voice)

Infinitive: to be drunk   *Present Participle:* being drunk
Perfect Infinitive: to have been drunk   *Past Participle:* been drunk

INDICATIVE MOOD

Pres.	I am drunk	we are drunk
	you are drunk	you are drunk
	he (she, it) is drunk	they are drunk
Pres. *Prog.*	I am being drunk	we are being drunk
	you are being drunk	you are being drunk
	he (she, it) is being drunk	they are being drunk
Pres. *Int.*	I do get drunk	we do get drunk
	you do get drunk	you do get drunk
	he (she, it) does get drunk	they do get drunk
Fut.	I shall be drunk	we shall be drunk
	you will be drunk	you will be drunk
	he (she, it) will be drunk	they will be drunk
Fut.	I will be drunk *(P)*	we will be drunk *(P)*
	you shall be drunk *(C)*	you shall be drunk *(C)*
	he (she, it) shall be drunk *(C)*	they shall be drunk *(C)*
Past	I was drunk	we were drunk
	you were drunk	you were drunk
	he (she, it) was drunk	they were drunk
Past *Prog.*	I was being drunk	we were being drunk
	you were being drunk	you were being drunk
	he (she, it) was being drunk	they were being drunk
Past *Int.*	I did get drunk	we did get drunk
	you did get drunk	you did get drunk
	he (she, it) did get drunk	they did get drunk
Pres. *Perf.*	I have been drunk	we have been drunk
	you have been drunk	you have been drunk
	he (she, it) has been drunk	they had been drunk
Past *Perf.*	I had been drunk	we had been drunk
	you had been drunk	you had been drunk
	he (she, it) had been drunk	they had been drunk
Fut. *Perf.*	I shall have been drunk	we shall have been drunk
	you will have been drunk	you will have been drunk
	he (she, it) will have been drunk	they will have been drunk

IMPERATIVE MOOD
be drunk

SUBJUNCTIVE MOOD

Pres.	if I be drunk	if we be drunk
	if you be drunk	if you be drunk
	if he (she, it) be drunk	if they be drunk
Past	if I were drunk	if we were drunk
	if you were drunk	if you were drunk
	if he (she, it) were drunk	if they were drunk
Fut.	if I should be drunk	if we should be drunk
	if you should be drunk	if you should be drunk
	if he (she, it) should be drunk	if they should be drunk

to drive (active voice)

Principal Parts: drive, driving, drove, driven

Infinitive: to drive   *Present Participle:* driving
Perfect Infinitive: to have driven   *Past Participle:* driven

INDICATIVE MOOD

Pres.	I drive	we drive
	you drive	you drive
	he (she, it) drives	they drive
Pres. Prog.	I am driving	we are driving
	you are driving	you are driving
	he (she, it) is driving	they are driving
Pres. Int.	I do drive	we do drive
	you do drive	you do drive
	he (she, it) does drive	they do drive
Fut.	I shall drive	we shall drive
	you will drive	you will drive
	he (she, it) will drive	they will drive
Fut.	I will drive *(P)*	we will drive *(P)*
	you shall drive *(C)*	you shall drive *(C)*
	he (she, it) shall drive *(C)*	they shall drive *(C)*
Past	I drove	we drove
	you drove	you drove
	he (she, it) drove	they drove
Past Prog.	I was driving	we were driving
	you were driving	you were driving
	he (she, it) was driving	they were driving
Past Int.	I did drive	we did drive
	you did drive	you did drive
	he (she, it) did drive	they did drive
Pres. Perf.	I have driven	we have driven
	you have driven	you have driven
	he (she, it) has driven	they have driven
Past Perf.	I had driven	we had driven
	you had driven	you had driven
	he (she, it) had driven	they had driven
Fut. Perf.	I shall have driven	we shall have driven
	you will have driven	you will have driven
	he (she, it) will have driven	they will have driven

IMPERATIVE MOOD
drive

SUBJUNCTIVE MOOD

Pres.	if I drive	if we drive
	if you drive	if you drive
	if he (she, it) drive	if they drive
Past	if I drove	if we drove
	if you drove	if you drove
	if he (she, it) drove	if they drove
Fut.	if I should drive	if we should drive
	if you should drive	if you should drive
	if he (she, it) should drive	if they should drive

(passive voice)

Infinitive: to be driven   *Present Participle:* being driven
Perfect Infinitive: to have been driven   *Past Participle:* been driven

INDICATIVE MOOD

Pres. I am driven	we are driven
you are driven	you are driven
he (she, it) is driven	they are driven
Pres. I am being driven	we are being driven
Prog. you are being driven	you are being driven
he (she, it) is being driven	they are being driven
Pres. I do get driven	we do get driven
Int. you do get driven	you do get driven
he (she, it) does get driven	they do get driven
Fut. I shall be driven	we shall be driven
you will be driven	you will be driven
he (she, it) will be driven	they will be driven
Fut. I will be driven *(P)*	we will be driven *(P)*
you shall be driven *(C)*	you shall be driven *(C)*
he (she, it) shall be driven *(C)*	they shall be driven *(C)*
Past I was driven	we were driven
you were driven	you were driven
he (she, it) was driven	they were driven
Past I was being driven	we were being driven
Prog. you were being driven	you were being driven
he (she, it) was being driven	they were being driven
Past I did get driven	we did get driven
Int. you did get driven	you did get driven
he (she, it) did get driven	they did get driven
Pres. I have been driven	we have been driven
Perf. you have been driven	you have been driven
he (she, it) has been driven	they have been driven
Past I had been driven	we had been driven
Perf. you had been driven	you had been driven
he (she, it) had been driven	they had been driven
Fut. I shall have been driven	we shall have been driven
Perf. you will have been driven	you will have been driven
he (she, it) will have been driven	they will have been driven

IMPERATIVE MOOD
be driven

SUBJUNCTIVE MOOD

Pres. if I be driven	if we be driven
if you be driven	if you be driven
if he (she, it) be driven	if they be driven
Past if I were driven	if we were driven
if you were driven	if you were driven
if he (she, it) were driven	if they were driven
Fut. if I should be driven	if we should be driven
if you should be driven	if you should be driven
if he (she, it) should be driven	if they should be driven

to eat (active voice)

Infinitive: to eat   *Present Participle:* eating
Perfect Infinitive: to have eaten   *Past Participle:* eaten

INDICATIVE MOOD

Pres.	I eat	we eat
	you eat	you eat
	he (she, it) eats	they eat
Pres.	I am eating	we are eating
Prog.	you are eating	you are eating
	he (she, it) is eating	they are eating
Pres.	I do eat	we do eat
Int.	you do eat	you do eat
	he (she, it) does eat	they do eat
Fut.	I shall eat	we shall eat
	you will eat	you will eat
	he (she, it) will eat	they will eat
Fut.	I will eat *(P)*	we will eat *(P)*
	you shall eat *(C)*	you shall eat *(C)*
	he (she, it) shall eat *(C)*	they shall eat *(C)*
Past	I ate	we ate
	you ate	you ate
	he (she, it) ate	they ate
Past	I was eating	we were eating
Prog.	you were eating	you were eating
	he (she, it) was eating	they were eating
Past	I did eat	we did eat
Int.	you did eat	you did eat
	he (she, it) did eat	they did eat
Pres.	I have eaten	we have eaten
Perf.	you have eaten	you have eaten
	he (she, it) has eaten	they have eaten
Past	I had eaten	we had eaten
Perf.	you had eaten	you had eaten
	he (she, it) had eaten	they had eaten
Fut.	I shall have eaten	we shall have eaten
Perf.	you will have eaten	you will have eaten
	he (she, it) will have eaten	they will have eaten

IMPERATIVE MOOD
eat

SUBJUNCTIVE MOOD

Pres.	if I eat	if we eat
	if you eat	if you eat
	if he (she, it) eat	if they eat
Past	if I ate	if we ate
	if you ate	if you ate
	if he (she, it) ate	if they ate
Fut.	if I should eat	if we should eat
	if you should eat	if you should eat
	if he (she, it) should eat	if they should eat

(passive voice)

Infinitive: to be eaten   *Present Participle:* being eaten
Perfect Infinitive: to have been eaten   *Past Participle:* been eaten

INDICATIVE MOOD

Pres.	I am eaten	we are eaten
	you are eaten	you are eaten
	he (she, it) is eaten	they are eaten
Pres. *Prog.*	I am being eaten	we are being eaten
	you are being eaten	you are being eaten
	he (she, it) is being eaten	they are being eaten
Pres. *Int.*	I do get eaten	we do get eaten
	you do get eaten	you do get eaten
	he (she, it) does get eaten	they do get eaten
Fut.	I shall be eaten	we shall be eaten
	you will be eaten	you will be eaten
	he (she, it) will be eaten	they will be eaten
Fut.	I will be eaten *(P)*	we will be eaten *(P)*
	you shall be eaten *(C)*	you shall be eaten *(C)*
	he (she, it) shall be eaten *(C)*	they shall be eaten *(C)*
Past	I was eaten	we were eaten
	you were eaten	you were eaten
	he (she, it) was eaten	they were eaten
Past *Prog.*	I was being eaten	we were being eaten
	you were being eaten	you were being eaten
	he (she, it) was being eaten	they were being eaten
Past *Int.*	I did get eaten	we did get eaten
	you did get eaten	you did get eaten
	he (she, it) did get eaten	they did get eaten
Pres. *Perf.*	I have been eaten	we have been eaten
	you have been eaten	you have been eaten
	he (she, it) has been eaten	they have been eaten
Past *Perf.*	I had been eaten	we had been eaten
	you had been eaten	you had been eaten
	he (she, it) had been eaten	they had been eaten
Fut. *Perf.*	I shall have been eaten	we shall have been eaten
	you will have been eaten	you will have been eaten
	he (she, it) will have been eaten	they will have been eaten

IMPERATIVE MOOD
be eaten

SUBJUNCTIVE MOOD

Pres.	if I be eaten	if we be eaten
	if you be eaten	if you be eaten
	if he (she, it) be eaten	if they be eaten
Past	if I were eaten	if we were eaten
	if you were eaten	if you were eaten
	if he (she, it) were eaten	if they were eaten
Fut.	if I should be eaten	if we should be eaten
	if you should be eaten	if you should be eaten
	if he (she, it) should be eaten	if they should be eaten

to fall

Infinitive: to fall   *Present Participle:* falling
Perfect Infinitive: to have fallen   *Past Participle:* fallen

INDICATIVE MOOD

Pres.	I fall	we fall
	you fall	you fall
	he (she, it) falls	they fall
Pres.	I am falling	we are falling
Prog.	you are falling	you are falling
	he (she, it) is falling	they are falling
Pres.	I do fall	we do fall
Int.	you do fall	you do fall
	he (she, it) does fall	they do fall
Fut.	I shall fall	we shall fall
	you will fall	you will fall
	he (she, it) will fall	they will fall
Fut.	I will fall *(P)*	we will fall *(P)*
	you shall fall *(C)*	you shall fall *(C)*
	he (she, it) shall fall *(C)*	they shall fall *(C)*
Past	I fell	we fell
	you fell	you fell
	he (she, it) fell	they fell
Past	I was falling	we were falling
Prog.	you were falling	you were falling
	he (she, it) was falling	they were falling
Past	I did fall	we did fall
Int.	you did fall	you did fall
	he (she, it) did fall	they did fall
Pres.	I have fallen	we have fallen
Perf.	you have fallen	you have fallen
	he (she, it) has fallen	they have fallen
Past	I had fallen	we had fallen
Perf.	you had fallen	you had fallen
	he (she, it) had fallen	they had fallen
Fut.	I shall have fallen	we shall have fallen
Perf.	you will have fallen	you will have fallen
	he (she, it) will have fallen	they will have fallen

IMPERATIVE MOOD
fall

SUBJUNCTIVE MOOD

Pres.	if I fall	if we fall
	if you fall	if you fall
	if he (she, it) fall	if they fall
Past	if I fell	if we fell
	if you fell	if you fell
	if he (she, it) fell	if they fell
Fut.	if I should fall	if we should fall
	if you should fall	if you should fall
	if he (she, it) should fall	if they should fall

To fall is an intransitive verb.

It does not take an object.

It describes actions, but the action is self-contained.

Like other intransitive verbs, it may be followed by adverbs, adverbial phrases and clauses describing the how, why, when, and where of the action:

HOW: The rain fell *slowly*. (adverb)

WHY: He fell *because he could not keep his balance*. (adverbial clause)

WHEN: Leaves fall *in the autumn*. (adverbial phrase)

WHERE: He fell *off the ladder*. (adverbial phrase)

to feed (active voice)   *Principal Parts:* feed, feeding, fed, fed

Infinitive: to feed   *Present Participle:* feeding
Perfect Infinitive: to have fed   *Past Participle:* fed

INDICATIVE MOOD

Pres.	I feed	we feed
	you feed	you feed
	he (she, it) feeds	they feed
Pres.	I am feeding	we are feeding
Prog.	you are feeding	you are feeding
	he (she, it) is feeding	they are feeding
Pres.	I do feed	we do feed
Int.	you do feed	you do feed
	he (she, it) does feed	they do feed
Fut.	I shall feed	we shall feed
	you will feed	you will feed
	he (she, it) will feed	they will feed
Fut.	I will feed *(P)*	we will feed *(P)*
	you shall feed *(C)*	you shall feed *(C)*
	he (she, it) shall feed *(C)*	they shall feed *(C)*
Past	I fed	we fed
	you fed	you fed
	he (she, it) fed	they fed
Past	I was feeding	we were feeding
Prog.	you were feeding	you were feeding
	he (she, it) was feeding	they were feeding
Past	I did feed	we did feed
Int.	you did feed	you did feed
	he (she, it) did feed	they did feed
Pres.	I have fed	we have fed
Perf.	you have fed	you have fed
	he (she, it) has fed	they have fed
Past	I had fed	we had fed
Perf.	you had fed	you had fed
	he (she, it) had fed	they had fed
Fut.	I shall have fed	we shall have fed
Perf.	you will have fed	you will have fed
	he (she, it) will have fed	they will have fed

IMPERATIVE MOOD
feed

SUBJUNCTIVE MOOD

Pres.	if I feed	if we feed
	if you feed	if you feed
	if he (she, it) feed	if they feed
Past	if I fed	if we fed
	if you fed	if you fed
	if he (she, it) fed	if they fed
Fut.	if I should feed	if we should feed
	if you should feed	if you should feed
	if he (she, it) should feed	if they should feed

(passive voice)

Infinitive: to be fed   *Present Participle:* being fed
Perfect Infinitive: to have been fed   *Past Participle:* been fed

INDICATIVE MOOD

Pres.	I am fed	we are fed
	you are fed	you are fed
	he (she, it) is fed	they are fed
Pres.	I am being fed	we are being fed
Prog.	you are being fed	you are being fed
	he (she, it) is being fed	they are being fed
Pres.	I do get fed	we do get fed
Int.	you do get fed	you do get fed
	he (she, it) does get fed	they do get fed
Fut.	I shall be fed	we shall be fed
	you will be fed	you will be fed
	he (she, it) will be fed	they will be fed
Fut.	I will be fed *(P)*	we will be fed *(P)*
	you shall be fed *(C)*	you shall be fed *(C)*
	he (she, it) shall be fed *(C)*	they shall be fed *(C)*
Past	I was fed	we were fed
	you were fed	you were fed
	he (she, it) was fed	they were fed
Past	I was being fed	we were being fed
Prog.	you were being fed	you were being fed
	he (she, it) was being fed	they were being fed
Past	I did get fed	we did get fed
Int.	you did get fed	you did get fed
	he (she, it) did get fed	they did get fed
Pres.	I have been fed	we have been fed
Perf.	you have been fed	you have been fed
	he (she, it) has been fed	they have been fed
Past	I had been fed	we had been fed
Perf.	you had been fed	you had been fed
	he (she, it) had been fed	they had been fed
Fut.	I shall have been fed	we shall have been fed
Perf.	you will have been fed	you will have been fed
	he (she, it) will have been fed	they will have been fed

IMPERATIVE MOOD
be fed

SUBJUNCTIVE MOOD

Pres.	if I be fed	if we be fed
	if you be fed	if you be fed
	if he (she, it) be fed	if they be fed
Past	if I were fed	if we were fed
	if you were fed	if you were fed
	if he (she, it) were fed	if they were fed
Fut.	if I should be fed	if we should be fed
	if you should be fed	if you should be fed
	if he (she, it) should be fed	if they should be fed

to fight (active voice)   *Principal Parts:* fight, fighting, fought, fought

Infinitive: to fight   *Present Participle:* fighting
Perfect Infinitive: to have fought   *Past Participle:* fought

INDICATIVE MOOD

Pres.	I fight	we fight
	you fight	you fight
	he (she, it) fights	they fight
Pres. Prog.	I am fighting	we are fighting
	you are fighting	you are fighting
	he (she, it) is fighting	they are fighting
Pres. Int.	I do fight	we do fight
	you do fight	you do fight
	he (she, it) does fight	they do fight
Fut.	I shall fight	we shall fight
	you will fight	you will fight
	he (she, it) will fight	they will fight
Fut.	I will fight *(P)*	we will fight *(P)*
	you shall fight *(C)*	you shall fight *(C)*
	he (she, it) shall fight *(C)*	they shall fight *(C)*
Past	I fought	we fought
	you fought	you fought
	he (she, it) fought	they fought
Past Prog.	I was fighting	we were fighting
	you were fighting	you were fighting
	he (she, it) was fighting	they were fighting
Past Int.	I did fight	we did fight
	you did fight	you did fight
	he (she, it) did fight	they did fight
Pres. Perf.	I have fought	we have fought
	you have fought	you have fought
	he (she, it) has fought	they have fought
Past Perf.	I had fought	we had fought
	you had fought	you had fought
	he (she, it) had fought	they had fought
Fut. Perf.	I shall have fought	we shall have fought
	you will have fought	you will have fought
	he (she, it) will have fought	they will have fought

IMPERATIVE MOOD
fight

SUBJUNCTIVE MOOD

Pres.	if I fight	if we fight
	if you fight	if you fight
	if he (she, it) fight	if they fight
Past	if I fought	if we fought
	if you fought	if you fought
	if he (she, it) fought	if they fought
Fut.	if I should fight	if we should fight
	if you should fight	if you should fight
	if he (she, it) should fight	if they should fight

Infinitive: to be fought   *Present Participle:* being fought
Perfect Infinitive: to have been fought   *Past Participle:* been fought

INDICATIVE MOOD

Pres.	I am fought	we are fought
	you are fought	you are fought
	he (she, it) is fought	they are fought
Pres. Prog.	I am being fought	we are being fought
	you are being fought	you are being fought
	he (she, it) is being fought	they are being fought
Pres. Int.	I do get fought	we do get fought
	you do get fought	you do get fought
	he (she, it) does get fought	they do get fought
Fut.	I shall be fought	we shall be fought
	you will be fought	you will be fought
	he (she, it) will be fought	they will be fought
Fut.	I will be fought *(P)*	we will be fought *(P)*
	you shall be fought *(C)*	you shall be fought *(C)*
	he (she, it) shall be fought *(C)*	they shall be fought *(C)*
Past	I was fought	we were fought
	you were fought	you were fought
	he (she, it) was fought	they were fought
Past Prog.	I was being fought	we were being fought
	you were being fought	you were being fought
	he (she, it) was being fought	they were being fought
Past Int.	I did get fought	we did get fought
	you did get fought	you did get fought
	he (she, it) did get fought	they did get fought
Pres. Perf.	I have been fought	we have been fought
	you have been fought	you have been fought
	he (she, it) has been fought	they have been fought
Past Perf.	I had been fought	we had been fought
	you had been fought	you had been fought
	he (she, it) had been fought	they had been fought
Fut. Perf.	I shall have been fought	we shall have been fought
	you will have been fought	you will have been fought
	he (she, it) will have been fought	they will have been fought

IMPERATIVE MOOD
be fought

SUBJUNCTIVE MOOD

Pres.	if I be fought	if we be fought
	if you be fought	if you be fought
	if he (she, it) be fought	if they be fought
Past	if I were fought	if we were fought
	if you were fought	if you were fought
	if he (she, it) were fought	if they were fought
Fut.	if I should be fought	if we should be fought
	if you should be fought	if you should be fought
	if he (she, it) should be fought	if they should be fought

to find (active voice)   *Principal Parts:* find, finding, found, found

Infinitive: to find   *Present Participle:* finding
Perfect Infinitive: to have found   *Past Participle:* found

INDICATIVE MOOD

Pres.	I find	we find
	you find	you find
	he (she, it) finds	they find
Pres.	I am finding	we are finding
Prog.	you are finding	you are finding
	he (she, it) is finding	they are finding
Pres.	I do find	we do find
Int.	you do find	you do find
	he (she, it) does find	they do find
Fut.	I shall find	we shall find
	you will find	you will find
	he (she, it) will find	they will find
Fut.	I will find *(P)*	we will find *(P)*
	you shall find *(C)*	you shall find *(C)*
	he (she, it) shall find *(C)*	they shall find *(C)*
Past	I found	we found
	you found	you found
	he (she, it) found	they found
Past	I was finding	we were finding
Prog.	you were finding	you were finding
	he (she, it) was finding	they were finding
Past	I did find	we did find
Int.	you did find	you did find
	he (she, it) did find	they did find
Pres.	I have found	we have found
Perf.	you have found	you have found
	he (she, it) has found	they have found
Past	I had found	we had found
Perf.	you had found	you had found
	he (she, it) had found	they had found
Fut.	I shall have found	we shall have found
Perf.	you will have found	you will have found
	he (she, it) will have found	they will have found

IMPERATIVE MOOD
find

SUBJUNCTIVE MOOD

Pres.	if I find	if we find
	if you find	if you find
	if he (she, it) find	if they find
Past	if I found	if we found
	if you found	if you found
	if he (she, it) found	if they found
Fut.	if I should find	if we should find
	if you should find	if you should find
	if he (she, it) should find	if they should find

(passive voice)

Infinitive: to be found *Present Participle:* being found
Perfect Infinitive: to have been found *Past Participle:* been found

INDICATIVE MOOD

Pres.	I am found	we are found
	you are found	you are found
	he (she, it) is found	they are found
Pres. Prog.	I am being found	we are being found
	you are being found	you are being found
	he (she, it) is being found	they are being found
Pres. Int.	I do get found	we do get found
	you do get found	you do get found
	he (she, it) does get found	they do get found
Fut.	I shall be found	we shall be found
	you will be found	you will be found
	he (she, it) will be found	they will be found
Fut.	I will be found *(P)*	we will be found *(P)*
	you shall be found *(C)*	you shall be found *(C)*
	he (she, it) shall be found *(C)*	they shall be found *(C)*
Past	I was found	we were found
	you were found	you were found
	he (she, it) was found	they were found
Past Prog.	I was being found	we were being found
	you were being found	you were being found
	he (she, it) was being found	they were being found
Past Int.	I did get found	we did get found
	you did get found	you did get found
	he (she, it) did get found	they did get found
Pres. Perf.	I have been found	we have been found
	you have been found	you have been found
	he (she, it) has been found	they have been found
Past Perf.	I had been found	we had been found
	you had been found	you had been found
	he (she, it) had been found	they had been found
Fut. Perf.	I shall have been found	we shall have been found
	you will have been found	you will have been found
	he (she, it) will have been found	they will have been found

IMPERATIVE MOOD
be found

SUBJUNCTIVE MOOD

Pres.	if I be found	if we be found
	if you be found	if you be found
	if he (she, it) be found	if they be found
Past	if I were found	if we were found
	if you were found	if you were found
	if he (she, it) were found	if they were found
Fut.	if I should be found	if we should be found
	if you should be found	if you should be found
	if he (she, it) should be found	if they should be found

to flee

Principal Parts: flee, fleeing, fled, fled

Infinitive: to flee   *Present Participle:* fleeing
Perfect Infinitive: to have fled   *Past Participle:* fled

INDICATIVE MOOD

Pres.	I flee	we flee
	you flee	you flee
	he (she, it) flees	they flee
Pres. *Prog.*	I am fleeing	we are fleeing
	You are fleeing	you are fleeing
	he (she, it) is fleeing	they are fleeing
Pres. *Int.*	I do flee	we do flee
	you do flee	you do flee
	he (she, it) does flee	they do flee
Fut.	I shall flee	we shall flee
	you will flee	you will flee
	he (she, it) will flee	they will flee
Fut.	I will flee *(P)*	we will flee *(P)*
	you shall flee *(C)*	you shall flee *(C)*
	he (she, it) shall flee *(C)*	they shall flee *(C)*
Past	I fled	we fled
	you fled	you fled
	he (she, it) fled	they fled
Past *Prog.*	I was fleeing	we were fleeing
	you were fleeing	you were fleeing
	he (she, it) was fleeing	they were fleeing
Past *Int.*	I did flee	we did flee
	you did flee	you did flee
	he (she, it) did flee	they did flee
Pres. *Perf.*	I have fled	we have fled
	you have fled	you have fled
	he (she, it) has fled	they have fled
Past *Perf.*	I had fled	we had fled
	you had fled	you had fled
	he (she, it) had fled	they had fled
Fut. *Perf.*	I shall have fled	we shall have fled
	you will have fled	you will have fled
	he (she, it) will have fled	they will have fled

IMPERATIVE MOOD
flee

SUBJUNCTIVE MOOD

Pres.	if I flee	if we flee
	if you flee	if you flee
	if he (she, it) flee	if they flee
Past	if I fled	if we fled
	if you fled	if you fled
	if he (she, it) fled	if they fled
Fut.	if I should flee	if we should flee
	if you should flee	if you should flee
	if he (she, it) should flee	if they should flee

To flee is an intransitive verb.

It does not take an object.

It describes action, but the action is self-contained.

Like other intransitive verbs, it may be followed by adverbs, adverbial phrases and clauses describing the how, why, when, and where of the action:

HOW: The thieves fled *quickly*. (adverb)

WHY: He fled *because he was wanted for murder*. (adverbial clause)

WHEN: The army will flee *when it meets the enemy*. (adverbial clause)

WHERE: He fled *into the forest*. (adverbial phrase)

to fling (active voice)　　　　*Principal Parts:* fling, flinging, flung, flung

Infinitive: to fling　　　　　　　　　　*Present Participle:* flinging
Perfect Infinitive: to have flung　　　　　*Past Participle:* flung

INDICATIVE MOOD

Pres.	I fling	we fling
	you fling	you fling
	he (she, it) flings	they fling
Pres.	I am flinging	we are flinging
Prog.	you are flinging	you are flinging
	he (she, it) is flinging	they are flinging
Pres.	I do fling	we do fling
Int.	you do fling	you do fling
	he (she, it) does fling	they do fling
Fut.	I shall fling	we shall fling
	you will fling	you will fling
	he (she, it) will fling	they will fling
Fut.	I will fling *(P)*	we will fling *(P)*
	you shall fling *(C)*	you shall fling *(C)*
	he (she, it) shall fling *(C)*	they shall fling *(C)*
Past	I flung	we flung
	you flung	you flung
	he (she, it) flung	they flung
Past	I was flinging	we were flinging
Prog.	you were flinging	you were flinging
	he (she, it) was flinging	they were flinging
Past	I did fling	we did fling
Int.	you did fling	you did fling
	he (she, it) did fling	they did fling
Pres.	I have flung	we have flung
Perf.	you have flung	you have flung
	he (she, it) has flung	they have flung
Past	I had flung	we had flung
Perf.	you had flung	you had flung
	he (she, it) had flung	they had flung
Fut.	I shall have flung	we shall have flung
Perf.	you will have flung	you will have flung
	he (she, it) will have flung	they will have flung

IMPERATIVE MOOD
fling

SUBJUNCTIVE MOOD

Pres.	if I fling	if we fling
	if you fling	if you fling
	if he (she, it) fling	if they fling
Past	if I flung	if we flung
	if you flung	if you flung
	if he (she, it) flung	if they flung
Fut.	if I should fling	if we should fling
	if you should fling	if you should fling
	if he (she, it) should fling	if they should fling

Infinitive: to be flung   *Present Participle:* being flung
Perfect Infinitive: to have been flung   *Past Participle:* been flung

INDICATIVE MOOD

Pres.	I am flung
	you are flung
	he (she, it) is flung

we are flung
you are flung
they are flung

Pres. Prog.	I am being flung
	you are being flung
	he (she, it) is being flung

we are being flung
you are being flung
they are being flung

Pres.
Int.
I do get flung
you do get flung
he (she, it) does get flung

we do get flung
you do get flung
they do get flung

Fut.
I shall be flung
you will be flung
he (she, it) will be flung

we shall be flung
you will be flung
they will be flung

Fut.
I will be flung *(P)*
you shall be flung *(C)*
he (she, it) shall be flung *(C)*

we will be flung *(P)*
you shall be flung *(C)*
they shall be flung *(C)*

Past
I was flung
you were flung
he (she, it) was flung

we were flung
you were flung
they were flung

Past
Prog.
I was being flung
you were being flung
he (she, it) was being flung

we were being flung
you were being flung
they were being flung

Past
Int.
I did get flung
you did get flung
he (she, it) did get flung

we did get flung
you did get flung
they did get flung

Pres.
Perf.
I have been flung
you have been flung
he (she, it) has been flung

we have been flung
you have been flung
they have been flung

Past
Perf.
I had been flung
you had been flung
he (she, it) had been flung

we had been flung
you had been flung
they had been flung

Fut.
Perf.
I shall have been flung
you will have been flung
he (she, it) will have been flung

we shall have been flung
you will have been flung
they will have been flung

IMPERATIVE MOOD
be flung

SUBJUNCTIVE MOOD

Pres.
if I be flung
if you be flung
if he (she, it) be flung

if we be flung
if you be flung
if they be flung

Past
if I were flung
if you were flung
if he (she, it) were flung

if we were flung
if you were flung
if they were flung

Fut.
if I should be flung
if you should be flung
if he (she, it) should be flung

if we should be flung
if you should be flung
if they should be flung

to fly (active voice)   *Principal Parts:* fly, flying, flew, flown

Infinitive: to fly   *Present Participle:* flying
Perfect Infinitive: to have flown   *Past Participle:* flown

INDICATIVE MOOD

Pres.	I fly	we fly
	you fly	you fly
	he (she, it) flies	they fly
Pres.	I am flying	we are flying
Prog.	you are flying	you are flying
	he (she, it) is flying	they are flying
Pres.	I do fly	we do fly
Int.	you do fly	you do fly
	he (she, it) does fly	they do fly
Fut.	I shall fly	we shall fly
	you will fly	you will fly
	he (she, it) will fly	they will fly
Fut.	I will fly *(P)*	we will fly *(P)*
	you shall fly *(C)*	you shall fly *(C)*
	he (she, it) shall fly *(C)*	they shall fly *(C)*
Past	I flew	we flew
	you flew	you flew
	he (she, it) flew	they flew
Past	I was flying	we were flying
Prog.	you were flying	you were flying
	he (she, it) was flying	they were flying
Past	I did fly	we did fly
Int.	you did fly	you did fly
	he (she, it) did fly	they did fly
Pres.	I have flown	we have flown
Perf.	you have flown	you have flown
	he (she, it) has flown	they have flown
Past	I had flown	we had flown
Perf.	you had flown	you had flown
	he (she, it) had flown	they had flown
Fut.	I shall have flown	we shall have flown
Perf.	you will have flown	you will have flown
	he (she, it) will have flown	they will have flown

IMPERATIVE MOOD
fly

SUBJUNCTIVE MOOD

Pres.	if I fly	if we fly
	if you fly	if you fly
	if he (she, it) fly	if they fly
Past	if I flew	if we flew
	if you flew	if you flew
	if he (she, it) flew	if they flew
Fut.	if I should fly	if we should fly
	if you should fly	if you should fly
	if he (she, it) should fly	if they should fly

(passive voice)

Infinitive: to be flown   *Present Participle:* being flown
Perfect Infinitive: to have been flown   *Past Participle:* been flown

INDICATIVE MOOD

Pres.	I am flown	we are flown
	you are flown	you are flown
	he (she, it) is flown	they are flown
Pres. Prog.	I am being flown	we are being flown
	you are being flown	you are being flown
	he (she, it) is being flown	they are being flown
Pres. Int.	I do get flown	we do get flown
	you do get flown	you do get flown
	he (she, it) does get flown	they do get flown
Fut.	I shall be flown	we shall be flown
	you will be flown	you will be flown
	he (she, it) will be flown	they will be flown
Fut.	I will be flown *(P)*	we will be flown *(P)*
	you shall be flown *(C)*	you shall be flown *(C)*
	he (she, it) shall be flown *(C)*	they shall be flown *(C)*
Past	I was flown	we were flown
	you were flown	you were flown
	he (she, it) was flown	they were flown
Past Prog.	I was being flown	we were being flown
	you were being flown	you were being flown
	he (she, it) was being flown	they were being flown
Past Int.	I did get flown	we did get flown
	you did get flown	you did get flown
	he (she, it) did get flown	they did get flown
Pres. Perf.	I have been flown	we have been flown
	you have been flown	you have been flown
	he (she, it) has been flown	they have been flown
Past Perf.	I had been flown	we had been flown
	you had been flown	you had been flown
	he (she, it) had been flown	they had been flown
Fut. Perf.	I shall have been flown	we shall have been flown
	you will have been flown	you will have been flown
	he (she, it) will have been flown	they will have been flown

IMPERATIVE MOOD
be flown

SUBJUNCTIVE MOOD

Pres.	if I be flown	if we be flown
	if you be flown	if you be flown
	if he (she, it) be flown	if they be flown
Past	if I were flown	if we were flown
	if you were flown	if you were flown
	if he (she, it) were flown	if they were flown
Fut.	if I should be flown	if we should be flown
	if you should be flown	if you should be flown
	if he (she, it) should be flown	if they should be flown

to forbid (active voice) *Principal Parts:* forbid, forbidding, forbade (forbad), forbidden

Infinitive: to forbid *Present Participle:* forbidding
Perfect Infinitive: to have forbidden *Past Participle:* forbidden

INDICATIVE MOOD

Pres.	I forbid	we forbid
	you forbid	you forbid
	he (she, it) forbids	they forbid
Pres.	I am forbidding	we are forbidding
Prog.	you are forbidding	you are forbidding
	he (she, it) is forbidding	they are forbidding
Pres.	I do forbid	we do forbid
Int.	you do forbid	you do forbid
	he (she, it) does forbid	they do forbid
Fut.	I shall forbid	we shall forbid
	you will forbid	you will forbid
	he (she, it) will forbid	they will forbid
Fut.	I will forbid *(P)*	we will forbid *(P)*
	you shall forbid *(C)*	you shall forbid *(C)*
	he (she, it) shall forbid *(C)*	they shall forbid *(C)*
Past	I forbade, forbad	we forbade, forbad
	you forbade, forbad	you forbade, forbad
	he (she, it) forbade, forbad	they forbade, forbad
Past	I was forbidding	we were forbidding
Prog.	you were forbidding	you were forbidding
	he (she, it) was forbidding	they were forbidding
Past	I did forbid	we did forbid
Int.	you did forbid	you did forbid
	he (she, it) did forbid	they did forbid
Pres.	I have forbidden	we have forbidden
Perf.	you have forbidden	you have forbidden
	he (she, it) has forbidden	they have forbidden
Past	I had forbidden	we had forbidden
Perf.	you had forbidden	you had forbidden
	he (she, it) had forbidden	they had forbidden
Fut.	I shall have forbidden	we shall have forbidden
Perf.	you will have forbidden	you will have forbidden
	he (she, it) will have forbidden	they will have forbidden

IMPERATIVE MOOD
forbid

SUBJUNCTIVE MOOD

Pres.	if I forbid	if we forbid
	if you forbid	if you forbid
	if he (she, it) forbid	if they forbid
Past	if I forbade, forbad	if we forbade, forbad
	if you forbade, forbad	if you forbade, forbad
	if he (she, it) forbade, forbad	if they forbade, forbad
Fut.	if I should forbid	if we should forbid
	if you should forbid	if you should forbid
	if he (she, it) should forbid	if they should forbid

(passive voice)

Infinitive: to be forbidden   *Present Participle:* being forbidden
Perfect Infinitive: to have been forbidden   *Past Participle:* been forbidden

INDICATIVE MOOD

Pres.	I am forbidden	we are forbidden
	you are forbidden	you are forbidden
	he (she, it) is forbidden	they are forbidden
Pres. Prog.	I am being forbidden	we are being forbidden
	you are being forbidden	you are being forbidden
	he (she, it) is being forbidden	they are being forbidden
Pres. Int.	I do get forbidden	we do get forbidden
	you do get forbidden	you do get forbidden
	he (she, it) does get forbidden	they do get forbidden
Fut.	I shall be forbidden	we shall be forbidden
	you will be forbidden	you will be forbidden
	he (she, it) will be forbidden	they will be forbidden
Fut.	I will be forbidden *(P)*	we will be forbidden *(P)*
	you shall be forbidden *(C)*	you shall be forbidden *(C)*
	he (she, it) shall be forbidden *(C)*	they shall be forbidden *(C)*
Past	I was forbidden	we were forbidden
	you were forbidden	you were forbidden
	he (she, it) was forbidden	they were forbidden
Past Prog.	I was being forbidden	we were being forbidden
	you were being forbidden	you were being forbidden
	he (she, it) was being forbidden	they were being forbidden
Past Int.	I did get forbidden	we did get forbidden
	you did get forbidden	you did get forbidden
	he (she, it) did get forbidden	they did get forbidden
Pres. Perf.	I have been forbidden	we have been forbidden
	you have been forbidden	you have been forbidden
	he (she, it) has been forbidden	they have been forbidden
Past Perf.	I had been forbidden	we had been forbidden
	you had been forbidden	you had been forbidden
	he (she, it) had been forbidden	they had been forbidden
Fut. Perf.	I shall have been forbidden	we shall have been forbidden
	you will have been forbidden	you will have been forbidden
	he (she, it) will have been forbidden	they will have been forbidden

IMPERATIVE MOOD
be forbidden

SUBJUNCTIVE MOOD

Pres.	if I be forbidden	if we be forbidden
	if you be forbidden	if you be forbidden
	if he (she, it) be forbidden	if they be forbidden
Past	if I were forbidden	if we were forbidden
	if you were forbidden	if you were forbidden
	if he (she, it) were forbidden	if they were forbidden
Fut.	if I should be forbidden	if we should be forbidden
	if you should be forbidden	if you should be forbidden
	if he (she, it) should be forbidden	if they should be forbidden

to forget (active voice)

Principal Parts: forget, forgetting, forgot, forgotten (forgot)

Infinitive: to forget
Perfect Infinitive: to have forgotten

Present Participle: forgetting
Past Participle: forgotten, forgot

INDICATIVE MOOD

Pres. I forget	we forget
you forget	you forget
he (she, it) forgets	they forget
Pres. I am forgetting	we are forgetting
Prog. you are forgetting	you are forgetting
he (she, it) is forgetting	they are forgetting
Pres. I do forget	we do forget
Int. you do forget	you do forget
he (she, it) does forget	they do forget
Fut. I shall forget	we shall forget
you will forget	you will forget
he (she, it) will forget	they will forget
Fut. I will forget *(P)*	we will forget *(P)*
you shall forget *(C)*	you shall forget *(C)*
he (she, it) shall forget *(C)*	they shall forget *(C)*
Past I forgot	we forgot
you forgot	you forgot
he (she, it) forgot	they forgot
Past I was forgetting	we were forgetting
Prog. you were forgetting	you were forgetting
he (she, it) was forgetting	they were forgetting
Past I did forget	we did forget
Int. you did forget	you did forget
he (she, it) did forget	they did forget
Pres. I have forgotten, forgot	we have forgotten, forgot
Perf. you have forgotten, forgot	you have forgotten, forgot
he (she, it) has forgotten, forgot	they have forgotten, forgot
Past I had forgotten, forgot	we had forgotten, forgot
Perf. you had forgotten, forgot	you had forgotten, forgot
he (she, it) had forgotten, forgot	they had forgotten, forgot
Fut. I shall have forgotten, forgot	we shall have forgotten, forgot
Perf. you will have forgotten, forgot	you will have forgotten, forgot
he (she, it) will have forgotten, forgot	they will have forgotten, forgot

IMPERATIVE MOOD
forget

SUBJUNCTIVE MOOD

Pres. if I forget	if we forget
if you forget	if you forget
if he (she, it) forget	if they forget
Past if I forgot	if we forgot
if you forgot	if you forgot
if he (she, it) forgot	if they forgot
Fut. if I should forget	if we should forget
if you should forget	if you should forget
if he (she, it) should forget	if they should forget

(passive voice)

Infinitive: to be forgotten
Perfect Infinitive: to have been forgotten
Present Participle: being forgotten
Past Participle: been forgotten

INDICATIVE MOOD

Pres.	I am forgotten, forgot you are forgotten, forgot he (she, it) is forgotten, forgot	we are forgotten, forgot you are forgotten, forgot they are forgotten, forgot
Pres. Prog.	I am being forgotten, forgot you are being forgotten, forgot he (she, it) is being forgotten, forgot	we are being forgotten, forgot you are being forgotten, forgot they are being forgotten, forgot
Pres. Int.	I do get forgotten, forgot you do get forgotten, forgot he (she, it) does get forgotten, forgot	we do get forgotten, forgot you do get forgotten, forgot they do get forgotten, forgot
Fut.	I shall be forgotten, forgot you will be forgotten, forgot he (she, it) will be forgotten, forgot	we shall be forgotten, forgot you will be forgotten, forgot they will be forgotten, forgot
Fut.	I will be forgotten, forgot *(P)* you shall be forgotten, forgot *(C)* he (she, it) shall be forgotten, forgot *(C)*	we will be forgotten, forgot *(P)* you shall be forgotten, forgot *(C)* they shall be forgotten, forgot *(C)*
Past	I was forgotten, forgot you were forgotten, forgot he (she, it) was forgotten, forgot	we were forgotten, forgot you were forgotten, forgot they were forgotten, forgot
Past Prog.	I was being forgotten, forgot you were being forgotten, forgot he (she, it) was being forgotten, forgot	we were being forgotten, forgot you were being forgotten, forgot they were being forgotten, forgot
Past Int.	I did get forgotten, forgot you did get forgotten, forgot he (she, it) did get forgotten, forgot	we did get forgotten, forgot you did get forgotten, forgot they did get forgotten, forgot
Pres. Perf.	I have been forgotten, forgot you have been forgotten, forgot he (she, it) has been forgotten, forgot	we have been forgotten, forgot you have been forgotten, forgot they have been forgotten, forgot
Past Perf.	I had been forgotten, forgot you had been forgotten, forgot he (she, it) had been forgotten, forgot	we had been forgotten, forgot you had been forgotten, forgot they have been forgotten, forgot
Fut. Perf.	I shall have been forgotten, forgot you will have been forgotten, forgot he (she, it) will have been forgotten, forgot	we shall have been forgotten, forgot you will have been forgotten, forgot they will have been forgotten, forgot

IMPERATIVE MOOD
be forgotten

SUBJUNCTIVE MOOD

Pres.   if I be forgotten, forgot   if we be forgotten, forgot
if you be forgotten, forgot   if you be forgotten, forgot
if he (she, it) be forgotten, forgot   if they be forgotten, forgot

Past   if I were forgotten, forgot   if we were forgotten, forgot
if you were forgotten, forgot   if you were forgotten, forgot
if he (she, it) were forgotten, forgot   if they were forgotten, forgot

Fut.   if I should be forgotten, forgot   if we should be forgotten, forgot
if you should be forgotten, forgot   if you should be forgotten, forgot
if he (she, it) should be forgotten,   if they should be forgotten,
    forgot   forgot

Typical Verb Usages

The verb *to forget* offers convenient illustrations of the many shades of meaning made possible by the different voices, moods, and tenses of English verbs.

Active Voice

Present: I *forget* nearly everything I learn.

Present Progressive: She *is* always *forgetting* to bring her notebook.

Present Intensive: You certainly *do forget* a great deal.

Future: You *will* probably *forget* me before long.

Future (Promise): I *will* never *forget* you.

Future (Command): The observers of this crime *shall forget* what they have seen or they will live to regret it.

Past: John *forgot* to lock the door.

Past Progressive: The children *were* always *forgetting* to drink their milk.

Past Intensive: They really *did forget* to drink their milk.

Present Perfect: The old man *has forgotten* his childhood.

Past Perfect: I *had forgotten* that I promised to meet you.

Future Perfect: When winter comes, I *shall have forgotten* our summer vacation.

SUBJUNCTIVE MOOD

Present: *If* I *forget* to meet you, go without me.

Past: *If* they *forgot* their tickets, they weren't able to hear the concert.

Future: *If* I *should forget* to leave a key, go to my neighbor's house.

Passive voice

Present: Telephone numbers *are* easily *forgotten*.

Present Progressive: I *am being forgotten* by all my friends.

Present Intensive: Your directions really *do get forgotten* easily.

Future: The words of the song *will be forgotten* very quickly.

Future (Promise): I will so live that I *will* not *be forgotten*.

Future (Command): Your bad habits *shall be forgotten*!

Past: The novel *was forgotten* by most people.

Past Progressive: The lessons *were being forgotten* almost as quickly as they were learned.

Past Intensive: You *did* not *get forgotten* after all.

Past Perfect: All the old times *have been forgotten*.

Future Perfect: When you have reached my age, your youth *will have been forgotten*.

SUBJUNCTIVE MOOD

Present: *If* his words *be forgotten*, he will have spoken in vain.

Past: *If* you *were forgotten*, it was through no fault of mine.

Future: *If* the lesson *should be forgotten*, it can be easily learned again.

to forgive (active voice)   *Principal Parts:* forgive, forgiving,
                                                                    forgave, forgiven

---

Infinitive: to forgive   *Present Participle:* forgiving
Perfect Infinitive: to have forgiven   *Past Participle:* forgiven

INDICATIVE MOOD

Pres.	I forgive	we forgive
	you forgive	you forgive
	he (she, it) forgives	they forgive
Pres.	I am forgiving	we are forgiving
Prog.	you are forgiving	you are forgiving
	he (she, it) is forgiving	they are forgiving
Pres.	I do forgive	we do forgive
Int.	you do forgive	you do forgive
	he (she, it) does forgive	they do forgive
Fut.	I shall forgive	we shall forgive
	you will forgive	you will forgive
	he (she, it) will forgive	they will forgive
Fut.	I will forgive *(P)*	we will forgive *(P)*
	you shall forgive *(C)*	you shall forgive *(C)*
	he (she, it) shall forgive *(C)*	they shall forgive *(C)*
Past	I forgave	we forgave
	you forgave	you forgave
	he (she, it) forgave	they forgave
Past	I was forgiving	we were forgiving
Prog.	you were forgiving	you were forgiving
	he (she, it) was forgiving	they were forgiving
Past	I did forgive	we did forgive
Int.	you did forgive	you did forgive
	he (she, it) did forgive	they did forgive
Pres.	I have forgiven	we have forgiven
Perf.	you have forgiven	you have forgiven
	he (she, it) has forgiven	they have forgiven
Past	I had forgiven	we had forgiven
Perf.	you had forgiven	you had forgiven
	he (she, it) had forgiven	they had forgiven
Fut.	I shall have forgiven	we shall have forgiven
Perf.	you will have forgiven	you will have forgiven
	he (she, it) will have forgiven	they will have forgiven

IMPERATIVE MOOD
forgive

SUBJUNCTIVE MOOD

Pres.	if I forgive	if we forgive
	if you forgive	if you forgive
	if he (she, it) forgive	if they forgive
Past	if I forgave	if we forgave
	if you forgave	if you forgave
	if he (she, it) forgave	if they forgave
Fut.	if I should forgive	if we should forgive
	if you should forgive	if you should forgive
	if he (she, it) should forgive	if they should forgive

186

Infinitive: to be forgiven   *Present Participle:* being forgiven
Perfect Infinitive: to have been forgiven   *Past Participle:* been forgiven

INDICATIVE MOOD

Pres.	I am forgiven you are forgiven he (she, it) is forgiven	we are forgiven you are forgiven they are forgiven
Pres. *Prog.*	I am being forgiven you are being forgiven he (she, it) is being forgiven	we are being forgiven you are being forgiven they are being forgiven
Pres. *Int.*	I do get forgiven you do get forgiven he (she, it) does get forgiven	we do get forgiven you do get forgiven they do get forgiven
Fut.	I shall be forgiven you will be forgiven he (she, it) will be forgiven	we shall be forgiven you will be forgiven they will be forgiven
Fut.	I will be forgiven *(P)* you shall be forgiven *(C)* he (she, it) shall be forgiven *(C)*	we will be forgiven *(P)* you shall be forgiven *(C)* they shall be forgiven *(C)*
Past	I was forgiven you were forgiven he (she, it) was forgiven	we were forgiven you were forgiven they were forgiven
Past *Prog.*	I was being forgiven you were being forgiven he (she, it) was being forgiven	we were being forgiven you were being forgiven they were being forgiven
Past *Int.*	I did get forgiven you did get forgiven he (she, it) did get forgiven	we did get forgiven you did get forgiven they did get forgiven
Pres. *Perf.*	I have been forgiven you have been forgiven he (she, it) has been forgiven	we have been forgiven you have been forgiven they have been forgiven
Past *Perf.*	I had been forgiven you had been forgiven he (she, it) had been forgiven	we had been forgiven you had been forgiven they had been forgiven
Fut. *Perf.*	I shall have been forgiven you will have been forgiven he (she, it) will have been forgiven	we shall have been forgiven you will have been forgiven they will have been forgiven

IMPERATIVE MOOD
be forgiven

SUBJUNCTIVE MOOD

Pres.	if I be forgiven if you be forgiven if he (she, it) be forgiven	if we be forgiven if you be forgiven if they be forgiven
Past	if I were forgiven if you were forgiven if he (she, it) were forgiven	if we were forgiven if you were forgiven if they were forgiven
Fut.	if I should be forgiven if you should be forgiven if he (she, it) should be forgiven	if we should be forgiven if you should be forgiven if they should be forgiven

to forsake (active voice)   *Principal Parts:* forsake, forsaking, forsook,   forsaken

Infinitive: to forsake   *Present Participle:* forsaking
Perfect Infinitive: to have forsaken   *Past Participle:* forsaken

INDICATIVE MOOD

Pres.	I forsake	we forsake
	you forsake	you forsake
	he (she, it) forsakes	they forsake

Pres.	I am forsaking	we are forsaking
Prog.	you are forsaking	you are forsaking
	he (she, it) is forsaking	they are forsaking

Pres.	I do forsake	we do forsake
Int.	you do forsake	you do forsake
	he (she, it) does forsake	they do forsake

Fut.	I shall forsake	we shall forsake
	you will forsake	you will forsake
	he (she, it) will forsake	they will forsake

Fut.	I will forsake *(P)*	we will forsake *(P)*
	you shall forsake *(C)*	you shall forsake *(C)*
	he (she, it) shall forsake *(C)*	they shall forsake *(C)*

Past	I forsook	we forsook
	you forsook	you forsook
	he (she, it) forsook	they forsook

Past	I was forsaking	we were forsaking
Prog.	you were forsaking	you were forsaking
	he (she, it) was forsaking	they were forsaking

Past	I did forsake	we did forsake
Int.	you did forsake	you did forsake
	he (she, it) did forsake	they did forsake

Pres.	I have forsaken	we have forsaken
Perf.	you have forsaken	you have forsaken
	he (she, it) has forsaken	they have forsaken

Past	I had forsaken	we had forsaken
Perf.	you had forsaken	you had forsaken
	he (she, it) had forsaken	they had forsaken

Fut.	I shall have forsaken	we shall have forsaken
Perf.	you will have forsaken	you will have forsaken
	he (she, it) will have forsaken	they will have forsaken

IMPERATIVE MOOD
forsake

SUBJUNCTIVE MOOD

Pres.	if I forsake	if we forsake
	if you forsake	if you forsake
	if he (she, it) forsake	if they forsake

Past	if I forsook	if we forsook
	if you forsook	if you forsook
	if he (she, it) forsook	if they forsook

Fut.	if I should forsake	if we should forsake
	if you should forsake	if you should forsake
	if he (she, it) should forsake	if they should forsake

Infinitive: to be forsaken   *Present Participle:* being forsaken
Perfect Infinitive: to have been forsaken   *Past Participle:* been forsaken

INDICATIVE MOOD

Pres.	I am forsaken	we are forsaken
	You are forsaken	you are forsaken
	he (she, it) is forsaken	they are forsaken
Pres.	I am being forsaken	we are being forsaken
Prog.	You are being forsaken	you are being forsaken
	he (she, it) is being forsaken	they are being forsaken
Pres.	I do get forsaken	we do get forsaken
Int.	you do get forsaken	you do get forsaken
	he (she, it) does get forsaken	they do get forsaken
Fut.	I shall be forsaken	we shall be forsaken
	you will be forsaken	you will be forsaken
	he (she, it) will be forsaken	they will be forsaken
Fut.	I will be forsaken *(P)*	we will be forsaken *(P)*
	you shall be forsaken *(C)*	you shall be forsaken *(C)*
	he (she, it) shall be forsaken *(C)*	they shall be forsaken *(C)*
Past	I was forsaken	we were forsaken
	you were forsaken	you were forsaken
	he (she, it) was forsaken	they were forsaken
Past	I was being forsaken	we were being forsaken
Prog.	you were being forsaken	you were being forsaken
	he (she, it) was being forsaken	they were being forsaken
Past	I did get forsaken	we did get forsaken
Int.	you did get forsaken	you did get forsaken
	he (she, it) did get forsaken	they did get forsaken
Pres.	I have been forsaken	we have been forsaken
Perf.	you have been forsaken	you have been forsaken
	he (she, it) has been forsaken	they have been forsaken
Past	I had been forsaken	we had been forsaken
Perf.	you had been forsaken	you had been forsaken
	he (she, it) had been forsaken	they had been forsaken
Fut.	I shall have been forsaken	we shall have been forsaken
Perf.	you will have been forsaken	you will have been forsaken
	he (she, it) will have been forsaken	they will have been forsaken

IMPERATIVE MOOD
be forsaken

SUBJUNCTIVE MOOD

Pres.	if I be forsaken	if we be forsaken
	if you be forsaken	if you be forsaken
	if you were forsaken	if they be forsaken
Past	if I were forsaken	if we were forsaken
	if you were forsaken	if you were forsaken
	if he (she, it) were forsaken	if they were forsaken
Fut.	if I should be forsaken	if we should be forsaken
	if you should be forsaken	if you should be forsaken
	if he (she, it) should be forsaken	if they should be forsaken

to freeze (active voice)   *Principal Parts:* freeze, freezing, froze, frozen

Infinitive: to freeze   *Present Participle:* freezing
Perfect Infinitive: to have frozen   *Past Participle:* frozen

INDICATIVE MOOD

Pres.	I freeze	we freeze
	you freeze	you freeze
	he (she, it) freezes	they freeze
Pres.	I am freezing	we are freezing
Prog.	you are freezing	you are freezing
	he (she, it) is freezing	they are freezing
Pres.	I do freeze	we do freeze
Int.	you do freeze	you do freeze
	he (she, it) does freeze	they do freeze
Fut.	I shall freeze	we shall freeze
	you will freeze	you will freeze
	he (she, it) will freeze	they will freeze
Fut.	I will freeze *(P)*	we will freeze *(P)*
	you shall freeze *(C)*	you shall freeze *(C)*
	he (she, it) shall freeze *(C)*	they shall freeze *(C)*
Past	I froze	we froze
	you froze	you froze
	he (she, it) froze	they froze
Past	I was freezing	we were freezing
Prog.	you were freezing	you were freezing
	he (she, it) was freezing	they were freezing
Past	I did freeze	we did freeze
Int.	you did freeze	you did freeze
	he (she, it) did freeze	they did freeze
Pres.	I have frozen	we have frozen
Perf.	you have frozen	you have frozen
	he (she, it) has frozen	they have frozen
Past	I had frozen	we had frozen
Perf.	you had frozen	you had frozen
	he (she, it) had frozen	they had frozen
Fut.	I shall have frozen	we shall have frozen
Perf.	you will have frozen	you will have frozen
	he (she, it) will have frozen	they will have frozen

IMPERATIVE MOOD
freeze

SUBJUNCTIVE MOOD

Pres.	if I freeze	if we freeze
	if you freeze	if you freeze
	if he (she, it) freeze	if they freeze
Past	if I froze	if we froze
	if you froze	if you froze
	if he (she, it) froze	if they froze
Fut.	if I should freeze	if we should freeze
	if you should freeze	if you should freeze
	if he (she, it) should freeze	if they should freeze

Infinitive: to be frozen

Perfect Infinitive: to have been frozen

Present Participle: being frozen

Past Participle: been frozen

INDICATIVE MOOD

Pres.	I am frozen	we are frozen
	you are frozen	you are frozen
	he (she, it) is frozen	they are frozen
Pres.	I am being frozen	we are being frozen
Prog.	you are being frozen	you are being frozen
	he (she, it) is being frozen	they are being frozen
Pres.	I do get frozen	we do get frozen
Int.	you do get frozen	you do get frozen
	he (she, it) does get frozen	they do get frozen
Fut.	I shall be frozen	we shall be frozen
	you will be frozen	you will be frozen
	he (she, it) will be frozen	they will be frozen
Fut.	I will be frozen *(P)*	we will be frozen *(P)*
	you shall be frozen *(C)*	you shall be frozen *(C)*
	he (she, it) shall be frozen *(C)*	they shall be frozen *(C)*
Past	I was frozen	we were frozen
	you were frozen	you were frozen
	he (she, it) was frozen	they were frozen
Past	I was being frozen	we were being frozen
Prog.	you were being frozen	you were being frozen
	he (she, it) was being frozen	they were being frozen
Past	I did get frozen	we did get frozen
Int.	you did get frozen	you did get frozen
	he (she, it) did get frozen	they did get frozen
Pres.	I have been frozen	we have been frozen
Perf.	you have been frozen	you have been frozen
	he (she, it) has been frozen	they have been frozen
Past	I had been frozen	we had been frozen
Perf.	you had been frozen	you had been frozen
	he (she, it) had been frozen	they had been frozen
Fut.	I shall have been frozen	we shall have been frozen
Perf.	you will have been frozen	you will have been frozen
	he (she, it) will have been frozen	they will have been frozen

IMPERATIVE MOOD
be frozen

SUBJUNCTIVE MOOD

Pres.	if I be frozen	if we be frozen
	if you be frozen	if you be frozen
	if he (she, it) be frozen	if they be frozen
Past	if I were frozen	if we were frozen
	if you were frozen	if you were frozen
	if he (she, it) were frozen	if they were frozen
Fut.	if I should be frozen	if we should be frozen
	if you should be frozen	if you should be frozen
	if he (she, it) should be frozen	if they should be frozen

191

to get (active voice)

Principal Parts: get, getting, got, got (gotten)

Infinitive: to get
Perfect Infinitive: to have got, gotten

Present Participle: getting
Past Participle: got, gotten

INDICATIVE MOOD

Pres.	I get	we get
	you get	you get
	he (she, it) gets	they get
Pres. Prog.	I am getting	we are getting
	you are getting	you are getting
	he (she, it) is getting	they are getting
Pres. Int.	I do get	we do get
	you do get	you do get
	he (she, it) does get	they do get
Fut.	I shall get	we shall get
	you will get	you will get
	he (she, it) will get	they will get
Fut.	I will get *(P)*	we will get *(P)*
	you shall get *(C)*	you shall get *(C)*
	he (she, it) shall get *(C)*	they shall get *(C)*
Past	I got	we got
	you got	you got
	he (she, it) got	they got
Past Prog.	I was getting	we were getting
	you were getting	you were getting
	he (she, it) was getting	they were getting
Past Int.	I did get	we did get
	you did get	you did get
	he (she, it) did get	they did get
Pres. Perf.	I have got, gotten	we have got, gotten
	you have got, gotten	you have got, gotten
	he (she, it) has got, gotten	they have got, gotten
Past Perf.	I had got, gotten	we had got, gotten
	you had got, gotten	you had got, gotten
	he (she, it) had got, gotten	they had got, gotten
Fut. Perf.	I shall have got, gotten	we shall have got, gotten
	you will have got, gotten	you will have got, gotten
	he (she, it) will have got, gotten	they will have got, gotten

IMPERATIVE MOOD
get

SUBJUNCTIVE MOOD

Pres.	if I get	if we get
	if you get	if you get
	if he (she, it) get	if they get
Past	if I got	if we got
	if you got	if you got
	if he (she, it) got	if they got
Fut.	if I should get	if we should get
	if you should get	if you should get
	if he (she, it) should get	if they should get

Infinitive: to be gotten   *Present Participle:* being gotten
Perfect Infinitive: to have been gotten   *Past Participle:* been gotten

INDICATIVE MOOD

Pres.	I am gotten	we are gotten
	you are gotten	you are gotten
	he (she, it) is gotten	they are gotten
Pres.	I am being gotten	we are being gotten
Prog.	you are being gotten	you are being gotten
	he (she, it) is being gotten	they are being gotten
Pres.	I do get gotten	we do get gotten
Int.	you do get gotten	you do get gotten
	he (she, it) does get gotten	they do get gotten
Fut.	I shall be gotten	we shall be gotten
	you will be gotten	you will be gotten
	he (she, it) will be gotten	they will be gotten
Fut.	I will be gotten *(P)*	we will be gotten *(P)*
	you shall be gotten *(C)*	you shall be gotten *(C)*
	he (she, it) shall be gotten *(C)*	they shall be gotten *(C)*
Past	I was gotten	we were gotten
	you were gotten	you were gotten
	he (she, it) was gotten	they were gotten
Past	I was being gotten	we were being gotten
Prog.	you were being gotten	you were being gotten
	he (she, it) was being gotten	they were being gotten
Past	I did get gotten	we did get gotten
Int.	you did get gotten	you did get gotten
	he (she, it) did get gotten	they did get gotten
Pres.	I have been gotten	we have been gotten
Perf.	you have been gotten	you have been gotten
	he (she, it) has been gotten	they have been gotten
Past	I had been gotten	we had been gotten
Perf.	you had been gotten	you had been gotten
	he (she, it) had been gotten	they had been gotten
Fut.	I shall have been gotten	we shall have been gotten
Perf.	you will have been gotten	you will have been gotten
	he (she, it) will have been gotten	they will have been gotten

IMPERATIVE MOOD
be gotten

SUBJUNCTIVE MOOD

Pres.	if I be gotten	if we be gotten
	if you be gotten	if you be gotten
	if he (she, it) be gotten	if they be gotten
Past	if I were gotten	if we were gotten
	if you were gotten	if you were gotten
	if he (she, it) were gotten	if they were gotten
Fut.	if I should be gotten	if we should be gotten
	if you should be gotten	if you should be gotten
	if he (she, it) should be gotten	if they should be gotten

to give (active voice) *Principal Parts:* give, giving, gave, given

Infinitive: to give *Present Participle:* giving
Perfect Infinitive: to have given *Past Participle:* given

INDICATIVE MOOD

Pres.	I give	we give

Pres. I give
you give
he (she, it) gives

we give
you give
they give

Pres.
Prog. I am giving
you are giving
he (she, it) is giving

we are giving
you are giving
they are giving

Pres.
Int. I do give
you do give
he (she, it) does give

we do give
you do give
they do give

Fut. I shall give
you will give
he (she, it) will give

we shall give
you will give
they will give

Fut. I will give *(P)*
you shall give *(C)*
he (she, it) shall give *(C)*

we will give *(P)*
you shall give *(C)*
they shall give *(C)*

Past I gave
you gave
he (she, it) gave

we gave
you gave
they gave

Past
Prog. I was giving
you were giving
he (she, it) was giving

we were giving
you were giving
they were giving

Past
Int. I did give
you did give
he (she, it) did give

we did give
you did give
they did give

Pres.
Perf. I have given
you have given
he (she, it) has given

we have given
you have given
they have given

Past
Perf. I had given
you had given
he (she, it) had given

we had given
you had given
they had given

Fut.
Perf. I shall have given
you will have given
he (she, it) will have given

we shall have given
you will have given
they will have given

IMPERATIVE MOOD
give

SUBJUNCTIVE MOOD

Pres. if I give
if you give
if he (she, it) give

if we give
if you give
if they give

Past if I gave
if you gave
if he (she, it) gave

if we gave
if you gave
if they gave

Fut. if I should give
if you should give
if he (she, it) should give

if we should give
if you should give
if they should give

(passive voice)

Infinitive: to be given	*Present Participle:* being given
Perfect Infinitive: to have been given	*Past Participle:* been given

INDICATIVE MOOD

Pres.	I am given	we are given
	you are given	you are given
	he (she, it) is given	they are given
Pres.	I am being given	we are being given
Prog.	you are being given	you are being given
	he (she, it) is being given	they are being given
Pres.	I do get given	we do get given
Int.	you do get given	you do get given
	he (she, it) does get given	they do get given
Fut.	I shall be given	we shall be given
	you will be given	you will be given
	he (she, it) will be given	they will be given
Fut.	I will be given *(P)*	we will be given *(P)*
	you shall be given *(C)*	you shall be given *(C)*
	he (she, it) shall be given *(C)*	they shall be given *(C)*
Past	I was given	we were given
	you were given	you were given
	he (she, it) was given	they were given
Past	I was being given	we were being given
Prog.	you were being given	you were being given
	he (she, it) was being given	they were being given
Past	I did get given	we did get given
Int.	you did get given	you did get given
	he (she, it) did get given	they did get given
Pres.	I have been given	we have been given
Perf.	you have been given	you have been given
	he (she, it) has been given	they have been given
Past	I had been given	we had been given
Perf.	you had been given	you had been given
	he (she, it) had been given	they had been given
Fut.	I shall have been given	we shall have been given
Perf.	you will have been given	you will have been given
	he (she, it) will have been given	they will have been given

IMPERATIVE MOOD

be given

SUBJUNCTIVE MOOD

Pres.	if I be given	if we be given
	if you be given	if you be given
	if he (she, it) be given	if they be given
Past	if I were given	if we were given
	if you were given	if you were given
	if he (she, it) were given	if they were given
Fut.	if I should be given	if we should be given
	if you should be given	if you should be given
	if he (she, it) should be given	if they should be given

Infinitive: to go   *Present Participle:* going
Perfect Infinitive: to have gone   *Past Participle:* gone

INDICATIVE MOOD

Pres.	I go	we go
	you go	you go
	he (she, it) goes	they go
Pres. Prog.	I am going	we are going
	you are going	you are going
	he (she, it) is going	they are going
Pres. Int.	I do go	we do go
	you do go	you do go
	he (she, it) does go	they do go
Fut.	I shall go	we shall go
	you will go	you will go
	he (she, it) will go	they will go
Fut.	I will go *(P)*	we will go *(P)*
	you shall go *(C)*	you shall go *(C)*
	he (she, it) shall go *(C)*	they shall go *(C)*
Past	I went	we went
	you went	you went
	he (she, it) went	they went
Past Prog.	I was going	we were going
	you were going	you were going
	he (she, it) was going	they were going
Past Int.	I did go	we did go
	you did go	you did go
	he (she, it) did go	they did go
Pres. Perf.	I have gone	we have gone
	you have gone	you have gone
	he (she, it) has gone	they have gone
Past Perf.	I had gone	we had gone
	you had gone	you had gone
	he (she, it) had gone	they had gone
Fut. Perf.	I shall have gone	we shall have gone
	you will have gone	you will have gone
	he (she, it) will have gone	they will have gone

IMPERATIVE MOOD
go

SUBJUNCTIVE MOOD

Pres.	if I go	if we go
	if you go	if you go
	if he (she, it) go	if they go
Past	if I went	if we went
	if you went	if you went
	if he (she, it) went	if they went
Fut.	if I should go	if we should go
	if you should go	if you should go
	if he (she, it) should go	if they should go

To go is an intransitive verb.

It does not take an object.
It describes action, but the action is self-contained.
Like other intransitive verbs, it may be followed by adverbs, adverbial phrases and clauses describing the how, why, when, and where of the action:

HOW: They will go *slowly*. (adverb)

WHY: Mary went *to meet her mother*. (adverbial phrase)

WHEN: All the birds will have gone *when winter comes*. (adverbial clause)

WHERE: The evening sun goes *down*. (adverb)

to grow (active voice)   *Principal Parts:* grow, growing, grew, grown

Infinitive: to grow   *Present Participle:* growing
Perfect Infinitive: to have grown   *Past Participle:* grown

INDICATIVE MOOD

Pres.	I grow	we grow
	you grow	you grow
	he (she, it) grows	they grow
Pres.	I am growing	we are growing
Prog.	you are growing	you are growing
	he (she, it) is growing	they are growing
Pres.	I do grow	we do grow
Int.	you do grow	you do grow
	he (she, it) does grow	they do grow
Fut.	I shall grow	we shall grow
	you will grow	you will grow
	he (she, it) will grow	they will grow
Fut.	I will grow *(P)*	we will grow *(P)*
	you shall grow *(C)*	you shall grow *(C)*
	he (she, it) shall grow *(C)*	they shall grow *(C)*
Past	I grew	we grew
	you grew	you grew
	he (she, it) grew	they grew
Past	I was growing	we were growing
Prog.	you were growing	you were growing
	he (she, it) was growing	they were growing
Past	I did grow	we did grow
Int.	you did grow	you did grow
	he (she, it) did grow	they did grow
Pres.	I have grown	we have grown
Perf.	you have grown	you have grown
	he (she, it) has grown	they have grown
Past	I had grown	we had grown
Perf.	you had grown	you had grown
	he (she, it) had grown	they had grown
Fut.	I shall have grown	we shall have grown
Perf.	you will have grown	you will have grown
	he (she, it) will have grown	they will have grown

IMPERATIVE MOOD
grow

SUBJUNCTIVE MOOD

Pres.	if I grow	if we grow
	if you grow	if you grow
	if he (she, it) grow	if they grow
Past	if I grew	if we grew
	if you grew	if you grew
	if he (she, it) grew	if they grew
Fut.	if I should grow	if we should grow
	if you should grow	if you should grow
	if he (she, it) should grow	if they should grow

Infinitive: to be grown
Perfect Infinitive: to have been grown

Present Participle: being grown
Past Participle: been grown

INDICATIVE MOOD

Pres.	I am grown	we are grown
	you are grown	you are grown
	he (she, it) is grown	they are grown
Pres. Prog.	I am being grown	we are being grown
	you are being grown	you are being grown
	he (she, it) is being grown	they are being grown
Pres. Int.	I do get grown	we do get grown
	you do get grown	you do get grown
	he (she, it) does get grown	they do get grown
Fut.	I shall be grown	we shall be grown
	you will be grown	you will be grown
	he (she, it) will be grown	they will be grown
Fut.	I will be grown *(P)*	we will be grown *(P)*
	you shall be grown *(C)*	you shall be grown *(C)*
	he (she, it) shall be grown *(C)*	they shall be grown *(C)*
Past	I was grown	we were grown
	you were grown	you were grown
	he (she, it) was grown	they were grown
Past Prog.	I was being grown	we were being grown
	you were being grown	you were being grown
	he (she, it) was being grown	they were being grown
Past Int.	I did get grown	we did get grown
	you did get grown	you did get grown
	he (she, it) did get grown	they did get grown
Pres. Perf.	I have been grown	we have been grown
	you have been grown	you have been grown
	he (she, it) has been grown	they have been grown
Past Perf.	I had been grown	we had been grown
	you had been grown	you had been grown
	he (she, it) had been grown	they had been grown
Fut. Perf.	I shall have been grown	we shall have been grown
	you will have been grown	you will have been grown
	he (she, it) will have been grown	they will have been grown

IMPERATIVE MOOD
be grown

SUBJUNCTIVE MOOD

Pres.	if I be grown	if we be grown
	if you be grown	if you be grown
	if he (she, it) be grown	if they be grown
Past	if I were grown	if we were grown
	if you were grown	if you were grown
	if he (she, it) were grown	if they were grown
Fut.	if I should be grown	if we should be grown
	if you should be grown	if you should be grown
	if he (she, it) should be grown	if they should be grown

199

to hang (active voice)　　*Principal Parts:* hang, hanging, hung, hung
(to fasten to an elevated point)

Infinitive: to hang　　　　　　　　　　　*Present Participle:* hanging
Perfect Infinitive: to have hung　　　　　　　*Past Participle:* hung

INDICATIVE MOOD

Pres.	I hang	we hang
	you hang	you hang
	he (she, it) hangs	they hang
Pres.	I am hanging	we are hanging
Prog.	you are hanging	you are hanging
	he (she, it) is hanging	they are hanging
Pres.	I do hang	we do hang
Int.	you do hang	you do hang
	he (she, it) does hang	they do hang
Fut.	I shall hang	we shall hang
	you will hang	you will hang
	he (she, it) will hang	they will hang
Fut.	I will hang *(P)*	we will hang *(P)*
	you shall hang *(C)*	you shall hang *(C)*
	he (she, it) shall hang *(C)*	they shall hang *(C)*
Past	I hung	we hung
	you hung	you hung
	he (she, it) hung	they hung
Past	I was hanging	we were hanging
Prog.	you were hanging	you were hanging
	he (she, it) was hanging	they were hanging
Past	I did hang	we did hang
Int.	you did hang	you did hang
	he (she, it) did hang	they did hang
Pres.	I have hung	we have hung
Perf.	you have hung	you have hung
	he (she, it) has hung	they have hung
Past	I had hung	we had hung
Perf.	you had hung	you had hung
	he (she, it) had hung	they had hung
Fut.	I shall have hung	we shall have hung
Perf.	you will have hung	you will have hung
	he (she, it) will have hung	they will have hung

IMPERATIVE MOOD
hang

SUBJUNCTIVE MOOD

Pres.	if I hang	if we hang
	if you hang	if you hang
	if he (she, it) hang	if they hang
Past	if I hung	if we hung
	if you hung	if you hung
	if he (she, it) hung	if they hung
Fut.	if I should hang	if we should hang
	if you should hang	if you should hang
	if he (she, it) should hang	if they should hang

(passive voice)

Infinitive: to be hung   *Present Participle:* to be hung
Perfect Infinitive: to have been hung   *Past Participle:* been hung

INDICATIVE MOOD

Pres.	I am hung	we are hung
	you are hung	you are hung
	he (she, it) is hung	they are hung
Pres. Prog.	I am being hung	we are being hung
	you are being hung	you are being hung
	he (she, it) is being hung	they are being hung
Pres. Int.	I do get hung	we do get hung
	you do get hung	you do get hung
	he (she, it) does get hung	they do get hung
Fut.	I shall be hung	we shall be hung
	you will be hung	you will be hung
	he (she, it) will be hung	they will be hung
Fut.	I will be hung *(P)*	we will be hung *(P)*
	you shall be hung *(C)*	you shall be hung *(C)*
	he (she, it) shall be hung *(C)*	they shall be hung *(C)*
Past	I was hung	we were hung
	you were hung	you were hung
	he (she, it) was hung	they were hung
Past Prog.	I was being hung	we were being hung
	you were being hung	you were being hung
	he (she, it) was being hung	they were being hung
Past Int.	I did get hung	we did get hung
	you did get hung	you did get hung
	he (she, it) did get hung	they did get hung
Pres. Perf.	I have been hung	we have been hung
	you have been hung	you have been hung
	he (she, it) has been hung	they have been hung
Past Perf.	I had been hung	we had been hung
	you had been hung	you had been hung
	he (she, it) had been hung	they had been hung
Fut. Perf.	I shall have been hung	we shall have been hung
	you will have been hung	you will have been hung
	he (she, it) will have been hung	they will have been hung

IMPERATIVE MOOD
be hung

SUBJUNCTIVE MOOD

Pres.	if I be hung	if we be hung
	if you be hung	if you be hung
	if he (she, it) be hung	if they be hung
Past	if I were hung	if we were hung
	if you were hung	if you were hung
	if he (she, it) were hung	if they were hung
Fut.	if I should be hung	if we should be hung
	if you should be hung	if you should be hung
	if he (she, it) should be hung	if they should be hung

to hang (active voice)   *Principal Parts:* hang, hanging, hanged,
                                                  hanged (executed)

Infinitive: to hang   *Present Participle:* hanging
Perfect Infinitive: to have hanged   *Past Participle:* hanged

INDICATIVE MOOD

Pres.	I hang	we hang
	you hang	you hang
	he (she, it) hang	they hang
Pres.	I am hanging	we are hanging
Prog.	you are hanging	you are hanging
	he (she, it) is hanging	they are hanging
Pres.	I do hang	we do hang
Int.	you do hang	you do hang
	he (she, it) does hang	they do hang
Fut.	I shall hang	we shall hang
	you will hang	you will hang
	he (she, it) will hang	they will hang
Fut.	I will hang *(P)*	we will hang *(P)*
	you shall hang *(C)*	you shall hang *(C)*
	he (she, it) shall hang *(C)*	they shall hang *(C)*
Past	I hanged	we hanged
	you hanged	you hanged
	he (she, it) hanged	they hanged
Past	I was hanging	we were hanging
Prog.	you were hanging	you were hanging
	he (she, it) was hanging	they were hanging
Past	I did hang	we did hang
Int.	you did hang	you did hang
	he (she, it) did hang	they did hang
Pres.	I have hanged	we have hanged
Perf.	you have hanged	you have hanged
	he (she, it) has hanged	they have hanged
Past	I had hanged	we had hanged
Perf.	you had hanged	you had hanged
	he (she, it) had hanged	they had hanged
Fut.	I shall have hanged	we shall have hanged
Perf.	you will have hanged	you will have hanged
	he (she, it) will have hanged	they will have hanged

IMPERATIVE MOOD
hang

SUBJUNCTIVE MOOD

Pres.	if I hang	if we hang
	if you hang	if you hang
	if he (she, it) hang	if they hang
Past	if I hanged	if we hanged
	if you hanged	if you hanged
	if he (she, it) hanged	if they hanged
Fut.	if I should hang	if we should hang
	if you should hang	if you should hang
	if he (she, it) should hang	if they should hang

Infinitive: to be hanged   *Present Participle:* being hanged
Perfect Infinitive: to have been hanged   *Past Participle:* been hanged

INDICATIVE MOOD

Pres.	I am hanged	we are hanged
	you are hanged	you are hanged
	he (she, it) is hanged	they are hanged
Pres.	I am being hanged	we are being hanged
Prog.	you are being hanged	you are being hanged
	he (she, it) is being hanged	they are being hanged
Pres.	I do get hanged	we do get hanged
Int.	you do get hanged	you do get hanged
	he (she, it) does get hanged	they do get hanged
Fut.	I shall be hanged	we shall be hanged
	you will be hanged	you will be hanged
	he (she, it) will be hanged	they will be hanged
Fut.	I will be hanged *(P)*	we will be hanged *(P)*
	you shall be hanged *(C)*	you shall be hanged *(C)*
	he (she, it) shall be hanged *(C)*	they shall be hanged *(C)*
Past	I was hanged	we were hanged
	you were hanged	you were hanged
	he (she, it) was hanged	they were hanged
Past	I was being hanged	we were being hanged
Prog.	you were being hanged	you were being hanged
	he (she, it) was being hanged	they were being hanged
Past	I did get hanged	we did get hanged
Int.	you did get hanged	you did get hanged
	he (she, it) did get hanged	they did get hanged
Pres.	I have been hanged	we have been hanged
Perf.	you have been hanged	you have been hanged
	he (she, it) has been hanged	they have been hanged
Past	I had been hanged	we had been hanged
Perf.	you had been hanged	you had been hanged
	he (she, it) had been hanged	they had been hanged
Fut.	I shall have been hanged	we shall have been hanged
Perf.	you will have been hanged	you will have been hanged
	he (she, it) will have been hanged	they will have been hanged

IMPERATIVE MOOD
be hanged

SUBJUNCTIVE MOOD

Pres.	if I be hanged	if we be hanged
	if you be hanged	if you be hanged
	if he (she, it) be hanged	if they be hanged
Past	if I were hanged	if we were hanged
	if you were hanged	if you were hanged
	if he (she, it) were hanged	if they were hanged
Fut.	if I should be hanged	if we should be hanged
	if you should be hanged	if you should be hanged
	if he (she, it) should be hanged	if they should be hanged

to have (active voice)   *Principal Parts:* have, having, had, had

---

Infinitive: to have   *Present Participle:* having
Perfect Infinitive: to have had   *Past Participle:* had

INDICATIVE MOOD

Pres.	I have	we have
	you have	you have
	he (she, it) has	they have
Pres.	I am having	we are having
Prog.	you are having	you are having
	he (she, it) is having	they are having
Pres.	I do have	we do have
Int.	you do have	you do have
	he (she, it) does have	they do have
Fut.	I shall have	we shall have
	you will have	you will have
	he (she, it) will have	they will have
Fut.	I will have *(P)*	we will have *(P)*
	you shall have *(C)*	you shall have *(C)*
	he (she, it) shall have *(C)*	they shall have *(C)*
Past	I had	we had
	you had	you had
	he (she, it) had	they had
Past	I was having	we were having
Prog.	you were having	you were having
	he (she, it) was having	they were having
Past	I did have	we did have
Int.	you did have	you did have
	he (she, it) did have	they did have
Pres.	I have had	we have had
Perf.	you have had	you have had
	he (she, it) has had	they have had
Past	I had had	we had had
Perf.	you had had	you had had
	he (she, it) had had	they had had
Fut.	I shall have had	you shall have had
Perf.	you will have had	you will have had
	he (she, it) will have had	they will have had

IMPERATIVE MOOD
have

SUBJUNCTIVE MOOD

Pres.	if I have	if we have
	if you have	if you have
	if he (she, it) have	if they have
Past	if I had	if we had
	if you had	if you had
	if he (she, it) had	if they had
Fut.	if I should have	if we should have
	if you should have	if you should have
	if he (she, it) should have	if they would have

Infinitive: to be had
Present Participle: being had

Perfect Infinitive: to have been had
Past Participle: been had

INDICATIVE MOOD

Pres.	I am had	we are had
	you are had	you are had
	he (she, it) is had	they are had

Pres. Prog.	I am being had	we are being had
	you are being had	you are being had
	he (she, it) is being had	they are being had

Pres. Int.	I do get had	we do get had
	you do get had	you do get had
	he (she, it) does get had	they do get had

Fut.	I shall be had	we shall be had
	you will be had	you will be had
	he (she, it) will be had	they will be had

Fut.	I will be had *(P)*	we will be had *(P)*
	you shall be had *(C)*	you shall be had *(C)*
	he (she, it) shall be had *(C)*	they shall be had *(C)*

Past	I was had	we were had
	you were had	you were had
	he (she, it) was had	they were had

Past Prog.	I was being had	we were being had
	you were being had	you were being had
	he (she, it) was being had	they were being had

Past Int.	I did get had	we did get had
	you did get had	you did get had
	he (she, it) did get had	they did get had

Pres. Perf.	I have been had	we have been had
	you have been had	you have been had
	he (she, it) has been had	they had been had

Past. Perf.	I had been had	we had been had
	you had been had	you had been had
	he (she, it) had been had	they had been had

Fut. Perf.	I shall have been had	we shall have been had
	you will have been had	you will have been had
	he (she, it) will have been had	they will have been had

IMPERATIVE MOOD
be had

SUBJUNCTIVE MOOD

Pres.	if I be had	if we be had
	if you be had	if you be had
	if he (she, it) be had	if they be had

Past	if I were had	if we were had
	if you were had	if you were had
	if he (she, it) were had	if they were had

Fut.	if I should be had	if we should be had
	if you should be had	if you should be had
	if he (she, it) should be had	if they should be had

to hear (active voice)   *Principal Parts:* hear, hearing, heard, heard

Infinitive: to hear   *Present Participle:* **hearing**
Perfect Infinitive: to have heard   *Past Participle:* **heard**

INDICATIVE MOOD

Pres.	I hear	we hear
	you hear	you hear
	he (she, it) hears	they hear
Pres.	I am hearing	we are hearing
Prog.	you are hearing	you are hearing
	he (she, it) is hearing	they are hearing
Pres.	I do hear	we do hear
Int.	you do hear	you do hear
	he (she, it) does hear	they do hear
Fut.	I shall hear	we shall hear
	you will hear	you will hear
	he (she, it) will hear	they will hear
Fut.	I will hear *(P)*	we will hear *(P)*
	you shall hear *(C)*	you shall hear *(C)*
	he (she, it) shall hear *(C)*	they shall hear *(C)*
Past	I heard	we heard
	you heard	you heard
	he (she, it) heard	they heard
Past	I was hearing	we were hearing
Prog.	you were hearing	you were hearing
	he (she, it) was hearing	they were hearing
Past	I did hear	we did hear
Int.	you did hear	you did hear
	he (she, it) did hear	they did hear
Pres.	I have heard	we have heard
Perf.	you have heard	you have heard
	he (she, it) has heard	they have heard
Past	I had heard	we had heard
Perf.	you had heard	you had heard
	he (she, it) had heard	they had heard
Fut.	I shall have heard	we shall have heard
Perf.	you will have heard	you will have heard
	he (she, it) will have heard	they will have heard

IMPERATIVE MOOD
hear

SUBJUNCTIVE MOOD

Pres.	if I hear	if we hear
	if you hear	if you hear
	if he (she, it) hear	if they hear
Past	if I heard	if we heard
	if you heard	if you heard
	if he (she, it) heard	if they heard
Fut.	if I should hear	if we should hear
	if you should hear	if you should hear
	if he (she, it) should hear	if they should hear

(passive voice)

Infinitive: **to be heard**   *Present Participle:* **being heard**
Perfect Infinitive: **to have been heard**   *Past Participle:* **been heard**

INDICATIVE MOOD

Pres.
I am heard / we are heard
you are heard / you are heard
he (she, it) is heard / they are heard

Pres. Prog.
I am being heard / we are being heard
you are being heard / you are being heard
he (she, it) is being heard / they are being heard

Pres. Int.
I do get heard / we do get heard
you do get heard / you do get heard
he (she, it) does get heard / they do get heard

Fut.
I shall be heard / we shall be heard
you will be heard / you will be heard
he (she, it) will be heard / they will be heard

Fut.
I will be heard *(P)* / we will be heard *(P)*
you shall be heard *(C)* / you shall be heard *(C)*
he (she, it) shall be heard *(C)* / they shall be heard *(C)*

Past
I was heard / we were heard
you were heard / you were heard
he (she, it) was heard / they were heard

Past Prog.
I was being heard / we were being heard
you were being heard / you were being heard
he (she, it) was being heard / they were being heard

Past Int.
I did get heard / we did get heard
you did get heard / you did get heard
he (she, it) did get heard / they did get heard

Pres. Perf.
I have been heard / we have been heard
you have been heard / you have been heard
he (she, it) has been heard / they have been heard

Past Perf.
I had been heard / we had been heard
you had been heard / you had been heard
he (she, it) had been heard / they had been heard

Fut. Perf.
I shall have been heard / we shall have been heard
you will have been heard / you will have been heard
he (she, it) will have been heard / they will have been heard

IMPERATIVE MOOD
be heard

SUBJUNCTIVE MOOD

Pres.
if I be heard / if we be heard
if you be heard / if you be heard
if he (she, it) be heard / if they be heard

Past
if I were heard / if we were heard
if you were heard / if you were heard
if he (she, it) were heard / if they were heard

Fut.
if I should be heard / if we should be heard
if you should be heard / if you should be heard
if he (she, it) should be heard / if they should be heard

to hit (active voice) *Principal Parts:* hit, hitting, hit, hit

Infinitive: to hit *Present Participle:* hitting
Perfect Infinitive: to have hit *Past Participle:* hit

INDICATIVE MOOD

Pres.	I hit	we hit
	you hit	you hit
	he (she, it) hits	they hit
Pres.	I am hitting	we are hitting
Prog.	you are hitting	you are hitting
	he (she, it) is hitting	they are hitting
Pres.	I do hit	we do hit
Int.	you do hit	you do hit
	he (she, it) does hit	they do hit
Fut.	I shall hit	we shall hit
	you will hit	you will hit
	he (she, it) will hit	they will hit
Fut.	I will hit *(P)*	we will hit *(P)*
	you shall hit *(C)*	you shall hit *(C)*
	he (she, it) shall hit *(C)*	they shall hit *(C)*
Past	I hit	we hit
	you hit	you hit
	he (she, it) hit	they hit
Past	I was hitting	we were hitting
Prog.	you were hitting	you were hitting
	he (she, it) was hitting	they were hitting
Past	I did hit	we did hit
Int.	you did hit	you did hit
	he (she, it) did hit	they did hit
Pres.	I have hit	we have hit
Perf.	you have hit	you have hit
	he (she, it) has hit	they have hit
Past.	I had hit	we had hit
Perf.	you had hit	you had hit
	he (she, it) had hit	they had hit
Fut.	I shall have hit	we shall have hit
Perf.	you will have hit	you will have hit
	he (she, it) will have hit	they will have hit

IMPERATIVE MOOD
hit

SUBJUNCTIVE MOOD

Pres.	if I hit	if we hit
	if you hit	if you hit
	if he (she, it) hit	if they hit
Past	if I hit	if we hit
	if you hit	if you hit
	if he (she, it) hit	if they hit
Fut.	if I should hit	if we should hit
	if you should hit	if you should hit
	if he (she, it) should hit	if they should hit

Infinitive: to be hit   *Present Participle:* being hit
Perfect Infinitive: to have been hit   *Past Participle:* been hit

INDICATIVE MOOD

Pres.	I am hit	we are hit
	you are hit	you are hit
	he (she, it) is hit	they are hit
Pres. Prog.	I am being hit	we are being hit
	you are being hit	you are being hit
	he (she, it) is being hit	they are being hit
Pres. Int.	I do get hit	we do get hit
	you do get hit	you do get hit
	he (she, it) does get hit	they do get hit
Fut.	I shall be hit	we shall be hit
	you will be hit	you will be hit
	he (she, it) will be hit	they will be hit
Fut.	I will be hit *(P)*	we will be hit *(P)*
	you shall be hit *(C)*	you shall be hit *(C)*
	he (she, it) shall be hit *(C)*	they shall be hit *(C)*
Past	I was hit	we were hit
	you were hit	you were hit
	he (she, it) was hit	they were hit
Past Prog.	I was being hit	we were being hit
	you were being hit	you were being hit
	he (she, it) was being hit	they were being hit
Past Int.	I did get hit	we did get hit
	you did get hit	you did get hit
	he (she, it) did get hit	they did get hit
Pres. Perf.	I have been hit	we have been hit
	you have been hit	you have been hit
	he (she, it) have been hit	they have been hit
Past Perf.	I had been hit	we had been hit
	you had been hit	you had been hit
	he (she, it) had been hit	they had been hit
Fut. Perf.	I shall have been hit	we shall have been hit
	you will have been hit	you will have been hit
	he (she, it) will have been hit	they will have been hit

IMPERATIVE MOOD
be hit

SUBJUNCTIVE MOOD

Pres.	if I be hit	if we be hit
	if you be hit	if you be hit
	if he (she, it) be hit	if they be hit
Past	if I were hit	if we were hit
	if you were hit	if you were hit
	if he (she, it) were hit	if they were hit
Fut.	if I should be hit	if we should be hit
	if you should be hit	if you should be hit
	if he (she, it) should be hit	if they should be hit

to hold (active voice)   *Principal Parts:* hold, holding, held, held

---

Infinitive: to hold   *Present Participle:* holding
Perfect Infinitive: to have held   *Past Participle:* held

INDICATIVE MOOD

Pres.	I hold	we hold
	you hold	you hold
	he (she, it) holds	they hold
Pres.	I am holding	we are holding
Prog.	you are holding	you are holding
	he (she, it) is holding	they are holding
Pres.	I do hold	we do hold
Int.	you do hold	you do hold
	he (she, it) does hold	they do hold
Fut.	I shall hold	we shall hold
	you will hold	you will hold
	he (she, it) will hold	they will hold
Fut.	I will hold *(P)*	we will hold *(P)*
	you shall hold *(C)*	you shall hold *(C)*
	he (she, it) shall hold *(C)*	they shall hold *(C)*
Past	I held	we held
	you held	you held
	he (she, it) held	they held
Past	I was holding	we were holding
Prog.	you were holding	you were holding
	he (she, it) was holding	they were holding
Past	I did hold	we did hold
Int.	you did hold	you did hold
	he (she, it) did hold	they did hold
Pres.	I have held	we have held
Perf.	you have held	you have held
	he (she, it) has held	they have held
Past	I had held	we had held
Perf.	you had held	you had held
	he (she, it) had held	they had held
Fut.	I shall have held	we shall have held
Perf.	you will have held	you will have held
	he (she, it) will have held	they will have held

IMPERATIVE MOOD
hold

SUBJUNCTIVE MOOD

Pres.	if I hold	if we hold
	if you hold	if you hold
	if he (she, it) hold	if they hold
Past	if I held	if we held
	if you held	if you held
	if he (she, it) held	if they held
Fut.	if I should hold	if we should hold
	if you should hold	if you should hold
	if he (she, it) should hold	if they should hold

(passive voice)

Infinitive: to be held   *Present Participle:* being held
Perfect Infinitive: to have been held   *Past Participle:* been held

INDICATIVE MOOD

Pres.	I am held	we are held
	you are held	you are held
	he (she, it) is held	they are held
Pres.	I am being held	we are being held
Prog.	you are being held	you are being held
	he (she, it) is being held	they are being held
Pres.	I do get held	we do get held
Int.	you do get held	you do get held
	he (she, it) does get held	they do get held
Fut.	I shall be held	we shall be held
	you will be held	you will be held
	he (she, it) will be held	they will be held
Fut.	I will be held *(P)*	we will be held *(P)*
	you shall be held *(C)*	you shall be held *(C)*
	he (she, it) shall be held *(C)*	they shall be held *(C)*
Past	I was held	we were held
	you were held	you were held
	he (she, it) was held	they were held
Past	I was being held	we were being held
Prog.	you were being held	you were being held
	he (she, it) was being held	they were being held
Past	I did get held	we did get held
Int.	you did get held	you did get held
	he (she, it) did get held	they did get held
Pres.	I have been held	we have been held
Perf.	you have been held	you have been held
	he (she, it) has been held	they have been held
Past	I had been held	we had been held
Perf.	you had been held	you had been held
	he (she, it) had been held	they had been held
Fut.	I shall have been held	we shall have been held
Perf.	you will have been held	you will have been held
	he (she, it) will have been held	they will have been held

IMPERATIVE MOOD
be held

SUBJUNCTIVE MOOD

Pres.	if I be held	if we be held
	if you be held	if you be held
	if he (she, it) be held	if they be held
Past	if I were held	if we were held
	if you were held	if you were held
	if he (she, it) were held	if they were held
Fut.	if I should be held	if we should be held
	if you should be held	if you should be held
	if he (she, it) should be held	if they should be held

to hurt (active voice)   *Principal Parts:* hurt, hurting, hurt, hurt

---

Infinitive: to hurt   *Present Participle:* hurting
Perfect Infinitive: to have hurt   *Past Participle:* hurt

INDICATIVE MOOD

Pres.	I hurt	we hurt
	you hurt	you hurt
	he (she, it) hurts	they hurt
Pres.	I am hurting	we are hurting
Prog.	you are hurting	you are hurting
	he (she, it) is hurting	they are hurting
Pres.	I do hurt	we do hurt
Int.	you do hurt	you do hurt
	he (she, it) does hurt	they do hurt
Fut.	I shall hurt	we shall hurt
	you will hurt	you will hurt
	he (she, it) will hurt	they will hurt
Fut.	I will hurt *(P)*	we will hurt *(P)*
	you shall hurt *(C)*	you shall hurt *(C)*
	he (she, it) shall hurt *(C)*	they shall hurt *(C)*
Past	I hurt	we hurt
	you hurt	you hurt
	he (she, it) hurt	they hurt
Past	I was hurting	we were hurting
Prog.	you were hurting	you were hurting
	he (she, it) was hurting	they were hurting
Past	I did hurt	we did hurt
Int.	you did hurt	you did hurt
	he (she, it) did hurt	they did hurt
Pres.	I have hurt	we have hurt
Perf.	you have hurt	you have hurt
	he (she, it) has hurt	they have hurt
Past.	I had hurt	we had hurt
Perf.	you had hurt	you had hurt
	he (she, it) has hurt	they had hurt
Fut.	I shall have hurt	we shall have hurt
Perf.	you will have hurt	you will have hurt
	he (she, it) will have hurt	they will have hurt

IMPERATIVE MOOD
hurt

SUBJUNCTIVE MOOD

Pres.	if I hurt	if we hurt
	if you hurt	if you hurt
	if he (she, it) hurt	if they hurt
Past	if I hurt	if we hurt
	if you hurt	if you hurt
	if he (she, it) hurt	if they hurt
Fut.	if I should hurt	if we should hurt
	if you should hurt	if you should hurt
	if he (she, it) should hurt	if they should hurt

Infinitive: to be hurt   *Present Participle:* being hurt
Perfect Infinitive: to have been hurt   *Past Participle:* been hurt

INDICATIVE MOOD

Pres.	I am hurt	we are hurt
	you are hurt	you are hurt
	he (she, it) is hurt	they are hurt
Pres. Prog.	I am being hurt	we are being hurt
	you are being hurt	you are being hurt
	he (she, it) is being hurt	they are being hurt
Pres. Int.	I do get hurt	we do get hurt
	you do get hurt	you do get hurt
	he (she, it) does get hurt	they do get hurt
Fut.	I shall be hurt	we shall be hurt
	you will be hurt	you will be hurt
	he (she, it) will be hurt	they will be hurt
Fut.	I will be hurt *(P)*	we will be hurt *(P)*
	you shall be hurt *(C)*	you shall be hurt *(C)*
	he (she, it) shall be hurt *(C)*	they shall be hurt *(C)*
Past	I was hurt	we were hurt
	you were hurt	you were hurt
	he (she, it) was hurt	they were hurt
Past Prog.	I was being hurt	we were being hurt
	you were being hurt	you were being hurt
	he (she, it) was being hurt	they were being hurt
Past Int.	I did get hurt	we did get hurt
	you did get hurt	you did get hurt
	he (she, it) did get hurt	they did get hurt
Pres. Perf.	I have been hurt	we have been hurt
	you have been hurt	you have been hurt
	he (she, it) has been hurt	they have been hurt
Past Perf.	I had been hurt	we had been hurt
	you had been hurt	you had been hurt
	he (she, it) had been hurt	they had been hurt
Fut. Perf.	I shall have been hurt	we shall have been hurt
	you will have been hurt	you will have been hurt
	he (she, it) will have been hurt	they will have been hurt

IMPERATIVE MOOD
be hurt

SUBJUNCTIVE MOOD

Pres.	if I be hurt	if we be hurt
	if you be hurt	if you be hurt
	if he (she, it) be hurt	if they be hurt
Past	if I were hurt	if we were hurt
	if you were hurt	if you were hurt
	if he (she, it) were hurt	if they were hurt
Fut.	if I should be hurt	if we should be hurt
	if you should be hurt	if you should be hurt
	if he (she, it) should be hurt	if they should be hurt

to kneel   *Principal Parts:* kneel, kneeling, knelt
                            (kneeled), knelt

Infinitive: to kneel   *Present Participle:* kneeling
Perfect Infinitive: to have knelt   *Past Participle:* knelt

INDICATIVE MOOD

Pres.	I kneel	we kneel
	you kneel	you kneel
	he (she, it) kneels	they kneel
Pres.	I am kneeling	we are kneeling
Prog.	you are kneeling	you are kneeling
	he (she, it) is kneeling	they are kneeling
Pres.	I do kneel	we do kneel
Int.	you do kneel	you do kneel
	he (she, it) does kneel	they do kneel
Fut.	I shall kneel	we shall kneel
	you will kneel	you will kneel
	he (she, it) will kneel	they will kneel
Fut.	I will kneel *(P)*	we will kneel *(P)*
	you shall kneel *(C)*	you shall kneel *(C)*
	he (she, it) shall kneel *(C)*	they shall kneel *(C)*
Past	I knelt, kneeled	we knelt, kneeled
	you knelt, kneeled	you knelt, kneeled
	he (she, it) knelt, kneeled	they knelt, kneeled
Past	I was kneeling	we were kneeling
Prog.	you were kneeling	you were kneeling
	he (she, it) was kneeling	they were kneeling
Past	I did kneel	we did kneel
Int.	you did kneel	you did kneel
	he (she, it) did kneel	they did kneel
Pres.	I have knelt	we have knelt
Perf.	you have knelt	you have knelt
	he (she, it) has knelt	they have knelt
Past	I had knelt	we had knelt
Perf.	you had knelt	you had knelt
	he (she, it) had knelt	they had knelt
Fut.	I shall have knelt	we shall have knelt
Perf.	you will have knelt	you will have knelt
	he (she, it) will have knelt	they will have knelt

IMPERATIVE MOOD
kneel

SUBJUNCTIVE MOOD

Pres.	if I kneel	if we kneel
	if you kneel	if you kneel
	if he (she, it) kneel	if they kneel
Past	if I knelt	if we knelt
	if you knelt	if you knelt
	if he (she, it) knelt	if they knelt
Fut.	if I should kneel	if we should kneel
	if you should kneel	if you should kneel
	if he (she, it) should kneel	if they should kneel

To kneel is an intransitive verb.

It does not take an object.

It describes action, but the action is self-contained.

Like other intransitive verbs, it may be followed by adverbs, adverbial phrases and clauses describing the how, why, when, and where of the action:

HOW: The congregation knelt *slowly*. (adverb)

WHY: The people will kneel *to pray*. (adverbial phrase)

WHEN: I *always* kneel *when I say my prayers*. (adverb and adverbial clause)

WHERE: The page knelt *in front of the king*. (adverbial phrase)

to know (active voice)

Infinitive: to know   *Present Participle:* knowing
Perfect Infinitive: to have known   *Past Participle:* known

INDICATIVE MOOD

Pres.	I know	we know
	you know	you know
	he (she, it) knows	they know

Pres. Int.	I do know	we do know
	you do know	you do know
	he (she, it) does know	they do know

Fut.	I shall know	we shall know
	you will know	you will know
	he (she, it) will know	they will know

Fut.	I will know *(P)*	we will know *(P)*
	you shall know *(C)*	you shall know *(C)*
	he (she, it) shall know *(C)*	they shall know *(C)*

Past	I knew	we knew
	you knew	you knew
	he (she, it) knew	they knew

Past Int.	I did know	we did know
	you did know	you did know
	he (she, it) did know	they did know

Pres. Perf.	I have known	we have known
	you have known	you have known
	he (she, it) has known	they have known

Past Perf.	I had known	we had known
	you had known	you had known
	he (she, it) had known	they had known

Fut. Perf.	I shall have known	we shall have known
	you will have known	you will have known
	he (she, it) will have known	they will have known

IMPERATIVE MOOD
know

SUBJUNCTIVE MOOD

Pres.	if I know	if we know
	if you know	if you know
	if he (she, it) know	if they know

Past	if I knew	if we knew
	if you knew	if you knew
	if he (she, it) knew	if they knew

Fut.	if I should know	if we should know
	if you should know	if you should know
	if he (she, it) should know	if they should know

Infinitive: to be known   *Present Participle:* being known
Perfect Infinitive: to have been known   *Past Participle:* been known

INDICATIVE MOOD

Pres.	I am known	we are known
	you are known	you are known
	he (she, it) is known	they are known
Pres.	I am being known	we are being known
	you are being known	you are being known
	he (she, it) is being known	they are being known
Pres.	I do get known	we do get known
Int.	you do get known	you do get known
	he (she, it) does get known	they do get known
Fut.	I shall be known	we shall be known
	you will be known	you will be known
	he (she, it) will be known	they will be known
Fut.	I will be known *(P)*	we will be known *(P)*
	you shall be known *(C)*	you shall be known *(C)*
	he (she, it) shall be known *(C)*	they shall be known *(C)*
Past	I was known	we were known
	you were known	you were known
	he (she, it) was known	they were known
Past	I was being known	we were being known
Prog.	you were being known	you were being known
	he (she, it) was being known	they were being known
Past	I did get known	we did get known
Int.	you did get known	you did get known
	he (she, it) did get known	they did get known
Pres.	I have been known	we have been known
Perf.	you have been known	you have been known
	he (she, it) has been known	they have been known
Past	I had been known	we had been known
Perf.	you had been known	you had been known
	he (she, it) had been known	they had been known
Fut.	I shall have been known	we shall have been known
Perf.	you will have been known	you will have been known
	he (she, it) will have been known	they will have been known

IMPERATIVE MOOD
be known

SUBJUNCTIVE MOOD

Pres.	if I be known	if we be known
	if you be known	if you be known
	if he (she, it) be known	if they be known
Past	if I were known	if we were known
	if you were known	if you were known
	if he (she, it) were known	if they were known
Fut.	if I should be known	if we should be known
	if you should be known	if you should be known
	if he (she, it) should be known	if they should be known

to lay (active voice)   *Principal Parts:* lay, laying, laid, laid

Infinitive: to lay   *Present Participle:* laying
Perfect Infinitive: to have laid   *Past Participle:* laid

INDICATIVE MOOD

Pres.	I lay	we lay
	you lay	you lay
	he (she, it) lays	they lay
Pres. Prog.	I am laying	we are laying
	you are laying	you are laying
	he (she, it) is laying	they are laying
Pres. Int.	I do lay	we do lay
	you do lay	you do lay
	he (she, it) does lay	they do lay
Fut.	I shall lay	we shall lay
	you will lay	you will lay
	he (she, it) will lay	they will lay
Fut.	I will lay *(P)*	we will lay *(P)*
	you shall lay *(C)*	you shall lay *(C)*
	he (she, it) shall lay *(C)*	they shall lay *(C)*
Past	I laid	we laid
	you laid	you laid
	he (she, it) laid	they laid
Past Prog.	I was laying	we were laying
	you were laying	you were laying
	he (she, it) was laying	they were laying
Past Int.	I did lay	we did lay
	you did lay	you did lay
	he (she, it) did lay	they did lay
Pres. Perf.	I have laid	we have laid
	you have laid	you have laid
	he (she, it) has laid	they have laid
Past Perf.	I had laid	we had laid
	you had laid	you had laid
	he (she, it) had laid	they had laid
Fut. Perf.	I shall have laid	we shall have laid
	you will have laid	you will have laid
	he (she, it) will have laid	they will have laid

IMPERATIVE MOOD
lay

SUBJUNCTIVE MOOD

Pres.	if I lay	if we lay
	if you lay	if you lay
	if he (she, it) lay	if they lay
Past	if I laid	if we laid
	if you laid	if you laid
	if he (she, it) laid	if they laid
Fut.	if I should lay	if we should lay
	if you should lay	if you should lay
	if he (she, it) should lay	if they should lay

(passive voice)

Infinitive: to be laid

Perfect Infinitive: to have been laid

Past Participle: been laid

Present Participle: being laid

INDICATIVE MOOD

Pres.	I am laid	we are laid
	you are laid	you are laid
	he (she, it) is laid	they are laid
Pres. Prog.	I am being laid	we are being laid
	you are being laid	you are being laid
	he (she, it) is being laid	they are being laid
Pres. Int.	I do get laid	we do get laid
	you do get laid	you do get laid
	he (she, it) does get laid	they do get laid
Fut.	I shall be laid	we shall be laid
	you will be laid	you will be laid
	he (she, it) will be laid	they will be laid
Fut.	I will be laid *(P)*	we will be laid *(P)*
	you shall be laid *(C)*	you shall be laid *(C)*
	he (she, it) shall be laid *(C)*	they shall be laid *(C)*
Past	I was laid	we were laid
	you were laid	you were laid
	he (she, it) was laid	they were laid
Past Prog.	I was being laid	we were being laid
	you were being laid	you were being laid
	he (she, it) was being laid	they were being laid
Past Int.	I did get laid	we did get laid
	you did get laid	you did get laid
	he (she, it) did get laid	they did get laid
Pres. Perf.	I have been laid	we have been laid
	you have been laid	you have been laid
	he (she, it) has been laid	they have been laid
Past Perf.	I had been laid	we had been laid
	you had been laid	you had been laid
	he (she, it) had been laid	they had been laid
Fut. Perf.	I shall have been laid	we shall have been laid
	you will have been laid	you will have been laid
	he (she, it) will have been laid	they will have been laid

IMPERATIVE MOOD
be laid

SUBJUNCTIVE MOOD

Pres.	if I be laid	if we be laid
	if you be laid	if you be laid
	if he (she, it) be laid	if they be laid
Past	if I were laid	if we were laid
	if you were laid	if you were laid
	if he (she, it) were laid	if they were laid
Fut.	if I should be laid	if we should be laid
	if you should be laid	if you should be laid
	if he (she, it) should be laid	if they should be laid

to lead (active voice)   *Principal Parts:* lead, leading, led, led

Infinitive: to lead   *Present Participle:* leading
Perfect Infinitive: to have led   *Past Participle:* led

INDICATIVE MOOD

Pres.	I lead	we lead
	you lead	you lead
	he (she, it) leads	they lead
Pres.	I am leading	we are leading
Prog.	you are leading	you are leading
	he (she, it) is leading	they are leading
Pres.	I do lead	we do lead
Int.	you do lead	you do lead
	he (she, it) does lead	they do lead
Fut.	I shall lead	we shall lead
	you will lead	you will lead
	he (she, it) will lead	they will lead
Fut.	I will lead *(P)*	we will lead *(P)*
	you shall lead *(C)*	you shall lead *(C)*
	he (she, it) shall lead *(C)*	they shall lead *(C)*
Past	I led	we led
	you led	you led
	he (she, it) led	they led
Past	I was leading	we were leading
Prog.	you were leading	you were leading
	he (she, it) was leading	they were leading
Past	I did lead	we did lead
Int.	you did lead	you did lead
	he (she, it) did lead	they did lead
Pres.	I have led	we have led
Perf.	you have led	you have led
	he (she, it) has led	they have led
Past	I had led	we had led
Perf.	you had led	you had led
	he (she, it) had led	they had led
Fut.	I shall have led	we shall have led
Perf.	you will have led	you will have led
	he (she, it) will have led	they will have led

IMPERATIVE MOOD
lead

SUBJUNCTIVE MOOD

Pres.	if I lead	if we lead
	if you lead	if you lead
	if he (she, it) lead	if they lead
Past	if I led	if we led
	if you led	if you led
	if he (she, it) led	if they led
Fut.	if I should lead	if we should lead
	if you should lead	if you should lead
	if he (she, it) should lead	if they should lead

Infinitive: to be led   *Present Participle:* being led
Perfect Infinitive: to have been led   *Past Participle:* been led

INDICATIVE MOOD

Pres.	I am led	we are led
	you are led	you are led
	he (she, it) is led	they are led
Pres.	I am being led	we are being led
Prog.	you are being led	you are being led
	he (she, it) is being led	they are being led
Pres.	I do get led	we do get led
Int.	you do get led	you do get led
	he (she, it) does get led	they do get led
Fut.	I shall be led	we shall be led
	you will be led	you will be led
	he (she, it) will be led	they will be led
Fut.	I will be led *(P)*	we will be led *(P)*
	you shall be led *(C)*	you shall be led *(C)*
	he (she, it) shall be led *(C)*	they shall be led *(C)*
Past	I was led	we were led
	you were led	you were led
	he (she, it) was led	they were led
Past	I was being led	we were being led
Prog.	you were being led	you were being led
	he (she, it) was being led	they were being led
Past	I did get led	we did get led
Int.	you did get led	you did get led
	he (she, it) did get led	they did get led
Pres.	I have been led	we have been led
Perf.	you have been led	you have been led
	he (she, it) has been led	they have been led
Past	I had been led	we had been led
Perf.	you had been led	you had been led
	he (she, it) had been led	they had been led
Fut.	I shall have been led	we shall have been led
Perf.	you will have been led	you will have been led
	he (she, it) will have been led	they will have been led

IMPERATIVE MOOD
be led

SUBJUNCTIVE MOOD

Pres.	if I be led	if we be led
	if you be led	if you be led
	if he (she, it) be led	if they be led
Past	if I were led	if we were led
	if you were led	if you were led
	if he (she, it) were led	if they were led
Fut.	if I should be led	if we should be led
	if you should be led	if you should be led
	if he (she, it) should be led	if they should be led

to leap *Principal Parts:* leap, leaping, leaped (leapt),
leaped (leapt)

Infinitive: to leap   *Present Participle:* leaping
Perfect Infinitive: to have leaped (leapt)   *Past Participle:* leaped (leapt)

INDICATIVE MOOD

Pres.	I leap	we leap
	you leap	you leap
	he (she, it) leaps	they leap
Pres.	I am leaping	we are leaping
Prog.	you are leaping	you are leaping
	he (she, it) is leaping	they are leaping
Pres.	I do leap	we do leap
Int.	you do leap	you do leap
	he (she, it) do leap	they do leap
Fut.	I shall leap	we shall leap
	you will leap	you will leap
	he (she, it) will leap	they will leap
Fut.	I will leap *(P)*	we will leap *(P)*
	you shall leap *(C)*	you shall leap *(C)*
	he (she, it) shall leap *(C)*	they shall leap *(C)*
Past	I leaped, leapt	we leaped, leapt
	you leaped, leapt	you leaped, leapt
	he (she, it) leaped, leapt	they leaped, leapt
Past	I was leaping	we were leaping
Prog.	you were leaping	you were leaping
	he (she, it) was leaping	they were leaping
Past	I did leap	we did leap
Int.	you did leap	you did leap
	he (she, it) did leap	they did leap
Pres.	I have leaped, leapt	we have leaped, leapt
Perf.	you have leaped, leapt	you have leaped, leapt
	he (she, it) has leaped, leapt	they have leaped, leapt
Past	I had leaped, leapt	we had leaped, leapt
Perf.	you had leaped, leapt	you had leaped, leapt
	he (she, it) had leaped, leapt	they had leaped, leapt
Fut.	I shall have leaped, leapt	we shall have leaped, leapt
Perf.	you will have leaped, leapt	you will have leaped, leapt
	he (she, it) will have leaped, leapt	they will have leaped, leapt

IMPERATIVE MOOD
leap

SUBJUNCTIVE MOOD

Pres.	if I leap	if we leap
	if you leap	if you leap
	if he (she, it) leap	if they leap
Past	if I leaped, leapt	if we leaped, leapt
	if you leaped, leapt	if you leaped, leapt
	if he (she, it) leaped, leapt	if they leaped, leapt
Fut.	if I should leap	if we should leap
	if you should leap	if you should leap
	if he (she, it) should leap	if they should leap

To leap is an intransitive verb.

It does not take an object.
It describes action, but the action is self-contained.
Like other intransitive verbs, it may be followed by adverbs, adverbial phrases and clauses describing the how, when, and where of the action:

HOW: The dancers leapt *vigorously*. (adverb)
WHY: They leapt *for joy*. (adverbial phrase)
WHEN: The fish will be leaping *as soon as the ice leaves the lake*. (adverbial clause)
WHERE: I shall leap *into my bed*. (adverbial phrase)

to leave (active voice)   *Principal Parts: leave, leaving, left, left*

Infinitive: to leave   *Present Participle:* leaving
Perfect Infinitive: to have left   *Past Participle:* left

INDICATIVE MOOD

Pres. I leave	we leave
you leave	you leave
he (she, it) leaves	they leave
Pres. I am leaving	we are leaving
Prog. you are leaving	you are leaving
he (she, it) is leaving	they are leaving
Pres. I do leave	we do leave
Int. you do leave	you do leave
he (she, it) does leave	they do leave
Fut. I shall leave	we shall leave
you will leave	you will leave
he (she, it) will leave	they will leave
Fut. I will leave *(P)*	we will leave *(P)*
you shall leave *(C)*	you shall leave *(C)*
he (she, it) shall leave *(C)*	they shall leave *(C)*
Past I left	we left
you left	you left
he (she, it) left	they left
Past I was leaving	we were leaving
Prog. you were leaving	you were leaving
he (she, it) was leaving	they were leaving
Past I did leave	we did leave
Int. you did leave	you did leave
he (she, it) did leave	they did leave
Pres. I have left	we have left
Perf. you have left	you have left
he (she, it) has left	they have left
Past I had left	we had left
Perf. you had left	you had left
he (she, it) had left	they had left
Fut. I shall have left	we shall have left
you will have left	you will have left
he (she, it) will have left	they will have left

IMPERATIVE MOOD
leave

SUBJUNCTIVE MOOD

Pres. if I leave	if we leave
if you leave	if you leave
if he (she, it) leave	if they leave
Past if I left	if we left
if you left	if you left
if he (she, it) left	if they left
Fut. if I should leave	if we should leave
if you should leave	if you should leave
if he (she, it) should leave	if they should leave

Infinitive: to be left   *Present Participle:* being left
Perfect Infinitive: to have been left   *Past Participle:* been left

INDICATIVE MOOD

Pres.	I am left	we are left
	you are left	you are left
	he (she, it) is left	they are left
Pres. Prog.	I am being left	we are being left
	you are being left	you are being left
	he (she, it) is being left	they are being left
Pres. Int.	I do get left	we do get left
	you do get left	you do get left
	he (she, it) does get left	they do get left
Fut.	I shall be left	we shall be left
	you will be left	you will be left
	he (she, it) will be left	they will be left
Fut.	I will be left *(P)*	we will be left *(P)*
	you shall be left *(C)*	you shall be left *(C)*
	he (she, it) shall be left *(C)*	they shall be left *(C)*
Past	I was left	we were left
	you were left	you were left
	he (she, it) was left	they were left
Past Prog.	I was being left	we were being left
	you were being left	you were being left
	he (she, it) was being left	they were being left
Past Int.	I did get left	we did get left
	you did get left	you did get left
	he (she, it) did get left	they did get left
Pres. Perf.	I have been left	we have been left
	you have been left	you have been left
	he (she, it) has been left	they have been left
Past Perf.	I had been left	we had been left
	you had been left	you had been left
	he (she, it) had been left	they had been left
Fut. Perf.	I shall have been left	we shall have been left
	you will have been left	you will have been left
	he (she, it) will have been left	they will have been left

IMPERATIVE MOOD
be left

SUBJUNCTIVE MOOD

Pres.	if I be left	if we be left
	if you be left	if you be left
	if he (she, it) be left	if they be left
Past	if I were left	if we were left
	if you were left	if you were left
	if he (she, it) were left	if they were left
Fut.	if I should be left	if we should be left
	if you should be left	if you should be left
	if he (she, it) should be left	if they should be left

to lend (active voice)

Principal Parts: lend, lending, lent, lent

Infinitive: to lend

Perfect Infinitive: to have lent

Present Participle: lending

Past Participle: been lent

INDICATIVE MOOD

Pres.	I lend	we lend
	you lend	you lend
	he (she, it) lends	they lend

Pres. Prog.	I am lending	we are lending
	you are lending	you are lending
	he (she, it) is lending	they are lending

Pres. Int.	I do lend	we do lend
	you do lend	you do lend
	he (she, it) does lend	they do lend

Fut.	I shall lend	we shall lend
	you will lend	you will lend
	he (she, it) will lend	they will lend

Fut.	I will lend *(P)*	we will lend *(P)*
	you shall lend *(C)*	you shall lend *(C)*
	he (she, it) shall lend *(C)*	they shall lend *(C)*

Past	I lent	we lent
	you lent	you lent
	he (she, it) lent	they lent

Past Prog.	I was lending	we were lending
	you were lending	you were lending
	he (she, it) was lending	they were lending

Past Int.	I did lend	we did lend
	you did lend	you did lend
	he (she, it) did lend	they did lend

Pres. Perf.	I have lent	we have lent
	you have lent	you have lent
	he (she, it) has lent	they have lent

Past Perf.	I had lent	we had lent
	you had lent	you had lent
	he (she, it) had lent	they had lent

Fut. Perf.	I shall have lent	we shall have lent
	you will have lent	you will have lent
	he (she, it) will have lent	they will have lent

IMPERATIVE MOOD
lend

SUBJUNCTIVE MOOD

Pres.	if I lend	if we lend
	if you lend	if you lend
	if he (she, it) lend	if they lend

Past	if I lent	if we lent
	if you lent	if you lent
	if he (she, it) lent	if they lent

Fut.	if I should lend	if we should lend
	if you should lend	if you should lend
	if he (she, it) should lend	if they should lend

(passive voice)

Infinitive: to be lent   *Present Participle:* being lent
Perfect Infinitive: to have been lent   *Past Participle:* been lent

INDICATIVE MOOD

Pres.	I am lent	we are lent
	you are lent	you are lent
	he (she, it) is lent	they are lent
Pres. Prog.	I am being lent	we are being lent
	you are being lent	you are being lent
	he (she, it) is being lent	they are being lent
Pres. Int.	I do get lent	we do get lent
	you do get lent	you do get lent
	he (she, it) does get lent	they do get lent
Fut.	I shall be lent	we shall be lent
	you will be lent	you will be lent
	he (she, it) will be lent	they will be lent
Fut.	I will be lent *(P)*	we will be lent *(P)*
	you shall be lent *(C)*	you shall be lent *(C)*
	he (she, it) shall be lent *(C)*	they shall be lent *(C)*
Past	I was lent	we were lent
	you were lent	you were lent
	he (she, it) was lent	they were lent
Past Prog.	I was being lent	we were being lent
	you were being lent	you were being lent
	he (she, it) was being lent	they were being lent
Past Int.	I did get lent	we did get lent
	you did get lent	you did get lent
	he (she, it) did get lent	they did get lent
Pres. Perf.	I have been lent	we have been lent
	you have been lent	you have been lent
	he (she, it) has been lent	they have been lent
Past Perf.	I had been lent	we had been lent
	you had been lent	you had been lent
	he (she, it) had been lent	they had been lent
Fut. Perf.	I shall have been lent	we shall have been lent
	you will have been lent	you will have been lent
	he (she, it) will have been lent	they will have been lent

IMPERATIVE MOOD
be lent

SUBJUNCTIVE MOOD

Pres.	if I be lent	if we be lent
	if you be lent	if you be lent
	if he (she, it) be lent	if they be lent
Past	if I were lent	if we were lent
	if you were lent	if you were lent
	if he (she, it) were lent	if they were lent
Fut.	if I should be lent	if we should be lent
	if you should be lent	if you should be lent
	if he (she, it) should be lent	if they should be lent

to let (active voice)

Principal Parts: let, letting, let, let

Infinitive: to let
Perfect Infinitive: to have let

Present Participle: letting
Past Participle: let

INDICATIVE MOOD

Pres.	I let	we let
	you let	you let
	he (she, it) lets	they let
Pres.	I am letting	we are letting
Prog.	you are letting	you are letting
	he (she, it) is letting	they are letting
Pres.	I do let	we do let
Int.	you do let	you do let
	he (she, it) does let	they do let
Fut.	I shall let	we shall let
	you will let	you will let
	he (she, it) will let	they will let
Fut.	I will let *(P)*	we will let *(P)*
	you shall let *(C)*	you shall let *(C)*
	he (she, it) shall let *(C)*	they shall let *(C)*
Past	I let	we let
	you let	you let
	he (she, it) lets	they let
Past	I was letting	we were letting
Prog.	you were letting	you were letting
	he (she, it) was letting	they were letting
Past	I did let	we did let
Int.	you did let	you did let
	he (she, it) did let	they did let
Pres.	I have let	we have let
Perf.	you have let	you have let
	he (she, it) has let	they have let
Past	I had let	we had let
Perf.	you had let	you had let
	he (she, it) had let	they had let
Fut.	I shall have let	we shall have let
Perf.	you will have let	you will have let
	he (she, it) will have let	they will have let

IMPERATIVE MOOD
let

SUBJUNCTIVE MOOD

Pres.	if I let	if we let
	if you let	if you let
	if he (she, it) let	if they let
Past	if I let	if we let
	if you let	if you let
	if he (she, it) let	if they let
Fut.	if I should let	if we should let
	if you should let	if you should let
	if he (she, it) should let	if they should let

Infinitive: to be let
Perfect Infinitive: to have been let

Present Participle: being let
Past Participle: been let

INDICATIVE MOOD

Pres.	I am let	we are let
	you are let	you are let
	he (she, it) is let	they are let
Pres. Prog.	I am being let	we are being let
	you are being let	you are being let
	he (she, it) is being let	they are being let
Pres. Int.	I do get let	we do get let
	you do get let	you do get let
	he (she, it) does get let	they do get let
Fut.	I shall be let	we shall be let
	you will be let	you will be let
	he (she, it) will be let	they will be let
Fut.	I will be let *(P)*	we will be let *(P)*
	you shall be let *(C)*	you shall be let *(C)*
	he (she, it) shall be let *(C)*	they shall be let *(C)*
Past	I was let	we were let
	you were let	you were let
	he (she, it) was let	they were let
Past Prog.	I was being let	we were being let
	you were being let	you were being let
	he (she, it) was being let	they were being let
Past Int.	I did get let	we did get let
	you did get let	you did get let
	he (she, it) did get let	they did get let
Pres. Perf.	I have been let	we have been let
	you have been let	you have been let
	he (she, it) has been let	they have been let
Past Perf.	I had been let	we had been let
	you had been let	you had been let
	he (she, it) had been let	they had been let
Fut. Perf.	I shall have been let	we shall have been let
	you will have been let	you will have been let
	he (she, it) will have been let	they will have been let

IMPERATIVE MOOD
be let

SUBJUNCTIVE MOOD

Pres.	if I be let	if we be let
	if you be let	if you be let
	if he (she, it) be let	if they be let
Past	if I were let	if we were let
	if you were let	if you were let
	if he (she, it) were let	if they were let
Fut.	if I should be let	if we should be let
	if you should be let	if you should be let
	if he (she, it) should be let	if they should be let

to lie

Infinitive: to lie *Present Participle:* lying
Perfect Infinitive: to have lain *Past Participle:* lain

INDICATIVE MOOD

Pres.	I lie	we lie
	you lie	you lie
	he (she, it) lies	they lie
Pres. Prog.	I am lying	we are lying
	you are lying	you are lying
	he (she, it) is lying	they are lying
Pres. Int.	I do lie	we do lie
	you do lie	you do lie
	he (she, it) does lie	they do lie
Fut.	I shall lie	we shall lie
	you will lie	you will lie
	he (she, it) will lie	they will lie
Fut.	I will lie *(P)*	we will lie *(P)*
	you shall lie *(C)*	you shall lie *(C)*
	he (she, it) shall lie *(C)*	they shall lie *(C)*
Past	I lay	we lay
	you lay	you lay
	he (she, it) lay	they lay
Past Prog.	I was lying	we were lying
	you were lying	you were lying
	he (she, it) was lying	they were lying
Past Int.	I did lay	we did lay
	you did lay	you did lay
	he (she, it) did lay	they did lay
Pres. Perf.	I have lain	we have lain
	you have lain	you have lain
	he (she, it) has lain	they have lain
Past Perf.	I had lain	we had lain
	you had lain	you had lain
	he (she, it) had lain	they had lain
Fut. Perf.	I shall have lain	we shall have lain
	you will have lain	you will have lain
	he (she, it) will have lain	they will have lain

IMPERATIVE MOOD
lay

SUBJUNCTIVE MOOD

Pres.	if I lie	if we lie
	if you lie	if you lie
	if he (she, it) lie	if they lie
Past	if I lay	if we lay
	if you lay	if you lay
	if he (she, it) lay	if they lay
Fut.	if I should lie	if we should lie
	if you should lie	if you should lie
	if he (she, it) should lie	if they should lie

To lie is an intransitive verb.

It does not take an object.
It describes action, but the action is self-contained.
Like other intransitive verbs, it may be followed by adverbs, adverbial phrases and clauses describing the how, why, when, and where of the action:

HOW: The body lay *in a strange position*. (adverbial phrase)
WHY: She will lie down *to take a nap*. (adverbial phrase)
WHEN: The books have lain untouched *ever since I bought them*. (adverbial clause)
WHERE: It seemed best to lie *low*. (adverb)

to lose (active voice)

Principal Parts: lose, losing, lost, lost

Infinitive: to lose
Perfect Infinitive: to have lost

Present Participle: losing
Past Participle: lost

INDICATIVE MOOD

Pres.	I lose	we lose
	you lose	you lose
	he (she, it) loses	they lose
Pres.	I am losing	we are losing
Prog.	you are losing	you are losing
	he (she, it) is losing	they are losing
Pres.	I do lose	we do lose
Int.	you do lose	you do lose
	he (she, it) does lose	they do lose
Fut.	I shall lose	we shall lose
	you will lose	you will lose
	he (she, it) will lose	they will lose
Fut.	I will lose *(P)*	we will lose *(P)*
	you shall lose *(C)*	you shall lose *(C)*
	he (she, it) shall lose *(C)*	they shall lose *(C)*
Past	I lost	we lost
	you lost	you lost
	he (she, it) lost	they lost
Past	I was losing	we were losing
Prog.	you were losing	you were losing
	he (she, it) was losing	they were losing
Past	I did lose	we did lose
Int.	you did lose	you did lose
	he (she, it) did lose	they did lose
Pres.	I have lost	we have lost
Perf.	you have lost	you have lost
	he (she, it) has lost	they have lost
Past	I had lost	we had lost
Perf.	you had lost	you had lost
	he (she, it) had lost	they had lost
Fut.	I shall have lost	we shall have lost
Perf.	you will have lost	you will have lost
	he (she, it) will have lost	they will have lost

IMPERATIVE MOOD
lose

SUBJUNCTIVE MOOD

Pres.	if I lose	if we lose
	if you lose	if you lose
	if he (she, it) lose	if they lose
Past	if I lost	if we lost
	if you lost	if you lost
	if he (she, it) lost	if they lost
Fut.	if I should lose	if we should lose
	if you should lose	if you should lose
	if he (she, it) should lose	if they should lose

Infinitive: to be lost

Perfect Infinitive: to have been lost

Present Participle: being lost

Past Participle: been lost

INDICATIVE MOOD

Pres.	I am lost	we are lost
	you are lost	you are lost
	he (she, it) is lost	they are lost
Pres. Prog.	I am being lost	we are being lost
	you are being lost	you are being lost
	he (she, it) is being lost	they are being lost
Pres. Int.	I do get lost	we do get lost
	you do get lost	you do get lost
	he (she, it) does get lost	they do get lost
Fut.	I shall be lost	we shall be lost
	you will be lost	you will be lost
	he (she, it) will be lost	they will be lost
Fut.	I will be lost *(P)*	we will be lost *(P)*
	you shall be lost *(C)*	you shall be lost *(C)*
	he (she, it) shall be lost *(C)*	they shall be lost *(C)*
Past	I was lost	we were lost
	you were lost	you were lost
	he (she, it) was lost	they were lost
Past Prog.	I was being lost	we were being lost
	you were being lost	you were being lost
	he (she, it) was being lost	they were being lost
Past Int.	I did get lost	we did get lost
	you did get lost	you did get lost
	he (she, it) did get lost	they did get lost
Pres. Perf.	I have been lost	we have been lost
	you have been lost	you have been lost
	he (she, it) has been lost	they have been lost
Past Perf.	I had been lost	we had been lost
	you had been lost	you had been lost
	he (she, it) had been lost	they had been lost
Fut. Perf.	I shall have been lost	we shall have been lost
	you will have been lost	you will have been lost
	he (she, it) will have been lost	they will have been lost

IMPERATIVE MOOD
be lost

SUBJUNCTIVE MOOD

Pres.	if I be lost	if we be lost
	if you be lost	if you be lost
	if he (she, it) be lost	if they be lost
Past	if I were lost	if we were lost
	if you were lost	if you were lost
	if he (she, it) were lost	if they were lost
Fut.	if I should be lost	if we should be lost
	if you should be lost	if you should be lost
	if he (she, it) should be lost	if they should be lost

to make (active voice)

Principal Parts: make, making, made, made

Infinitive: to make
Perfect Infinitive: to have made

Present Participle: making
Past Participle: made

INDICATIVE MOOD

Pres.	I make	we make
	you make	you make
	he (she, it) makes	they make

Pres. Prog.	I am making	we are making
	you are making	you are making
	he (she, it) is making	they are making

Pres. Int.	I do make	we do make
	you do make	you do make
	he (she, it) does make	they do make

Fut.	I shall make	we shall make
	you will make	you will make
	he (she, it) will make	they will make

Fut.	I will make *(P)*	we will make *(P)*
	you shall make *(C)*	you shall make *(C)*
	he (she, it) shall make *(C)*	they shall make *(C)*

Past	I made	we made
	you made	you made
	he (she, it) made	they made

Past Prog.	I was making	we were making
	you were making	you were making
	he (she, it) was making	they were making

Past Int.	I did make	we did make
	you did make	you did make
	he (she, it) did make	they did make

Pres. Perf.	I have made	we have made
	you have made	you have made
	he (she, it) has made	they have made

Past Perf.	I had made	we had made
	you had made	you had made
	he (she, it) had made	they had made

Fut. Perf.	I shall have made	we shall have made
	you will have made	you will have made
	he (she, it) will have made	they will have made

IMPERATIVE MOOD
make

SUBJUNCTIVE MOOD

Pres.	if I make	if we make
	if you make	if you make
	if he (she, it) make	if they make

Past	if I made	if we made
	if you made	if you made
	if he (she, it) made	if they made

Fut.	if I should make	if we should make
	if you should make	if you should make
	if he (she, it) should make	if they should make

(passive voice)

Infinitive: to be made *Present Participle:* being made
Perfect Infinitive: to have been made *Past Participle:* been made

INDICATIVE MOOD

Pres.	I am made	we are made
	you are made	you are made
	he (she, it) is made	they are made
Pres.	I am being made	we are being made
Prog.	you are being made	you are being made
	he (she, it) is being made	they are being made
Pres.	I do get made	we do get made
Int.	you do get made	you do get made
	he (she, it) does get made	they do get made
Fut.	I shall be made	we shall be made
	you will be made	you will be made
	he (she, it) will be made	they will be made
Fut.	I will be made *(P)*	we will be made *(P)*
	you shall be made *(C)*	you shall be made *(C)*
	he (she, it) shall be made *(C)*	they shall be made *(C)*
Past	I was made	we were made
	you were made	you were made
	he (she, it) was made	they were made
Past	I was being made	we were being made
Prog.	you were being made	you were being made
	he (she, it) was being made	they were being made
Past	I did get made	we did get made
Int.	you did get made	you did get made
	he (she, it) did get made	they did get made
Pres.	I have been made	we have been made
Perf.	you have been made	you have been made
	he (she, it) has been made	they have been made
Past	I had been made	we had been made
Perf.	you had been made	you had been made
	he (she, it) had been made	they had been made
Fut.	I shall have been made	we shall have been made
Perf.	you will have been made	you will have been made
	he (she, it) will have been made	they will have been made

IMPERATIVE MOOD
be made

SUBJUNCTIVE MOOD

Pres.	if I be made	if we be made
	if you be made	if you be made
	if he (she, it) be made	if they be made
Past	if I were made	if we were made
	if you were made	if you were made
	if he (she, it) were made	if they were made
Fut.	if I should be made	if we should be made
	if you should be made	if you should be made
	if he (she, it) should be made	if they should be made

Principal Parts: meet, meeting, met, met

Infinitive: to meet   *Present Participle:* meeting
Perfect Infinitive: to have met   *Past Participle:* met

INDICATIVE MOOD

Pres.	I meet	we meet
	you meet	you meet
	he (she, it) meets	they meet
Pres.	I am meeting	we are meeting
Prog.	you are meeting	you are meeting
	he (she, it) is meeting	they are meeting
Pres.	I do meet	we do meet
Int.	you do meet	you do meet
	he (she, it) does meet	they do meet
Fut.	I shall meet	we shall meet
	you will meet	you will meet
	he (she, it) will meet	they will meet
Fut.	I will meet *(P)*	we will meet *(P)*
	you shall meet *(C)*	you shall meet *(C)*
	he (she, it) shall meet *(C)*	they shall meet *(C)*
Past	I met	we met
	you met	you met
	he (she, it) met	they met
Past	I was meeting	we were meeting
Prog.	you were meeting	you were meeting
	he (she, it) was meeting	they were meeting
Past	I did meet	we did meet
Int.	you did meet	you did meet
	he (she, it) did meet	they did meet
Pres.	I have met	we have met
Perf.	you have met	you have met
	he (she, it) has met	they have met
Past	I had met	we had met
Perf.	you had met	you had met
	he (she, it) had met	they had met
Fut.	I shall have met	we shall have met
Perf.	you will have met	you will have met
	he (she, it) will have met	they will have met

IMPERATIVE MOOD
meet

SUBJUNCTIVE MOOD

Pres.	if I meet	if we meet
	if you meet	if you meet
	if he (she, it) meet	if they meet
Past	if I met	if we met
	if you met	if you met
	if he (she, it) met	if they met
Fut.	if I should meet	if we should meet
	if you should meet	if you should meet
	if he (she, it) should meet	if they should meet

(passive voice)

Infinitive: to be met   *Present Participle:* being met
Perfect Infinitive: to have been met   *Past Participle:* been met

INDICATIVE MOOD

Pres.	I am met	we are met
	you are met	you are met
	he (she, it) is met	they are met
Pres. *Prog.*	I am being met	we are being met
	you are being met	you are being met
	he (she, it) is being met	they are being met
Pres. *Int.*	I do get met	we do get met
	you do get met	you do get met
	he (she, it) does get met	they do get met
Fut.	I shall be met	we shall be met
	you will be met	you will be met
	he (she, it) will be met	they will be met
Fut.	I will be met *(P)*	we will be met *(P)*
	you shall be met *(C)*	you shall be met *(C)*
	he (she, it) shall be met *(C)*	they shall be met *(C)*
Past	I was met	we were met
	you were met	you were met
	he (she, it) was met	they were met
Past *Prog.*	I was being met	we were being met
	you were being met	you were being met
	he (she, it) was being met	they were being met
Past *Int.*	I did get met	we did get met
	you did get met	you did get met
	he (she, it) did get met	they did get met
Pres. *Perf.*	I have been met	we have been met
	you have been met	you have been met
	he (she, it) had been met	they have been met
Past *Perf.*	I had been met	we had been met
	you had been met	you had been met
	he (she, it) had been met	they had been met
Fut. *Perf.*	I shall have been met	we shall have been met
	you will have been met	you will have been met
	he (she, it) will have been met	they will have been met

IMPERATIVE MOOD
be met

SUBJUNCTIVE MOOD

Pres.	if I be met	if we be met
	if you be met	if you be met
	if he (she, it) be met	if they be met
Past	if I were met	if we were met
	if you were met	if you were met
	if he (she, it) were met	if they were met
Fut.	if I should be met	if we should be met
	if you should be met	if you should be met
	if he (she, it) should be met	if they should be met

to pay (active voice)   *Principal Parts:* pay, paying, paid, paid

Infinitive: to pay   *Present Participle:* paying
Perfect Infinitive: to have paid   *Past Participle:* paid

INDICATIVE MOOD

Pres.	I pay	we pay
	you pay	you pay
	he (she, it) pays	they pay
Pres.	I am paying	we are paying
Prog.	you are paying	you are paying
	he (she, it) is paying	they are paying
Pres.	I do pay	we do pay
Int.	you do pay	you do pay
	he (she, it) does pay	they do pay
Fut.	I shall pay	we shall pay
	you will pay	you will pay
	he (she, it) will pay	they will pay
Fut.	I will pay *(P)*	we will pay *(P)*
	you shall pay *(C)*	you shall pay *(C)*
	he (she, it) shall pay *(C)*	they shall pay *(C)*
Past	I paid	we paid
	you paid	you paid
	he (she, it) paid	they paid
Past	I was paying	we were paying
Prog.	you were paying	you were paying
	he (she, it) was paying	they were paying
Past	I did pay	we did pay
Int.	you did pay	you did pay
	he (she, it) did pay	they did pay
Pres.	I have paid	we have paid
Perf.	you have paid	you have paid
	he (she, it) has paid	they have paid
Past	I had paid	we had paid
Perf.	you had paid	you had paid
	he (she, it) had paid	they had paid
Fut.	I shall have paid	we shall have paid
Perf.	you will have paid	you will have paid
	he (she, it) will have paid	they will have paid

IMPERATIVE MOOD
pay

SUBJUNCTIVE MOOD

Pres.	if I pay	if we pay
	if you pay	if you pay
	if he (she, it) pay	if they pay
Past	if I paid	if we paid
	if you paid	if you paid
	if he (she, it) paid	if they paid
Fut.	if I should pay	if we should pay
	if you should pay	if you should pay
	if he (she, it) should pay	if they should pay

238

(passive voice)

Infinitive: to be paid
Perfect Infinitive: to have been paid

Present Participle: being paid
Past Participle: been paid

INDICATIVE MOOD

Pres.	I am paid you are paid he (she, it) is paid	we are paid you are paid they are paid
Pres. *Prog.*	I am being paid you are being paid he (she, it) is being paid	we are being paid you are being paid they are being paid
Pres. *Int.*	I do get paid you do get paid he (she, it) does get paid	we do get paid you do get paid they do get paid
Fut.	I shall be paid you will be paid he (she, it) will be paid	we shall be paid you will be paid they will be paid
Fut.	I will be paid *(P)* you shall be paid *(C)* he (she, it) shall be paid *(C)*	we will be paid *(P)* you shall be paid *(C)* they shall be paid *(C)*
Past	I was paid you were paid he (she, it) was paid	we were paid you were paid they were paid
Past *Prog.*	I was being paid you were being paid he (she, it) was being paid	we were being paid you were being paid they were being paid
Past *Int.*	I did get paid you did get paid he (she, it) did get paid	we did get paid you did get paid they did get paid
Pres. *Perf.*	I have been paid you have been paid he (she, it) has been paid	we have been paid you have been paid they have been paid
Past *Perf.*	I had been paid you had been paid he (she, it) had been paid	we had been paid you had been paid they had been paid
Fut. *Perf.*	I shall have been paid you will have been paid he (she, it) will have been paid	we shall have been paid you will have been paid they will have been paid

IMPERATIVE MOOD
be paid

SUBJUNCTIVE MOOD

Pres.	if I be paid if you be paid if he (she, it) be paid	if we be paid if you be paid if they be paid
Past	if I were paid if you were paid if he (she, it) were paid	if we were paid if you were paid if they were paid
Fut.	if I should be paid if you should be paid if he (she, it) should be paid	if we should be paid if you should be paid if they should be paid

to put (active voice)　　　　*Principal Parts:* put, putting, put, put

Infinitive: to put　　　　　　　　　　*Present Participle:* putting
Perfect Infinitive: to have put　　　　　*Past Participle:* put

INDICATIVE MOOD

Pres.	I put	we put
	you put	you put
	he (she, it) puts	they put
Pres.	I am putting	we are putting
Prog.	you are putting	you are putting
	he (she, it) is putting	they are putting
Pres.	I do put	we do put
Int.	you do put	you do put
	he (she, it) does put	they do put
Fut.	I shall put	we shall put
	you will put	you will put
	he (she, it) will put	they will put
Fut.	I will put *(P)*	we will put *(P)*
	you shall put *(C)*	you shall put *(C)*
	he (she, it) shall put *(C)*	they shall put *(C)*
Past	I put	we put
	you put	you put
	he (she, it) put	they put
Past	I was putting	we were putting
Prog.	you were putting	you were putting
	he (she, it) was putting	they were putting
Past	I did put	we did put
Int.	you did put	you did put
	he (she, it) did put	they did put
Pres.	I have put	we have put
Perf.	you have put	you have put
	he (she, it) has put	they have put
Past	I had put	we had put
Perf.	you had put	you had put
	he (she, it) had put	they had put
Fut.	I shall have put	we shall have put
Perf.	you will have put	you will have put
	he (she, it) will have put	they will have put

IMPERATIVE MOOD
put

SUBJUNCTIVE MOOD

Pres.	if I put	if we put
	if you put	if you put
	if he (she, it) put	if they put
Past	if I put	if we put
	if you put	if you put
	if he (she, it) put	if they put
Fut.	if I should put	if we should put
	if you should put	if you should put
	if he (she, it) should put	if they should put

(passive voice)

Infinitive: to be put   *Present Participle:* being put
Perfect Infinitive: to have been put   *Past Participle:* been put

INDICATIVE MOOD

Pres.	I am put	we are put
	you are put	you are put
	he (she, it) is put	they are put
Pres.	I am being put	we are being put
Prog.	you are being put	you are being put
	he (she, it) is being put	they are being put
Pres.	I do get put	we do get put
Int.	you do get put	you do get put
	he (she, it) does get put	they do get put
Fut.	I shall be put	we shall be put
	you will be put	you will be put
	he (she, it) will be put	they will be put
Fut.	I will be put *(P)*	we will be put be put *(P)*
	you shall be put *(C)*	you shall be put *(C)*
	he (she, it) shall be put *(C)*	they shall be put *(C)*
Past	I was put	we were put
	you were put	you were put
	he (she, it) was put	they were put
Past	I was being put	we were being put
Prog.	you were being put	you were being put
	he (she, it) was being put	they were being put
Past	I did get put	we did get put
Int.	you did get put	you did get put
	he (she, it) did get put	they did get put
Pres.	I have been put	we have been put
Perf.	you have been put	you have been put
	he (she, it) has been put	they have been put
Past	I had been put	we had been put
Perf.	you had been put	you had been put
	he (she, it) had been put	they had been put
Fut.	I shall have been put	we shall have been put
Perf.	you will have been put	you will have been put
	he (she, it) will have been put	they will have been put

IMPERATIVE MOOD
be put

SUBJUNCTIVE MOOD

Pres.	if I be put	if we be put
	if you be put	if you be put
	if he (she, it) be put	if they be put
Past	if I were put	if we were put
	if you were put	if you were put
	if he (she, it) were put	if they were put
Fut.	if I should be put	if we should be put
	if you should be put	if you should be put
	if he (she, it) should be put	if they should be put

to read (active voice)   *Principal Parts:* read, reading, read, read

Infinitive: to read   *Present Participle:* reading
Perfect Infinitive: to have read   *Past Participle:* read

INDICATIVE MOOD

Pres.	I read	we read
	you read	you read
	he (she, it) reads	they read
Pres.	I am reading	we are reading
Prog.	you are reading	you are reading
	he (she, it) is reading	they are reading
Pres.	I do read	we do read
Int.	you do read	you do read
	he (she, it) does read	they do read
Fut.	I shall read	we shall read
	you will read	you will read
	he (she, it) will read	they will read
Fut.	I will read *(P)*	we will read *(P)*
	you shall read *(C)*	you shall read *(C)*
	he (she, it) shall read *(C)*	they shall read *(C)*
Past	I read	we read
	you read	you read
	he (she, it) read	they read
Past	I was reading	we were reading
Prog.	you were reading	you were reading
	he (she, it) was reading	they were reading
Past	I did read	we did read
Int.	you did read	you did read
	he (she, it) did read	they did read
Pres.	I have read	we have read
Perf.	you have read	you have read
	he (she, it) has read	they have read
Past	I had read	we had read
Perf.	you had read	you had read
	he (she, it) had read	they had read
Fut.	I shall have read	we shall have read
Perf.	you will have read	you will have read
	he (she, it) will have read	they will have read

IMPERATIVE MOOD
read

SUBJUNCTIVE MOOD

Pres.	if I read	if we read
	if you read	if you read
	if he (she, it) read	if they read
Past	if I read	if we read
	if you read	if you read
	if he (she, it) read	if they read
Fut.	if I should read	if we should read
	if you should read	if you should read
	if he (she, it) should read	if they should read

(passive voice)

Infinitive: to be read   *Present Participle:* being read
Perfect Infinitive: to have been read   *Past Participle:* been read

INDICATIVE MOOD

Pres.	I am read	we are read
	you are read	you are read
	he (she, it) is read	they are read
Pres.	I am being read	we are being read
Prog.	you are being read	you are being read
	he (she, it) is being read	they are being read
Pres.	I do get read	we do get read
Int.	you do get read	you do get read
	he (she, it) does get read	they do get read
Fut.	I shall be read	we shall be read
	you will be read	you will be read
	he (she, it) will be read	they will be read
Fut.	I will be read *(P)*	we will be read *(P)*
	you shall be read *(C)*	you shall be read *(C)*
	he (she, it) shall be read *(C)*	they shall be read *(C)*
Past	I was read	we were read
	you were read	you were read
	he (she, it) was read	they were read
Past	I was being read	we were being read
Prog.	you were being read	you were being read
	he (she, it) was being read	they were being read
Past	I did get read	we did get read
Int.	you did get read	you did get read
	he (she, it) did get read	they did get read
Pres.	I have been read	we have been read
Perf.	you have been read	you have been read
	he (she, it) has been read	they have been read
Past	I had been read	we had been read
Perf.	you had been read	you had been read
	he (she, it) had been read	they had been read
Fut.	I shall have been read	we shall have been read
Perf.	you will have been read	you will have been read
	he (she, it) will have been read	they will have been read

IMPERATIVE MOOD
be read

SUBJUNCTIVE MOOD

Pres.	if I be read	if we be read
	if you be read	if you be read
	if he (she, it) be read	if they be read
Past	if I were read	if we were read
	if you were read	if you were read
	if he (she, it) were read	if they were read
Fut.	if I should be read	if we should be read
	if you should be read	if you should be read
	if he (she, it) should be read	if they should be read

to rend (active voice)   *Principal Parts:* rend, rending, rent, rent

Infinitive: to rend   *Present Participle:* rending
Perfect Infinitive: to have rent   *Past Participle:* rent

INDICATIVE MOOD

Pres.	I rend	we rend
	you rend	you rend
	he (she, it) rends	they rend
Pres.	I am rending	we are rending
Prog.	you are rending	you are rending
	he (she, it) is rending	they are rending
Pres.	I do rend	we do rend
Int.	you do rend	you do rend
	he (she, it) does rend	they do rend
Fut.	I shall rend	we shall rend
	you will rend	you will rend
	he (she, it) will rend	they will rend
Fut.	I will rend *(P)*	we will rend *(P)*
	you shall rend *(C)*	you shall rend *(C)*
	he (she, it) shall rend *(C)*	they shall rend *(C)*
Past	I rent	we rent
	you rent	you rent
	he (she, it) rent	they rent
Past	I was rending	we were rending
Prog.	you were rending	you were rending
	he (she, it) was rending	they were rending
Past	I did rend	we did rend
Int.	you did rend	you did rend
	he (she, it) did rend	they did rend
Pres.	I have rent	we have rent
Perf.	you have rent	you have rent
	he (she, it) has rent	they have rent
Past	I had rent	we had rent
Perf.	you had rent	you had rent
	he (she, it) had rent	they had rent
Fut.	I shall have rent	we shall have rent
Perf.	you will have rent	you will have rent
	he (she, it) will have rent	they will have rent

IMPERATIVE MOOD
rend

SUBJUNCTIVE MOOD

Pres.	if I rend	if we rend
	if you rend	if you rend
	if he (she, it) rend	if they rend
Past	if I rent	if we rent
	if you rent	if you rent
	if he (she, it) rent	if they rent
Fut.	if I should rend	if we should rend
	if you should rend	if you should rend
	if he (she, it) should rend	if they should rend

(passive voice)

Infinitive: to be rent

Perfect Infinitive: to have been rent

Present Participle: being rent

Past Participle: been rent

INDICATIVE MOOD

Pres.	I am rent	we are rent
	you are rent	you are rent
	he (she, it) is rent	they are rent
Pres. Prog.	I am being rent	we are being rent
	you are being rent	you are being rent
	he (she, it) is being rent	they are being rent
Pres. Int.	I do get rent	we do get rent
	you do get rent	you do get rent
	he (she, it) does get rent	they do get rent
Fut.	I shall be rent	we shall be rent
	you will be rent	you will be rent
	he (she, it) will be rent	they will be rent
Fut.	I will be rent *(P)*	we will be rent *(P)*
	you shall be rent *(C)*	you shall be rent *(C)*
	he (she, it) shall be rent *(C)*	they shall be rent *(C)*
Past	I was rent	we were rent
	you were rent	you were rent
	he (she, it) was rent	they were rent
Past Prog.	I was being rent	we were being rent
	you were being rent	you were being rent
	he (she, it) was being rent	they were being rent
Past Int.	I did get rent	we did get rent
	you did get rent	you did get rent
	he (she, it) did get rent	they did get rent
Pres. Perf.	I have been rent	we have been rent
	you have been rent	you have been rent
	he (she, it) has been rent	they have been rent
Past Perf.	I had been rent	we had been rent
	you had been rent	you had been rent
	he (she, it) had been rent	they had been rent
Fut. Perf.	I shall have been rent	we shall have been rent
	you will have been rent	you will have been rent
	he (she, it) will have been rent	they will have been rent

IMPERATIVE MOOD

be rent

SUBJUNCTIVE MOOD

Pres.	if I be rent	if we be rent
	if you be rent	if you be rent
	if he (she, it) be rent	if they be rent
Past	if I were rent	if we were rent
	if you were rent	if you were rent
	if he (she, it) were rent	if they were rent
Fut.	if I should be rent	if we should be rent
	if you should be rent	if you should be rent
	if he (she, it) should be rent	if they should be rent

to ride (active voice)   *Principal Parts:* ride, riding, rode, ridden

Infinitive: to ride   *Present Participle:* riding
Perfect Infinitive: to have ridden   *Past Participle:* ridden

INDICATIVE MOOD

Pres.	I ride	we ride
	you ride	you ride
	he (she, it) rides	they ride
Pres.	I am riding	we are riding
Prog.	you are riding	you are riding
	he (she, it) is riding	they are riding
Pres.	I do ride	we do ride
Int.	you do ride	you do ride
	he (she, it) does ride	they do ride
Fut.	I shall ride	we shall ride
	you will ride	you will ride
	he (she, it) will ride	they will ride
Fut.	I will ride *(P)*	we will ride *(P)*
	you shall ride *(C)*	you shall ride *(C)*
	he (she, it) shall ride *(C)*	they shall ride *(C)*
Past	I rode	we rode
	you rode	you rode
	he (she, it) rode	they rode
Past	I was riding	we were riding
Prog.	you were riding	you were riding
	he (she, it) was riding	they were riding
Past	I did ride	we did ride
Int.	you did ride	you did ride
	he (she, it) did ride	they did ride
Pres.	I have ridden	we have ridden
Perf.	you have ridden	you have ridden
	he (she, it) has ridden	they have ridden
Past	I had ridden	we had ridden
Perf.	you had ridden	you had ridden
	he (she, it) had ridden	they had ridden
Fut.	I shall have ridden	we shall have ridden
Perf.	you will have ridden	you will have ridden
	he (she, it) will have ridden	they will have ridden

IMPERATIVE MOOD
ride

SUBJUNCTIVE MOOD

Pres.	if I ride	if we ride
	if you ride	if you ride
	if he (she, it) ride	if they ride
Past	if I rode	if we rode
	if you rode	if you rode
	if he (she, it) rode	if they rode
Fut.	if I should ride	if we should ride
	if you should ride	if you should ride
	if he (she, it) should ride	if they should ride

Infinitive: to be ridden   *Present Participle:* being ridden
Perfect Infinitive: to have been ridden   *Past Participle:* been ridden

INDICATIVE MOOD

Pres.	I am ridden	we are ridden
	you are ridden	you are ridden
	he (she, it) is ridden	they are ridden
Pres.	I am being ridden	we are being ridden
Prog.	you are being ridden	you are being ridden
	he (she, it) is being ridden	they are being ridden
Pres.	I do get ridden	we do get ridden
Int.	you do get ridden	you do get ridden
	he (she, it) does get ridden	they do get ridden
Fut.	I shall be ridden	we shall be ridden
	you will be ridden	you will be ridden
	he (she, it) will be ridden	they will be ridden
Fut.	I will be ridden *(P)*	we will be ridden *(P)*
	you shall be ridden *(C)*	you shall be ridden *(C)*
	he (she, it) shall be ridden *(C)*	they shall be ridden *(C)*
Past	I was ridden	we were ridden
	you were ridden	you were ridden
	he (she, it) was ridden	they were ridden
Past	I was being ridden	we were being ridden
Prog.	you were being ridden	you were being ridden
	he (she, it) was being ridden	they were being ridden
Past	I did get ridden	we did get ridden
Int.	you did get ridden	you did get ridden
	he (she, it) did get ridden	they did get ridden
Pres.	I have been ridden	we have been ridden
Perf.	you have been ridden	you have been ridden
	he (she, it) has been ridden	they have been ridden
Past	I had been ridden	we had been ridden
Perf.	you had been ridden	you had been ridden
	he (she, it) had been ridden	they had been ridden
Fut.	I shall have been ridden	we shall have been ridden
Perf.	you will have been ridden	you will have been ridden
	he (she, it) will have been ridden	they will have been ridden

IMPERATIVE MOOD
be ridden

SUBJUNCTIVE MOOD

Pres.	if I be ridden	if we be ridden
	if you be ridden	if you be ridden
	if he (she, it) be ridden	if they be ridden
Past	if I were ridden	if we were ridden
	if you were ridden	if you were ridden
	if he (she, it) were ridden	if they were ridden
Fut.	if I should be ridden	if we should be ridden
	if you should be ridden	if you should be ridden
	if he (she, it) should be ridden	if they should be ridden

to ring (active voice)

Principal Parts: ring, ringing, rang, rung

Infinitive: to ring
Perfect Infinitive: to have rung

Present Participle: ringing
Past Participle: rung

INDICATIVE MOOD

Pres.	I ring	we ring
	you ring	you ring
	he (she, it) rings	they ring
Pres. *Prog.*	I am ringing	we are ringing
	you are ringing	you are ringing
	he (she, it) is ringing	they are ringing
Pres. *Int.*	I do ring	we do ring
	you do ring	you do ring
	he (she, it) does ring	they do ring
Fut.	I shall ring	we shall ring
	you will ring	you will ring
	he (she, it) will ring	they will ring
Fut.	I will ring *(P)*	we will ring *(P)*
	you shall ring *(C)*	you shall ring *(C)*
	he (she, it) shall ring *(C)*	they shall ring *(C)*
Past	I rang	we rang
	you rang	you rang
	he (she, it) rang	they rang
Past *Prog.*	I was ringing	we were ringing
	you were ringing	you were ringing
	he (she, it) was ringing	they were ringing
Past *Int.*	I did ring	we did ring
	you did ring	you did ring
	he (she, it) did ring	they did ring
Pres. *Perf.*	I have rung	we have rung
	you have rung	you have rung
	he (she, it) has rung	they have rung
Past *Perf.*	I had rung	we had rung
	you had rung	you had rung
	he (she, it) had rung	they had rung
Fut. *Perf.*	I shall have rung	we shall have rung
	you will have rung	you will have rung
	he (she, it) will have rung	they will have rung

IMPERATIVE MOOD
ring

SUBJUNCTIVE MOOD

Pres.	if I ring	if we ring
	if you ring	if you ring
	if he (she, it) ring	if they ring
Past	if I rang	if we rang
	if you rang	if you rang
	if he (she, it) rang	if they rang
Fut.	if I should ring	if we should ring
	if you should ring	if you should ring
	if he (she, it) should ring	if they should ring

(passive voice)

Infinitive: to be rung *Present Participle:* being rung
Perfect Infinitive: to have been rung *Past Participle:* been rung

INDICATIVE MOOD

Pres.	I am rung	we are rung
	you are rung	you are rung
	he (she, it) is rung	they are rung
Pres.	I am being rung	we are being rung
Prog.	you are being rung	you are being rung
	he (she, it) is being rung	they are being rung
Pres.	I do get rung	we do get rung
Int.	you do get rung	you do get rung
	he (she, it) does get rung	they do get rung
Fut.	I shall be rung	we shall be rung
	you will be rung	you will be rung
	he (she, it) will be rung	they will be rung
Fut.	I will be rung *(P)*	we will be rung *(P)*
	you shall be rung *(C)*	you shall be rung *(C)*
	he (she, it) shall be rung *(C)*	they shall be rung *(C)*
Past	I was rung	we were rung
	you were rung	you were rung
	he (she, it) was rung	they were rung
Past	I was being rung	we were being rung
Prog.	you were being rung	you were being rung
	he (she, it) was being rung	they were being rung
Past	I did get rung	we did get rung
Int.	you did get rung	you did get rung
	he (she, it) did get rung	they did get rung
Pres.	I have been rung	we have been rung
Perf.	you have been rung	you have been rung
	he (she, it) has been rung	they have been rung
Past	I had been rung	we had been rung
Perf.	you had been rung	you had been rung
	he (she, it) had been rung	they had been rung
Fut.	I shall have been rung	we shall have been rung
Perf.	you will have been rung	you will have been rung
	he (she, it) will have been rung	they will have been rung

IMPERATIVE MOOD
be rung

SUBJUNCTIVE MOOD

Pres.	if I be rung	if we be rung
	if you be rung	if you be rung
	if he (she, it) be rung	if they be rung
Past	if I were rung	if we were rung
	if you were rung	if you were rung
	if he (she, it) were rung	if they were rung
Fut.	if I should be rung	if we should be rung
	if you should be rung	if you should be rung
	if he (she, it) should be rung	if they should be rung

Infinitive: to rise   *Present Participle:* rising
Perfect Infinitive: to have risen   *Past Participle:* risen

INDICATIVE MOOD

Pres.	I rise	we rise
	you rise	you rise
	he (she, it) rises	they rise
Pres.	I am rising	we are rising
Prog.	you are rising	you are rising
	he (she, it) is rising	they are rising
Pres.	I do rise	we do rise
Int.	you do rise	you do rise
	he (she, it) does rise	they do rise
Fut.	I shall rise	we shall rise
	you will rise	you will rise
	he (she, it) will rise	they will rise
Fut.	I will rise *(P)*	we will rise *(P)*
	you shall rise *(C)*	you shall rise *(C)*
	he (she, it) shall rise *(C)*	they shall rise *(C)*
Past	I rose	we rose
	you rose	you rose
	he (she, it) rose	they rose
Past	I was rising	we were rising
Prog.	you were rising	you were rising
	he (she, it) was rising	they were rising
Past	I did rise	we did rise
Int.	you did rise	you did rise
	he (she, it) did rise	they did rise
Pres.	I have risen	we have risen
Perf.	you have risen	you have risen
	he (she, it) has risen	they have risen
Past	I had risen	we had risen
Perf.	you had risen	you had risen
	he (she, it) had risen	they had risen
Fut.	I shall have risen	we shall have risen
Perf.	you will have risen	you will have risen
	he (she, it) will have risen	they will have risen

IMPERATIVE MOOD
rise

SUBJUNCTIVE MOOD

Pres.	if I rise	if we rise
	if you rise	if you rise
	if he (she, it) rise	if they rise
Past	if I rose	if we rose
	if you rose	if you rose
	if he (she, it) rose	if they rose
Fut.	if I should rise	if we should rise
	if you should rise	if you should rise
	if he (she, it) should rise	if they should rise

To rise is an intransitive verb.

It does not take an object.
It describes action, but the action is self-contained.
Like other intransitive verbs, it may be followed by adverbs, adverbial phrases and clauses describing the how, why, when, and where of the action.
HOW: The sun rose *brilliantly*. (adverb)
WHY: He rose *to address the audience*. (adverbial phrase)
WHEN: I always rise *when the alarm rings*. (adverbial clause)
WHERE: The moon has risen *above the horizon*. (adverbial phrase)

to run (active voice)   *Principal Parts:* run, running, ran, run

Infinitive: to run   *Present Participle:* running
Perfect Infinitive: to have run   *Past Participle:* run

INDICATIVE MOOD

Pres.	I run	we run
	you run	you run
	he (she, it) runs	they run
Pres.	I am running	we are running
Prog.	you are running	you are running
	he (she, it) is running	they are running
Pres.	I do run	we do run
Int.	you do run	you do run
	he (she, it) does run	they do run
Fut.	I shall run	we shall run
	you will run	you will run
	he (she, it) will run	they will run
Fut.	I will run *(P)*	we will run *(P)*
	you shall run *(C)*	you shall run *(C)*
	he (she, it) shall run *(C)*	they shall run *(C)*
Past	I ran	we ran
	you ran	you ran
	he (she, it) ran	they ran
Past	I was running	we were running
Prog.	you were running	you were running
	he (she, it) was running	they were running
Past	I did run	we did run
Int.	you did run	you did run
	he (she, it) did run	they did run
Pres.	I have run	we have run
Perf.	you have run	you have run
	he (she, it) has run	they have run
Past	I had run	we had run
Perf.	you had run	you had run
	he (she, it) had run	they had run
Fut.	I shall have run	we shall have run
Perf.	you will have run	you will have run
	he (she, it) will have run	they will have run

IMPERATIVE MOOD
run

SUBJUNCTIVE MOOD

Pres.	if I run	if we run
	if you run	if you run
	if he (she, it) run	if they run
Past	if I ran	if we ran
	if you ran	if you ran
	if he (she, it) ran	if they ran
Fut.	if I should run	if we should run
	if you should run	if you should run
	if he (she, it) should run	if they should run

Infinitive: to be run   *Present Participle:* being run
Perfect Infinitive: to have been run   *Past Participle:* been run

INDICATIVE MOOD

Pres.	I am run	we are run
	you are run	you are run
	he (she, it) is run	they are run

Pres. Prog.	I am being run	we are being run
	you are being run	you are being run
	he (she, it) is being run	they are being run

Pres. Int.	I do get run	we do get run
	you do get run	you do get run
	he (she, it) does get run	they do get run

Fut.	I shall be run	we shall be run
	you will be run	you will be run
	he (she, it) will be run	they will be run

Fut.	I will be run *(P)*	we will be run *(P)*
	you shall be run *(C)*	you shall be run *(C)*
	he (she, it) shall be run *(C)*	they shall be run *(C)*

Past	I was run	we were run
	you were run	you were run
	he (she, it) was run	they were run

Past Prog.	I was being run	we were being run
	you were being run	you were being run
	he (she, it) was being run	they were being run

Past Int.	I did get run	we did get run
	you did get run	you did get run
	he (she, it) did get run	they did get run

Pres. Perf.	I have been run	we have been run
	you have been run	you have been run
	he (she, it) has been run	they have been run

Past Perf.	I had been run	we had been run
	you had been run	you had been run
	he (she, it) had been run	they had been run

Fut. Perf.	I shall have been run	we shall have been run
	you will have been run	you will have been run
	he (she, it) will have been run	they will have been run

IMPERATIVE MOOD
be run

SUBJUNCTIVE MOOD

Pres.	if I be run	if we be run
	if you be run	if you be run
	if he (she, it) be run	if they be run

Past	if I were run	if we were run
	if you were run	if you were run
	if he (she, it) were run	if they were run

Fut.	if I should be run	if we should be run
	if you should be run	if you should be run
	if he (she, it) should be run	if they should be run

to say (active voice) — *Principal Parts:* say, saying, said, said

Infinitive: to say   *Present Participle:* saying
Perfect Infinitive: to have said   *Past Participle:* said

INDICATIVE MOOD

Pres.	I say	we say
	you say	you say
	he (she, it) says	they say
Pres.	I am saying	we are saying
Prog.	you are saying	you are saying
	he (she, it) is saying	they are saying
Pres.	I do say	we do say
Int.	you do say	you do say
	he (she, it) does say	they do say
Fut.	I shall say	we shall say
	you will say	you will say
	he (she, it) will say	they will say
Fut.	I will say *(P)*	we will say *(P)*
	you shall say *(C)*	you shall say *(C)*
	he (she, it) shall say *(C)*	they shall say *(C)*
Past	I said	we said
	you said	you said
	he (she, it) said	they said
Past	I was saying	we were saying
Prog.	you were saying	you were saying
	he (she, it) was saying	they were saying
Past	I did say	we did say
Int.	you did say	you did say
	he (she, it) did say	they did say
Pres.	I have said	we have said
Perf.	you have said	you have said
	he (she, it) has said	they have said
Past	I had said	we had said
Perf.	you had said	you had said
	he (she, it) had said	they had said
Fut.	I shall have said	we shall have said
Perf.	you will have said	you will have said
	he (she, it) will have said	they will have said

IMPERATIVE MOOD
say

SUBJUNCTIVE MOOD

Pres.	if I say	if we say
	if you say	if you say
	if he (she, it) say	if they say
Past	if I said	if we said
	if you said	if you said
	if he (she, it) said	if they said
Fut.	if I should say	if we should say
	if you should say	if you should say
	if he (she, it) should say	if they should say

(passive voice)

Infinitive: to be said   *Present Participle:* being said
Perfect Infinitive: to have been said   *Past Participle:* been said

INDICATIVE MOOD

Pres. I am said
you are said
he (she, it) is said

we are said
you are said
they are said

Pres.
Prog. I am being said
you are being said
he (she, it) is being said

we are being said
you are being said
they are being said

Pres.
Int. I do get said
you do get said
he (she, it) does get said

we do get said
you do get said
they do get said

Fut. I shall be said
you will be said
he (she, it) will be said

we shall be said
you will be said
they will be said

Fut. I will be said *(P)*
you shall be said *(C)*
he (she, it) shall be said *(C)*

we will be said *(P)*
you shall be said *(C)*
they shall be said *(C)*

Past I was said
you were said
he (she, it) was said

we were said
you were said
they were said

Past
Prog. I was being said
you were being said
he (she, it) was being said

we were being said
you were being said
they were being said

Past
Int. I did get said
you did get said
he (she, it) did get said

we did get said
you did get said
they did get said

Pres.
Perf. I have been said
you have been said
he (she, it) has been said

we have been said
you have been said
they have been said

Past
Perf. I had been said
you had been said
he (she, it) had been said

we have been said
you had been said
they had been said

Fut.
Perf. I shall have been said
you will have been said
he (she, it) will have been said

we shall have been said
you will have been said
they will have been said

IMPERATIVE MOOD
be said

SUBJUNCTIVE MOOD

Pres. if I be said
if you be said
if he (she, it) be said

if we be said
if you be said
if they be said

Past if I were said
if you were said
if he (she, it) were said

if we were said
if you were said
if they were said

Fut. if I should be said
if you should be said
if he (she, it) should be said

if we should be said
if you should be said
if they should be said

to see (active voice)

Principal Parts: see, seeing, saw, seen

Infinitive: to see
Perfect Infinitive: to have seen

Present Participle: seeing
Past Participle: seen

INDICATIVE MOOD

Pres.	I see	we see
	you see	you see
	he (she, it) sees	they see
Pres.	I am seeing	we are seeing
Prog.	you are seeing	you are seeing
	he (she, it) is seeing	they are seeing
Pres.	I do see	we do see
Int.	you do see	you do see
	he (she, it) does see	they do see
Fut.	I shall see	we shall see
	you will see	you will see
	he (she, it) will see	they will see
Fut.	I will see *(P)*	we will see *(P)*
	you shall see *(C)*	you shall see *(C)*
	he (she, it) shall see *(C)*	they shall see *(C)*
Past	I saw	we saw
	you saw	you saw
	he (she, it) saw	they saw
Past	I was seeing	we were seeing
Prog.	you were seeing	you were seeing
	he (she, it) was seeing	they were seeing
Past	I did see	we did see
Int.	you did see	you did see
	he (she, it) did see	they did see
Pres.	I have seen	we have seen
Perf.	you have seen	you have seen
	he (she, it) has seen	they have seen
Past	I had seen	we had seen
Perf.	you had seen	you had seen
	he (she, it) had seen	they had seen
Fut.	I shall have seen	we shall have seen
Perf.	you will have seen	you will have seen
	he (she, it) will have seen	they will have seen

IMPERATIVE MOOD
see

SUBJUNCTIVE MOOD

Pres.	if I see	if we see
	if you see	if you see
	if he (she, it) see	if they see
Past	if I saw	if we saw
	if you saw	if you saw
	if he (she, it) saw	if they saw
Fut.	if I should see	if we should see
	if you should see	if you should see
	if he (she, it) should see	if they should see

(passive voice)

Infinitive: to be seen

Perfect Infinitive: to have been seen

Present Participle: being seen

Past Participle: been seen

INDICATIVE MOOD

Pres.	I am seen	we are seen
	you are seen	you are seen
	he (she, it) is seen	they are seen
Pres.	I am being seen	we are being seen
Prog.	you are being seen	you are being seen
	he (she, it) is being seen	they are being seen
Pres.	I do get seen	we do get seen
Int.	you do get seen	you do get seen
	he (she, it) does get seen	they do get seen
Fut.	I shall be seen	we shall be seen
	you will be seen	you will be seen
	he (she, it) will be seen	they will be seen
Fut.	I will be seen *(P)*	we will be seen *(P)*
	you shall be seen *(C)*	you shall be seen *(C)*
	he (she, it) shall be seen *(C)*	they shall be seen *(C)*
Past	I was seen	we were seen
	you were seen	you were seen
	he (she, it) was seen	they were seen
Past	I was being seen	we were being seen
Prog.	you were being seen	you were being seen
	he (she, it) was being seen	they were being seen
Past	I did get seen	we did get seen
Int.	you did get seen	you did get seen
	he (she, it) did get seen	they did get seen
Pres.	I have been seen	we have been seen
Perf.	you have been seen	you have been seen
	he (she, it) has been seen	they have been seen
Past	I had been seen	we had been seen
Perf.	you had been seen	you had been seen
	he (she, it) had been seen	they had been seen
Fut.	I shall have been seen	we shall have been seen
Perf.	you will have been seen	you will have been seen
	he (she, it) will have been seen	they will have been seen

IMPERATIVE MOOD
be seen

SUBJUNCTIVE MOOD

Pres.	if I be seen	if we be seen
	if you be seen	if you be seen
	if he (she, it) be seen	if they be seen
Past	if I were seen	if we were seen
	if you were seen	if you were seen
	if he (she, it) were seen	if they were seen
Fut.	if I should be seen	if we should be seen
	if you should be seen	if you should be seen
	if he (she, it) should be seen	if they should be seen

to seek (active voice) — *Principal Parts:* seek, seeking, sought, sought

Infinitive: to seek   *Present Participle:* seeking
Perfect Infinitive: to have sought   *Past Participle:* sought

INDICATIVE MOOD

Pres.	I seek	we seek
	you seek	you seek
	he (she, it) seeks	they seek
Pres. Prog.	I am seeking	we are seeking
	you are seeking	you are seeking
	he (she, it) is seeking	they are seeking
Pres. Int.	I do seek	we do seek
	you do seek	you do seek
	he (she, it) does seek	they do seek
Fut.	I shall seek	we shall seek
	you will seek	you will seek
	he (she, it) will seek	they will seek
Fut.	I will seek *(P)*	we will seek *(P)*
	you shall seek *(C)*	you shall seek *(C)*
	he (she, it) shall seek *(C)*	they shall seek *(C)*
Past	I sought	we sought
	you sought	you sought
	he (she, it) sought	they sought
Past Prog.	I was seeking	we were seeking
	you were seeking	you were seeking
	he (she, it) was seeking	they were seeking
Past Int.	I did seek	we did seek
	you did seek	you did seek
	he (she, it) did seek	they did seek
Pres. Perf.	I have sought	we have sought
	you have sought	you have sought
	he (she, it) has sought	they have sought
Past Perf.	I had sought	we had sought
	you had sought	you had sought
	he (she, it) had sought	they had sought
Fut. Perf.	I shall have sought	we shall have sought
	you will have sought	you will have sought
	he (she, it) will have sought	they will have sought

IMPERATIVE MOOD
seek

SUBJUNCTIVE MOOD

Pres.	if I seek	if we seek
	if you seek	if you seek
	if he (she, it) seek	if they seek
Past	if I sought	if we sought
	if you sought	if you sought
	if he (she, it) sought	if they sought
Fut.	if I should seek	if we should seek
	if you should seek	if you should seek
	if he (she, it) should seek	if they should seek

(passive voice)

Infinitive: to be sought *Present Participle:* being sought
Perfect Infinitive: to have been sought *Past Participle:* been sought

INDICATIVE MOOD

Pres.	I am sought	we are sought
	you are sought	you are sought
	he (she, it) is sought	they are sought
Pres.	I am being sought	we are being sought
Prog.	you are being sought	you are being sought
	he (she, it) is being sought	they are being sought
Pres.	I do get sought	we do get sought
Int.	you do get sought	you do get sought
	he (she, it) does get sought	they do get sought
Fut.	I shall be sought	we shall be sought
	you will be sought	you will be sought
	he (she, it) will be sought	they will be sought
Fut.	I will be sought *(P)*	we will be sought *(P)*
	you shall be sought *(C)*	you shall be sought *(C)*
	he (she, it) shall be sought *(C)*	they shall be sought *(C)*
Past	I was sought	we were sought
	you were sought	you were sought
	he (she, it) was sought	they were sought
Past	I was being sought	we were being sought
Prog.	you were being sought	you were being sought
	he (she, it) was being sought	they were being sought
Past	I did get sought	we did get sought
Int.	you did get sought	you did get sought
	he (she, it) did get sought	they did get sought
Pres.	I have been sought	we have been sought
Perf.	you have been sought	you have been sought
	he (she, it) has been sought	they have been sought
Past	I had been sought	we had been sought
Perf.	you had been sought	you had been sought
	he (she, it) had been sought	they had been sought
Fut.	I shall have been sought	we shall have been sought
Perf.	you will have been sought	you shall have been sought
	he (she, it) will have been sought	they will have been sought

IMPERATIVE MOOD
be sought

SUBJUNCTIVE MOOD

Pres.	if I be sought	if we be sought
	if you be sought	if you be sought
	if he (she, it) be sought	if they be sought
Past	if I were sought	if we were sought
	if you were sought	if you were sought
	if he (she, it) were sought	if they were sought
Fut.	if I should be sought	if we should be sought
	if you should be sought	if you should be sought
	if he (she, it) should be sought	if they should be sought

to sell (active voice)   *Principal Parts:* sell, selling, sold, sold

Infinitive: to sell   *Present Participle:* selling
Perfect Infinitive: to have sold   *Past Participle:* sold

INDICATIVE MOOD

Pres.	I sell	we sell
	you sell	you sell
	he (she, it) sells	they sell
Pres. Prog.	I am selling	we are selling
	you are selling	you are selling
	he (she, it) is selling	they are selling
Pres. Int.	I do sell	we do sell
	you do sell	you do sell
	he (she, it) does sell	they do sell
Fut.	I shall sell	we shall sell
	you will sell	you will sell
	he (she, it) will sell	they will sell
Fut.	I will sell *(P)*	we will sell *(P)*
	you shall sell *(C)*	you shall sell *(C)*
	he (she, it) shall sell *(C)*	they shall sell *(C)*
Past	I sold	we sold
	you sold	you sold
	he (she, it) sold	they sold
Past Prog.	I was selling	we were selling
	you were selling	you were selling
	he (she, it) was selling	they were selling
Past Int.	I did sell	we did sell
	you did sell	you did sell
	he (she, it) did sell	they did sell
Pres. Perf.	I have sold	we have sold
	you have sold	you have sold
	he (she, it) has sold	they have sold
Past Perf.	I had sold	we had sold
	you had sold	you had sold
	he (she, it) had sold	they had old
Fut. Perf.	I shall have sold	we shall have sold
	you will have sold	you will have sold
	he (she, it) will have sold	they will have sold

IMPERATIVE MOOD
sell

SUBJUNCTIVE MOOD

Pres.	if I sell	if we sell
	if you sell	if you sell
	if he (she, it) sell	if they sell
Past	if I sold	if we sold
	if you sold	if you sold
	if he (she, it) sold	if they sold
Fut.	if I should sell	if we should sell
	if you should sell	if you should sell
	if he (she, it) should sell	if they should sell

Infinitive: to be sold   *Present Participle:* being sold
Perfect Infinitive: to have been sold   *Past Participle:* been sold

INDICATIVE MOOD

Pres. I am sold   we are sold
you are sold   you are sold
he (she, it) is sold   they are sold

Pres. I am being sold   we are being sold
Prog. you are being sold   you are being sold
he (she, it) is being sold   they are being sold

Pres. I do get sold   we do get sold
Int. you do get sold   you do get sold
he (she, it) does get sold   they do get sold

Fut. I shall be sold   we shall be sold
you will be sold   you will be sold
he (she, it) will be sold   they will be sold

Fut. I will be sold *(P)*   we will be sold *(P)*
you shall be sold *(C)*   you shall be sold *(C)*
he (she, it) shall be sold *(C)*   they shall be sold *(C)*

Past I was sold   we were sold
you were sold   you were sold
he (she, it) was sold   they were sold

Past I was being sold   we were being sold
Prog. you were being sold   you were being sold
he (she, it) was being sold   they were being sold

Past I did get sold   we did get sold
Int. you did get sold   you did get sold
he (she, it) did get sold   they did get sold

Pres. I have been sold   we have been sold
Perf. you have been sold   you have been sold
he (she, it) has been sold   they have been sold

Past I had been sold   we had been sold
Perf. you had been sold   you had been sold
he (she, it) had been sold   they had been sold

Fut. I shall have been sold   we shall have been sold
Perf. you will have been sold   you will have been sold
he (she, it) will have been sold   they will have been sold

IMPERATIVE MOOD
be sold

SUBJUNCTIVE MOOD

Pres. if I be sold   if we be sold
if you be sold   if you be sold
if he (she, it) be sold   if they be sold

Past if I were sold   if we were sold
if you were sold   if you were sold
if he (she, it) were sold   if they were sold

Fut. if I should be sold   if we should be sold
if you should be sold   if you should be sold
if he (she, it) should be sold   if they should be sold

to send (active voice)

Principal Parts: send, sending, sent, sent

Infinitive: to send

Perfect Infinitive: to have sent

Present Participle: sending

Past Participle: sent

INDICATIVE MOOD

Pres.	I send	we send
	you send	you send
	he (she, it) sends	they send
Pres.	I am sending	we are sending
Prog.	you are sending	you are sending
	he (she, it) is sending	they are sending
Pres.	I do send	we do send
Int.	you do send	you do send
	he (she, it) does send	they do send
Fut.	I shall send	we shall send
	you will send	you will send
	he (she, it) will send	they will send
Fut.	I will send *(P)*	we will send *(P)*
	you shall send *(C)*	you shall send *(C)*
	he (she, it) shall send *(C)*	they shall send *(C)*
Past	I sent	we sent
	you sent	you sent
	he (she, it) sent	they sent
Past	I was sending	we were sending
Prog.	you were sending	you were sending
	he (she, it) was sending	they were sending
Past	I did send	we did send
Int.	you did send	you did send
	he (she, it) did send	they did send
Pres.	I have sent	we have sent
Perf.	you have sent	you have sent
	he (she, it) has sent	they have sent
Past	I had sent	we had sent
Perf.	you had sent	you had sent
	he (she, it) had sent	they had sent
Fut.	I shall have sent	we shall have sent
Perf.	you will have sent	you will have sent
	he (she, it) will have sent	they will have sent

IMPERATIVE MOOD
send

SUBJUNCTIVE MOOD

Pres.	if I send	if we send
	if you send	if you send
	if he (she, it) send	if they send
Past	if I sent	if we sent
	if you sent	if you sent
	if he (she, it) sent	if they sent
Fut.	if I should send	if we should send
	if you should send	if you should send
	if he (she, it) should send	if they should send

Infinitive: to be sent   *Present Participle:* being sent
Perfect Infinitive: to have been sent   *Past Participle:* been sent

INDICATIVE MOOD

Pres.	I am sent	we are sent
	you are sent	you are sent
	he (she, it) is sent	they are sent
Pres.	I am being sent	we are being sent
Prog.	you are being sent	you are being sent
	he (she, it) is being sent	they are being sent
Pres.	I do get sent	we do get sent
Int.	you do get sent	you do get sent
	he (she, it) does get sent	they do get sent
Fut.	I shall be sent	we shall be sent
	you will be sent	you will be sent
	he (she, it) will be sent	they will be sent
Fut.	I will be sent *(P)*	we will be sent *(P)*
	you shall be sent *(C)*	you shall be sent *(C)*
	he (she, it) shall be sent *(C)*	they shall be sent *(C)*
Past	I was sent	we were sent
	you were sent	you were sent
	he (she, it) was sent	they were sent
Past	I was being sent	we were being sent
Prog.	you were being sent	you were being sent
	he (she, it) was being sent	they were being sent
Past	I did get sent	we did get sent
Int.	you did get sent	you did get sent
	he (she, it) did get sent	they did get sent
Pres.	I have been sent	we have been sent
Perf.	you have been sent	you have been sent
	he (she, it) has been sent	they have been sent
Past	I had been sent	we had been sent
Perf.	you had been sent	you had been sent
	he (she, it) had been sent	they had been sent
Fut.	I shall have been sent	we shall have been sent
Perf.	you will have been sent	you will have been sent
	he (she, it) will have been sent	they will have been sent

IMPERATIVE MOOD
be sent

SUBJUNCTIVE MOOD

Pres.	if I be sent	if we be sent
	if you be sent	if you be sent
	if he (she, it) be sent	if they be sent
Past	if I were sent	if we were sent
	if you were sent	if you were sent
	if he (she, it) were sent	if they were sent
Fut.	if I should be sent	if we should be sent
	if you should be sent	if you should be sent
	if he (she, it) should be sent	if they should be sent

to set (active voice)   *Principal Parts:* set, setting, set, set

Infinitive: to set   *Present Participle:* setting
Perfect Infinitive: to have set   *Past Participle:* set

INDICATIVE MOOD

Pres.	I set	we set
	you set	you set
	he (she, it) sets	they set
Pres.	I am setting	we are setting
Prog.	you are setting	you are setting
	he (she, it) is setting	they are setting
Pres.	I do set	we do set
Int.	you do set	you do set
	he (she, it) does set	they do set
Fut.	I shall set	we shall set
	you will set	you will set
	he (she, it) will set	they will set
Fut.	I will set *(P)*	we will set *(P)*
	you shall set *(C)*	you shall set *(C)*
	he (she, it) shall set *(C)*	they shall set *(C)*
Past	I set	we set
	you set	you set
	he (she, it) set	they set
Past	I was setting	we were setting
Prog.	you were setting	you were setting
	he (she, it) was setting	they were setting
Past	I did set	we did set
Int.	you did set	you did set
	he (she, it) did set	they did set
Pres.	I have set	we have set
Perf.	you have set	you have set
	he (she, it) has set	they have set
Past	I had set	we had set
Perf.	you had set	you had set
	he (she, it) had set	they had set
Fut.	I shall have set	we shall have set
Perf.	you will have set	you will have set
	he (she, it) will have set	they will have set

IMPERATIVE MOOD
set

SUBJUNCTIVE MOOD

Pres.	if I set	if we set
	if you set	if you set
	if he (she, it) set	if they set
Past	if I set	if we set
	if you set	if you set
	if he (she, it) set	if they set
Fut.	if I should set	if we should set
	if you should set	if you should set
	if he (she, it) should set	if they should set

Infinitive: to be set   *Present Participle:* being set
Perfect Infinitive: to have been set   *Past Participle:* been set

INDICATIVE MOOD

Pres.	I am set	we are set
	you are set	you are set
	he (she, it) is set	they are set
Pres.	I am being set	we are being set
Prog.	you are being set	you are being set
	he (she, it) is being set	they are being set
Pres.	I do get set	we do get set
Int.	you do get set	you do get set
	he (she, it) does get set	they do get set
Fut.	I shall be set	we shall be set
	you will be set	you will be set
	he (she, it) will be set	they will be set
Fut.	I will be set *(P)*	we will be set *(P)*
	you shall be set *(C)*	you shall be set *(C)*
	he (she, it) shall be set *(C)*	they shall be set *(C)*
Past	I was set	we were set
	you were set	you were set
	he (she, it) was set	they were set
Past	I was being set	we were being set
Prog.	you were being set	you were being set
	he (she, it) was being set	they were being set
Past	I did get set	we did get set
Int.	you did get set	you did get set
	he (she, it) did get set	they did get set
Pres.	I have been set	we have been set
Perf.	you have been set	you have been set
	he (she, it) has been set	they have been set
Past	I had been set	we had been set
Perf.	you had been set	you had been set
	he (she, it) had been set	they had been set
Fut.	I shall have been set	we shall have been set
Pref.	you will have been set	you will have been set
	he (she, it) will have been set	they will have been set

IMPERATIVE MOOD
be set

SUBJUNCTIVE MOOD

Pres.	if I be set	if we be set
	if you be set	if you be set
	if he (she, it) be set	if they be set
Past	if I were set	if we were set
	if you were set	if you were set
	if he (she, it) were set	if they were set
Fut.	if I should be set	if we should be set
	if you should be set	if you should be set
	if he (she, it) should be set	if they should be set

to shake (active voice) *Principal Parts:* shake, shaking, shook, shaken

Infinitive: to shake *Present Participle:* shaking
Perfect Infinitive: to have shaken *Past Participle:* shaken

INDICATIVE MOOD

Pres.	I shake	we shake
	you shake	you shake
	he (she, it) shakes	they shake
Pres Prog.	I am shaking	we are shaking
	you are shaking	you are shaking
	he (she, it) is shaking	they are shaking
Pres. Int.	I do shake	we do shake
	you do shake	you do shake
	he (she, it) does shake	they do shake
Fut.	I shall shake	we shall shake
	you will shake	you will shake
	he (she, it) will shake	they will shake
Fut.	I will shake *(P)*	we will shake *(P)*
	you shall shake *(C)*	you shall shake *(C)*
	he (she, it) shall shake *(C)*	they shall shake *(C)*
Past	I shook	we shook
	you shook	you shook
	he (she, it) shook	they shook
Past Prog.	I was shaking	we were shaking
	you were shaking	you were shaking
	he (she, it) was shaking	they were shaking
Past Int.	I did shake	we did shake
	you did shake	you did shake
	he (she, it) did shake	they did shake
Pres. Perf.	I have shaken	we have shaken
	you have shaken	you have shaken
	he (she, it) has shaken	they have shaken
Past Perf.	I had shaken	we had shaken
	you had shaken	you had shaken
	he (she, it) had shaken	they had shaken
Fut. Perf.	I shall have shaken	we shall have shaken
	you will have shaken	you will have shaken
	he (she, it) will have shaken	they will have shaken

IMPERATIVE MOOD
shake

SUBJUNCTIVE MOOD

Pres.	if I shake	if we shake
	if you shake	if you shake
	if he (she, it) shake	if they shake
Past	if I shook	if we shook
	if you shook	if you shook
	if he (she, it) shook	if they shook
Fut.	if I should shake	if we should shake
	if you should shake	if you should shake
	if he (she, it) should shake	if they should shake

266

(passive voice)

Infinitive: to be shaken   *Present Participle:* being shaken
Perfect Infinitive: to have been shaken   *Past Participle:* been shaken

INDICATIVE MOOD

Pres.	I am shaken	we are shaken
	you are shaken	you are shaken
	he (she, it) is shaken	they are shaken
Pres. Prog.	I am being shaken	we are being shaken
	you are being shaken	you are being shaken
	he (she, it) is being shaken	they are being shaken
Pres. Int.	I do get shaken	we do get shaken
	you do get shaken	you do get shaken
	he (she, it) does get shaken	they do get shaken
Fut.	I shall be shaken	we shall be shaken
	you will be shaken	you will be shaken
	he (she, it) will be shaken	they will be shaken
Fut.	I will be shaken *(P)*	we will be shaken *(P)*
	you shall be shaken *(C)*	you shall be shaken *(C)*
	he (she, it) shall be shaken *(C)*	they shall be shaken *(C)*
Past	I was shaken	we were shaken
	you were shaken	you were shaken
	he (she, it) was shaken	they were shaken
Past Prog.	I was being shaken	we were being shaken
	you were being shaken	you were being shaken
	he (she, it) was being shaken	they were being shaken
Past Int.	I did get shaken	we did get shaken
	you did get shaken	you did get shaken
	he (she, it) did get shaken	they did get shaken
Pres. Perf.	I have been shaken	we have been shaken
	you have been shaken	you have been shaken
	he (she, it) has been shaken	they have been shaken
Past Perf.	I had been shaken	we had been shaken
	you had been shaken	you had been shaken
	he (she, it) had been shaken	they had been shaken
Fut. Perf.	I shall have been shaken	we shall have been shaken
	you will have been shaken	you will have been shaken
	he (she, it) will have been shaken	they will have been shaken

IMPERATIVE MOOD
be shaken

SUBJUNCTIVE MOOD

Pres.	if I be shaken	if we be shaken
	if you be shaken	if you be shaken
	if he (she, it) be shaken	if they be shaken
Past	if I were shaken	if we were shaken
	if you were shaken	if you were shaken
	if he (she, it) were shaken	if they were shaken
Fut.	if I should be shaken	if we should be shaken
	if you should be shaken	if you should be shaken
	if he (she, it) should be shaken	if they should be shaken

to shine (active voice)   *Principal Parts:* shine, shining, shone (shined),
shone (shined)

Infinitive: to shine   *Present Participle:* shining
Perfect Infinitive: to have shone, shined   *Past Participle:* shone, shined

INDICATIVE MOOD

Pres.	I shine	we shine
	you shine	you shine
	he (she, it) shines	they shine
Pres.	I am shining	we are shining
Prog.	you are shining	you are shining
	he (she, it) is shining	they are shining
Pres.	I do shine	we do shine
Int.	you do shine	you do shine
	he (she, it) does shine	they do shine
Fut.	I shall shine	we shall shine
	you will shine	you will shine
	he (she, it) will shine	they will shine
Fut.	I will shine *(P)*	we will shine *(P)*
	you shall shine *(C)*	you shall shine *(C)*
	he (she, it) shall shine *(C)*	they shall shine *(C)*
Past	I shone, shined	we shone, shined
	you shone, shined	you shone, shined
	he (she, it) shone, shined	they shone, shined
Past	I was shining	we were shining
Prog.	you were shining	you were shining
	he (she, it) was shining	they were shining
Past	I did shine	we did shine
Int.	you did shine	you did shine
	he (she, it) did shine	they did shine
Pres.	I have shone, shined	we have shone, shined
Perf.	you have shone, shined	you have shone, shined
	he (she, it) has shone, shined	they have shone, shined
Past	I had shone, shined	we had shone, shined
Perf.	you had shone, shined	you had shone, shined
	he (she, it) had shone, shined	they had shone, shined
Fut.	I shall have shone, shined	we shall have shone, shined
Perf.	you will have shone, shined	you will have shone, shined
	he (she, it) will have shone, shined	they will have shone, shined

IMPERATIVE MOOD
shine

SUBJUNCTIVE MOOD

Pres.	if I shine	if we shine
	if you shine	if you shine
	if he (she, it) shine	if they shine
Past	if I shone, shined	if we shone, shined
	if you shone, shined	if you shone, shined
	if he (she, it) shone, shined	if they shone, shined
Fut.	if I should shine	if we should shine
	if you should shine	if you should shine
	if he (she, it) should shine	if they should shine

268

Infinitive: to be shone, shined   *Present Participle:* being shone, shined
Perfect Infinitive: to have been   *Past Participle:* been shone, shined
shone, shined

INDICATIVE MOOD

Pres. I am shone, shined	we are shone, shined
you are shone, shined	you are shone, shined
he (she, it) is shone, shined	they are shone, shined

Pres. I am being shone, shined	we are being shone, shined
Prog. you are being shone, shined	you are being shone, shined
he (she, it) is being shone, shined	they are being shone, shined

Pres. I do get shone, shined	we do get shone, shined
Int. you do get shone, shined	you do get shone, shined
he (she, it) does get shone, shined	they do get shone, shined

Fut. I shall be shone, shined	we shall be shone, shined
you will be shone, shined	you will be shone, shined
he (she, it) will be shone, shined	they will be shone, shined

Fut. I will be shone, shined *(P)*	we will be shone, shined *(P)*
you shall be shone, shined *(C)*	you shall be shone, shined *(C)*
he (she, it) shall be shone, shined *(C)*	they shall be shone, shined *(C)*

Past I was shone, shined	we were shone, shined
you were shone, shined	you were shone, shined
he (she, it) was shone, shined	they were shone, shined

Past I was being shone, shined	we were being shone, shined
Prog. you were being shone, shined	you were being shone, shined
he (she, it) was being shone, shined	they were being shone, shined

Past I did get shone, shined	we did get shone, shined
Int. you did get shone, shined	you did get shone, shined
he (she, it) did get shone, shined	they did get shone, shined

Pres. I have been shone, shined	we have been shone, shined
Perf. you have been shone, shined	you have been shone, shined
he (she, it) has been shone, shined	they have been shone, shined

Past I had been shone, shined	we had been shone, shined
Perf. you had been shone, shined	you had been shone, shined
he (she, it) had been shone, shined	they had been shone, shined

Fut. I shall have been shone, shined	we shall have been shone, shined
Perf. you will have been shone, shined	you will have been shone, shined
he (she, it) will have been shone, shined	they will have been shone, shined

IMPERATIVE MOOD
be shone, shined

SUBJUNCTIVE MOOD

Pres. if I be shone, shined	if we be shone, shined
if you be shone, shined	if you be shone, shined
if he (she, it) be shone, shined	if they be shone, shined

Past if I were shone, shined	if we were shone, shined
if you were shone, shined	if you were shone, shined
if he (she, it) were shone, shined	if they were shone, shined

Fut. if I should be shone, shined	if we should be shone, shined
if you should be shone, shined	if you should be shone, shined
if he (she, it) should be shone, shined	if they should be shone, shined

to shoot (active voice)　　*Principal Parts:* shoot, shooting, shot, shot

Infinitive: to shoot　　　　　　　　　*Present Participle:* shooting
Perfect Infinitive: to have shot　　　　　　*Past Participle:* shot

INDICATIVE MOOD

Pres.	I shoot	we shoot
	you shoot	you shoot
	he (she, it) shoots	they shoot
Pres.	I am shooting	we are shooting
Prog.	you are shooting	you are shooting
	he (she, it) is shooting	they are shooting
Pres.	I do shoot	we do shoot
Int.	you do shoot	you do shoot
	he (she, it) does shoot	they do shoot
Fut.	I shall shoot	we shall shoot
	you will shoot	you will shoot
	he (she, it) will shoot	they will shoot
Fut.	I will shoot *(P)*	we will shoot *(P)*
	you shall shoot *(C)*	you shall shoot *(C)*
	he (she, it) shall shoot *(C)*	they shall shoot *(C)*
Past	I shot	we shot
	you shot	you shot
	he (she, it) shot	they shot
Past	I was shooting	we were shooting
Prog.	you were shooting	you were shooting
	he (she, it) was shooting	they were shooting
Past	I did shoot	we did shoot
Int.	you did shoot	you did shoot
	he (she, it) did shoot	they did shoot
Pres.	I have shot	we have shot
Perf.	you have shot	you have shot
	he (she, it) has shot	they have shot
Past	I had shot	we had shot
Perf.	you had shot	you had shot
	he (she, it) had shot	they had shot
Fut.	I shall have shot	we shall have shot
Perf.	you will have shot	you will have shot
	he (she, it) will have shot	they will have shot

IMPERATIVE MOOD
shoot

SUBJUNCTIVE MOOD

Pres.	if I shoot	if we shoot
	if you shoot	if you shoot
	if he (she, it) shoot	if they shoot
Past	if I shot	if we shot
	if you shot	if you shot
	if he (she, it) shot	if they shot
Fut.	if I should shoot	if we should shoot
	if you should shoot	if you should shoot
	if he (she, it) should shoot	if they should shoot

(passive voice)

Infinitive: to be shot   *Present Participle:* being shot
Perfect Infinitive: to have been shot   *Past Participle:* been shot

INDICATIVE MOOD

Pres.	I am shot	we are shot
	you are shot	you are shot
	he (she, it) is shot	they are shot
Pres.	I am being shot	we are being shot
Prog.	you are being shot	you are being shot
	he (she, it) is being shot	they are being shot
Pres.	I do get shot	we do get shot
Int.	you do get shot	you do get shot
	he (she, it) does get shot	they do get shot
Fut.	I shall be shot	we shall be shot
	you will be shot	you will be shot
	he (she, it) will be shot	they will be shot
Fut.	I will be shot *(P)*	we will be shot *(P)*
	you shall be shot *(C)*	you shall be shot *(C)*
	he (she, it) shall be shot *(C)*	they shall be shot *(C)*
Past	I was shot	we were shot
	you were shot	you were shot
	he (she, it) was shot	they were shot
Past	I was being shot	we were being shot
Prog.	you were being shot	you were being shot
	he (she, it) was being shot	they were being shot
Past	I did get shot	we did get shot
Int.	you did get shot	you did get shot
	he (she, it) did get shot	they did get shot
Pres.	I have been shot	we have been shot
Perf.	you have been shot	you have been shot
	he (she, it) has been shot	they have been shot
Past	I had been shot	we had been shot
Perf.	you had been shot	you had been shot
	he (she, it) had been shot	they had been shot
Fut.	I shall have been shot	we shall have been shot
Perf.	you will have been shot	you will have been shot
	he (she, it) will have been shot	they will have been shot

IMPERATIVE MOOD
be shot

SUBJUNCTIVE MOOD

Pres.	if I be shot	if we be shot
	if you be shot	if you be shot
	if he (she, it) be shot	if they be shot
Past	if I were shot	if we were shot
	if you were shot	if you were shot
	if he (she, it) were shot	if they were shot
Fut.	if I should be shot	if we should be shot
	if you should be shot	if you should be shot
	if (she, it) should be shot	if they should be shot

to shrink (active voice)　　*Principal Parts:* shrink, shrinking, shrank
　　　　　　　　　　　　　　　　　　　(shrunk), shrunk (shrunken)

Infinitive: to shrink　　　　　　　　　　*Present Participle:* shrinking
Perfect Infinitive: to have shrunk (shrunken)　*Past Participle:* shrunk, shrunken

INDICATIVE MOOD

Pres.	I shrink	we shrink

Pres.
　I shrink　　　　　　　　　　　　we shrink
　you shrink　　　　　　　　　　　you shrink
　he (she, it) shrinks　　　　　　　they shrink

Pres.
Prog.
　I am shrinking　　　　　　　　　we are shrinking
　you are shrinking　　　　　　　　you are shrinking
　he (she, it) is shrinking　　　　　they are shrinking

Pres.
Int.
　I do shrink　　　　　　　　　　we do shrink
　you do shrink　　　　　　　　　you do shrink
　he (she, it) does shrink　　　　　they do shrink

Fut.
　I shall shrink　　　　　　　　　we shall shrink
　you will shrink　　　　　　　　you will shrink
　he (she, it) will shrink　　　　　they will shrink

Fut.
　I will shrink *(P)*　　　　　　　we will shrink *(P)*
　you shall shrink *(C)*　　　　　you shall shrink *(C)*
　he (she, it) shall shrink *(C)*　they shall shrink *(C)*

Past
　I shrank, shrunk　　　　　　　we shrank, shrunk
　you shrank, shrunk　　　　　　you shrank, shrunk
　he (she, it) shrank, shrunk　　they shrank, shrunk

Past
Prog.
　I was shrinking　　　　　　　we were shrinking
　you were shrinking　　　　　　you were shrinking
　he (she, it) was shrinking　　　they were shrinking

Past
Int.
　I did shrink　　　　　　　　　we did shrink
　you did shrink　　　　　　　　you did shrink
　he (she, it) did shrink　　　　they did shrink

Pres.
Perf.
　I have shrunk, shrunken　　　　we have shrunk, shrunken
　you have shrunk, shrunken　　　you have shrunk, shrunken
　he (she, it) has shrunk, shrunken　they have shrunk, shrunken

Past
Perf.
　I had shrunk, shrunken　　　　we had shrunk, shrunken
　you had shrunk, shrunken　　　you had shrunk, shrunken
　he (she, it) had shrunk, shrunken　they had shrunk, shrunken

Fut.
Perf.
　I shall have shrunk, shrunken　we shall have shrunk, shrunken
　you will have shrunk, shrunken　you will have shrunk, shrunken
　he (she, it) will have shrunk,　they will have shrunk, shrunken
　　shrunken

IMPERATIVE MOOD
shrink

SUBJUNCTIVE MOOD

Pres.
　if I shrink　　　　　　　　　if we shrink
　if you shrink　　　　　　　　if you shrink
　if he (she, it) shrink　　　　if they shrink

Past
　if I shrank　　　　　　　　if we shrank
　if you shrank　　　　　　　if you shrank
　if he (she, it) shrank　　　if they shrank

Fut.
　if I should shrink　　　　　if we should shrink
　if you should shrink　　　　if you should shrink
　if he (she, it) should shrink　if they should shrink

(passive voice)

Infinitive: to be shrunk, shrunken

Perfect Infinitive: to have been shrunk, shrunken

Present Participle: being shrunk, shrunken

Past Participle: been shrunk, shrunken

INDICATIVE MOOD

Pres. I am shrunk, shrunken	we are shrunk, shrunken
you are shrunk, shrunken	you are shrunk, shrunken
he (she, it) is shrunk, shrunken	they are shrunk, shrunken

Pres. I am being shrunk, shrunken	we are being shrunk, shrunken
Prog. you are being shrunk, shrunken	you are being shrunk, shrunken
he (she, it) is being shrunk, shrunken	they are being shrunk, shrunken

Pres. I do get shrunk, shrunken	we do get shrunk, shrunken
Int. you do get shrunk, shrunken	you do get shrunk, shrunken
he (she, it) does get shrunk, shrunken	they do get shrunk, shrunken

Fut. I shall be shrunk, shrunken	we shall be shrunk, shrunken
you will be shrunk, shrunken	you will be shrunk, shrunken
he (she, it) will be shrunk, shrunken	they will be shrunk, shrunken

Fut. I will be shrunk, shrunken *(P)*	we will be shrunk, shrunken *(P)*
you shall be shrunk, shrunken *(C)*	you shall be shrunk, shrunken *(C)*
he (she, it) shall be shrunk, shrunken *(C)*	they shall be shrunk, shrunken *(C)*

Past I was shrunk, shrunken	we were shrunk, shrunken
you were shrunk, shrunken	you were shrunk, shrunken
he (she, it) was shrunk, shrunken	they were shrunk, shrunken

Past I was being shrunk	we were being shrunk
Prog. you were being shrunk	you were being shrunk
he (she, it) was being shrunk	they were being shrunk

Past I did get shrunk, shrunken	we did get shrunk, shrunken
Int. you did get shrunk, shrunken	you did get shrunk, shrunken
he (she, it) did get shrunk, shrunken	they did get shrunk, shrunken

Pres. I have been shrunk, shrunken	we have been shrunk, shrunken
Perf. you have been shrunk, shrunken	you have been shrunk, shrunken
he (she, it) has been shrunk, shrunken	they have been shrunk, shrunken

Past I had been shrunk, shrunken	we had been shrunk, shrunken
Perf. you had been shrunk, shrunken	you had been shrunk, shrunken
he (she, it) had been shrunk, shrunken	they had been shrunk, shrunken

Fut. I shall have been shrunk, shrunken	we shall have been shrunk, shrunken
Perf. you will have been shrunk, shrunken	you will have been shrunk, shrunken
he (she, it) will have been shrunk, shrunken	they will have been shrunk, shrunken

(passive voice)

IMPERATIVE MOOD
be shrunk

SUBJUNCTIVE MOOD

Pres. if I be shrunk, shrunken
if you be shrunk, shrunken
if he (she, it) be shrunk, shrunken

if we be shrunk, shrunken
if you be shrunk, shrunken
if they be shrunk, shrunken

Past if I were shrunk, shrunken
if you were shrunk, shrunken
if he (she, it) were shrunk, shrunken

if we were shrunk, shrunken
if you were shrunk, shrunken
if they were shrunk, shrunken

Fut. if I should be shrunk, shrunken
if you should be shrunk, shrunken
if he (she, it) should be shrunk,
shrunken

if we should be shrunk, shrunken
if you should be shrunk, shrunken
if they should be shrunk,
shrunken

To shrink is a transitive and intransitive verb.

The verb *to shrink*, meaning to diminish in size, like a woolen sweater after being washed in hot water, is both a transitive and intransitive verb. As a transitive verb it describes the action of someone causing something to shrink: a person *shrinks* a sweater by putting it into hot water. As a result (passive voice) the sweater is shrunken by the person.

But *to shrink* is also an intransitive verb in the sense that the shrinking can be thought of as a self-contained action: "The sweater *is shrinking* in the hot water" or "My capital *is shrinking* every day because stock market prices are falling."

The verb also has a figurative meaning *to draw back*, implying *becoming smaller* or *attempting to become inconspicuous* as in the face of danger or embarrassment: "He *shrank* from a confrontation with his angry father."

to sing (active voice)   *Principal Parts:* sing, singing, sang, sung

Infinitive: to sing   *Present Participle:* singing
Perfect Infinitive: to have sung   *Past Participle:* sung

INDICATIVE MOOD

Pres.	I sing	we sing
	you sing	you sing
	he (she, it) sings	they sing
Pres.	I am singing	we are singing
Prog.	you are singing	you are singing
	he (she, it) is singing	they are singing
Pres.	I do sing	we do sing
Int.	you do sing	you do sing
	he (she, it) does sing	they do sing
Fut.	I shall sing	we shall sing
	you will sing	you will sing
	he (she, it) will sing	they will sing
Fut.	I will sing *(P)*	we will sing *(P)*
	you shall sing *(C)*	you shall sing *(C)*
	he (she, it) shall sing *(C)*	they shall sing *(C)*
Past	I sang	we sang
	you sang	you sang
	he (she, it) sang	they sang
Past	I was singing	we were singing
Prog.	you were singing	you were singing
	he (she, it) was singing	they were singing
Past	I did sing	we did sing
Int.	you did sing	you did sing
	he (she, it) did sing	they did sing
Pres.	I have sung	we have sung
Perf.	you have sung	you have sung
	he (she, it) has sung	they have sung
Past	I had sung	we had sung
Perf.	you had sung	you had sung
	he (she, it) had sung	they had sung
Fut.	I shall have sung	we shall have sung
Perf.	you will have sung	you will have sung
	he (she, it) will have sung	they will have sung

IMPERATIVE MOOD

sing

SUBJUNCTIVE MOOD

Pres.	if I sing	if we sing
	if you sing	if you sing
	if he (she, it) sing	if they sing
Past	if I sang	if we sang
	if you sang	if you sang
	if he (she, it) sang	if they sang
Fut.	if I should sing	if we should sing
	if you should sing	if you should sing
	if he (she, it) should sing	if they should sing

(passive voice)

Infinitive: to be sung *Present Participle:* being sung
Perfect Infinitive: to have been sung *Past Participle:* been sung

INDICATIVE MOOD

Pres.	I am sung	we are sung
	you are sung	you are sung
	he (she, it) is sung	they are sung
Pres. Prog.	I am being sung	we are being sung
	you are being sung	you are being sung
	he (she, it) is being sung	they are being sung
Pres. Int.	I do get sung	we do get sung
	you do get sung	you do get sung
	he (she, it) does get sung	they do get sung
Fut.	I shall be sung	we shall be sung
	you will be sung	you will be sung
	he (she, it) will be sung	they will be sung
Fut.	I will be sung *(P)*	we will be sung *(P)*
	you shall be sung *(C)*	you shall be sung *(C)*
	he (she, it) shall be sung *(C)*	they shall be sung *(C)*
Past	I was sung	we were sung
	you were sung	you were sung
	he (she, it) was sung	they were sung
Past Prog.	I was being sung	we were being sung
	you were being sung	you were being sung
	he (she, it) was being sung	they were being sung
Past Int.	I did get sung	we did get sung
	you did get sung	you did get sung
	he (she, it) did get sung	they did get sung
Pres. Perf.	I have been sung	we have been sung
	you have been sung	you have been sung
	he (she, it) has been sung	they have been sung
Past Perf.	I had been sung	we had been sung
	you had been sung	you had been sung
	he (she, it) had been sung	they had been sung
Fut. Perf.	I shall have been sung	we shall have been sung
	you will have been sung	you will have been sung
	he (she, it) will have been sung	they will have been sung

IMPERATIVE MOOD
be sung

SUBJUNCTIVE MOOD

Pres.	if I be sung	if we be sung
	if you be sung	if you be sung
	if he (she, it) be sung	if they be sung
Past	if I were sung	if we were sung
	if you were sung	if you were sung
	if he (she, it) were sung	if they were sung
Fut.	if I should be sung	if we should be sung
	if you should be sung	if you should be sung
	if he (she, it) should be sung	if they should be sung

to sink (active voice)   *Principal Parts:* sink, sinking, sank, sunk

Infinitive: to sink   *Present Participle:* sinking
Perfect Infinitive: to have sunk   *Past Participle:* sunk

INDICATIVE MOOD

Pres.	I sink	we sink
	you sink	you sink
	he (she, it) sinks	they sink
Pres.	I am sinking	we are sinking
Prog.	you are sinking	you are sinking
	he (she, it) is sinking	they are sinking
Pres.	I do sink	we do sink
Int.	you do sink	you do sink
	he (she, it) does sink	they do sink
Fut.	I shall sink	we shall sink
	you will sink	you will sink
	he (she, it) will sink	they will sink
Fut.	I will sink *(P)*	we will sink *(P)*
	you shall sink *(C)*	you shall sink *(C)*
	he (she, it) shall sink *(C)*	they shall sink *(C)*
Past	I sank	we sank
	you sank	you sank
	he (she, it) sank	they sank
Past	I was sinking	we were sinking
Prog.	you were sinking	you were sinking
	he (she, it) was sinking	they were sinking
Past	I did sink	we did sink
Int.	you did sink	you did sink
	he (she, it) did sink	they did sink
Pres.	I have sunk	we have sunk
Perf.	you have sunk	you have sunk
	he (she, it) has sunk	they have sunk
Past	I had sunk	we had sunk
Perf.	you had sunk	you had sunk
	he (she, it) had sunk	they had sunk
Fut.	I shall have sunk	we shall have sunk
Perf.	you will have sunk	you will have sunk
	he (she, it) will have sunk	they will have sunk

IMPERATIVE MOOD
sink

SUBJUNCTIVE MOOD

Pres.	if I sink	if we sink
	if you sink	if you sink
	if he (she, it) sink	if they sink
Past	if I sank	if we sank
	if you sank	if you sank
	if he (she, it) sank	if they sank
Fut.	if I should sink	if we should sink
	if you should sink	if you should sink
	if he (she, it) should sink	if they should sink

Infinitive: to be sunk   *Present Participle:* being sunk
Perfect Infinitive: to have been sunk   *Past Participle:* been sunk

INDICATIVE MOOD

Pres.	I am sunk	we are sunk
	you are sunk	you are sunk
	he (she, it) is sunk	they are sunk
Pres.	I am being sunk	we are being sunk
Prog.	you are being sunk	you are being sunk
	he (she, it) is being sunk	they are being sunk
Pres.	I do get sunk	we do get sunk
Int.	you do get sunk	you do get sunk
	he (she, it) does get sunk	they do get sunk
Fut.	I shall be sunk	we shall be sunk
	you will be sunk	you will be sunk
	he (she, it) will be sunk	they will be sunk
Fut.	I will be sunk *(P)*	we will be sunk *(P)*
	you shall be sunk *(C)*	you shall be sunk *(C)*
	he (she, it) shall be sunk *(C)*	they shall be sunk *(C)*
Past	I was sunk	we were sunk
	you were sunk	you were sunk
	he (she, it) was sunk	they were sunk
Past	I was being sunk	we were being sunk
Prog.	you were being sunk	you were being sunk
	he (she, it) was being sunk	they were being sunk
Past	I did get sunk	we did get sunk
Int.	you did get sunk	you did get sunk
	he (she, it) did get sunk	they did get sunk
Pres.	I have been sunk	we have been sunk
Perf.	you have been sunk	you have been sunk
	he (she, it) has been sunk	they have been sunk
Past	I had been sunk	we had been sunk
Perf.	you had been sunk	you had been sunk
	he (she, it) had been sunk	they had been sunk
Fut.	I shall have been sunk	we shall have been sunk
Perf.	you will have been sunk	you will have been sunk
	he (she, it) will have been sunk	they will have been sunk

IMPERATIVE MOOD
be sunk

SUBJUNCTIVE MOOD

Pres.	if I be sunk	if we be sunk
	if you be sunk	if you be sunk
	if he (she, it) be sunk	if they be sunk
Past	if I were sunk	if we were sunk
	if you were sunk	if you were sunk
	if he (she, it) were sunk	if they were sunk
Fut.	if I should be sunk	if we should be sunk
	if you should be sunk	if you should be sunk
	if he (she, it) should be sunk	if they should be sunk

Infinitive: to sit   *Present Participle:* sitting
Perfect Infinitive: to have sat   *Past Participle:* sat

INDICATIVE MOOD

Pres.	I sit	we sit
	you sit	you sit
	he (she, it) sits	they sit
Pres.	I am sitting	we are sitting
Prog.	you are sitting	you are sitting
	he (she, it) is sitting	they are sitting
Pres.	I do sit	we do sit
Int.	you do sit	you do sit
	he (she, it) does sit	they do sit
Fut.	I shall sit	we shall sit
	you will sit	you will sit
	he (she, it) will sit	they will sit
Fut.	I will sit *(P)*	we will sit *(P)*
	you shall sit *(C)*	you shall sit *(C)*
	he (she, it) shall sit *(C)*	they shall sit *(C)*
Past	I sat	we sat
	you sat	you sat
	he (she, it) sat	they sat
Past	I was sitting	we were sitting
Prog.	you were sitting	you were sitting
	he (she, it) was sitting	they were sitting
Past	I did sit	we did sit
Int.	you did sit	you did sit
	he (she, it) did sit	they did sit
Pres.	I have sat	we have sat
Perf.	you have sat	you have sat
	he (she, it) has sat	they have sat
Past	I had sat	we had sat
Perf.	you had sat	you had sat
	he (she, it) had sat	they had sat
Fut.	I shall have sat	we shall have sat
Perf.	you will have sat	you will have sat
	he (she, it) will have sat	they will have sat

IMPERATIVE MOOD
sit

SUBJUNCTIVE MOOD

Pres.	if I sit	if we sit
	if you sit	if you sit
	if he (she, it) sit	if they sit
Past	if I sat	if we sat
	if you sat	if you sat
	if he (she, it) sat	if they sat
Fut.	if I should sit	if we should sit
	if you should sit	if you should sit
	if he (she, it) should sit	if they should sit

To sit is an intransitive verb.

It does not take an object.
It describes action, but the action is self-contained.
Like other intransitive verbs, it may be followed by adverbs, adverbial phrases and clauses describing the how, why, when, and where of the action:

HOW: John, sit *straight!* (adverb)
WHY: They were sitting *because they were tired*. (adverbial clause)
WHEN: I expect to be sitting *all day*. (adverbial phrase)
WHERE: The baby sat *on a high chair*. (adverbial phrase)

to slay (active voice)   *Principal Parts:* slay, slaying, slew, slain

Infinitive: to slay   *Present Participle:* slaying
Perfect Infinitive: to have slain   *Past Participle:* slain

INDICATIVE MOOD

Pres.	I slay	we slay
	you slay	you slay
	he (she, it) slays	they slay
Pres.	I am slaying	we are slaying
Prog.	you are slaying	you are slaying
	he (she, it) is slaying	they are slaying
Pres.	I do slay	we do slay
Int.	you do slay	you do slay
	he (she, it) does slay	they do slay
Fut.	I shall slay	we shall slay
	you will slay	you will slay
	he (she, it) will slay	they will slay
Fut.	I will slay *(P)*	we will slay *(P)*
	you shall slay *(C)*	you shall slay *(C)*
	he (she, it) shall slay *(C)*	they shall slay *(C)*
Past	I slew	we slew
	you slew	you slew
	he (she, it) slew	they slew
Past	I was slaying	we were slaying
Prog.	you were slaying	you were slaying
	he (she, it) was slaying	they were slaying
Past	I did slay	we did slay
Int.	you did slay	you did slay
	he (she, it) did slay	they did slay
Pres.	I have slain	we have slain
Perf.	you have slain	you have slain
	he (she, it) has slain	they have slain
Past	I had slain	we had slain
Perf.	you had slain	you had slain
	he (she, it) had slain	they had slain
Fut.	I shall have slain	we shall have slain
Perf.	you will have slain	you will have slain
	he (she, it) will have slain	they will have slain

IMPERATIVE MOOD
slay

SUBJUNCTIVE MOOD

Pres.	if I slay	if we slay
	if you slay	if you slay
	if he (she, it) slay	if they slay
Past	if I slew	if we slew
	if you slew	if you slew
	if he (she, it) slew	if they slew
Fut.	if I should slay	if we should slay
	if you should slay	if you should slay
	if he (she, it) should slay	if they should slay

(passive voice)

Infinitive: to be slain
Perfect Infinitive: to have been slain

Present Participle: being slain
Past Participle: been slain

INDICATIVE MOOD

Pres.	I am slain	we are slain
	you are slain	you are slain
	he (she, it) is slain	they are slain
Pres. *Prog.*	I am being slain	we are being slain
	you are being slain	you are being slain
	he (she, it) is being slain	they are being slain
Pres. *Int.*	I do get slain	we do get slain
	you do get slain	you do get slain
	he (she, it) does get slain	they do get slain
Fut.	I shall be slain	we shall be slain
	you will be slain	you will be slain
	he (she, it) will be slain	they will be slain
Fut.	I will be slain *(P)*	we will be slain *(P)*
	you shall be slain *(C)*	you shall be slain *(C)*
	he (she, it) shall be slain *(C)*	they shall be slain *(C)*
Past	I was slain	we were slain
	you were slain	you were slain
	he (she, it) was slain	they were slain
Past *Prog.*	I was being slain	we were being slain
	you were being slain	you were being slain
	he (she, it) was being slain	they were being slain
Past *Int.*	I did get slain	we did get slain
	you did get slain	you did get slain
	he (she, it) did get slain	they did get slain
Pres. *Perf.*	I have been slain	we have been slain
	you have been slain	you have been slain
	he (she, it) has been slain	they have been slain
Past *Perf.*	I had been slain	we had been slain
	you had been slain	you had been slain
	he (she, it) had been slain	they had been slain
Fut. *Perf.*	I shall have been slain	we shall have been slain
	you will have been slain	you will have been slain
	he (she, it) will have been slain	they will have been slain

IMPERATIVE MOOD
be slain

SUBJUNCTIVE MOOD

Pres.	if I be slain	if we be slain
	if you be slain	if you be slain
	if he (she, it) be slain	if they be slain
Past	if I were slain	if we were slain
	if you were slain	if you were slain
	if he (she, it) were slain	if they were slain
Fut.	if I should be slain	if we should be slain
	if you should be slain	if you should be slain
	if he (she, it) should be slain	if they should be slain

Infinitive: to sleep   *Present Participle:* sleeping
Perfect Infinitive: to have slept   *Past Participle:* slept

INDICATIVE MOOD

Pres.   I sleep   we sleep
       you sleep   you sleep
       he (she, it) sleeps   they sleep

Pres.	I sleep	we sleep
	you sleep	you sleep
	he (she, it) sleeps	they sleep
Pres. Prog.	I am sleeping	we are sleeping
	you are sleeping	you are sleeping
	he (she, it) is sleeping	they are sleeping
Pres. Int.	I do sleep	we do sleep
	you do sleep	you do sleep
	he (she, it) does sleep	they do sleep
Fut.	I shall sleep	we shall sleep
	you will sleep	you will sleep
	he (she, it) will sleep	they will sleep
Fut.	I will sleep *(P)*	we will sleep *(P)*
	you shall sheep *(C)*	you shall sleep *(C)*
	he (she, it) shall sleep *(C)*	they shall sleep *(C)*
Past	I slept	we slept
	you slept	you slept
	he (she, it) slept	they slept
Past Prog.	I was sleeping	we were sleeping
	you were sleeping	you were sleeping
	he (she, it) was sleeping	they were sleeping
Past Int.	I did sleep	we did sleep
	you did sleep	you did sleep
	he (she, it) did sleep	they did sleep
Pres. Perf.	I have slept	we have slept
	you have slept	you have slept
	he (she, it) has slept	they have slept
Past Perf.	I had slept	we had slept
	you had slept	you had slept
	he (she, it) had slept	they had slept
Fut. Perf.	I shall have slept	we shall have slept
	you will have slept	you will have slept
	he (she, it) will have slept	they will have slept

IMPERATIVE MOOD
sleep

SUBJUNCTIVE MOOD

Pres.	if I sleep	if we sleep
	if you sleep	if you sleep
	if he (she, it) sleep	if they sleep
Past	if I slept	if we slept
	if you slept	if you slept
	if he (she, it) slept	if they slept
Fut.	if I should sleep	if we should sleep
	if you should sleep	if you should sleep
	if he (she, it) should sleep	if they should sleep

To sleep is an intransitive verb.

It does not take an object.

It describes action, but the action is self-contained.

Like other intransitive verbs, it may be followed by adverbs, adverbial phrases and clauses describing the how, why, when, and where of the action:

HOW: Sleep *well*. (adverb)

WHY: She was sleeping *because she was tired*. (adverbial clause)

WHEN: Most people sleep *at night*. (adverbial phrase)

WHERE: I always sleep *when I ride on a train*. (adverbial clause)

to slide (active voice) *Principal Parts:* slide, sliding, slid, slid

Infinitive: to slide *Present Participle:* sliding
Perfect Infinitive: to have slid *Past Participle:* slid

INDICATIVE MOOD

Pres.	I slide	we slide
	you slide	you slide
	he (she, it) slides	they slide
Pres.	I am sliding	we are sliding
Prog.	you are sliding	you are sliding
	he (she, it) is sliding	they are sliding
Pres.	I do slide	we do slide
Int.	you do slide	you do slide
	he (she, it) does slide	they do slide
Fut.	I shall slide	we shall slide
	you will slide	you will slide
	he (she, it) will slide	they will slide
Fut.	I will slide *(P)*	we will slide *(P)*
	you shall slide *(C)*	you shall slide *(C)*
	he (she, it) shall slide *(C)*	they shall slide *(C)*
Past	I slid	we slid
	you slid	you slid
	he (she, it) slid	they slid
Past	I was sliding	we were sliding
Prog.	you were sliding	you were sliding
	he (she, it) was sliding	they were sliding
Past	I did slide	we did slide
Int.	you did slide	you did slide
	he (she, it) did slide	they did slide
Pres.	I have slid	we have slid
Perf.	you have slid	you have slid
	he (she, it) has slid	they have slid
Past	I had slid	we had slid
Perf.	you had slid	you had slid
	he (she, it) had slid	they had slid
Fut.	I shall have slid	we shall have slid
Perf.	you will have slid	you will have slid
	he (she, it) will have slid	they will have slid

IMPERATIVE MOOD
slide

SUBJUNCTIVE MOOD

Pres.	if I slide	if we slide
	if you slide	if you slide
	if he (she, it) slide	if they slide
Past	if I slid	if we slid
	if you slid	if you slid
	if he (she, it) slid	if they slid
Fut.	if I should slide	if we should slide
	if you should slide	if you should slide
	if he (she, it) should slide	if they should slide

(passive voice)

Infinitive: to be slid

Present Participle: being slid

Perfect Infinitive: to have been slid

Past Participle: been slid

INDICATIVE MOOD

Pres.	I am slid	we are slid
	you are slid	you are slid
	he (she, it) is slid	they are slid

Pres. Prog.	I am being slid	we are being slid
	you are being slid	you are being slid
	he (she, it) is being slid	they are being slid

Pres. Int.	I do get slid	we do get slid
	you do get slid	you do get slid
	he (she, it) does get slid	they do get slid

Fut.	I shall be slid	we shall be slid
	you will be slid	you will be slid
	he (she, it) will be slid	they will be slid

Fut.	I will be slid *(P)*	we will be slid *(P)*
	you shall be slid *(C)*	you shall be slid *(C)*
	he (she, it) shall be slid *(C)*	they shall be slid *(C)*

Past	I was slid	we were slid
	you were slid	you were slid
	he (she, it) was slid	they were slid

Past Prog.	I was being slid	we were being slid
	you were being slid	you were being slid
	he (she, it) was being slid	they were being slid

Past Int.	I did get slid	we did get slid
	you did get slid	you did get slid
	he (she, it) did get slid	they did get slid

Pres. Perf.	I have been slid	we have been slid
	you have been slid	you have been slid
	he (she, it) has been slid	they have been slid

Past Perf.	I had been slid	we had been slid
	you had been slid	you had been slid
	he (she, it) had been slid	they had been slid

Fut. Perf.	I shall have been slid	we shall have been slid
	you will have been slid	you will have been slid
	he (she, it) will have been slid	they will have been slid

IMPERATIVE MOOD
be slid

SUBJUNCTIVE MOOD

Pres.	if I be slid	if we be slid
	if you be slid	if you be slid
	if he (she, it) be slid	if they be slid

Past	if I were slid	if we were slid
	if you were slid	if you were slid
	if he (she, it) were slid	if they were slid

Fut.	if I should be slid	if we should be slid
	if you should be slid	if you should be slid
	if he (she, it) should be slid	if they should be slid

to speak (active voice)

Principal Parts: speak, speaking, spoke, spoken

Infinitive: to speak
Perfect Infinitive: to have spoken

Present Participle: speaking
Past Participle: spoken

INDICATIVE MOOD

Pres.	I speak	we speak
	you speak	you speak
	he (she, it) speaks	they speak
Pres. Prog.	I am speaking	we are speaking
	you are speaking	you are speaking
	he (she, it) is speaking	they are speaking
Pres. Int.	I do speak	we do speak
	you do speak	you do speak
	he (she, it) does speak	they do speak
Fut.	I shall speak	we shall speak
	you will speak	you will speak
	he (she, it) will speak	they will speak
Fut.	I will speak *(P)*	we will speak *(P)*
	you shall speak *(C)*	you shall speak *(C)*
	he (she, it) shall speak *(C)*	they shall speak *(C)*
Past	I spoke	we spoke
	you spoke	you spoke
	he (she, it) spoke	they spoke
Past Prog.	I was speaking	we were speaking
	you were speaking	you were speaking
	he (she, it) was speaking	they were speaking
Past Int.	I did speak	we did speak
	you did speak	you did speak
	he (she, it) did speak	they did speak
Pres. Perf.	I have spoken	we have spoken
	you have spoken	you have spoken
	he (she, it) has spoken	they have spoken
Past Perf.	I had spoken	we had spoken
	you had spoken	you had spoken
	he (she, it) had spoken	they had spoken
Fut. Perf.	I shall have spoken	we shall have spoken
	you will have spoken	you will have spoken
	he (she, it) will have spoken	they will have spoken

IMPERATIVE MOOD
speak

SUBJUNCTIVE MOOD

Pres.	if I speak	if we speak
	if you speak	if you speak
	if he (she, it) speak	if they speak
Past	if I spoke	if we spoke
	if you spoke	if you spoke
	if he (she, it) spoke	if they spoke
Fut.	if I should speak	if we should speak
	if you should speak	if you should speak
	if he (she, it) should speak	if they should speak

Infinitive: to be spoken	*Present Participle:* being spoken
Perfect Infinitive: to have been spoken	*Past Participle:* been spoken

INDICATIVE MOOD

Pres.	I am spoken	we are spoken
	you are spoken	you are spoken
	he (she, it) is spoken	they are spoken
Pres.	I am being spoken	we are being spoken
Prog.	you are being spoken	you are being spoken
	he (she, it) is being spoken	they are being spoken
Pres.	I do get spoken	we do get spoken
Int.	you do get spoken	you do get spoken
	he (she, it) does get spoken	they do get spoken
Fut.	I shall be spoken	we shall be spoken
	you will be spoken	you will be spoken
	he (she, it) will be spoken	they will be spoken
Fut.	I will be spoken *(P)*	we will be spoken *(P)*
	you shall be spoken *(C)*	you shall be spoken *(C)*
	he (she, it) shall be spoken *(C)*	they shall be spoken *(C)*
Past	I was spoken	we were spoken
	you were spoken	you were spoken
	he (she, it) was spoken	they were spoken
Past	I was being spoken	we were being spoken
Prog.	you were being spoken	you were being spoken
	he (she, it) was being spoken	they were being spoken
Past	I did get spoken	we did get spoken
Int.	you did get spoken	you did get spoken
	he (she, it) did get spoken	they did get spoken
Pres.	I have been spoken	we have been spoken
Perf.	you have been spoken	you have been spoken
	he (she, it) has been spoken	they have been spoken
Past	I had been spoken	we had been spoken
Perf.	you had been spoken	you had been spoken
	he (she, it) had been spoken	they had been spoken
Fut.	I shall have been spoken	we shall have been spoken
Perf.	you will have been spoken	you will have been spoken
	he (she, it) will have been spoken	they will have been spoken

IMPERATIVE MOOD
be spoken

SUBJUNCTIVE MOOD

Pres.	if I be spoken	if we be spoken
	if you be spoken	if you be spoken
	if he (she, it) be spoken	if they be spoken
Past	if I were spoken	if we were spoken
	if you were spoken	if you were spoken
	if he (she, it) were spoken	if they were spoken
Fut.	if I should be spoken	if we should be spoken
	if you should be spoken	if you should be spoken
	if he (she, it) should be spoken	if they should be spoken

to spend (active voice)

Principal Parts: spend, spending, spent, spent

Infinitive: to spend
Perfect Infinitive: having spent

Present Participle: spending
Past Participle: spent

INDICATIVE MOOD

Pres.	I spend	we spend
	you spend	you spend
	he (she, it) spends	they spend
Pres.	I am spending	we are spending
Prog.	you are spending	you are spending
	he (she, it) is spending	they are spending
Pres.	I do spend	we do spend
Int.	you do spend	you do spend
	he (she, it) does spend	they do spend
Fut.	I shall spend	we shall spend
	you will spend	you will spend
	he (she, it) will spend	they will spend
Fut.	I will spend *(P)*	we will spend *(P)*
	you shall spend *(C)*	you shall spend *(C)*
	he (she, it) shall spend *(C)*	they shall spend *(C)*
Past	I spent	we spent
	you spent	you spent
	he (she, it) spent	they spent
Past	I was spending	we were spending
Prog.	you were spending	you were spending
	he (she, it) was spending	they were spending
Past	I did spend	we did spend
Int.	you did spend	you did spend
	he (she, it) did spend	they did spend
Pres.	I have spent	we have spent
Perf.	you have spent	you have spent
	he (she, it) has spent	they have spent
Past	I had spent	we had spent
Perf.	you had spent	you had spent
	he (she, it) had spent	they had spent
Fut.	I shall have spent	we shall have spent
Perf.	you will have spent	you will have spent
	he (she, it) will have spent	they will have spent

IMPERATIVE MOOD
spend

SUBJUNCTIVE MOOD

Pres.	if I spend	if we spend
	if you spend	if you spend
	if he (she, it) spend	if they spend
Past	if I spent	if we spent
	if you spent	if you spent
	if he (she, it) spent	if they spent
Fut.	if I should spend	if we should spend
	if you should spend	if you should spend
	if he (she, it) should spend	if they should spend

290

Infinitive: to be spent   *Present Participle:* being spent
Perfect Infinitive: to have been spent   *Past Participle:* been spent

INDICATIVE MOOD

Pres.	I am spent	we are spent
	you are spent	you are spent
	he (she, it) is spent	they are spent
Pres.	I am being spent	we are being spent
Prog.	you are being spent	you are being spent
	he (she, it) is being spent	they are being spent
Pres.	I do get spent	we do get spent
Int.	you do get spent	you do get spent
	he (she, it) does get spent	they do get spent
Fut.	I shall be spent	we shall be spent
	you will be spent	you will be spent
	he (she, it) will be spent	they will be spent
Fut.	I will be spent *(P)*	we will be spent *(P)*
	you shall be spent *(C)*	you shall be spent *(C)*
	he (she, it) shall be spent *(C)*	they shall be spent *(C)*
Past	I was spent	we were spent
	you were spent	you were spent
	he (she, it) was spent	they were spent
Past	I was being spent	we were being spent
Prog.	you were being spent	you were being spent
	he (she, it) was being spent	they were being spent
Past	I did get spent	we did get spent
Int.	you did get spent	you did get spent
	he (she, it) did get spent	they did get spent
Pres.	I have been spent	we have been spent
Perf.	you have been spent	you have been spent
	he (she, it) has been spent	they have been spent
Past	I had been spent	we had been spent
Perf.	you had been spent	you had been spent
	he (she, it) had been spent	they had been spent
Fut.	I shall have been spent	we shall have been spent
Perf.	you will have been spent	you will have been spent
	he (she, it) will have been spent	they will have been spent

IMPERATIVE MOOD
be spent

SUBJUNCTIVE MOOD

Pres.	if I be spent	if we be spent
	if you be spent	if you be spent
	if he (she, it) be spent	if they be spent
Past	if I were spent	if we were spent
	if you were spent	if you were spent
	if he (she, it) were spent	if they were spent
Fut.	if I should be spent	if we should be spent
	if you should be spent	if you should be spent
	if he (she, it) should be spent	if they should be spent

to spin (active voice)   *Principal Parts:* spin, spinning, spun, spun

Infinitive: to spin   *Present Participle:* spinning
Perfect Infinitive: to have spun   *Past Participle:* spun

INDICATIVE MOOD

Pres.	I spin	we spin
	you spin	you spin
	he (she, it) spins	they spin
Pres.	I am spinning	we are spinning
Prog.	you are spinning	you are spinning
	he (she, it) is spinning	they are spinning
Pres.	I do spin	we do spin
Int.	you do spin	you do spin
	he (she, it) does spin	they do spin
Fut.	I shall spin	we shall spin
	you will spin	you will spin
	he (she, it) will spin	they will spin
Fut.	I will spin *(P)*	we will spin *(P)*
	you shall spin *(C)*	you shall spin *(C)*
	he (she, it) shall spin *(C)*	they shall spin *(C)*
Past	I spun	we spun
	you spun	you spun
	he (she, it) spun	they spun
Past	I was spinning	we were spinning
Prog.	you were spinning	you were spinning
	he (she, it) was spinning	they were spinning
Past	I did spin	we did spin
Int.	you did spin	you did spin
	he (she, it) did spin	they did spin
Pres.	I have spun	we have spun
Perf.	you have spun	you have spun
	he (she, it) has spun	they have spun
Past	I had spun	we had spun
Perf.	you had spun	you had spun
	he (she, it) had spun	they had spun
Fut.	I shall have spun	we shall have spun
Perf.	you will have spun	you will have spun
	he (she, it) will have spun	they will have spun

IMPERATIVE MOOD
spin

SUBJUNCTIVE MOOD

Pres.	if I spin	if we spin
	if you spin	if you spin
	if he (she, it) spin	if they spin
Past	if I spin	if we spin
	if you spin	if you spin
	if he (she, it) spin	if they spin
Fut.	if I should spin	if we should spin
	if you should spin	if you should spin
	if he (she, it) should spin	if they should spin

Infinitive: to be spun   *Present Participle:* being spun
Perfect Infinitive: to have been spun   *Past Participle:* been spun

INDICATIVE MOOD

Pres.	I am spun	we are spun
	you are spun	you are spun
	he (she, it) is spun	they are spun
Pres.	I am being spun	we are being spun
Prog.	you are being spun	you are being spun
	he (she, it) is being spun	they are being spun
Pres.	I do get spun	we do get spun
Int.	you do get spun	you do get spun
	he (she, it) does get spun	they do get spun
Fut.	I shall be spun	we shall be spun
	you will be spun	you will be spun
	he (she, it) will be spun	they will be spun
Fut.	I will be spun *(P)*	we will be spun *(P)*
	you shall be spun *(C)*	you shall be spun *(C)*
	he (she, it) shall be spun *(C)*	they shall be spun *(C)*
Past	I was spun	we were spun
	you were spun	you were spun
	he (she, it) was spun	they were spun
Past	I was being spun	we were being spun
Prog.	you were being spun	you were being spun
	he (she, it) was being spun	they were being spun
Past	I did get spun	we did get spun
Int.	you did get spun	you did get spun
	he (she, it) did get spun	they did get spun
Pres.	I have been spun	we have been spun
Perf.	you have been spun	you have been spun
	he (she, it) has been spun	they have been spun
Past	I had been spun	we had been spun
Perf.	you had been spun	you had been spun
	he (she, it) had been spun	they had been spun
Fut.	I shall have been spun	we shall have been spun
Perf.	you will have been spun	you will have been spun
	he (she, it) will have been spun	they will have been spun

IMPERATIVE MOOD
be spun

SUBJUNCTIVE MOOD

Pres.	if I be spun	if we be spun
	if you be spun	if you be spun
	if he (she, it) be spun	if they be spun
Past	if I were spun	if we were spun
	if you were spun	if you were spun
	if he (she, it) were spun	if they were spun
Fut.	if I should be spun	if we should be spun
	if you should be spun	if you should be spun
	if he (she, it) should be spun	if they should be spun

to spring (active voice)

Principal Parts: spring, springing, sprang (sprung), sprung

Infinitive: to spring
Perfect Infinitive: to have sprung

Present Participle: springing
Past Participle: sprung

INDICATIVE MOOD

Pres.	I spring	we spring
	you spring	you spring
	he (she, it) springs	they spring
Pres. *Prog.*	I am springing	we are springing
	you are springing	you are springing
	he (she, it) is springing	they are springing
Pres. *Int.*	I do spring	we do spring
	you do spring	you do spring
	he (she, it) does spring	they do spring
Fut.	I shall spring	we shall spring
	you will spring	you will spring
	he (she, it) will spring	they will spring
Fut.	I will spring *(P)*	we will spring *(P)*
	you shall spring *(C)*	you shall spring *(C)*
	he (she, it) shall spring *(C)*	they shall spring *(C)*
Past	I sprang, sprung	we sprang, sprung
	you sprang, sprung	you sprang, sprung
	he (she, it) sprang, sprung	they sprang, sprung
Past *Prog.*	I was springing	we were springing
	you were springing	you were springing
	he (she, it) was springing	they were springing
Past *Int.*	I did spring	we did spring
	you did spring	you did spring
	he (she, it) did spring	they did spring
Pres. *Perf.*	I have sprung	we have sprung
	you have sprung	you have sprung
	he (she, it) has sprung	they have sprung
Past *Perf.*	I had sprung	we had sprung
	you had sprung	you had sprung
	he (she, it) had sprung	they had sprung
Fut. *Perf.*	I shall have sprung	we shall have sprung
	you will have sprung	you will have sprung
	he (she, it) will have sprung	they will have sprung

IMPERATIVE MOOD
spring

SUBJUNCTIVE MOOD

Pres.	if I spring	if we spring
	if you spring	if you spring
	if he (she, it) spring	if they spring
Past	if I sprang, sprung	if we sprang, sprung
	if you sprang, sprung	if you sprang, sprung
	if he (she, it) sprang, sprung	if they sprang, sprung
Fut.	if I should spring	if we should spring
	if you should spring	if you should spring
	if he (she, it) should spring	if they should spring

Infinitive: to be sprung   *Present Participle:* being sprung
Perfect Infinitive: to have been sprung   *Past Participle:* been sprung

INDICATIVE MOOD

Pres.	I am sprung	we are sprung
	you are sprung	you are sprung
	he (she, it) is sprung	they are sprung
Pres.	I am being sprung	we are being sprung
Prog.	you are being sprung	you are being sprung
	he (she, it) is being sprung	they are being sprung
Pres.	I do get sprung	we do get sprung
Int.	you do sprung	you do get sprung
	he (she, it) does get sprung	they do get sprung
Fut.	I shall be sprung	we shall be sprung
	you will be sprung	you will be sprung
	he (she, it) will be sprung	they will be sprung
Fut.	I will be sprung *(P)*	we will be sprung *(P)*
	you shall be sprung *(C)*	you shall be sprung *(C)*
	he (she, it) shall be sprung *(C)*	they shall be sprung *(C)*
Past	I was sprung	we were sprung
	you were sprung	you were sprung
	he (she, it) was sprung	they were sprung
Past	I was being sprung	we were being sprung
Prog.	you were being sprung	you were being sprung
	he (she, it) was being sprung	they were being sprung
Past	I did get sprung	we did get sprung
Int.	you did get sprung	you did get sprung
	he (she, it) did get sprung	they did get sprung
Pres.	I have been sprung	we have been sprung
Perf.	you have been sprung	you have been sprung
	he (she, it) has been sprung	they have been sprung
Past	I had been sprung	we had been sprung
Perf.	you had been sprung	you had been sprung
	he (she, it) had been sprung	they had been sprung
Fut.	I shall have been sprung	we shall have been sprung
Perf.	you will have been sprung	you will have been sprung
	he (she, it) will have been sprung	they will have been sprung

IMPERATIVE MOOD
be sprung

SUBJUNCTIVE MOOD

Pres.	if I be sprung	if we be sprung
	if you be sprung	if you be sprung
	if he (she, it) be sprung	if they be sprung
Past	if I were sprung	if we were sprung
	if you were sprung	if you were sprung
	if he (she, it) were sprung	if they were sprung
Fut.	if I should be sprung	if we should be sprung
	if you should be sprung	if you should be sprung
	if he (she, it) should be sprung	if they should be sprung

to steal (active voice) *Principal Parts:* steal, stealing, stole, stolen

Infinitive: to steal *Present Participle:* stealing
Perfect Infinitive: to have stolen *Past Participle:* stolen

INDICATIVE MOOD

Pres.	I steal	we steal
	you steal	you steal
	he (she, it) steals	they steal
Pres.	I am stealing	we are stealing
Prog.	you are stealing	you are stealing
	he (she, it) is stealing	they are stealing
Pres.	I do steal	we do steal
Int.	you do steal	you do steal
	he (she, it) does steal	they do steal
Fut.	I shall steal	we shall steal
	you will steal	you will steal
	he (she, it) will steal	they will steal
Fut.	I will steal *(P)*	we will steal *(P)*
	you shall steal *(C)*	you shall steal *(C)*
	he (she, it) shall steal *(C)*	they shall steal *(C)*
Past	I stole	we stole
	you stole	you stole
	he (she, it) stole	they stole
Past	I was stealing	we were stealing
Prog.	you were stealing	you were stealing
	he (she, it) was stealing	they were stealing
Past	I did steal	we did steal
Int.	you did steal	you did steal
	he (she, it) did steal	they did steal
Pres.	I have stolen	we have stolen
Perf.	you have stolen	you have stolen
	he (she, it) has stolen	they have stolen
Past	I had stolen	we had stolen
Perf.	you had stolen	you had stolen
	he (she, it) had stolen	they had stolen
Fut.	I shall have stolen	we shall have stolen
Perf.	you will have stolen	you will have stolen
	he (she, it) will have stolen	they will have stolen

IMPERATIVE MOOD
steal

SUBJUNCTIVE MOOD

Pres.	if I steal	if we steal
	if you steal	if you steal
	if he (she, it) steal	if they steal
Past	if I stole	if we stole
	if you stole	if you stole
	if he (she, it) stole	if they stole
Fut.	if I should steal	if we should steal
	if you should steal	if you should steal
	if he (she, it) should steal	if they should steal

(passive voice)

Infinitive: to be stolen   *Present Participle:* being stolen
Perfect Infinitive: to have been stolen   *Past Participle:* been stolen

INDICATIVE MOOD

Pres.	I am stolen	we are stolen
	you are stolen	you are stolen
	he (she, it) is stolen	they are stolen
Pres. *Prog.*	I am being stolen	we are being stolen
	you are being stolen	you are being stolen
	he (she, it) is being stolen	they are being stolen
Pres. *Int.*	I do get stolen	we do get stolen
	you do get stolen	you do get stolen
	he (she, it) does get stolen	they do get stolen
Fut.	I shall be stolen	we shall be stolen
	you will be stolen	you will be stolen
	he (she, it) will be stolen	they will be stolen
Fut.	I will be stolen *(P)*	we will be stolen *(P)*
	you shall be stolen *(C)*	you shall be stolen *(C)*
	he (she, it) shall be stolen *(C)*	they shall be stolen *(C)*
Past	I was stolen	we were stolen
	you were stolen	you were stolen
	he (she, it) was stolen	they were stolen
Past *Prog.*	I was being stolen	we were being stolen
	you were being stolen	you were being stolen
	he (she, it) was being stolen	they were being stolen
Past *Int.*	I did get stolen	we did get stolen
	you did get stolen	you did get stolen
	he (she, it) did get stolen	they did get stolen
Pres. *Perf.*	I have been stolen	we have been stolen
	you have been stolen	you have been stolen
	he (she, it) has been stolen	they have been stolen
Past *Perf.*	I had been stolen	we had been stolen
	you had been stolen	you had been stolen
	he (she, it) had been stolen	they had been stolen
Fut. *Perf.*	I shall have been stolen	we shall have been stolen
	you will have been stolen	you will have been stolen
	he (she, it) will have been stolen	they will have been stolen

IMPERATIVE MOOD
be stolen

SUBJUNCTIVE MOOD

Pres.	if I be stolen	if we be stolen
	if you be stolen	if you be stolen
	if he (she, it) be stolen	if they be stolen
Past	if I were stolen	if we were stolen
	if you were stolen	if you were stolen
	if he (she, it) were stolen	if they were stolen
Fut.	if I should be stolen	if we should be stolen
	if you should be stolen	if you should be stolen
	if he (she, it) should be stolen	if they should be stolen

to stick (active voice)

Principal Parts: stick, sticking, stuck, stuck

Infinitive: to stick

Perfect Infinitive: to have stuck

Present Participle: sticking

Past Participle: stuck

INDICATIVE MOOD

Pres.	I stick	we stick
	you stick	you stick
	he (she, it) sticks	they stick
Pres. Prog.	I am sticking	we are sticking
	you are sticking	you are sticking
	he (she, it) is sticking	they are sticking
Pres. Int.	I do stick	we do stick
	you do stick	you do stick
	he (she, it) does stick	they do stick
Fut.	I shall stick	we shall stick
	you will stick	you will stick
	he (she, it) will stick	they will stick
Fut.	I will stick *(P)*	we will stick *(P)*
	you shall stick *(C)*	you shall stick *(C)*
	he (she, it) shall stick *(C)*	they shall stick *(C)*
Past	I stuck	we stuck
	you stuck	you stuck
	he (she, it) stuck	they stuck
Past Prog.	I was sticking	we were sticking
	you were sticking	you were sticking
	he (she, it) was sticking	they were sticking
Past Int.	I did stick	we did stick
	you did stick	you did stick
	he (she, it) did stick	they did stick
Pres. Perf.	I have stuck	we have stuck
	you have stuck	you have stuck
	he (she, it) has stuck	they have stuck
Past Perf.	I had stuck	we had stuck
	you had stuck	you had stuck
	he (she, it) had stuck	they had stuck
Fut. Perf.	I shall have stuck	we shall have stuck
	you will have stuck	you will have stuck
	he (she, it) will have stuck	they will have stuck

IMPERATIVE MOOD

stick

SUBJUNCTIVE MOOD

Pres.	if I stick	if we stick
	if you stick	if you stick
	if he (she, it) stick	if they stick
Past	if I stuck	if we stuck
	if you stuck	if you stuck
	if he (she, it) stuck	if they stuck
Fut.	if I should stick	if we should stick
	if you should stick	if you should stick
	if he (she, it) should stick	if they should stick

298

(passive voice)

Infinitive: to be stuck *Present Participle:* being stuck
Perfect Infinitive: to have been stuck *Past Participle:* been stuck

INDICATIVE MOOD

Pres.	I am stuck	we are stuck
	you are stuck	you are stuck
	he (she, it) is stuck	they are stuck
Pres.	I am being stuck	we are being stuck
Prog.	you are being stuck	you are being stuck
	he (she, it) is being stuck	they are being stuck
Pres.	I do get stuck	we do get stuck
Int.	you do get stuck	you do get stuck
	he (she, it) does get stuck	they do get stuck
Fut.	I shall be stuck	we shall be stuck
	you will be stuck	you will be stuck
	he (she, it) will be stuck	they will be stuck
Fut.	I will be stuck *(P)*	we will be stuck *(P)*
	you shall be stuck *(C)*	you shall be stuck *(C)*
	he (she, it) shall be stuck *(C)*	they shall be stuck *(C)*
Past	I was stuck	we were stuck
	you were stuck	you were stuck
	he (she, it) was stuck	they were stuck
Past	I was being stuck	we were being stuck
Prog.	you were being stuck	you were being stuck
	he (she, it) was being stuck	they were being stuck
Past	I did get stuck	we did get stuck
Int.	you did get stuck	you did get stuck
	he (she, it) did get stuck	they did get stuck
Pres.	I have been stuck	we have been stuck
Perf.	you have been stuck	you have been stuck
	he (she, it) has been stuck	they have been stuck
Past	I had been stuck	we had been stuck
Perf.	you had been stuck	you had been stuck
	he (she, it) had been stuck	they had been stuck
Fut.	I shall have been stuck	we shall have been stuck
Perf.	you will have been stuck	you will have been stuck
	he (she, it) will have been stuck	they will have been stuck

IMPERATIVE MOOD
be stuck

SUBJUNCTIVE MOOD

Pres.	if I be stuck	if we be stuck
	if you be stuck	if you be stuck
	if he (she, it) be stuck	if they be stuck
Past	if I were stuck	if we were stuck
	if you were stuck	if you were stuck
	if he (she, it) were stuck	if they were stuck
Fut.	if I should be stuck	if we should be stuck
	if you should be stuck	if you should be stuck
	if he (she, it) should be stuck	if they should be stuck

Infinitive: to sting   *Present Participle:* stinging
Perfect Infinitive: to have stung   *Past Participle:* stung

INDICATIVE MOOD

Pres.	I sting	we sting
	you sting	you sting
	he (she, it) stings	they sting
Pres.	I am stinging	we are stinging
Prog.	you are stinging	you are stinging
	he (she, it) is stinging	they are stinging
Pres.	I do sting	we do sting
Int.	you do sting	you do sting
	he (she, it) does sting	they do sting
Fut.	I shall sting	we shall sting
	you will sting	you will sting
	he (she, it) will sting	they will sting
Fut.	I will sting *(P)*	we will sting *(P)*
	you shall sting *(C)*	you shall sting *(C)*
	he (she, it) shall sting *(C)*	they shall sting *(C)*
Past	I stung	we stung
	you stung	you stung
	he (she, it) stung	they stung
Past	I was stinging	we were stinging
Prog.	you were stinging	you were stinging
	he (she, it) was stinging	they were stinging
Past	I did sting	we did sting
Int.	you did sting	you did sting
	he (she, it) did sting	they did sting
Pres.	I have stung	we have stung
Perf.	you have stung	you have stung
	he (she, it) has stung	they have stung
Past	I had stung	we had stung
Perf.	you had stung	you had stung
	he (she, it) had stung	they had stung
Fut.	I shall have stung	we shall have stung
Perf.	you will have stung	you will have stung
	he (she, it) will have stung	they will have stung

IMPERATIVE MOOD
sting

SUBJUNCTIVE MOOD

Pres.	if I sting	if we sting
	if you sting	if you sting
	if he (she, it) sting	if they sting
Past	if I stung	if we stung
	if you stung	if you stung
	if he (she, it) stung	if they stung
Fut.	if I should sting	if we should sting
	if you should sting	if you should sting
	if he (she, it) should sting	if they should sting

(passive voice)

Infinitive: to be stung *Present Participle:* being stung
Perfect Infinitive: to have been stung *Past Participle:* been stung

INDICATIVE MOOD

Pres.	I am stung	we are stung
	you are stung	you are stung
	he (she, it) is stung	they are stung
Pres.	I am being stung	we are being stung
Prog.	you are being stung	you are being stung
	he (she, it) is being stung	they are being stung
Pres.	I do get stung	we do get stung
Int.	you do get stung	you do get stung
	he (she, it) does get stung	they do get stung
Fut.	I shall be stung	we shall be stung
	you will be stung	you will be stung
	he (she, it) will be stung	they will be stung
Fut.	I will be stung *(P)*	we will be stung *(P)*
	you shall be stung *(C)*	you shall be stung *(C)*
	he (she, it) shall be stung *(C)*	they shall be stung *(C)*
Past	I was stung	we were stung
	you were stung	you were stung
	he (she, it) was stung	they were stung
Past	I was being stung	we were being stung
Prog.	you were being stung	you were being stung
	he (she, it) was being stung	they were being stung
Past	I did get stung	we did get stung
Int.	you did get stung	you did get stung
	he (she, it) did get stung	they did get stung
Pres.	I have been stung	we have been stung
Perf.	you have been stung	you have been stung
	he (she, it) has been stung	they have been stung
Past	I had been stung	we had been stung
Perf.	you had been stung	you had been stung
	he (she, it) had been stung	they had been stung
Fut.	I shall have been stung	we shall have been stung
Perf.	you will have been stung	you will have been stung
	he (she, it) will have been stung	they will have been stung

IMPERATIVE MOOD
be stung

SUBJUNCTIVE MOOD

Pres.	if I be stung	if we be stung
	if you be stung	if you be stung
	if he (she, it) be stung	if they be stung
Past	if I were stung	if we were stung
	if you were stung	if you were stung
	if he (she, it) were stung	if they were stung
Fut.	if I should be stung	if we should be stung
	if you should be stung	if you should be stung
	if he (she, it) should be stung	if they should be stung

to stride   *Principal Parts:* stride, striding, strode, stridden

Infinitive: to stride   *Present Participle:* striding
Perfect Infinitive: to have stridden   *Past Participle:* stridden

INDICATIVE MOOD

Pres.	I stride	we stride
	you stride	you stride
	he (she, it) strides	they stride
Pres.	I am striding	we are striding
Prog.	you are striding	you are striding
	he (she, it) is striding	they are striding
Pres.	I do stride	we do stride
Int.	you do stride	you do stride
	he (she, it) does stride	they do stride
Fut.	I shall stride	we shall stride
	you will stride	you will stride
	he (she, it) will stride	they will stride
Fut.	I will stride *(P)*	we will stride *(P)*
	you shall stride *(C)*	you shall stride *(C)*
	he (she, it) shall stride *(C)*	they shall stride *(C)*
Past	I strode	we strode
	you strode	you strode
	he (she, it) strode	they strode
Past	I was striding	we were striding
Prog.	you were striding	you were striding
	he (she, it) was striding	they were striding
Past	I did stride	we did stride
Int.	you did stride	you did stride
	he (she, it) did stride	they did stride
Pres.	I have stridden	we have stridden
Perf.	you have stridden	you have stridden
	he (she, it) has stridden	they have stridden
Past	I had stridden	we had stridden
Perf.	you had stridden	you had stridden
	he (she, it) had stridden	they had stridden
Fut.	I shall have stridden	we shall have stridden
Perf.	you will have stridden	you will have stridden
	he (she, it) will have stridden	they will have stridden

IMPERATIVE MOOD
stride

SUBJUNCTIVE MOOD

Pres.	if I stride	if we stride
	if you stride	if you stride
	if he (she, it) stride	if they stride
Past	if I strode	if we strode
	if you strode	if you strode
	if he (she, it) strode	if they strode
Fut.	if I should stride	if we should stride
	if you should stride	if you should stride
	if he (she, it) should stride	if they should stride

To stride is an intransitive verb.

It does not take an object.

It describes action, but the action is self-contained.

Like other intransitive verbs, it may be followed by adverbs, adverbial phrases and clauses describing the how, why, when, and where of the action:

HOW: The giant strode *mightily*. (adverb)

WHY: He was striding *to impress people with his vitality*. (adverbial phrase)

WHEN: Mephistopheles strode *when he left Arcadia to return to German soil*. (adverbial clause)

WHERE: I shall stride *into the room*. (adverbial phrase)

to strike (active voice)   *Principal Parts:* strike, striking, struck, struck (stricken)

Infinitive: to strike   *Present Participle:* striking
Perfect Infinitive: to have struck, stricken   *Past Participle:* struck, stricken

INDICATIVE MOOD

Pres.	I strike	we strike
	you strike	you strike
	he (she, it) strikes	they strike
Pres. Prog.	I am striking	we are striking
	you are striking	you are striking
	he (she, it) is striking	they are striking
Pres. Int.	I do strike	we do strike
	you do strike	you do strike
	he (she, it) does strike	they do strike
Fut.	I shall strike	we shall strike
	you will strike	you will strike
	he (she, it) will strike	they will strike
Fut.	I will strike *(P)*	we will strike *(P)*
	you shall strike *(C)*	you shall strike *(C)*
	he (she, it) shall strike *(C)*	they shall strike *(C)*
Past	I struck	we struck
	you struck	you struck
	he (she, it) struck	they struck
Past Prog.	I was striking	we were striking
	you were striking	you were striking
	he (she, it) was striking	they were striking
Past Int.	I did strike	we did strike
	you did strike	you did strike
	he (she, it) did strike	they did strike
Pres. Perf.	I have struck, stricken	we have struck, stricken
	you have struck, stricken	you have struck, stricken
	he (she, it) has struck, stricken	they have struck, stricken
Past Perf.	I had struck, stricken	we had struck, stricken
	you had struck, stricken	you had struck, stricken
	he (she, it) had struck, stricken	they had struck, stricken
Fut. Perf.	I shall have struck, stricken	we shall have struck, stricken
	you will have struck, stricken	you will have struck, stricken
	he (she, it) will have struck, stricken	they will have struck, stricken

IMPERATIVE MOOD
strike

SUBJUNCTIVE MOOD

Pres.	if I strike	if we strike
	if you strike	if you strike
	if he (she, it) strike	if they strike
Past	if I struck	if we struck
	if you struck	if you struck
	if he (she, it) struck	if they struck
Fut.	if I should strike	if we should strike
	if you should strike	if you should strike
	if he (she, it) should strike	if they should strike

(passive voice)

Infinitive: to be struck, stricken
Perfect Infinitive: to have been struck, stricken
Present Participle: being struck, stricken
Past Participle: struck, stricken

INDICATIVE MOOD

Pres.	I am struck, stricken	we are struck, stricken
	you are struck, stricken	you are struck, stricken
	he (she, it) is struck, stricken	they are struck, stricken
Pres. Prog.	I am being struck, stricken	we are being struck, stricken
	you are being struck, stricken	you are being struck, stricken
	he (she, it) is being struck, stricken	they are being struck, stricken
Pres. Int.	I do get struck, stricken	we do get struck, stricken
	you do get struck, stricken	you do get struck, stricken
	he (she, it) does get struck, stricken	they do get struck, stricken
Fut.	I shall be struck, stricken	we shall be struck, stricken
	you will be struck, stricken	you will be struck, stricken
	he (she, it) will be struck, stricken	they will be struck, stricken
Fut.	I will be struck, stricken *(P)*	we will be struck, stricken *(P)*
	you shall be struck, stricken *(C)*	you shall be struck, stricken *(C)*
	he (she, it) shall be struck, stricken *(C)*	they shall be struck, stricken *(C)*
Past	I was struck, stricken	we were struck, stricken
	you were struck, stricken	you were struck, stricken
	he (she, it) was struck, stricken	they were struck, stricken
Past Prog.	I was being struck, stricken	we were being struck, stricken
	you were being struck, stricken	you were being struck, stricken
	he (she, it) was being struck, stricken	they were being struck, stricken
Past Int.	I did get struck, stricken	we did get struck, stricken
	you did get struck, stricken	you did get struck, stricken
	he (she, it) did get struck, stricken	they did get struck, stricken
Pres. Perf.	I have been struck, stricken	we have been struck, stricken
	you have been struck, stricken	you have been struck, stricken
	he (she, it) has been struck, stricken	they have been struck, stricken
Past Perf.	I had been struck, stricken	we had been struck, stricken
	you had been struck, stricken	you had been struck, stricken
	he (she, it) had been struck, stricken	they had been struck, stricken
Fut. Perf.	I shall have been struck, stricken	we shall have been struck, stricken
	you will have been struck, stricken	you will have been struck, stricken
	he (she, it) will have been struck, stricken	they will have been struck, stricken

(passive voice)

IMPERATIVE MOOD
be struck

SUBJUNCTIVE MOOD

Pres. if I be struck, stricken
if you be struck, stricken
if he (she, it) be struck, stricken

if we be struck, stricken
if you be struck, stricken
if they be struck, stricken

Past if I were struck, stricken
if you were struck, stricken
if he (she, it) were struck, stricken

if we were struck, stricken
if you were struck, stricken
if they were struck, stricken

Fut. if I should be struck, stricken
if you should be struck, stricken
if he (she, it) should be struck, stricken

if we should be struck, stricken
if you should be struck, stricken
if they should be struck, stricken

Infinitive: to strive   *Present Participle:* striving
Perfect Infinitive: to have striven   *Past Participle:* striven

INDICATIVE MOOD

Pres.	I strive	we strive
	you strive	you strive
	he (she, it) strives	they strive
Pres.	I am striving	we are striving
Prog.	you are striving	you are striving
	he (she, it) is striving	they are striving
Pres.	I do strive	we do strive
Int.	you do strive	you do strive
	he (she, it) does strive	they do strive
Fut.	I shall strive	we shall strive
	you will strive	you will strive
	he (she, it) will strive	they will strive
Fut.	I will strive *(P)*	we will strive *(P)*
	you shall strive *(C)*	you shall strive *(C)*
	he (she, it) shall strive *(C)*	they shall strive *(C)*
Past	I strove	we strove
	you strove	you strove
	he (she, it) strove	they strove
Past	I was striving	we were striving
Prog.	you were striving	you were striving
	he (she, it) was striving	they were striving
Past	I did strive	we did strive
Int.	you did strive	you did strive
	he (she, it) did strive	they did strive
Pres.	I have striven	we have striven
Perf.	you have striven	you have striven
	he (she, it) has striven	they have striven
Past	I had striven	we had striven
Perf.	you had striven	you had striven
	he (she, it) had striven	they had striven
Fut.	I shall have striven	we shall have striven
Perf.	you will have striven	you will have striven
	he (she, it) will have striven	they will have striven

IMPERATIVE MOOD
strive

SUBJUNCTIVE MOOD

Pres.	if I strive	if we strive
	if you strive	if you strive
	if he (she, it) strive	if they strive
Past	if I strove	if we strove
	if you strove	if you strove
	if he (she, it) strove	if they strove
Fut.	if I should strive	if we should strive
	if you should strive	if you should strive
	if he (she, it) should strive	if they should strive

to swear (active voice)   *Principal Parts:* swear, swearing, swore, sworn

Infinitive: to swear   *Present Participle:* swearing
Perfect Infinitive: to have sworn   *Past Participle:* sworn

INDICATIVE MOOD

Pres.	I swear	we swear
	you swear	you swear
	he (she, it) swears	they swear
Pres.	I am swearing	we are swearing
Prog.	you are swearing	you are swearing
	he (she, it) is swearing	they are swearing
Pres.	I do swear	we do swear
Int.	you do swear	you do swear
	he (she, it) does swear	they do swear
Fut.	I shall swear	we shall swear
	you will swear	you will swear
	he (she, it) will swear	they will swear
Fut.	I will swear *(P)*	we will swear *(P)*
	you shall swear *(C)*	you shall swear *(C)*
	he (she, it) shall swear *(C)*	they shall swear *(C)*
Past	I swore	we swore
	you swore	you swore
	he (she, it) swore	they swore
Past	I was swearing	we were swearing
Prog.	you were swearing	you were swearing
	he (she, it) was swearing	they were swearing
Past	I did swear	we did swear
Int.	you did swear	you did swear
	he (she, it) did swear	they did swear
Pres.	I have sworn	we have sworn
Perf.	you have sworn	you have sworn
	he (she, it) has sworn	they have sworn
Past	I had sworn	we had sworn
Perf.	you had sworn	you had sworn
	he (she, it) had sworn	they had sworn
Fut.	I shall have sworn	we shall have sworn
Perf.	you will have sworn	you will have sworn
	he (she, it) will have sworn	they will have sworn

IMPERATIVE MOOD
swear

SUBJUNCTIVE MOOD

Pres.	if I swear	if we swear
	if you swear	if you swear
	if he (she, it) swear	if they swear
Past	if I swore	if we swore
	if you swore	if you swore
	if he (she, it) swore	if they swore
Fut.	if I should swear	if we should swear
	if you should swear	if you should swear
	if he (she, it) should swear	if they should swear

Infinitive: to be sworn   *Present Participle:* being sworn
Perfect Infinitive: to have been sworn   *Past Participle:* been sworn

INDICATIVE MOOD

Pres.	I am sworn	we are sworn
	you are sworn	you are sworn
	he (she, it) is sworn	they are sworn
Pres. Prog.	I am being sworn	we are being sworn
	you are being sworn	you are being sworn
	he (she, it) is being sworn	they are being sworn
Pres. Int.	I do get sworn	we do get sworn
	you do get sworn	you do get sworn
	he (she, it) does get sworn	they do get sworn
Fut.	I shall be sworn	we shall be sworn
	you will be sworn	you will be sworn
	he (she, it) will be sworn	they will be sworn
Fut.	I will be sworn (P)	we will be sworn (P)
	you shall be sworn (C)	you shall be sworn (C)
	he (she, it) shall be sworn (C)	they shall be sworn (C)
Past	I was sworn	we were sworn
	you were sworn	you were sworn
	he (she, it) was sworn	they were sworn
Past Prog.	I was being sworn	we were being sworn
	you were being sworn	you were being sworn
	he (she, it) was being sworn	they were being sworn
Past Int.	I did get sworn	we did get sworn
	you did get sworn	you did get sworn
	he (she, it) did get sworn	they did get sworn
Pres. Perf.	I have been sworn	we have been sworn
	you have been sworn	you have been sworn
	he (she, it) has been sworn	they have been sworn
Past Perf.	I had been sworn	we had been sworn
	you had been sworn	you had been sworn
	he (she, it) had been sworn	they had been sworn
Fut. Perf.	I shall have been sworn	we shall have been sworn
	you will have been sworn	you will have been sworn
	he (she, it) will have been sworn	they will have been sworn

IMPERATIVE MOOD
be sworn

SUBJUNCTIVE MOOD

Pres.	if I be sworn	if we be sworn
	if you be sworn	if you be sworn
	if he (she, it) be sworn	if they be sworn
Past	if I were sworn	if we were sworn
	if you were sworn	if you were sworn
	if he (she, it) were sworn	if they were sworn
Fut	if I should be sworn	if we should be sworn
	if you should be sworn	if you should be sworn
	if he (she, it) should be sworn	if they should be sworn

to sweat (active voice)   *Principal Parts:* sweat, sweating, sweat
                                          (sweated), sweated

Infinitive: to sweat   *Present Participle:* sweating
Perfect Infinitive: to have sweated   *Past Participle:* sweated

INDICATIVE MOOD

Pres.	I sweat	we sweat
	you sweat	you sweat
	he (she, it) sweats	they sweat
Pres.	I am sweating	we are sweating
Prog.	you are sweating	you are sweating
	he (she, it) is sweating	they are sweating
Pres.	I do sweat	we do sweat
Int.	you do sweat	you do sweat
	he (she, it) does sweat	they do sweat
Fut.	I shall sweat	we shall sweat
	you will sweat	you will sweat
	he (she, it) will sweat	they will sweat
Fut.	I will sweat *(P)*	we will sweat *(P)*
	you shall sweat *(C)*	you shall sweat *(C)*
	he (she, it) shall sweat *(C)*	they shall sweat *(C)*
Past	I sweat, sweated	we sweat, sweated
	you sweat, sweated	you sweat, sweated
	he (she, it) sweat, sweated	they sweat, sweated
Past	I was sweating	we were sweating
Prog.	you were sweating	you were sweating
	he (she, it) was sweating	they were sweating
Past	I did sweat	we did sweat
Int.	you did sweat	you did sweat
	he (she, it) did sweat	they did sweat
Pres.	I have sweated	we have sweated
Perf.	you have sweated	you have sweated
	he (she, it) has sweated	they have sweated
Past	I had sweated	we had sweated
Perf.	you had sweated	you had sweated
	he (she, it) had	they had sweated
Fut.	I shall have sweated	we shall have sweated
Perf.	you will have sweated	you will have sweated
	he (she, it) will have sweated	they will have sweated

IMPERATIVE MOOD
sweat

SUBJUNCTIVE MOOD

Pres.	if I sweat	if we sweat
	if you sweat	if you sweat
	if he (she, it) sweat	if they sweat
Past	if I sweat, sweated	if we sweat, sweated
	if you sweat, sweated	if you sweat, sweated
	if he (she, it) sweat, sweated	if they sweat, sweated
Fut.	if I should sweat	if we should sweat
	if you should sweat	if you should sweat
	if he (she, it) should sweat	if they should sweat

(passive voice)

Infinitive: to be sweated   *Present Participle:* being sweated
Perfect Infinitive: to have been sweated   *Past Participle:* been sweated

INDICATIVE MOOD

Pres.	I am sweated	we are sweated
	you are sweated	you are sweated
	he (she, it) is sweated	they are sweated
Pres.	I am being sweated	we are being sweated
Prog.	you are being sweated	you are being sweated
	he (she, it) is being sweated	they are being sweated
Pres.	I do get sweated	we do get sweated
Int.	you do get sweated	you do get sweated
	he (she, it) does get sweated	they do get sweated
Fut.	I shall be sweated	we shall be sweated
	you will be sweated	you will be sweated
	he (she, it) will be sweated	they will be sweated
Fut.	I will be sweated *(P)*	we will be sweated *(P)*
	you shall be sweated *(C)*	you shall be sweated *(C)*
	he (she, it) shall be sweated *(C)*	they shall be sweated *(C)*
Past	I was sweated	we were sweated
	you were sweated	you were sweated
	he (she, it) was sweated	they were sweated
Past	I was being sweated	we were being sweated
Prog.	you were being sweated	you were being sweated
	he (she, it) was being sweated	they were being sweated
Past	I did get sweated	we did get sweated
Int.	you did get sweated	you did get sweated
	he (she, it) did get sweated	they did get sweated
Pres.	I have been sweated	we have been sweated
Perf.	you have been sweated	you have been sweated
	he (she, it) has been sweated	they have been sweated
Past	I had been sweated	we had been sweated
Perf.	you had been sweated	you had been sweated
	he (she, it) had been sweated	they had been sweated
Fut.	I shall have been sweated	we shall have been sweated
Perf.	you will have been sweated	you will have been sweated
	he (she, it) will have been sweated	they will have been sweated

IMPERATIVE MOOD
be sweated

SUBJUNCTIVE MOOD

Pres.	if I be sweated	if we be sweated
	if you be sweated	if you be sweated
	if he (she, it) be sweated	if they be sweated
Past	if I were sweated	if we were sweated
	if you were sweated	if you were sweated
	if he (she, it) were sweated	if they were sweated
Fut.	if I should be sweated	if we should be sweated
	if you should be sweated	if you should be sweated
	if he (she, it) should be sweated	if they should be sweated

to sweep (active voice)   *Principal Parts:* sweep, sweeping, swept, swept

Infinitive: to sweep   *Present Participle:* sweeping
Perfect Infinitive: to have swept   *Past Participle:* swept

INDICATIVE MOOD

Pres.	I sweep	we sweep
	you sweep	you sweep
	he (she, it) sweeps	they sweep
Pres.	I am sweeping	we are sweeping
Prog.	you are sweeping	you are sweeping
	he (she, it) is sweeping	they are sweeping
Pres.	I do sweep	we do sweep
Int.	you do sweep	you do sweep
	he (she, it) does sweep	they do sweep
Fut.	I shall sweep	we shall sweep
	you will sweep	you will sweep
	he (she, it) will sweep	they will sweep
Fut.	I will sweep *(P)*	we will sweep *(P)*
	you shall sweep *(C)*	you shall sweep *(C)*
	he (she, it) shall sweep *(C)*	they shall sweep *(C)*
Past	I swept	we swept
	you swept	you swept
	he (she, it) swept	they swept
Past	I was sweeping	we were sweeping
Prog.	you were sweeping	you were sweeping
	he (she, it) was sweeping	they were sweeping
Past	I did sweep	we did sweep
Int.	you did sweep	you did sweep
	he (she, it) did sweep	they did sweep
Pres.	I have swept	we have swept
Perf.	you have swept	you have swept
	he (she, it) has swept	they have swept
Past	I had swept	we had swept
Perf.	you had swept	you had swept
	he (she, it) had swept	they had swept
Fut.	I shall have swept	we shall have swept
Perf.	you will have swept	you will have swept
	he (she, it) will have swept	they will have swept

IMPERATIVE MOOD
sweep

SUBJUNCTIVE MOOD

Pres.	if I sweep	if we sweep
	if you sweep	if you sweep
	if he (she, it) sweep	if they sweep
Past	if I swept	if we swept
	if you swept	if you swept
	if he (she, it) swept	if they swept
Fut.	if I should sweep	if we should sweep
	if you should sweep	if you should sweep
	if he (she, it) should sweep	if they should sweep

(passive voice)

Infinitive: to be swept   *Present Participle:* being swept
Perfect Infinitive: to have been swept   *Past Participle:* been swept

INDICATIVE MOOD

Pres.	I am swept	we are swept
	you are swept	you are swept
	he (she, it) is swept	they are swept

Pres. Prog. I am being swept — we are being swept
you are being swept — you are being swept
he (she, it) is being swept — they are being swept

Pres. Int. I do get swept — we do get swept
you do get swept — you do get swept
he (she, it) does get swept — they do get swept

Fut. I shall be swept — we shall be swept
you will be swept — you will be swept
he (she, it) will be swept — they will be swept

Fut. I will be swept *(P)* — we will be swept *(P)*
you shall be swept *(C)* — you shall be swept *(C)*
he (she, it) shall be swept *(C)* — they shall be swept *(C)*

Past I was swept — we were swept
you were swept — you were swept
he (she, it) was swept — they were swept

Past Prog. I was being swept — we were being swept
you were being swept — you were being swept
he (she, it) was being swept — they were being swept

Past Int. I did get swept — we did get swept
you did get swept — you did get swept
he (she, it) did get swept — they did get swept

Pres. Perf. I have been swept — we have been swept
you have been swept — you have been swept
he (she, it) has been swept — they have been swept

Past Perf. I had been swept — we had been swept
you had been swept — you had been swept
he (she, it) had been swept — they had been swept

Fut. Perf. I shall have been swept — we shall have been swept
you will have been swept — you will have been swept
he (she, it) will have been swept — they will have been swept

IMPERATIVE MOOD
be swept

SUBJUNCTIVE MOOD

Pres. if I be swept — if we be swept
if you be swept — if you be swept
if he (she, it) be swept — if they be swept

Past if I were swept — if we were swept
if you were swept — if you were swept
if he (she, it) were swept — if they were swept

Fut. if I should be swept — if we should be swept
if you should be swept — if you should be swept
if he (she, it) should be swept — if they should be swept

313

to swim (active voice)   *Principal Parts:* swim, swimming, swam,
                                                                        swum

---

Infinitive: to swim   *Present Participle:* swimming
Perfect Infinitive: to have swum   *Past Participle:* swum

INDICATIVE MOOD

Pres.	I swim	we swim
	you swim	you swim
	he (she, it) swims	they swim
Pres.	I am swimming	we are swimming
Prog.	you are swimming	you are swimming
	he (she, it) is swimming	they are swimming
Pres.	I do swim	we do swim
Int.	you do swim	you do swim
	he (she, it) does swim	they do swim
Fut.	I shall swim	we shall swim
	you will swim	you will swim
	he (she, it) will swim	they will swim
Fut.	I will swim *(P)*	we will swim *(P)*
	you shall swim *(C)*	you shall swim *(C)*
	he (she, it) shall swim *(C)*	they shall swim *(C)*
Past	I swam	we swam
	you swam	you swam
	he (she, it) swam	they swam
Past	I was swimming	we were swimming
Prog.	you were swimming	you were swimming
	he (she, it) was swimming	they were swimming
Past	I have swum	we have swum
Int.	you have swum	you have swum
	he (she, it) has swum	they have swum
Pres.	I have swum	we have swum
Perf.	you have swum	you have swum
	he (she, it) has swum	they have swum
Past	I had swum	we had swum
Perf.	you had swum	you had swum
	he (she, it) had swum	they had swum
Fut.	I shall have swum	we shall have swum
Perf.	you will have swum	you will have swum
	he (she, it) will have swum	they will have swum

IMPERATIVE MOOD
swim

SUBJUNCTIVE MOOD

Pres.	if I swim	if we swim
	if you swim	if you swim
	if he (she, it) swim	if they swim
Past	if I swam	if we swam
	if you swam	if you swam
	if he (she, it) swam	if they swam
Fut.	if I should swim	if we should swim
	if you should swim	if you should swim
	if he (she, it) should swim	if they should swim

(passive voice)

Infinitive: to be swum*   *Present Participle:* being swum
Perfect Infinitive: to have been swum   *Past Participle:* been swum

INDICATIVE MOOD

Pres.
I am swum
you are swum
he (she, it) is swum

we are swum
you are swum
they are swum

Pres.
Prog.
I am being swum
you are being swum
he (she, it) is being swum

we are being swum
you are being swum
they are being swum

Pres.
Int.
I do get swum
you do get swum
he (she, it) does get swum

we do get swum
you do get swum
they do get swum

Fut.
I shall be swum
you will be swum
he (she, it) will be swum

we shall be swum
you will be swum
they will be swum

Fut.
I will be swum *(P)*
you shall be swum *(C)*
he (she, it) shall be swum *(C)*

we will be swum *(C)*
you shall be swum *(C)*
they shall be swum *(C)*

Past
I was swum
you were swum
he (she, it) was swum

we were swum
you were swum
they were swum

Past
Prog.
I was being swum
you were being swum
he (she, it) was being swum

we were being swum
you were being swum
they were being swum

Past
Int.
I did get swum
you did get swum
he (she, it) did get swum

we did get swum
you did get swum
they did get swum

Pres.
Perf.
I have been swum
you have been swum
he (she, it) has been swum

we have been swum
you have been swum
they have been swum

Past
Perf.
I had been swum
you had been swum
he (she, it) had been swum

we had been swum
you had been swum
they had been swum

Fut.
Perf.
I shall have been swum
you will have been swum
he (she, it) will have been swum

we shall have been swum
you will have been swum
they will have been swum

IMPERATIVE MOOD
be swum

SUBJUNCTIVE MOOD

Pres.
if I be swum
if you be swum
if he (she, it) be swum

if we be swum
if you be swum
if they be swum

Past
if I were swum
if you were swum
if he (she, it) were swum

if we were swum
if you were swum
if they were swum

Fut.
if I should be swum
if you should be swum
if he (she, it) should be swum

if we should be swum
if you should be swum
if they should be swum

*Although grammatically correct, this form is rarely used.

to swing (active voice)   *Principal Parts:* swing, swinging, swung, swung

Infinitive: to swing   *Present Participle:* swinging
Perfect Infinitive: to have swung   *Past Participle:* swung

INDICATIVE MOOD

Pres.	I swing	we swing
	you swing	you swing
	he (she, it) swings	they swing
Pres.	I am swinging	we are swinging
Prog.	you are swinging	you are swinging
	he (she, it) is swinging	they are swinging
Pres.	I do swing	we do swing
Int.	you do swing	you do swing
	he (she, it) does swing	they do swing
Fut.	I shall swing	we shall swing
	you will swing	you will swing
	he (she, it) will swing	they will swing
Fut.	I will swing *(P)*	we will swing *(P)*
	you shall swing *(C)*	you shall swing *(C)*
	he (she, it) shall swing *(C)*	they shall swing *(C)*
Past	I swung	we swung
	you swung	you swung
	he (she, it) swung	they swung
Past	I was swinging	we were swinging
Prog.	you were swinging	you were swinging
	he (she, it) was swinging	they were swinging
Past	I did swing	we did swing
Int.	you did swing	you did swing
	he (she, it) did swing	they did swing
Pres.	I have swung	we have swung
Perf.	you have swung	you have swung
	he (she, it) has swung	they have swung
Past	I had swung	we had swung
Perf.	you had swung	you had swung
	he (she, it) had swung	they had swung
Fut.	I shall have swung	we shall have swung
Perf.	you will have swung	you will have swung
	he (she, it) will have swung	they will have swung

IMPERATIVE MOOD
swing

SUBJUNCTIVE MOOD

Pres.	if I swing	if we swing
	if you swing	if you swing
	if he (she, it) swing	if they swing
Past	if I swung	if we swung
	if you swung	if you swung
	if he (she, it) swung	if they swung
Fut.	if I should swing	if we should swing
	if you should swing	if you should swing
	if he (she, it) should swing	if they should swing

(passive voice)

Infinitive: to be swung   *Present Participle:* being swung
Perfect Infinitive: to have been swung   *Past Participle:* been swung

INDICATIVE MOOD

Pres.	I am swung	we are swung
	you are swung	you are swung
	he (she, it) is swung	they are swung
Pres.	I am being swung	we are being swung
Prog.	you are being swung	you are being swung
	he (she, it) is being swung	they are being swung
Pres.	I do get swung	we do get swung
Int.	you do get swung	you do get swung
	he (she, it) does get swung	they do get swung
Fut.	I shall be swung	we shall be swung
	you will be swung	you will be swung
	he (she, it) will be swung	they will be swung
Fut.	I will be swung *(P)*	we will be swung *(P)*
	you shall be swung *(C)*	you shall be swung *(C)*
	he (she, it) shall be swung *(C)*	they shall be swung *(C)*
Past	I was swung	we were swung
	you were swung	you were swung
	he (she, it) was swung	they were swung
Past	I was being swung	we were being swung
Prog.	you were being swung	you were being swung
	he (she, it) was being swung	they were being swung
Past	I did get swung	we did get swung
Int.	you did get swung	you did get swung
	he (she, it) did get swung	they did get swung
Pres.	I have been swung	we have been swung
Perf.	you have been swung	you have been swung
	he (she, it) has been swung	they have been swung
Past	I had been swung	we had been swung
Perf.	you had been swung	you had been swung
	he (she, it) had been swung	they had been swung
Fut.	I shall have been swung	we should have been swung
Perf.	you will have been swung	you will have been swung
	he (she, it) will have been swung	they will have been swung

IMPERATIVE MOOD
be swung

SUBJUNCTIVE MOOD

Pres.	if I be swung	if we be swung
	if you be swung	if you be swung
	if he (she, it) be swung	if they be swung
Past	if I were swung	if we were swung
	if you were swung	if you were swung
	if he (she, it) were swung	if they were swung
Fut.	if I should be swung	if we should be swung
	if you should be swung	if you should be swung
	if he (she, it) should be swung	if they should be swung

to take (active voice)

Principal Parts: take, taking, took, taken

Infinitive: to take
Perfect Infinitive: to have taken

Present Participle: taking
Past Participle: taken

INDICATIVE MOOD

Pres.	I take	we take
	you take	you take
	he (she, it) takes	they take
Pres.	I am taking	we are taking
Prog.	you are taking	you are taking
	he (she, it) is taking	they are taking
Pres.	I do take	we do take
Int.	you do take	you do take
	he (she, it) does take	they do take
Fut.	I shall take	we shall take
	you will take	you will take
	he (she, it) will take	they will take
Fut.	I will take *(P)*	we will take *(P)*
	you shall take *(C)*	you shall take *(C)*
	he (she, it) shall take *(C)*	they shall take *(C)*
Past	I took	we took
	you took	you took
	he (she, it) took	they took
Past	I was taking	we were taking
Prog.	you were taking	you were taking
	he (she, it) was taking	they were taking
Past	I did take	we did take
Int.	you did take	you did take
	he (she, it) did take	they did take
Pres.	I have taken	we have taken
Perf.	you have taken	you have taken
	he (she, it) has taken	they have taken
Past	I had taken	we had taken
Perf.	you had taken	you had taken
	he (she, it) had taken	they had taken
Fut.	I shall have taken	we shall have taken
Perf.	you will have taken	you will have taken
	he (she, it) will have taken	they will have taken

IMPERATIVE MOOD
take

SUBJUNCTIVE MOOD

Pres.	if I take	if we take
	if you take	if you take
	if he (she, it) take	if they take
Past	if I took	if we took
	if you took	if you took
	if he (she, it) took	if they took
Fut.	if I should take	if we should take
	if you should take	if you should take
	if he (she, it) should take	if they should take

(passive voice)

Infinitive: to be taken *Present Participle:* being taken
Perfect Infinitive: to have been taken *Past Participle:* been taken

INDICATIVE MOOD

Pres. I am taken
you are taken
he (she, it) is taken

we are taken
you are taken
they are taken

Pres.
Prog. I am being taken
you are being taken
he (she, it) is being taken

we are being taken
you are being taken
they are being taken

Pres.
Int. I do get taken
you do get taken
he (she, it) does get taken

we do get taken
you do get taken
they do get taken

Fut. I shall be taken
you will be taken
he (she, it) will be taken

we shall be taken
you will be taken
they will be taken

Fut. I will be taken *(P)*
you shall be taken *(C)*
he (she, it) shall be taken *(C)*

we will be taken *(P)*
you shall be taken *(C)*
they shall be taken *(C)*

Past I was taken
you were taken
he (she, it) was taken

we were taken
you were taken
they were taken

Past
Prog. I was being taken
you were being taken
he (she, it) was being taken

we were being taken
you were being taken
they were being taken

Past
Int. I did get taken
you did get taken
he (she, it) did get taken

we did get taken
you did get taken
they did get taken

Pres.
Perf. I have been taken
you have been taken
he (she, it) has been taken

we have been taken
you have been taken
they have been taken

Past
Perf. I had been taken
you had been taken
he (she, it) had been taken

we had been taken
you had been taken
they had been taken

Fut.
Perf. I shall have been taken
you will have been taken
he (she, it) will have been taken

we shall have been taken
you will have been taken
they will have been taken

IMPERATIVE MOOD
be taken

SUBJUNCTIVE MOOD

Pres. if I be taken
if you be taken
if he (she, it) be taken

if we be taken
if you be taken
if they be taken

Past if I were taken
if you were taken
if he (she, it) were taken

if we were taken
if you were taken
if they were taken

Fut. if I should be taken
if you should be taken
if he (she, it) should be taken

if we should be taken
if you should be taken
if they should be taken

to teach (active voice)   *Principal Parts:* teach, teaching, taught, taught

Infinitive: to teach   *Present Participle:* teaching
Perfect Infinitive: to have taught   *Past Participle:* taught

INDICATIVE MOOD

Pres.	I teach	we teach
	you teach	you teach
	he (she, it) teaches	they teach
Pres.	I am teaching	we are teaching
Prog.	you are teaching	you are teaching
	he (she, it) is teaching	they are teaching
Pres.	I do teach	we do teach
Int.	you do teach	you do teach
	he (she, it) does teach	they do teach
Fut.	I shall teach	we shall teach
	you will teach	you will teach
	he (she, it) will teach	they will teach
Fut.	I will teach *(P)*	we will teach *(P)*
	you shall teach *(C)*	you shall teach *(C)*
	he (she, it) shall teach *(C)*	they shall teach *(C)*
Past	I taught	we taught
	you taught	you taught
	he (she, it) taught	they taught
Past	I was teaching	we were teaching
Prog.	you were teaching	you were teaching
	he (she, it) was teaching	they were teaching
Past	I did teach	we did teach
Int.	you did teach	you did teach
	he (she, it) did teach	they did teach
Pres.	I have taught	we have taught
Perf.	you have taught	you have taught
	he (she, it) has taught	they have taught
Past	I had taught	we had taught
Perf.	you had taught	you had taught
	he (she, it) had taught	they had taught
Fut.	I shall have taught	we shall have taught
Perf.	you will have taught	you will have taught
	he (she, it) will have taught	they will have taught

IMPERATIVE MOOD
teach

SUBJUNCTIVE MOOD

Pres.	if I teach	if we teach
	if you teach	if you teach
	if he (she, it) teach	if they teach
Past	if I taught	if we taught
	if you taught	if you taught
	if he (she, it) taught	if they taught
Fut.	if I should teach	if we should teach
	if you should teach	if you should teach
	if he (she, it) should teach	if they should teach

(passive voice)

Infinitive: to be taught   *Present Participle:* being taught
Perfect Infinitive: to have been taught   *Past Participle:* been taught

INDICATIVE MOOD

Pres.	I am taught	we are taught
	you are taught	you are taught
	he (she, it) is taught	they are taught

Pres. Prog.	I am being taught	we are being taught
	you are being taught	you are being taught
	he (she, it) is being taught	they are being taught

Pres. Int.	I do get taught	we do get taught
	you do get taught	you do get taught
	he (she, it) does get taught	they do get taught

Fut.	I shall be taught	we shall be taught
	you will be taught	you will be taught
	he (she, it) will be taught	they will be taught

Fut.	I will be taught *(P)*	we will be taught *(P)*
	you shall be taught *(C)*	you shall be taught *(C)*
	he (she, it) shall be taught *(C)*	they shall be taught *(C)*

Past	I was taught	we were taught
	you were taught	you were taught
	he (she, it) was taught	they were taught

Past Prog.	I was being taught	we were being taught
	you were being taught	you were being taught
	he (she, it) was being taught	they were being taught

Past Int.	I did get taught	we did get taught
	you did get taught	you did get taught
	he (she, it) did get taught	they did get taught

Pres. Perf.	I have been taught	we have been taught
	you have been taught	you have been taught
	he (she, it) has been taught	they have been taught

Past Perf.	I had been taught	we had been taught
	you had been taught	you had been taught
	he (she, it) had been taught	they had been taught

Fut. Perf.	I shall have been taught	we shall have been taught
	you will have been taught	you will have been taught
	he (she, it) will have been taught	they will have been taught

IMPERATIVE MOOD
be taught

SUBJUNCTIVE MOOD

Pres.	if I be taught	if we be taught
	if you be taught	if you be taught
	if he (she, it) be taught	if they be taught

Past	if I were taught	if we were taught
	if you were taught	if you were taught
	if he (she, it) were taught	if they were taught

Fut.	if I should be taught	if we should be taught
	if you should be taught	if you should be taught
	if he (she, it) should be taught	if they should be taught

to tear (active voice) *Principal Parts:* tear, tearing, tore, torn

Infinitive: to tear *Present Participle:* tearing
Perfect Infinitive: to have torn *Past Participle:* torn

INDICATIVE MOOD

Pres. I tear	we tear
you tear	you tear
he (she, it) tears	they tear
Pres. I am tearing	we are tearing
Prog. you are tearing	you are tearing
he (she, it) is tearing	they are tearing
Pres. I do tear	we do tear
Int. you do tear	you do tear
he (she, it) does tear	they do tear
Fut. I shall tear	we shall tear
you will tear	you will tear
he (she, it) will tear	they will tear
Fut. I will tear *(P)*	we will tear *(P)*
you shall tear *(C)*	you shall tear *(C)*
he (she, it) shall tear *(C)*	they shall tear *(C)*
Past I tore	we tore
you tore	you tore
he (she, it) tore	they tore
Past I was tearing	we were tearing
Prog. you were tearing	you were tearing
he (she, it) was tearing	they were tearing
Past I did tear	we did tear
Int. you did tear	you did tear
he (she, it) did tear	they did tear
Pres. I have torn	we have torn
Perf. you have torn	you have torn
he (she, it) has torn	they have torn
Past I had torn	we had torn
Perf. you had torn	you had torn
he (she, it) had torn	they torn
Fut. I shall have torn	we shall have torn
Perf. you will have torn	you will have torn
he (she, it) will have torn	they will have torn

IMPERATIVE MOOD
tear

SUBJUNCTIVE MOOD

Pres. if I tear	if we tear
if you tear	if you tear
if he (she, it) tear	if they tear
Past if I tore	if we tore
if you tore	if you tore
if he (she, it) tore	if they tore
Fut. if I should tear	if we should tear
if you should tear	if you should tear
if he (she, it) should tear	if they should tear

(passive voice)

Infinitive: to be torn   *Present Participle:* being torn
Perfect Infinitive: to have been torn   *Past Participle:* been torn

INDICATIVE MOOD

Pres.	I am torn	we are torn
	you are torn	you are torn
	he (she, it) is torn	they are torn
Pres.	I am being torn	we are being torn
Prog.	you are being torn	you are being torn
	he (she, it) is being torn	they are being torn
Pres.	I do get torn	we do get torn
Int.	you do get torn	you do get torn
	he (she, it) does get torn	they do get torn
Fut.	I shall be torn	we shall be torn
	you will be torn	you will be torn
	he (she, it) will be torn	they will be torn
Fut.	I will be torn *(P)*	we will be torn *(P)*
	you shall be torn *(C)*	you shall be torn *(C)*
	he (she, it) shall be torn *(C)*	they shall be torn *(C)*
Past	I was torn	we were torn
	you were torn	you were torn
	he (she, it) was torn	they were torn
Past	I was being torn	we were being torn
Prog.	you were being torn	you were being torn
	he (she, it) was being torn	they were being torn
Past	I did get torn	we did get torn
Int.	you did get torn	you did get torn
	he (she, it) did get torn	they did get torn
Pres.	I have been torn	we have been torn
Perf.	you have been torn	you have been torn
	he (she, it) has been torn	they have been torn
Past	I had been torn	we had been torn
Perf.	you had been torn	you had been torn
	he (she, it) had been torn	they had been torn
Fut.	I shall have been torn	we shall have been torn
Perf.	you will have been torn	you will have been torn
	he (she, it) will have been torn	they will have been torn

IMPERATIVE MOOD
be torn

SUBJUNCTIVE MOOD

Pres.	if I be torn	if we be torn
	if you be torn	if you be torn
	if he (she, it) be torn	if they be torn
Past	if I were torn	if we were torn
	if you were torn	if you were torn
	if he (she, it) were torn	if they were torn
Fut.	if I should be torn	if we should be torn
	if you should be torn	if you should be torn
	if he (she, it) should be torn	if they should be torn

Infinitive: to tell   *Present Participle:* telling
Perfect Infinitive: to have told   *Past Participle:* told

INDICATIVE MOOD

Pres.	I tell	we tell
	you tell	you tell
	he (she, it) tells	they tell
Pres. Prog.	I am telling	we are telling
	you are telling	you are telling
	he (she, it) is telling	they are telling
Pres. Int.	I do tell	we do tell
	you do tell	you do tell
	he (she, it) does tell	they do tell
Fut.	I shall tell	we shall tell
	you will tell	you will tell
	he (she, it) will tell	they will tell
Fut.	I will tell *(P)*	we will tell *(P)*
	you shall tell *(C)*	you shall tell *(C)*
	he (she, it) shall tell *(C)*	they shall tell *(C)*
Past	I told	we told
	you told	you told
	he (she, it) told	they told
Past Prog.	I was telling	we were telling
	you were telling	you were telling
	he (she, it) was telling	they were telling
Past Int.	I did tell	we did tell
	you did tell	you did tell
	he (she, it) did tell	they did tell
Pres. Perf.	I have told	we have told
	you have told	you have told
	he (she, it) has told	they have told
Past Perf.	I had told	we had told
	you had told	you had told
	he (she, it) had told	they had told
Fut. Perf.	I shall have told	we shall have told
	you will have told	you will have told
	he (she, it) will have told	they will have told

IMPERATIVE MOOD
tell

SUBJUNCTIVE MOOD

Pres.	if I tell	if we tell
	if you tell	if you tell
	if he (she, it) tell	if they tell
Past	if I told	if we told
	if you told	if you told
	if he (she, it) told	if they told
Fut.	if I should tell	if we should tell
	if you should tell	if you should tell
	if he (she, it) should tell	if they should tell

(passive voice)

Infinitive: to be told   *Present Participle:* being told
Perfect Infinitive: to have been told   *Past Participle:* been told

INDICATIVE MOOD

Pres.	I am told	we are told
	you are told	you are told
	he (she, it) is told	they are told
Pres. *Prog.*	I am being told	we are being told
	you are being told	you are being told
	he (she, it) is being told	they are being told
Pres. *Int.*	I do get told	we do get told
	you do get told	you do get told
	he (she, it) does get told	they do get told
Fut.	I shall be told	we shall be told
	you will be told	you will be told
	he (she, it) will be told	they will be told
Fut.	I will be told *(P)*	we will be told *(P)*
	you shall be told *(C)*	you shall be told *(C)*
	he (she, it) shall be told *(C)*	they shall be told *(C)*
Past	I was told	we were told
	you were told	you were told
	he (she, it) was told	they were told
Past *Prog.*	I was being told	we were being told
	you were being told	you were being told
	he (she, it) was being told	they were being told
Past *Int.*	I did get told	we did get told
	you did get told	you did get told
	he (she, it) did get told	they did get told
Pres. *Perf.*	I have been told	we have been told
	you have been told	you have been told
	he (she, it) has been told	they have been told
Past *Perf.*	I had been told	we had been told
	you had been told	you had been told
	he (she, it) had been told	they had been told
Fut. *Perf.*	I shall have been told	we shall have been told
	you will have been told	you will have been told
	he (she, it) will have been told	they will have been told

IMPERATIVE MOOD
be told

SUBJUNCTIVE MOOD

Pres.	if I be told	if we be told
	if you be told	if you be told
	if he (she, it) be told	if they be told
Past	if I were told	if we were told
	if you were told	if you were told
	if he (she, it) were told	if they were told
Fut.	if I should be told	if we should be told
	if you should be told	if you should be told
	if he (she, it) should be told	if they should be told

to think (active voice) *Principal Parts:* think, thinking, thought, thought

Infinitive: to think *Present Participle:* thinking
Perfect Infinitive: to have thought *Past Participle:* thought

INDICATIVE MOOD

Pres.	I think	we think
	you think	you think
	he (she, it) thinks	they think
Pres. Prog.	I am thinking	we are thinking
	you are thinking	you are thinking
	he (she, it) is thinking	they are thinking
Pres. Int.	I do think	we do think
	you do think	you do think
	he (she, it) does think	they do think
Fut.	I shall think	we shall think
	you will think	you will think
	he (she, it) will think	they will think
Fut.	I will think *(P)*	we will think *(P)*
	you shall think *(C)*	you shall think *(C)*
	he (she, it) shall think *(C)*	they shall think *(C)*
Past	I thought	we thought
	you thought	you thought
	he (she, it) thought	they thought
Past Prog.	I was thinking	we were thinking
	you were thinking	you were thinking
	he (she, it) was thinking	they were thinking
Past Int.	I did think	we did think
	you did think	you did think
	he (she, it) did think	they did think
Pres. Perf.	I have thought	we have thought
	you have thought	you have thought
	he (she, it) has thought	they have thought
Past Perf.	I had thought	we had thought
	you had thought	you had thought
	he (she, it) had thought	they had thought
Fut. Perf.	I shall have thought	we shall have thought
	you will have thought	you will have thought
	he (she, it) will have thought	they will have thought

IMPERATIVE MOOD
think

SUBJUNCTIVE MOOD

Pres.	if I think	if we think
	if you think	if you think
	if he (she, it) think	if they think
Past	if I thought	if we thought
	if you thought	if you thought
	if he (she, it) thought	if they thought
Fut.	if I should think	if we should think
	if you should think	if you should think
	if he (she, it) should think	if they should think

(passive voice)

Infinitive: to be thought   *Present Participle:* being thought
Perfect Infinitive: to have been thought   *Past Participle:* been thought

INDICATIVE MOOD

Pres.	I am thought	we are thought
	you are thought	you are thought
	he (she, it) is thought	they are thought
Pres. *Prog.*	I am being thought	we are being thought
	you are being thought	you are being thought
	he (she, it) is being thought	they are being thought
Pres. *Int.*	I do get thought	we do get thought
	you do get thought	you do get thought
	he (she, it) does get thought	they do get thought
Fut.	I shall be thought	we shall be thought
	you will be thought	you will be thought
	he (she, it) will be thought	they will be thought
Fut.	I will be thought *(P)*	we will be thought *(P)*
	you shall be thought *(C)*	you shall be thought *(C)*
	he (she, it) shall be thought *(C)*	they shall be thought *(C)*
Past	I was thought	we were thought
	you were thought	you were thought
	he (she, it) was thought	they were thought
Past *Prog.*	I was being thought	we were being thought
	you were being thought	you were being thought
	he (she, it) was being thought	they were being thought
Past *Int.*	I did get thought	we did get thought
	you did get thought	you did get thought
	he (she, it) did get thought	they did get thought
Pres. *Perf.*	I have been thought	we have been thought
	you have been thought	you have been thought
	he (she, it) has been thought	they have been thought
Past *Perf.*	I had been thought	we had been thought
	you had been thought	you had been thought
	he (she, it) had been thought	they had been thought
Fut. *Perf.*	I shall have been thought	we shall have been thought
	you will have been thought	you will have been thought
	he (she, it) will have been thought	they will have been thought

IMPERATIVE MOOD
be thought

SUBJUNCTIVE MOOD

Pres.	if I be thought	if we be thought
	if you be thought	if you be thought
	if he (she, it) be thought	if they be thought
Past	if I were thought	if we were thought
	if you were thought	if you were thought
	if he (she, it) were thought	if they were thought
Fut.	if I should be thought	if we should be thought
	if you should be thought	if you should be thought
	if he (she, it) should be thought	if they should be thought

to thrive   *Principal Parts:* thrive, thriving, throve (thrived),
                                          thrived (thriven)

Infinitive: to thrive   *Present Participle:* thriving
Perfect Infinitive: to have thrived, thriven   *Past Participle:* thrived, thriven

INDICATIVE MOOD

Pres.	I thrive	we thrive
	you thrive	you thrive
	he (she, it) thrives	they thrive
Pres.	I am thriving	we are thriving
Prog.	you are thriving	you are thriving
	he (she, it) is thriving	they are thriving
Pres.	I do thrive	we do thrive
Int.	you do thrive	you do thrive
	he (she, it) does thrive	they do thrive
Fut.	I shall thrive	we shall thrive
	you will thrive	you will thrive
	he (she, it) will thrive	they will thrive
Fut.	I will thrive *(P)*	we will thrive *(P)*
	you shall thrive *(C)*	you shall thrive *(C)*
	he (she, it) shall thrive *(C)*	they shall thrive *(C)*
Past	I throve, thrived	we throve, thrived
	you throve, thrived	you throve, thrived
	he (she, it) throve, thrived	they throve, thrived
Past	I was thriving	we were thriving
Prog.	you were thriving	you were thriving
	he (she, it) was thriving	they were thriving
Past	I did thrive	we did thrive
Int.	you did thrive	you did thrive
	he (she, it) did thrive	they did thrive
Pres.	I have thrived, thriven	we have thrived, thriven
Perf.	you have thrived, thriven	you have thrived, thriven
	he (she, it) has thrived, thriven	they have thrived, thriven
Past	I had thrived, thriven	we had thrived, thriven
Perf.	you had thrived, thriven	you had thrived, thriven
	he (she, it) had thrived, thriven	they had thrived, thriven
Fut.	I shall have thrived, thriven	we shall have thrived, thriven
Perf.	you will have thrived, thriven	you will have thrived, thriven
	he (she, it) will have thrived, thriven	they will have thrived, thriven

IMPERATIVE MOOD
thrive

SUBJUNCTIVE MOOD

Pres.	if I thrive	if we thrive
	if you thrive	if you thrive
	if he (she, it) thrive	if they thrive
Past	if I throve, thrived	if we throve, thrived
	if you throve, thrived	if you throve, thrived
	if he (she, it) throve, thrived	if they throve, thrived
Fut.	if I should thrive	if we should thrive
	if you should thrive	if you should thrive
	if he (she, it) should thrive	if they should thrive

To thrive is an intransitive verb.

It does not take an object.

It describes action, but the action is self-contained.

Like other intransitive verbs, it may be followed by adverbs, adverbial phrases and clauses describing the how, why, when and where of the action:

HOW: The family has thriven *wonderfully*. (adverb)

WHY: The crops are thriving *because of the unusually warm weather*. (adverbial phrase)

WHEN: The animals will be thriving *when spring comes*. (adverbial clause)

WHERE: He was thriving *in his job at the bank*. (adverbial phrase)

to throw (active voice)

Principal Parts: throw, throwing, threw, thrown

Infinitive: to throw
Perfect Infinitive: to have thrown

Present Participle: throwing
Past Participle: thrown

INDICATIVE MOOD

Pres.	I throw	we throw
	you throw	you throw
	he (she, it) throw	they throw
Pres. Prog.	I am throwing	we are throwing
	you are throwing	you are throwing
	he (she, it) is throwing	they are throwing
Pres. Int.	I do throw	we do throw
	you do throw	you do throw
	he (she, it) does throw	they do throw
Fut.	I shall throw	we shall throw
	you will throw	you will throw
	he (she, it) will throw	they will throw
Fut.	I will throw *(P)*	we will throw *(P)*
	you shall throw *(C)*	you shall throw *(C)*
	he (she, it) shall throw *(C)*	they shall throw *(C)*
Past	I threw	we threw
	you threw	you threw
	he (she, it) threw	they threw
Past Prog.	I was throwing	we were throwing
	you were throwing	you were throwing
	he (she, it) was throwing	they were throwing
Past Int.	I did throw	we did throw
	you did throw	you did throw
	he (she, it) did throw	they did throw
Pres. Perf.	I have thrown	we have thrown
	you have thrown	you have thrown
	he (she, it) has thrown	they have thrown
Past Perf.	I had thrown	we had thrown
	you had thrown	you had thrown
	he (she, it) had thrown	they had thrown
Fut. Perf.	I shall have thrown	we shall have thrown
	you will have thrown	you will have thrown
	he (she, it) will have thrown	they will have thrown

IMPERATIVE MOOD
throw

SUBJUNCTIVE MOOD

Pres.	if I throw	if we throw
	if you throw	if you throw
	if he (she, it) throw	if they throw
Past	if I threw	if we threw
	if you threw	if you threw
	if he (she, it) threw	if they threw
Fut.	if I should throw	if we should throw
	if you should throw	if you should throw
	if he (she, it) should throw	if they should throw

330

Infinitive: to be thrown   *Present Participle:* being thrown
Perfect Infinitive: to have been thrown   *Past Participle:* been thrown

INDICATIVE MOOD

Pres.	I am thrown	we are thrown
	you are thrown	you are thrown
	he (she, it) is thrown	they are thrown
Pres. *Prog.*	I am being thrown	we are being thrown
	you are being thrown	you are being thrown
	he (she, it) is being thrown	they are being thrown
Pres. *Int.*	I do get thrown	we do get thrown
	you do get thrown	you do get thrown
	he (she, it) does get thrown	they do get thrown
Fut.	I shall be thrown	we shall be thrown
	you will be thrown	you will be thrown
	he (she, it) will be thrown	they will be thrown
Fut.	I will be thrown *(P)*	we will be thrown *(P)*
	you shall be thrown *(C)*	you shall be thrown *(C)*
	he (she, it) shall be thrown *(C)*	they shall be thrown *(C)*
Past	I was thrown	we were thrown
	you were thrown	you were thrown
	he (she, it) was thrown	they were thrown
Past *Prog.*	I was being thrown	we were being thrown
	you were being thrown	you were being thrown
	he (she, it) was being thrown	they were being thrown
Past *Int.*	I did get thrown	we did get thrown
	you did get thrown	you did get thrown
	he (she, it) did get thrown	they did get thrown
Pres. *Perf.*	I have been thrown	we have been thrown
	you have been thrown	you have been thrown
	he (she, it) has been thrown	they have been thrown
Past *Perf.*	I had been thrown	we had been thrown
	you had been thrown	you had been thrown
	he (she, it) had been thrown	they had been thrown
Fut. *Perf.*	I shall have been thrown	we shall have been thrown
	you will have been thrown	you will have been thrown
	he (she, it) will have been thrown	they will have been thrown

IMPERATIVE MOOD
be thrown

SUBJUNCTIVE MOOD

Pres.	if I be thrown	if we be thrown
	if you be thrown	if you be thrown
	if he (she, it) be thrown	if they be thrown
Past	if I were thrown	if we were thrown
	if you were thrown	if you were thrown
	if he (she, it) were thrown	if they were thrown
Fut.	if I should be thrown	if we should be thrown
	if you should be thrown	if you should be thrown
	if he (she, it) should be thrown	if they should be thrown

to wake (active voice)   *Principal Parts:* wake, waking, woke (waked),
                                              waked (wakened, woken)

Infinitive: to wake   *Present Participle:* waking
Perfect Infinitive: to have waked, wakened, woken   *Past Participle:* wakened,
                                                                           woken

INDICATIVE MOOD

Pres.	I wake	we wake
	you wake	you wake
	he (she, it) wake	they wake

Pres. I wake   we wake
       you wake   you wake
       he (she, it) wake   they wake

Pres.   I am waking   we are waking
Prog.   you are waking   you are waking
          he (she, it) is waking   they are waking

Pres.   I do wake   we do wake
Int.   you do wake   you do wake
          he (she, it) does wake   they do wake

Fut.   I shall wake   we shall wake
          you will wake   you will wake
          he (she, it) will wake   they will wake

Fut.   I will wake *(P)*   we will wake *(P)*
          you shall wake *(C)*   you shall wake *(C)*
          he (she, it) shall wake *(C)*   they shall wake *(C)*

Past   I woke   we woke
          you woke   you woke
          he (she, it) woke   they woke

Past   I was waking   we were waking
Prog.   you were waking   you were waking
          he (she, it) was waking   they were waking

Past   I did wake   we did wake
Int.   you did wake   you did wake
          he (she, it) did wake   they did wake

Pres.   I have waked, wakened, woken   we have waked, wakened, woken
Perf.   you have waked, wakened, woken   you have waked, wakened, woken
          he (she, it) has waked, wakened,   they have waked, wakened, woken
          woken

Past   I had waked, wakened, woken   we had waked, wakened, woken
Perf.   you had waked, wakened, woken   you had waked, wakened, woken
          he (she, it) had waked, wakened,   they had waked, wakened, woken
          woken

Fut.   I shall have waked, wakened,   we shall have waked, wakened,
          woken   woken
Perf.   you will have waked, wakened,   you will have waked, wakened,
          woken   woken
          he (she, it) will have waked,   they will have waked, wakened,
          wakened, woken   woken

to wake (active voice)

IMPERATIVE MOOD
wake

SUBJUNCTIVE MOOD

Pres.	if I wake	if we wake
	if you wake	if you wake
	if he (she, it) wake	if they wake
Past	if I woke	if we woke
	if you woke	if you woke
	if he (she, it) woke	if they woke
Fut.	if I should wake	if we should wake
	if you should wake	if you should wake
	if he (she, it) should wake	if they should wake

(passive voice)

Infinitive: to be waked, wakened, woken

Perfect Infinitive: to have been waked, wakened, woken

Present Participle: being waked, wakened, woken

Past Participle: been waked, wakened, woken

INDICATIVE MOOD

Pres.	I am waked, wakened, woken	we are waked, wakened, woken
	you are waked, wakened, woken	you are waked, wakened, woken
	he (she, it) is waked, wakened, woken	they are waked, wakened, woken
Pres. Prog.	I am being waked, wakened, woken	we are being waked, wakened, woken
	you are being waked, wakened, woken	you are being waked, wakened, woken
	he (she, it) is being waked, wakened, woken	they are being waked, wakened, woken
Pres. Int.	I do get waked, wakened, woken	we do get waked, wakened, woken
	you do get waked, wakened, woken	you do get waked, wakened, woken
	he (she, it) does get waked, wakened, woken	they do get waked, wakened, woken
Fut.	I shall be waked, wakened, woken	we shall be waked, wakened, woken
	you will be waked, wakened, woken	you will be waked, wakened, woken
	he (she, it) will be waked, wakened, woken	they will be waked, wakened, woken
Fut.	I will be waked, wakened, woken (P)	we will be waked, wakened, woken (P)
	you shall be waked, wakened, woken (C)	you shall be waked, wakened, woken (C)
	he (she, it) shall be waked, wakened, woken (C)	they shall be waked, wakened, woken (C)
Past	I was waked, wakened, woken	we were waked, wakened, woken
	you were waked, wakened, woken	you were waked, wakened, woken
	he (she, it) was waked, wakened, woken	they were waked, wakened, woken

Past. *Prog.*	I was being waked, wakened, woken	we were being waked, wakened, woken
	you were being waked, wakened, woken	you were being waked, wakened, woken
	he (she, it) was being waked, wakened, woken	they were being waked, wakened, woken
Past. *Int.*	I did get waked, wakened, woken	we did get waked, wakened, woken
	you did get waked, wakened, woken	you did get waked, wakened, woken
	he (she, it) did get waked, wakened, woken	they did get waked, wakened, woken
Pres. *Perf.*	I have been waked, wakened, woken	we have been waked, wakened, woken
	you have been waked, wakened, woken	you have been waked, wakened, woken
	he (she, it) has been waked, wakened, woken	they have been waked, wakened, woken
Past. *Perf.*	I had been waked, wakened, woken	we had been waked, wakened, woken
	you had been waked, wakened, woken	you had been waked, wakened, woken
	he (she, it) had been waked, wakened, woken	they had been waked, wakened, woken
Fut. *Perf.*	I shall have been waked, wakened, woken	we shall have been waked, wakened, woken
	you will have been waked, wakened, woken	you will have been waked, wakened, woken
	he (she, it) will have been waked, wakened, woken	they will have been waked, wakened, woken

IMPERATIVE MOOD

be waked

SUBJUNCTIVE MOOD

Pres.	if I be waked, wakened, woken	if we be waked, wakened, woken
	if you be waked, wakened, woken	if you be waked, wakened, woken
	if he (she, it) be waked, wakened, woken	if they be waked, wakened, woken
Past	if I were waked, wakened, woken	if we were waked, wakened, woken
	if you were waked, wakened, woken	if you were waked, wakened, woken
	if he (she, it) were waked, wakened, woken	if they were waked, wakened, woken
Fut.	if I should be waked, wakened, woken	if we should be waked, wakened, woken
	if you should be waked, wakened, woken	if you should be waked, wakened, woken
	if he (she, it) should be waked, wakened, woken	if they should be waked, wakened, woken

NOTE: The verb *to wake* is another form of the verb *to awake* (p. 106)

To wake is much more commonly used in English since *to awake* has a more formal connotation and poetic overtones: "I awake from dreams of thee." A similar usage pattern occurs in the verbs *to arise* and to *rise*.

to wear (active voice)   *Principal Parts:* wear, wearing, wore, worn

Infinitive: to wear   *Present Participle:* wearing
Perfect Infinitive: to have worn   *Past Participle:* worn

INDICATIVE MOOD

Pres.	I wear	we wear
	you wear	you wear
	he (she, it) wears	they wear
Pres. Prog.	I am wearing	we are wearing
	you are wearing	you are wearing
	he (she, it) is wearing	they are wearing
Pres. Int.	I do wear	we do wear
	you do wear	you do wear
	he (she, it) does wear	they do wear
Fut.	I shall wear	we shall wear
	you will wear	you will wear
	he (she, it) will wear	they will wear
Fut.	I will wear *(P)*	we will wear *(P)*
	you shall wear *(C)*	you shall wear *(C)*
	he (she, it) shall wear *(C)*	they shall wear *(C)*
Past	I wore	we wore
	you wore	you wore
	he (she, it) wore	they wore
Past Prog.	I was wearing	we were wearing
	you were wearing	you were wearing
	he (she, it) was wearing	they were wearing
Past Int.	I did wear	we did wear
	you did wear	you did wear
	he (she, it) did wear	they did wear
Pres. Perf.	I have worn	we have worn
	you have worn	you have worn
	he (she, it) has worn	they have worn
Past Perf.	I had worn	we had worn
	you had worn	you had worn
	he (she, it) had worn	they had worn
Fut. Perf.	I shall have worn	we shall have worn
	you will have worn	you will have worn
	he (she, it) will have worn	they will have worn

IMPERATIVE MOOD
wear

SUBJUNCTIVE MOOD

Pres.	if I wear	if we wear
	if you wear	if you wear
	if he (she, it) wear	if they wear
Past	if I wore	if we wore
	if you wore	if you wore
	if he (she, it) wore	if they wore
Fut.	if I should wear	if we should wear
	if you should wear	if you should wear
	if he (she, it) should wear	if they should wear

(passive voice)

Infinitive: to be worn   *Present Participle:* being worn
Perfect Infinitive: to have been worn   *Past Participle:* been worn

INDICATIVE MOOD

Pres.	I am worn	we are worn
	you are worn	you are worn
	he (she, it) is worn	they are worn
Pres. *Prog.*	I am being worn	we are being worn
	you are being worn	you are being worn
	he (she, it) is being worn	they are being worn
Pres. *Int.*	I do get worn	we do get worn
	you do get worn	you do get worn
	he (she, it) does get worn	they do get worn
Fut.	I shall be worn	we shall be worn
	you will be worn	you will be worn
	he (she, it) will be worn	they will be worn
Fut.	I will be worn *(P)*	we will be worn *(P)*
	you shall be worn *(C)*	you shall be worn *(C)*
	he (she, it) shall be worn *(C)*	they shall be worn *(C)*
Past	I was worn	we were worn
	you were worn	you were worn
	he (she, it) was worn	they were worn
Past *Prog.*	I was being worn	we were being worn
	you were being worn	you were being worn
	he (she, it) was being worn	they were being worn
Past *Int.*	I did get worn	we did get worn
	you did get worn	you did get worn
	he (she, it) did get worn	they did get worn
Pres. *Perf.*	I have been worn	we have been worn
	you have been worn	you have been worn
	he (she, it) has been worn	they have been worn
Past *Perf.*	I had been worn	we had been worn
	you had been worn	you had been worn
	he (she, it) had been worn	they had been worn
Fut. *Perf.*	I shall have been worn	we shall have been worn
	you will have been worn	you will have been worn
	he (she, it) will have been worn	they will have been worn

IMPERATIVE MOOD
be worn

SUBJUNCTIVE MOOD

Pres.	if I be worn	if we be worn
	if you be worn	if you be worn
	if he (she, it) be worn	if they be worn
Past	if I were worn	if we were worn
	if you were worn	if you were worn
	if he (she, it) were worn	if they were worn
Fut.	if I should be worn	if we should be worn
	if you should be worn	if you should be worn
	if he (she, it) should be worn	if they should be worn

to weave (active voice)   *Principal Parts:* weave, weaving, wove, woven

Infinitive: to weave   *Present Participle:* weaving
Perfect Infinitive: to have woven   *Past Participle:* woven

INDICATIVE MOOD

Pres.	I weave	we weave
	you weave	you weave
	he (she, it) weave	they weave

Pres. Prog.	I am weaving	we are weaving
	you are weaving	you are weaving
	he (she, it) is weaving	they are weaving

Pres. Int.	I do weave	we do weave
	you do weave	you do weave
	he (she, it) does weave	they do weave

Fut.	I shall weave	we shall weave
	you will weave	you will weave
	he (she, it) will weave	they will weave

Fut.	I will weave *(P)*	we will weave *(P)*
	you shall weave *(C)*	you shall weave *(C)*
	he (she, it) shall weave *(C)*	they shall weave *(C)*

Past	I wove	we wove
	you wove	you wove
	he (she, it) wove	they wove

Past Prog.	I was weaving	we were weaving
	you were weaving	you were weaving
	he (she, it) was weaving	they were weaving

Past Int.	I did weave	we did weave
	you did weave	you did weave
	he (she, it) did weave	they did weave

Pres. Perf.	I have woven	we have woven
	you have woven	you have woven
	he (she, it) has woven	they have woven

Past Perf.	I had woven	we had woven
	you had woven	you had woven
	he (she, it) had woven	they had woven

Fut. Perf.	I shall have woven	we shall have woven
	you will have woven	you will have woven
	he (she, it) will have woven	they will have woven

IMPERATIVE MOOD
weave

SUBJUNCTIVE MOOD

Pres.	if I weave	if we weave
	if you weave	if you weave
	if he (she, it) weave	if they weave

Past	if I wove	if we wove
	if you wove	if you wove
	if he (she, it) wove	if they wove

Fut.	if I should weave	if we should weave
	if you should weave	if you should weave
	if he (she, it) should weave	if they should weave

(passive voice)

Infinitive: to be woven   *Present Participle:* being woven
Perfect Infinitive: to have been woven   *Past Participle:* been woven

INDICATIVE MOOD

Pres.	I am woven	we are woven
	you are woven	you are woven
	he (she, it) is woven	they are woven
Pres.	I am being woven	we are being woven
Prog.	you are being woven	you are being woven
	he (she, it) is being woven	they are being woven
Pres.	I do get woven	we do get woven
Int.	you do get woven	you do get woven
	he (she, it) does get woven	they do get woven
Fut.	I shall be woven	we shall be woven
	you will be woven	you will be woven
	he (she, it) will be woven	they will be woven
Fut.	I will be woven *(P)*	we will be woven *(P)*
	you shall be woven *(C)*	you shall be woven *(C)*
	he (she, it) shall be woven *(C)*	they shall be woven *(C)*
Past	I was woven	we were woven
	you were woven	you were woven
	he (she, it) was woven	they were woven
Past	I was being woven	we were being woven
Prog.	you were being woven	you were being woven
	he (she, it) was being woven	they were being woven
Past	I did get woven	we did get woven
Int.	you did get woven	you did get woven
	he (she, it) did get woven	they did get woven
Pres.	I have been woven	we have been woven
Perf.	you have been woven	you have been woven
	he (she, it) has been woven	they have been woven
Past	I had been woven	we had been woven
Perf.	you had been woven	you had been woven
	he (she, it) had been woven	they had been woven
Fut.	I shall have been woven	we shall have been woven
Perf.	you will have been woven	you will have been woven
	he (she, it) will have been woven	they will have been woven

IMPERATIVE MOOD
be woven

SUBJUNCTIVE MOOD

Pres.	if I be woven	if we be woven
	if you be woven	if you be woven
	if he (she, it) be woven	if they be woven
Past	if I were woven	if we were woven
	if you were woven	if you were woven
	if he (she, it) were woven	if they were woven
Fut.	if I should be woven	if we should be woven
	if you should be woven	if you should be woven
	if he (she, it) should be woven	if they should be woven

to weep (active voice)   *Principal Parts:* weep, weeping, wept, wept

Infinitive: to weep   *Present Participle:* weeping
Perfect Infinitive: to have wept   *Past Participle:* wept

INDICATIVE MOOD

Pres.	I weep	we weep
	you weep	you weep
	he (she, it) weeps	they weep
Pres.	I am weeping	we are weeping
Prog.	you are weeping	you are weeping
	he (she, it) is weeping	they are weeping
Pres.	I do weep	we do weep
Int.	you do weep	you do weep
	he (she, it) does weep	they do weep
Fut.	I shall weep	we shall weep
	you will weep	you will weep
	he (she, it) will weep	they will weep
Fut.	I will weep *(P)*	we will weep *(P)*
	you shall weep *(C)*	you shall weep *(C)*
	he (she, it) shall weep *(C)*	they shall weep *(C)*
Past	I wept	we wept
	you wept	you wept
	he (she, it) wept	they wept
Past	I was weeping	we were weeping
Prog.	you were weeping	you were weeping
	he (she, it) was weeping	they were weeping
Past	I did weep	we did weep
Int.	you did weep	you did weep
	he (she, it) did weep	they did weep
Pres.	I have wept	we have wept
Perf.	you have wept	you have wept
	he (she, it) has wept	they have wept
Past	I had wept	we had wept
Perf.	you had wept	you had wept
	he (she, it) had wept	they had wept
Fut.	I shall have wept	we shall have wept
Perf.	you will have wept	you will have wept
	he (she, it) will have wept	they will have wept

IMPERATIVE MOOD
weep

SUBJUNCTIVE MOOD

Pres.	if I weep	if we weep
	if you weep	if you weep
	if he (she, it) weep	if they weep
Past	if I wept	if we wept
	if you wept	if you wept
	if he (she, it) wept	if they wept
Fut.	if I should weep	if we should weep
	if you should weep	if you should weep
	if he (she, it) should weep	if they should weep

Infinitive: to be wept   *Present Participle:* being wept
Perfect Infinitive: to have been wept   *Past Participle:* been wept

INDICATIVE MOOD

Pres.	I am wept	we are wept
	you are wept	you are wept
	he (she, it) is wept	they are wept
Pres.	I am being wept	we are being wept
Prog.	you are being wept	you are being wept
	he (she, it) he being wept	they are being wept
Pres.	I do get wept	we do get wept
Int.	you do get wept	you do get wept
	he (she, it) does get wept	they do get wept
Fut.	I shall be wept	we shall be wept
	you will be wept	you will be wept
	he (she, it) will be wept	they will be wept
Fut.	I will be wept *(P)*	we will be wept *(P)*
	you shall be wept *(C)*	you shall be wept *(C)*
	he (she, it) shall be wept *(C)*	they shall be wept *(C)*
Past	I was wept	we were wept
	you were wept	you were wept
	he (she, it) was wept	they were wept
Past	I was being wept	we were being wept
Prog.	you were being wept	you were being wept
	he (she, it) was being wept	they were being wept
Past	I did get wept	we did get wept
Int.	you did get wept	you did get wept
	he (she, it) did get wept	they did get wept
Pres.	I have been wept	we have been wept
Perf.	you have been wept	you have been wept
	he (she, it) has been wept	they have been wept
Past	I had been wept	we had been wept
Perf.	you had been wept	you had been wept
	he (she, it) had been wept	they had been wept
Fut.	I shall have been wept	we shall have been wept
Perf.	you will have been wept	you will have been wept
	he (she, it) will have been wept	they will have been wept

IMPERATIVE MOOD
be wept

SUBJUNCTIVE MOOD

Pres.	if I be wept	if we be wept
	if you be wept	if you be wept
	he (she, it) be wept	if they be wept
Past	if I were wept	if we were wept
	if you were wept	if you were wept
	he (she, it) were wept	if they were wept
Fut.	if I should be wept	if we should be wept
	if you should be wept	if you should be wept
	he (she, it) should be wept	if they should be wept

to win (active voice)　　　　*Principal Parts:* win, winning, won, won

---

Infinitive: to win　　　　　　　　　　*Present Participle:* winning
Perfect Infinitive: to have won　　　　*Past Participle:* won

INDICATIVE MOOD

Pres.	I win	we win
	you win	you win
	he (she, it) wins	they win
Pres.	I am winning	we are winning
Prog.	you are winning	you are winning
	he (she, it) is winning	they are winning
Pres.	I do win	we do win
Int.	you do win	you do win
	he (she, it) does win	they do win
Fut.	I shall win	we shall win
	you will win	you will win
	he (she, it) will win	they will win
Fut.	I will win *(P)*	we will win *(P)*
	you shall win *(C)*	you shall win *(C)*
	he (she, it) shall win *(C)*	they shall win *(C)*
Past	I won	we won
	you won	you won
	he (she, it) won	they won
Past	I was winning	we were winning
Prog.	you were winning	you were winning
	he (she, it) was winning	they were winning
Past	I did win	we did win
Int.	you did win	you did win
	he (she, it) did win	they did win
Pres.	I have won	we have won
Perf.	you have won	you have won
	he (she, it) has won	they have won
Past	I had won	we had won
Perf.	you had won	you had won
	he (she, it) had won	they had won
Fut.	I shall have won	we shall have won
Perf.	you will have won	you will have won
	he (she, it) will have won	they will have won

IMPERATIVE MOOD
win

SUBJUNCTIVE MOOD

Pres.	if I win	if we win
	if you win	if you win
	if he (she, it) win	if they win
Past	if I won	if we won
	if you won	if you won
	if he (she, it) won	if they won
Fut.	if I should win	if we should win
	if you should win	if you should win
	if he (she, it) should win	if they should win

Infinitive: to be won   *Present Participle:* being won
Perfect Infinitive: to have been won   *Past Participle:* been won

INDICATIVE MOOD

Pres. I am won	we are won
you are won	you are won
he (she, it) is won	they are won
Pres. I am being won	we are being won
Prog. you are being won	you are being won
he (she, it) is being won	they are being won
Pres. I do get won	we do get won
Int. you do get won	you do get won
he (she, it) does get won	they do get won
Fut. I shall be won	we shall be won
you will be won	you will be won
he (she, it) will be won	they will be won
Fut. I will be won *(P)*	we will be won *(P)*
you shall be won *(C)*	you shall be won *(C)*
he (she, it) shall be won *(C)*	they shall be won *(C)*
Past I was won	we were won
you were won	you were won
he (she, it) was won	they were won
Past I was being won	we were being won
Prog. you were being won	you were being won
he (she, it) was being won	they were being won
Past I did get won	we did get won
Int. you did get won	you did get won
he (she, it) did get won	they did get won
Pres. I have been won	we have been won
Perf. you have been won	you have been won
he (she, it) has been won	they have been won
Past I had been won	we had been won
Perf. you had been won	you had been won
he (she, it) had been won	they had been won
Fut. I shall have been won	we shall have been won
Perf. you will have been won	you will have been won
he (she, it) will have been won	they will have been won

IMPERATIVE MOOD
be won

SUBJUNCTIVE MOOD

Pres. if I be won	if we be won
if you be won	if you be won
if he (she, it) be won	if they be won
Past if I were won	if we were won
if you were won	if you were won
if he (she, it) were won	if they were won
Fut. if I should be won	if we should be won
if you should be won	if you should be won
if he (she, it) should be won	if they should be won

to wind (active voice)   *Principal Parts:* wind, winding, wound, wound

Infinitive: to wind   *Present Participle:* winding
Perfect Infinitive: to have wound   *Past Participle:* wound

INDICATIVE MOOD

Pres.	I wind	we wind
	you wind	you wind
	he (she, it) winds	they wind
Pres.	I am winding	we are winding
Prog.	you are winding	you are winding
	he (she, it) is winding	they are winding
Pres.	I do wind	we do wind
Int.	you do wind	you do wind
	he (she, it) does wind	they do wind
Fut.	I shall wind	we shall wind
	you will wind	you will wind
	he (she, it) will wind	they will wind
Fut.	I will wind *(P)*	we will wind *(P)*
	you shall wind *(C)*	you shall wind *(C)*
	he (she, it) shall wind *(C)*	they shall wind *(C)*
Past	I wound	we wound
	you wound	you wound
	he (she, it) wound	they wound
Past	I was winding	we were winding
Prog.	you were winding	you were winding
	he (she, it) was winding	they were winding
Past	I did wind	we did wind
Int.	you did wind	you did wind
	he (she, it) did wind	they did wind
Pres.	I have wound	we have wound
Perf.	you have wound	you have wound
	he (she, it) has wound	they have wound
Past	I had wound	we had wound
Perf.	you had wound	you had wound
	he (she, it) had wound	they had wound
Fut.	I shall have wound	we shall have wound
Perf.	you will have wound	you will have wound
	he (she, it) will have wound	they will have wound

IMPERATIVE MOOD
wind

SUBJUNCTIVE MOOD

Pres.	if I wind	if we wind
	if you wind	if you wind
	if he (she, it) wind	if they wind
Past	if I wound	if we wound
	if you wound	if you wound
	if he (she, it) wound	if they wound
Fut.	if I should wind	if we should wind
	if you should wind	if you should wind
	if he (she, it) should wind	if they should wind

(passive voice)

Infinitive: to be wound   *Present Participle:* being wound
Perfect Infinitive: to have been wound   *Past Participle:* been wound

INDICATIVE MOOD

Pres.
I am wound
you are wound
he (she, it) is wound

we are wound
you are wound
they are wound

Pres.
Prog.
I am being wound
you are being wound
he (she, it) he being wound

we are being wound
you are being wound
they are being wound

Pres.
Int.
I do get wound
you do get wound
he (she, it) does get wound

we do get wound
you do get wound
they do get wound

Fut.
I shall be wound
you will be wound
he (she, it) will be wound

we shall be wound
you will be wound
they will be wound

Fut.
I will be wound *(P)*
you shall be wound *(C)*
he (she, it) shall be wound *(C)*

we will be wound *(P)*
you shall be wound *(C)*
they shall be wound *(C)*

Past
I was wound
you were wound
he (she, it) was wound

we were wound
you were wound
they were wound

Past
Prog.
I was being wound
you were being wound
he (she, it) was being wound

we were being wound
you were being wound
they were being wound

Past
Int.
I did get wound
you did get wound
he (she, it) did get wound

we did get wound
you did get wound
they did get wound

Pres.
Perf.
I have been wound
you have been wound
he (she, it) has been wound

we have been wound
you have been wound
they have been wound

Past
Perf.
I had been wound
you had been wound
he (she, it) had been wound

we had been wound
you had been wound
they had been wound

Fut.
Perf.
I shall have been wound
you will have been wound
he (she, it) will have been wound

we shall have been wound
you will have been wound
they will have been wound

IMPERATIVE MOOD
be wound

SUBJUNCTIVE MOOD

Pres.
if I be wound
if you be wound
if he (she, it) be wound

if we be wound
if you be wound
if they be wound

Past
if I were wound
if you were wound
if he (she, it) were wound

if we were wound
if you were wound
if they were wound

Fut.
if I should be wound
if you should be wound
if he (she, it) should be wound

if we should be wound
if you should be wound
if they should be wound

to work (active voice)

Principal Parts: work, working, worked, worked

Infinitive: to work
Perfect Infinitive: to have worked

Present Participle: working
Past Participle: worked

INDICATIVE MOOD

Pres.	I work	we work
	you work	you work
	he (she, it) works	they work

Pres.	I am working	we are working
Prog.	you are working	you are working
	he (she, it) is working	they are working

Pres.	I do work	we do work
Int.	you do work	you do work
	he (she, it) does work	they do work

Fut.	I shall work	we shall work
	you will work	you will work
	he (she, it) will work	they will work

Fut.	I will work *(P)*	we will work *(P)*
	you shall work *(C)*	you shall work *(C)*
	he (she, it) shall work *(C)*	they shall work *(C)*

Past	I worked	we worked
	you worked	you worked
	he (she, it) worked	they worked

Past	I was working	we were working
Prog.	you were working	you were working
	he (she, it) was working	they were working

Past	I did work	we did work
Int.	you did work	you did work
	he (she, it) did work	they did work

Pres.	I have worked	we have worked
Perf.	you have worked	you have worked
	he (she, it) has worked	they have worked

Past	I had worked	we had worked
Perf.	you had worked	you had worked
	he (she, it) had worked	they had worked

Fut.	I shall have worked	we shall have worked
Perf.	you will have worked	you will have worked
	he (she, it) will have worked	they will have worked

IMPERATIVE MOOD
work

SUBJUNCTIVE MOOD

Pres.	if I work	if we work
	if you work	if you work
	if he (she, it) work	if they work

Past	if I worked	if we worked
	if you worked	if you worked
	if he (she, it) worked	if they worked

Fut.	if I should work	if we should work
	if you should work	if you should work
	if he (she, it) should work	if they should work

Infinitive: to be worked

Perfect Infinitive: to have been worked

Present Participle: being worked

Past Participle: been worked

INDICATIVE MOOD

Pres.	I am worked	we are worked
	you are worked	you are worked
	he (she, it) is worked	they are worked
Pres.	I am being worked	we are being worked
Prog.	you are being worked	you are being worked
	he (she, it) is being worked	they are being worked
Pres.	I do get worked	we do get worked
Int.	you do get worked	you do get worked
	he (she, it) does get worked	they do get worked
Fut.	I shall be worked	we shall be worked
	you will be worked	you will be worked
	he (she, it) will be worked	they will be worked
Fut.	I will be worked *(P)*	we will be worked *(P)*
	you shall be worked *(C)*	you shall be worked *(C)*
	he (she, it) shall be worked *(C)*	they shall be worked *(C)*
Past	I was worked	we were worked
	you were worked	you were worked
	he (she, it) was worked	they were worked
Past	I was being worked	we were being worked
Prog.	you were being worked	you were being worked
	he (she, it) was being worked	they were being worked
Past	I did get worked	we did get worked
Int.	you did get worked	you did get worked
	he (she, it) did get worked	they did get worked
Pres.	I have been worked	we have been worked
Perf.	you have been worked	you have been worked
	he (she, it) has been worked	they have been worked
Past	I had been worked	we had been worked
Perf.	you had been worked	you had been worked
	he (she, it) had been worked	they had been worked
Fut.	I shall have been worked	we shall have been worked
Perf.	you will have been worked	you will have been worked
	he (she, it) will have been worked	they will have been worked

IMPERATIVE MOOD

be worked

SUBJUNCTIVE MOOD

Pres.	if I be worked	if we be worked
	if you be worked	if you be worked
	if he (she, it) be worked	if they be worked
Past	if I were worked	if we were worked
	if you were worked	if you were worked
	if he (she, it) were worked	if they were worked
Fut.	if I should be worked	if we should be worked
	if you should be worked	if you should be worked
	if he (she, it) should be worked	if they should be worked

to wreak (active voice)   *Principal Parts:* wreak, wreaking, wrought, wrought

---

Infinitive: to wreak   *Present Participle:* wreaking
Perfect Infinitive: to have wrought   *Past Participle:* wrought

INDICATIVE MOOD

Pres.	I wreak	we wreak
	you wreak	you wreak
	he (she, it) wreaks	they wreak
Pres.	I am wreaking	we are wreaking
Prog.	you are wreaking	you are wreaking
	he (she, it) is wreaking	they are wreaking
Pres.	I do wreak	we do wreak
Int.	you do wreak	you do wreak
	he (she, it) does wreak	they do wreak
Fut.	I shall wreak	we shall wreak
	you will wreak	you will wreak
	he (she, it) will wreak	they will wreak
Fut.	I will wreak *(P)*	we will wreak *(P)*
	you shall wreak *(C)*	you shall wreak *(C)*
	he (she, it) shall wreak *(C)*	they shall wreak *(C)*
Past	I wrought	we wrought
	you wrought	you wrought
	he (she, it) wrought	they wrought
Past	I was wreaking	we were wreaking
Prog.	you were wreaking	you were wreaking
	he (she, it) was wreaking	they were wreaking
Past	I did wreak	we did wreak
Int.	you did wreak	you did wreak
	he (she, it) did wreak	they did wreak
Pres.	I have wrought	we have wrought
Perf.	you have wrought	you have wrought
	he (she, it) has wrought	they have wrought
Past	I had wrought	we had wrought
Perf.	you had wrought	you had wrought
	he (she, it) had wrought	they had wrought
Fut.	I shall have wrought	we shall have wrought
Perf.	you will have wrought	you will have wrought
	he (she, it) will have wrought	they will have wrought

IMPERATIVE MOOD
wreak

SUBJUNCTIVE MOOD

Pres.	if I wreak	if we wreak
	if you wreak	if you wreak
	if he (she, it) wreak	if they wreak
Past	if I wrought	if we wrought
	if you wrought	if you wrought
	if he (she, it) wrought	if they wrought
Fut.	if I should wreak	if we should wreak
	if you should wreak	if you should wreak
	if he (she, it) should wreak	if they should wreak

Infinitive: to be wrought   *Present Participle:* being wrought
Perfect Infinitive: to have been wrought   *Past Participle:* been wrought

INDICATIVE MOOD

Pres. I am wrought	we are wrought
you are wrought	you are wrought
he (she, it) is wrought	they are wrought
Pres. I am being wrought	we are being wrought
Prog. you are being wrought	you are being wrought
he (she, it) is being wrought	they are being wrought
Pres. I do get wrought	we do get wrought
Int. you do get wrought	you do get wrought
he (she, it) does get wrought	they do get wrought
Fut. I shall be wrought	we shall be wrought
you will be wrought	you will be wrought
he (she, it) will be wrought	they will be wrought
Fut. I will be wrought *(P)*	we will be wrought *(P)*
you shall be wrought *(C)*	you shall be wrought *(C)*
he (she, it) shall be wrought *(C)*	they shall be wrought *(C)*
Past I was wrought	we were wrought
you were wrought	you were wrought
he (she, it) was wrought	they were wrought
Past I was being wrought	we were being wrought
Prog. you were being wrought	you were being wrought
he (she, it) was being wrought	they were being wrought
Past I did get wrought	we did get wrought
Int. you did get wrought	you did get wrought
he (she, it) did get wrought	they did get wrought
Pres. I have been wrought	we have been wrought
Perf. you have been wrought	you have been wrought
he (she, it) has been wrought	they have been wrought
Past I had been wrought	we had been wrought
Perf. you had been wrought	you had been wrought
he (she, it) had been wrought	they had been wrought
Fut. I shall have been wrought	we shall have been wrought
Perf. you will have been wrought	you will have been wrought
he (she, it) will have been wrought	they will have been wrought

IMPERATIVE MOOD
be wrought

SUBJUNCTIVE MOOD

Pres. if I be wrought	if we be wrought
if you be wrought	if you be wrought
if he (she, it) be wrought	if they be wrought
Past if I were wrought	if we were wrought
if you were wrought	if you were wrought
if he (she, it) were wrought	if they were wrought
Fut. if I should be wrought	if we should be wrought
if you should be wrought	if you should be wrought
if he (she, it) should be wrought	if they should be wrought

to wring (active voice) *Principal Parts:* wring, wringing, wrung, wrung

Infinitive: to wring   *Present Participle:* wringing
Perfect Infinitive: to have wrung   *Past Participle:* wrung

INDICATIVE MOOD

Pres.	I wring	we wring
	you wring	you wring
	he (she, it) wrings	they wring
Pres. Prog.	I am wringing	we are wringing
	you are wringing	you are wringing
	he (she, it) is wringing	they are wringing
Pres. Int.	I do wring	we do wring
	you do wring	you do wring
	he (she, it) does wring	they do wring
Fut.	I shall wring	we shall wring
	you will wring	you will wring
	he (she, it) will wring	they will wring
Fut.	I will wring *(P)*	we will wring *(P)*
	you shall wring *(C)*	you shall wring *(C)*
	he (she, it) shall wring *(C)*	they shall wring *(C)*
Past	I wrung	we wrung
	you wrung	you wrung
	he (she, it) wrung	they wrung
Past Prog.	I was wringing	we were wringing
	you were wringing	you were wringing
	he (she, it) was wringing	they were wringing
Past Int.	I did wring	we did wring
	you did wring	you did wring
	he (she, it) did wring	they did wring
Pres. Perf.	I have wrung	we have wrung
	you have wrung	you have wrung
	he (she, it) has wrung	they have wrung
Past Perf.	I had wrung	we had wrung
	you had wrung	you had wrung
	he (she, it) had wrung	they had wrung
Fut. Perf.	I shall have wrung	we shall have wrung
	you will have wrung	you will have wrung
	he (she, it) will have wrung	they will have wrung

IMPERATIVE MOOD
wring

SUBJUNCTIVE MOOD

Pres.	if I wring	if we wring
	if you wring	if you wring
	if he (she, it) wring	if they wring
Past	if I wrung	if we wrung
	if you wrung	if you wrung
	if he (she, it) wrung	if they wrung
Fut.	if I should wring	if we should wring
	if you should wring	if you should wring
	if he (she, it) should wring	if they should wring

Infinitive: to be wrung   *Present Participle:* being wrung
Perfect Infinitive: to have been wrung   *Past Participle:* been wrung

INDICATIVE MOOD

Pres.   I am wrung   we are wrung
you are wrung   you are wrung
he (she, it) is wrung   they are wrung

Pres.   I am being wrung   we are being wrung
Prog.   you are being wrung   you are being wrung
he (she, it) is being wrung   they are being wrung

Pres.   I do get wrung   we do get wrung
Int.   you do get wrung   you do get wrung
he (she, it) does get wrung   they do get wrung

Fut.   I shall be wrung   we shall be wrung
you will be wrung   you will be wrung
he (she, it) will be wrung   they will be wrung

Fut.   I will be wrung *(P)*   we will be wrung *(P)*
you shall be wrung *(C)*   you shall be wrung *(C)*
he (she, it) shall be wrung *(C)*   they shall be wrung *(C)*

Past   I was wrung   we were wrung
you were wrung   you were wrung
he (she, it) was wrung   they were wrung

Past   I was being wrung   we were being wrung
Prog.   you were being wrung   you were being wrung
he (she, it) was being wrung   they were being wrung

Past   I did get wrung   we did get wrung
Int.   you did get wrung   you did get wrung
he (she, it) did get wrung   they did get wrung

Pres.   I have been wrung   we have been wrung
Perf.   you have been wrung   you have been wrung
he (she, it) has been wrung   they have been wrung

Past   I had been wrung   we had been wrung
Perf.   you had been wrung   you had been wrung
he (she, it) had been wrung   they had been wrung

Fut.   I shall have been wrung   we shall have been wrung
Perf.   you will have been wrung   you will have been wrung
he (she, it) will have been wrung   they will have been wrung

IMPERATIVE MOOD
be wrung

SUBJUNCTIVE MOOD

Pres.   if I be wrung   if we be wrung
if you be wrung   if you be wrung
if he (she, it) be wrung   if they be wrung

Past   if I were wrung   if we were wrung
if you were wrung   if you were wrung
if he (she, it) were wrung   if they were wrung

Fut.   if I should be wrung   if we should be wrung
if you should be wrung   if you should be wrung
if he (she, it) should be wrung   if they should be wrung

to write (active voice)   *Principal Parts:* write, writing, wrote, written

---

Infinitive: to write   *Present Participle:* writing
Perfect Infinitive: to have written   *Past Participle:* written

INDICATIVE MOOD

Pres.	I write	we write
	you write	you write
	he (she, it) writes	they write
Pres.	I am writing	we are writing
Prog.	you are writing	you are writing
	he (she, it) is writing	they are writing
Pres.	I do write	we do write
Int.	you do write	you do write
	he (she, it) does write	they do write
Fut.	I shall write	we shall write
	you will write	you will write
	he (she, it) will write	they will write
Fut.	I will write *(P)*	we will write *(P)*
	you shall write *(C)*	you shall write *(C)*
	he (she, it) shall write *(C)*	they shall write *(C)*
Past	I wrote	we wrote
	you wrote	you wrote
	he (she, it) wrote	they wrote
Past	I was writing	we were writing
Prog.	you were writing	you were writing
	he (she, it) was writing	they were writing
Past	I did write	we did write
Int.	you did write	you did write
	he (she, it) did write	they did write
Pres.	I have written	we have written
Perf.	you have written	you have written
	he (she, it) has written	they have written
Past	I had written	we had written
Perf.	you had written	you had written
	he (she, it) had written	they had written
Fut.	I shall have written	we shall have written
Perf.	you will have written	you will have written
	he (she, it) will have written	they will have written

IMPERATIVE MOOD
write

SUBJUNCTIVE MOOD

Pres.	if I write	if we write
	if you write	if you write
	if he (she, it) write	if they write
Past	if I wrote	if we wrote
	if you wrote	if you wrote
	if he (she, it) wrote	if they wrote
Fut.	if I should write	if we should write
	if you should write	if they should write
	if he (she, it) should write	if you should write

Infinitive: to be written   *Present Participle:* being written
Perfect Infinitive: to have been written   *Past Participle:* been written

INDICATIVE MOOD

Pres.	I am written	we are written
	you are written	you are written
	he (she, it) is written	they are written
Pres. Prog.	I am being written	we are being written
	you are being written	you are being written
	he (she, it) is being written	they are being written
Pres. Int.	I do get written	we do get written
	you do get written	you do get written
	he (she, it) does get written	they do get written
Fut.	I shall be written	we shall be written
	you will be written	you will be written
	he (she, it) will be written	they will be written
Fut.	I will be written *(P)*	we will be written *(P)*
	you shall be written *(C)*	you shall be written *(C)*
	he (she, it) shall be written *(C)*	they shall be written *(C)*
Past	I was written	we were written
	you were written	you were written
	he (she, it) was written	they were written
Past Prog.	I was being written	we were being written
	you were being written	you were being written
	he (she, it) was being written	they were being written
Past Int.	I did get written	we did get written
	you did get written	you did get written
	he (she, it) did get written	they did get written
Pres. Perf.	I have been written	we have been written
	you have been written	you have been written
	he (she, it) has been written	they have been written
Past Perf.	I had been written	we had been written
	you had been written	you had been written
	he (she, it) had been written	they had been written
Fut. Perf.	I shall have been written	we shall have been written
	you will have been written	you will have been written
	he (she, it) will have been written	they will have been written

IMPERATIVE MOOD
be written

SUBJUNCTIVE MOOD

Pres.	if I be written	if we be written
	if you be written	if you be written
	if he (she, it) be written	if they be written
Past	if I were written	if we were written
	if you were written	if you were written
	if he (she, it) were written	if they were written
Fut.	if I should be written	if we should be written
	if you should be written	if you should be written
	if he (she, it) should be written	if they should be written